Old Runcorn

by

H.F. Starkey

Halton Borough Council

In Memory of Michael

Contents

Introduction ....

Acknowledgements ....

Chapter

1	The Evidence of Prehistoric Settlement	1
2	Norman Rule	7
3	The Medieval Community	17
4	Norton Priory	35
5	Matters of Religion	43
6	The Civil War	57
7	Parson Versus People	85
8	New Churches and Chapels	95
9	The Parish Constable and the Overseers	105
10	The Bridgewater Canal	125
11	Runcorn, A Health Resort	133
12	Victorian Runcorn	139
13	The Coming of Industry	147
14	The Coming of the Railway	165
15	The Port of Runcorn	173
16	The Improvement Commissioners	193
17	Social Activity	205
18	The Twentieth Century	211

Index 225

Illustrations

Runcorn Township in 1782 .... *facing page i*

The medieval Parish Church .... *iii*

Striated boulder from the Ice Age .... *facing page 1*

Pre-historic axe-hammer found at Weston Point 1

Lead seal of Pope Boniface IX 12

"Abbey Cottage" on Mount Pleasant 14

Charter of Runcorn Ferry 16

Halton Castle 1800 27

Halton Castle 1900 32

Norman doorway, Norton Priory 34

Wall arcade, Norton Priory 36

Statue of St. Christopher, Norton Priory 40

Dug-out chest from Norton Priory 40

Norton Priory Mansion House 41

Canon Alfred Maitland Wood 54

Halton township 17th century 56

Ruins of Halton Castle 18th century 61

Seneschal's House, Halton 66

The Old Hall, High Street 67

17th century timber framed cottages, Halton 68

Village cross and Old Hall, Weston 69

The Green, Halton 71

Castle Hotel, Halton 72

Rocksavage gatehouse 76

Hallwood 78

Sir John Chesshyre's Library, Halton 79, 80

Alms Houses, Halton Hill 82

Early 19th century Runcorn 84

Medieval Parish Church showing 1802 rebuilding 88

Interior of medieval Parish Church 89

Mr. Master's Parish School 93

All Saints Parish Church 95

Christ Church, Weston Point 99

St. Paul's Wesleyan Methodist Church 101

Halton Road Chapel 103

Trinity Chapel, Halton 103

First Town Hall of 1831 116

Runcorn Windmill 119

Pre-industrial Runcorn 122

Top Locks in the early 1930s 124

Sir Richard Brooke 127

Bridgewater House 128

Old Quay Canal and locks 131

Belvedere boarding houses 133

Bathing parties and parkland at
    Runcorn about 1830 136

Runcorn Town Bridge 138

Narrow-boat women 138

Halton Ladies' Club 1909 143

Pavement pot seller, turn of the century 145

Weston Quarry tramroad 148

A local quarry 150

The launch of the "Despatch" May 1886 152

Highfield Tannery in the 1960s 153

Halton Grange 155

Vacuum plant, Salt Union, Weston Point 161

Dredging for coal, Bridgewater Canal 163

Telford's design for Runcorn Bridge 166

The railway bridge under construction in 1864 169

Railway bridge shortly after completion, 1868 170

Bridgewater docks and Duke's house 172

Old Quay Docks in 1840 175

Three-masted barque, Bridgewater Docks 177

Two masted Mersey "jigger" flats 178

Fishing smacks on the upper Mersey 178

River tug "Earl of Ellesmere" 180

Bridgewater Docks 1886 181

Runcorn schooner "Gleaner" 182

Narrow boats in 1905 183

Runcorn to Latchford Canal in 1888 185

"Noah's Ark Café" 186

Excavating Manchester Ship Canal 1891 187

Narrow beam Bridgewater Canal tug 188

Ocean going vessel passing Old
    Quay swing bridge 190

Ferry crossing and old baths 191

The waterworks pumping station
    on Runcorn Heath 195

Lowe's Court, off Cooper Street 198

Old houses in Pool Lane 199

Runcorn waterfront about 1870 201

Crescent Row 202

Whit Monday procession in 1924 204

Tableau advertising biscuits and bakery, 1926 204

Staff of the "Palace" in 1920s 209

Last ferryman in 1905 212

Transporter Bridge first crossing, 1905 .... 213, 214

Runcorn Coat of Arms 223

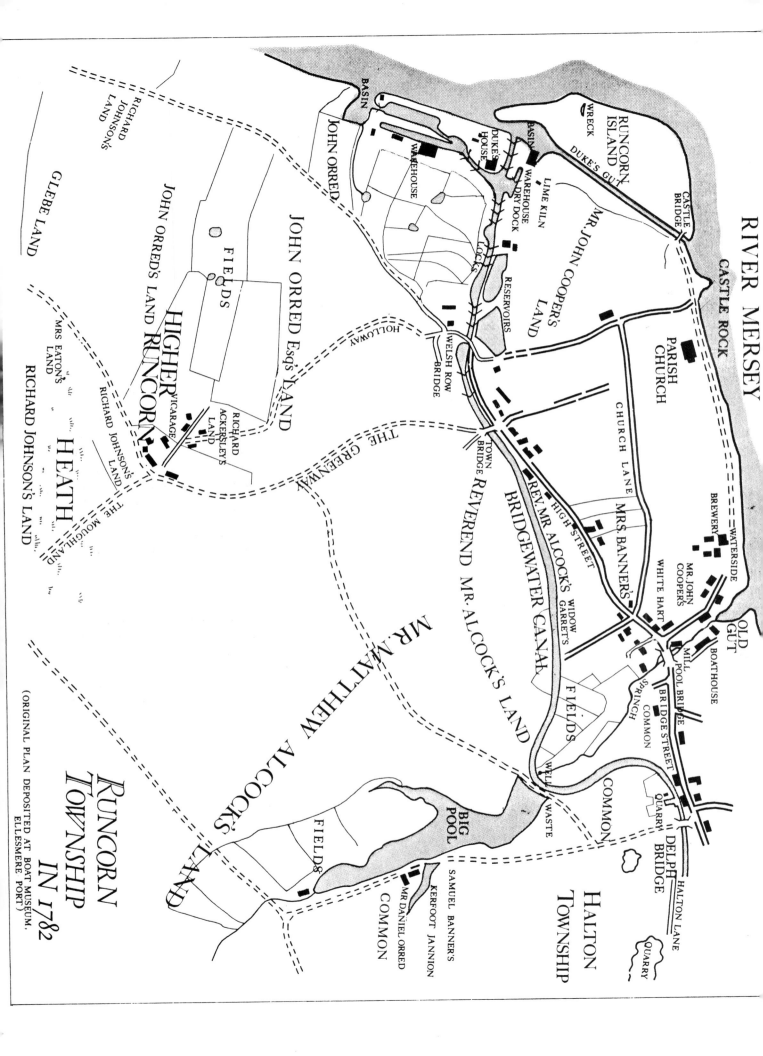

RIVER MERSEY

CASTLE ROCK

RUNCORN ISLAND

WRECK

DUKE'S GUT

CASTLE BRIDGE

BASIN

DUKE'S HOUSE

BASIN

WAREHOUSE

WAREHOUSE DRY DOCK

LIME KILN

MR. JOHN COOPER'S LAND

LOCKS

RESERVOIRS

JOHN ORRED

JOHN ORRED

PARISH CHURCH

HOLLOWAY

WELSH ROW BRIDGE

CHURCH LANE

JOHN ORRED Esq's LAND

FIELDS

THE GREENWAY

TOWN BRIDGE

REV. MR. ALCOCK'S

BRIDGEWATER CANAL

MRS. BANNER'S

BREWERY

WATERSIDE

HIGHER RUNCORN

VICARAGE

RICHARD ACKERSLEY'S LAND

HIGH STREET

WIDOW GARRET'S

MR. JOHN COOPER'S

WHITE HART

JOHN ORRED'S LAND

REVEREND MR. ALCOCK'S LAND

OLD GUT

BOATHOUSE

MILL

POOL BRIDGE

BRIDGE STREET

SPRINCH

COMMON

RICHARD JOHNSON'S LAND

FIELDS

THE MOUGHLAND

WELL

WASTE

BIG POOL

FIELDS

COMMON

QUARRY

DELPH BRIDGE

HALTON LANE

QUARRY

HALTON TOWNSHIP

MRS. EATON'S LAND

RICHARD JOHNSON'S LAND

GLEBE LAND

HEATH

RICHARD JOHNSON'S LAND

MR. MATTHEW ALCOCK'S LAND

SAMUEL BANNER'S

KERFOOT JANNION

MR DANIEL ORRED

COMMON

RUNCORN TOWNSHIP IN 1782

(ORIGINAL PLAN DEPOSITED AT BOAT MUSEUM, ELLESMERE PORT)

Introduction

Unaccountably, the only major work concerned with the history of Runcorn was written as long ago as 1887 and yet, in the hundred years to elapse since Charles Nickson published his book, the public's interest in the story of this locality has grown enormously.

It has been said that the study of local history is rather like examining the past through a microscope. Certainly the written histories of most small towns are severely local in content, often being little more than collections of trivia of interest only to local people. However, Runcorn's story differs from these in that the town has played a significant role in national affairs. Throughout the Industrial Revolution it was at the forefront of developments as a vital centre of communications on the country's inland waterways system and in two World Wars, local industry made an essential contribution to the nation's war effort.

In attempting to convey something of the day-to-day life of ordinary folk throughout successive ages, problems concerning balance and emphasis are bound to occur. For instance, a writer may make much of an obscure local event which happened centuries ago, simply because it is new evidence discovered as the result of laborious and painstaking research and yet the same author may treat a more recent event of national importance in an abbreviated manner because all the essential details are readily available at the local library. So it is with this present work where it can be seen that a great deal of easily accessible twentieth century material has been markedly condensed to form the shortest section of the book. Furthermore, it might be argued with justification, that there is much about Runcorn and rather less of Halton township, whereas for many centuries the latter was the more important settlement. Perhaps, in the not too distant future, a study of the archives of the Duchy of Lancaster will produce findings which will redress the balance to disclose Halton's richer heritage.

Undoubtedly, the most crucial date in Runcorn's history was 1964 when it was designated a New Town. Although profound changes have since transformed the appearance and character of old Runcorn and its neighbourhood out of all recognition, this book does not relate these important events because they are well documented and the detailed records are available for public scrutiny. Furthermore, the continuing development of the new town and its merger with the Borough of Widnes to form the Borough of Halton in 1974, constitute an entirely new urban project, the consequence of which only time can assess. For that reason these momentous events have been left for some future historian to recount and 1964 has been selected as the most appropriate date at which to end this narrative of old Runcorn.

Finally it must be stated that 'Old Runcorn' was written not to satisfy an academic readership but in response to requests from many local people who have attended my lectures over the years. It is my hope that the book will interest young people and in particular, those new town folk who, like the author, came to settle in the town and wondered about its history.

Acknowledgements

In gathering together a mass of information from documents, maps, old newspapers and published works, the author is acutely aware of the fragmentary nature of much of the material. Often the records are incomplete, accounts of events which occurred centuries ago may be one-sided or biased and certainly, there is still plenty of primary source evidence scattered throughout the country's libraries and archives where it remains yet to be discovered. No local history is ever complete and every year new detail of Runcorn's past is coming to light. Any history is only as good as its sources. Fortunately I have been helped by many well-informed people who have taken the trouble to enlighten me and who have supplied much of the essential detail needed to illuminate the Runcorn of the past.

Among my friends, old and new, I am indebted to Runcornians; Mrs E Dutton, Mr. B Findlow, Mrs E Grisdale, Miss E Hough, Mr. P Johnson, the late Mr. A D Jones, Mr. & Mrs A Marsh, the late Mr. Alan Mack, the late Mrs E Pollard, Mr. John Thompson, Mrs M Snookes and Canon Donald Thomas. I have obtained useful information from Mr. G Locke, Mr. D Pearce and Mrs B Tough, all of Widnes as well as from Mr. T Hazlehurst of Warrington and Mr. T V Jackson of Grappenhall. Miss Eileen Simpson of the Cheshire County Record Office and Mr. Rhys Williams, former Archaeological Officer to Cheshire, drew my attention to important local records. Mr. Paul Booth of Liverpool University was most generous in supplying me with detail from his own research as was Dr Gordon Rintoul, the Director of Catalyst, the Museum of the Chemical Industry. I have received useful advice from Mr. W E Leathwood and Mr. Mike Eddison both of whom read the manuscript. My thanks are also due to my typist, Mrs Rosalind Denton and to Mr. L J Starkey for photography.

I have been heavily dependent on the assistance of the staffs at the Cheshire County Record Office, Catalyst, the Museum of the Chemical Industry, Norton Priory Museum, the Boat Museum, Ellesmere Port and the public libraries in Runcorn, Widnes and Warrington.

To Mr. Gordon Oakes PC, MP, I owe a great deal, both for his efforts in promoting the publication of the book and also for his encouraging observations which induced me to embark on the project in the first place.

I acknowledge an overriding debt to my wife, not only for her assistance in the unenviable task of checking the manuscript but also for her boundless patience during the years that I have been absorbed in antiquity.

Above all, I have a special obligation to Halton Borough Council for publishing this book and to Alex Cowan, the Principal Administrative Officer of the Council, for all his assistance.

Designed and typeset by
P & M Farrington, Tarporley 733506

Runcorn

"Now a poore hamlet by a salt creke" John Leland "The Itinerary" 1540

"Runcorn, where now we see nothing but a fair Parish Church, a Parsonage and a few scattered tenements" Daniel King "The Vale Royal of England" 1656

"Lovers of botany may find a pleasing variety of plants both maritime and inland varieties in the vicinity of this place" John Aikin "A Description of the Country from Thirty to Forty Miles Around Manchester" 1795

"I took a sail up to Runcorn and I admire it more than any other watering place I have seen" Ellen Weeton "Journal of a Governess" 1817

"Runcorn has always been celebrated for its situation being surrounded by a beautifully romantic and picturesque scenery. It has also the advantages of a salubrious air and a mild temperature" Reverend G Fowler "A Visitor's Guide to Runcorn and its Vicinity" 1834

"A meagre, uninteresting, shabby brick town with irregular streets, not village-like but paved and looking like a dwarfed, stunted city" Nathaniel Hawthorne "Our Old Home" 1863

"With the exception of the railway and canal works there is nothing to be seen" J Murray "Handbook for Cheshire and Shropshire" 1879

The medieval Parish Church of Runcorn as seen from the north-east.
The painting was made by the Reverend J. Allen about 1835.

One of the many striated boulders (erratic stones) which were deposited locally during the retreat of the glaciers in the Ice Age. This one is now a decorative feature in the new Runcorn.

Chapter 1
The Evidence of Prehistoric Settlement

With the last retreat of the Ice Age over ten thousand years ago, the bleak arctic conditions in prehistoric Britain began to change and the polar landscape of Cheshire was during the passage of thousands of years, gradually transformed from icy tundra into a region of dense forest with areas of peat-moss and marsh. Oaks predominated, with the pedunculate oak thriving across most of the county whilst the durmast oak flourished on the well-drained soils. The wych elm, the ash and the lime also proliferated, while everywhere scrublands of hazel became established.

The glaciers left deposits of debris across the landscape. Boulders, some of great size, had been carried by the ice from the mountains of Scotland and northern England. Smoothed and rounded by the movement and pressure of the ice, granite boulders were left lying on the sandstone beds of north Cheshire. These alien stones, sometimes called 'erratics', were deposited hundreds of miles away from their natural sites. Some of these striated boulders have been found in Runcorn and without doubt they are the oldest items of historical interest in the district. One great white stone was until recently a feature of the gardens at the New Town shopping centre and other, smaller stones, some almost black in colour, were to be found in old Runcorn where they had been set into the ground to serve as fenders to protect gate-posts and walls from damage caused by cart wheels.

The earliest man-made objects found locally date from the period about 5,000 years to 3,500 years BC. Flint tools have been discovered at Frodsham and struck flakes of flint have been found on Halton Hill and in Norton village. During the archaeological excavations carried out in Norton village in the 1970s, a quantity of waste flints together with one or two which had been worked to produce serrated blades were discovered. As flints do not occur naturally in any of Cheshire's rocks but are associated with the chalk lands in the south and east of England, it is certain that either the finished tools or the raw flints were imported into the county. Small quantities of flint were carried by the glacial ice from Northern Ireland and some flint tools which have been found in Wirral have their origin in Ireland. This suggests that prehistoric man had

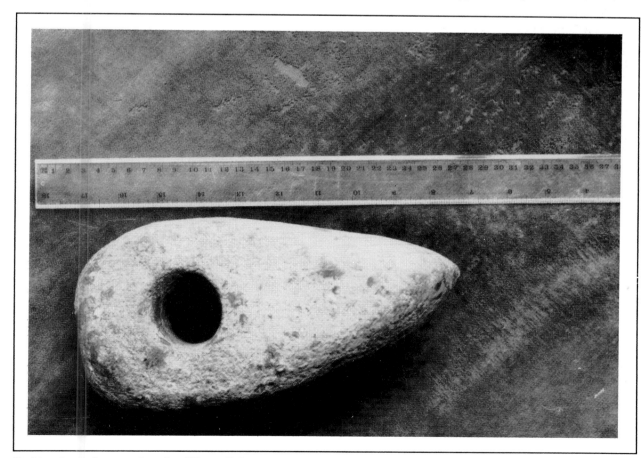

Prehistoric axe-hammer found at Weston Point.

developed trade routes and communications far more complex than has previously been believed. Neolithic pottery shards of a type found in Cumbria have been excavated in Norton village.

The flint tools prove the presence of a primitive people who had not learned to cultivate the land but who relied on their fishing and hunting skills in order to provide their food and clothing. Some years ago a massive perforated axe-hammer of a later period was found at Weston Point. This polished tool or weapon was fashioned from sheared dolerite, an igneous rock which is to be found at Langdale Pike in Cumbria and at Penmaenmawr. A few years ago a similar axe-hammer was discovered at Dutton.

From the Bronze Age we have a single item. A socketed bronze axe was found at Runcorn in 1892 during the construction of the Manchester Ship Canal. The looped axe or palstave belongs to the middle bronze period and a suggested date is about 1000 BC.

It was believed until fairly recently that Cheshire remained virtually unpopulated even into late prehistoric times and certainly, evidence of permanent settlement is hard to find until we come to consider the Iron Age period. From about 500 BC a Celtic people formed tribal groups in various parts of the county. The early Iron Age was a period of continual warfare and the remains of ancient defences in the form of hill forts are still obvious at Helsby Hill, at Bradley and Woodhouses Hill and at Eddisbury near Delamere forest. These hilly areas provided ideal sites for the building of formidable earthworks and it is reasonable to assume that Halton Hill was fortified to be used as a place of refuge in times of war but all traces of a fort there have been obliterated by subsequent building. However, it must be said that the only other evidence of Iron Age man yet found in this immediate district is a late Celtic or Brigantian coin found near Halton Castle.

The Celtic Brythons or Britons were a more developed people than any who had preceded them. A pastoral people, nomadic at first, they eventually settled to cultivate small fields. They reared cattle and horses, could spin and weave, used iron implements and tools and learned to use coinage in order to promote trade. The Celts used a Brythonic language which has been perpetuated in some Cheshire place names and in many dialect words still in common use.

It was these people who dominated Cheshire until the arrival of the Roman legions. Although the Britons, or Celts or Cornovii, as the Romans called them, were to be subject to Roman rule for over three hundred and thirty years, their culture survived the occupation and they were to prevail in Cheshire for another two hundred years until they were overwhelmed in the Anglian invasions early in the seventh century.

The Roman Presence

By AD45 the Roman occupation of southern and eastern England had been consolidated and the legions moved north into the territory lying between the Pennine lands of the Brigantians and the Ordovices and the Deceangli of North Wales. The area around Chester was strategically important to Paulinus in his operations to conquer Anglesey and in AD60 he began his march from his headquarters at Deva (Chester). Deva became the base for the Second Legion which was replaced by the Twentieth Legion in AD87.

From Deva a network of military roads was constructed throughout what is now Cheshire and gradually Roman settlement took place at Middlewich, which is believed to have been the Roman 'Salinae', at Northwich (Condate) and at Wilderspool, Warrington (Veratinum). The road from Chester to Warrington was built to the most convenient crossing place of the Mersey and its route was probably that taken by the modern road which passes through Helsby, Frodsham and Daresbury.

After Chester, Wilderspool was the most important Roman centre of the region. Wilderspool was vital for north-south communications and it developed into an important industrial centre. Ample evidence of extensive Roman occupation came to light during the construction of the Bridgewater Canal in the eighteenth century and the Manchester Ship Canal in the nineteenth. Many artifacts have been found on the site of the Wilderspool brewery. Pottery, coins, dressed stone, domestic utensils and evidence of metal founding and glass manufacture were discovered. Without doubt Wilderspool was a Roman settlement of some consequence.

There is also some evidence of shipping on the upper reaches of the river Mersey during the first century of the Roman occupation. William Camden, the great Elizabethan antiquary writing in 1590, records the finding of twenty inscribed Roman lead 'sowes' which were unearthed when "pursuing a vein of marl" at the river's edge at Norton. The lead pigs no longer exist but Camden has given a precise description of the ingots. The earliest was dated AD76 and it bore the stamp DE. CEANG. which indicates that the lead was mined in the territory of the Deceangli in North Wales. Other ingots had lettering showing that they were cast between AD84 and AD96.

Camden says that the lead pigs were "long in forme and four square" and in a hollow impressed at the upper end of each, was an inscription giving its source. On some the abbreviated inscriptions read:

IMP. DOMIT. AVG. GER.,

DE CEANG.

On others, IMP. VESP. VII. T. IMP V COSS. When completed, the full wording reads, IMP(ERATORE) DOMIT(IANO) AUG(USTO) GER(MANICO) DE CEANG(IS) IMP(ERATORE) VESP(ASIANO) VII T(ITO) IMP(ERATORE) V CO(N)S(ULIBU)S

Most probably the lead was part of the cargo of a Roman vessel which was trading to Wilderspool. However, the Cheshire historian, W. Thompson Watkin, suggests the possibility that the lead was intended for a Roman station situated on Halton Hill.

Of course Roman surveyors would have explored the possibility of making a crossing of the Mersey at the narrows of Runcorn Gap and indeed, there is indisputable evidence of Roman occupation in this immediate district. In 1936, the archaeologists J.P. Droop and R. Newstead carried out excavations on a sloping site to the north of Halton Brow about 350 metres below Halton Castle. They found signs of a Roman settlement and concluded the site was a temporary camp protected by a ditch which had been cut partly through sandstone and partly through clay. The archaeologists were unable to determine the southern limits of the site but they estimated that the ditch probably encircled a camp of about an acre. Pottery finds dated the camp to the late third or early fourth century AD.

The development of Runcorn New Town threatened to destroy the site and in 1967 the Ministry of Public Buildings and Works made funds available for further exploration and the work was undertaken by students from Manchester University. Mechanical excavation was carried out in an attempt to discover the full extent of the ditch discovered in 1936. That part of the ditch which had been cut through sandstone was found to be V-shaped in form and it had been lined with puddled clay. The ditch was found to enclose an area considerably larger than that supposed by Newstead and Droop. The new excavation proved that the encampment was in excess of three and a half acres but its southern boundary could not be located and it was concluded that it lies under the houses on the north side of Halton Brow or under the road

itself. The new dig yielded few artifacts but two small fragments of second century Samian ware and a quern stone were discovered.

The 1967 excavations proved that the site was occupied much earlier than had been previously believed. Because of the length of the occupation, the site must have been more than a temporary military camp. The assymetrical shape, the unmilitary nature of the ditch and the lack of ramparts and gates, suggest that the Halton Brow site was an agricultural settlement similar to the one found at Tallington in Lincolnshire. The Roman Camp at Halton Brow has been built over and the ground is now occupied by the houses and flats of Caesar's Close, Roman Close and Centurion Row.

Undoubtedly Roman soldiers encamped on Halton Hill. From this elevated position it would be possible to observe movement over a wide area of Merseyside. There is a late seventeenth century reference to 'Roman' remains on Halton Hill and also to a military road leading to them. In 1699 a Mr. Stones investigated the area around Halton Castle and he came to the conclusion that, *"The castle is situated at one angle of the (Roman) station ... and from this angle, both the line of the Roman vallum and its corresponding fosse, have been continued with their usual regularity in the form of a parallelogram to the extent of nearly forty statute acres."* Stones admits that *"only obscure and imperfect traces could be discerned"* and we are not told in which angle of the Roman camp the Norman castle was placed. No vestige of Roman building is apparent today but if Stones' dimensions are correct and the site did cover forty acres, then there is no doubt that the station was more than a temporary earthwork. Stones' unscientific observations with their inconclusive comments cannot be accepted with any degree of certainty but it is possible that at some future date archaeological exploration could enhance our knowledge of activity on Halton Hill during the period of Roman occupation.

Throughout all English counties accounts of ancient trackways and roads, allegedly Roman, are numerous. The origins of most so-called Roman roads date from the medieval period and later. Few can be traced back to the occupation. One such 'Roman' road was unearthed in Runcorn a hundred years ago. In 1884 a paved road was discovered half a metre under the surface of a field at the south end of the Big Pool. A length of roadway was exposed to reveal a three metre-wide causeway paved with boulders and having a convex surface. The line of the road pointed towards Weston village, up what was known as Sprinch Valley or Pool Valley. In the eighteenth century, during the construction of the Bridgewater Canal an embankment had been built across the small stream which flowed down the valley and this caused the formation of the pool. Investigation by probing to a depth of 1.5 metres proved that the road dipped towards the pool. Thomas Watkin decided that the discovery merited a mention in his 'Roman Cheshire'. He believed that the causeway was ancient in origin and that it had been in use until the canal was built. He thought it "best to put the fact on record ... though it is doubtful whether Roman". Watkin was puzzled. He could not account for so well-made a surface on a minor country lane. The local newspapers of the time however expressed no doubts. They emphatically pronounced the find to be the remains of a Roman road. But firm evidence of Roman commercial and military activity in this immediate district is non-existent. Watkin, in his 'Roman Lancashire' does mention a ferry or ford from Ditton to Runcorn which communicated with the Roman camp on Halton Hill but he gives no authority for its existence. Of the Roman occupation in what is now Runcorn and Halton there is little more to add. There have been few random finds. In 1907 a Mr. Roeder exhibited a Roman coin of the Emperor Domitian at a meeting of the Cheshire Antiquarian Society. The coin had been found nine metres below the sand of the river bed during excavations near to the Runcorn railway bridge and a fourth century coin of the Emperor Constantine was found by a schoolboy in a field at Weston in 1950. In recent years groups using metal detecting equipment have been active in the district and although definite evidence is not yet available there have been reports that Roman artifacts have been discovered at Dutton.

During the period of the Roman occupation our part of Cheshire was sparsely settled and there was little coming and going away from the major arterial roads. To the west of Halton Hill the terrain remained a wild, wooded region and three centuries of Roman rule left little evidence of their occupation. When the legions left Britain about the year 410 AD the landscape of north Cheshire was as it had been on their arrival centuries before. The panoramic view from Runcorn Hill in every direction presented a still and silent landscape with hardly a sign to indicate the presence of man. Perhaps smoke might be seen rising from an unseen dwelling in the distance and it might be possible to discern the scar of a muddy trackway disappearing in the direction of Halton. In the river bed at low tide the posts of a fish garth might be visible but it was heavily wooded country and the few small fields and homesteads would probably be completely hidden from sight among the trees. The region belonged to the deer and the wild boar and for

centuries to come, wolves would make sporadic attacks on farm stock.

Runcorn Burgh

For a period of more than two centuries after the withdrawal of the Roman legions the history of Britain is almost totally obscure. In the complete absence of documents and reliable accounts of events, we must rely on the archaeologist to attempt to throw light on the Dark Ages. However, despite the increase in scientific excavation which has taken place in the Runcorn area since 1971 we have, as yet, no finds from which we can hazard a guess as to the extent of the Anglo-Saxon settlement between the Mersey and the Weaver.

The Anglo-Saxon invaders had reached Cheshire by the end of the sixth century when the foundation of the Saxon kingdom of Mercia was taking place to the south of the county. Within a hundred years the power of Mercia increased and Cheshire was absorbed into the kingdom. Mercia, in its turn, was conquered in 829AD by Wessex, one of whose kings, Egbert, is usually acknowledged to have been the first King of all England.

Throughout the Dark Ages the landscape changed little and for the most part, large areas of the county remained uncultivated woodland and marsh but a study of Anglian place names gives some indication of English colonisation. Halton, Sutton, Stockham, Norton and Frodsham are names of Anglo-Saxon origin. Runcorn was 'ruman cofan' - a spacious cove or bay. The Mersey derives its name from the old English 'maeres ea' meaning boundary river. Daresbury is a personal name and a fortified place 'Deore's burgh'. Walton means 'the farm of the Welsh'. The former pre-eminence of Halton is obvious from the naming of the settlements which surrounded it. Norton is the 'north farm'; Aston, the 'east farm'; Sutton 'south farm' and Weston 'west farm'.

Even though the Anglo-Saxon period of the Dark Ages was of long duration, our knowledge from historical and archaeological sources is scanty but we do know that the population density hereabouts was thin and only Frodsham was a settlement of local importance.

During the reigns of King Alfred and his son Edward the Elder, the Vikings invaded Cheshire. The Norse came from the west from their bases in Ireland and the Isle of Man, whilst the Danes attacked from the east. In order to frustrate a Norse-Danish amalgamation, King Edward and his sister Ethelfleda built a line of forts or 'burghs' from Chester to Manchester. The Anglo-Saxon Chronicle tells us that Ethelfleda reinforced the defences of the Iron Age hill fort of Eddisbury in 914 and in the following year she built a burgh at Runcorn. These strongpoints were the responsibility of the local population. The settlements had to provide the garrisons and maintain the defences. It was expected that the men of the burghs would take quick action against Viking raiding parties without calling for help from the King's army. From the burghs, attacks could be launched to destroy small mobile enemy parties before they could join with others to become a larger force and a more serious threat. Action could also be taken in order to block the enemy's line of retreat. The Mersey became the boundary river between English Mercia and Scandinavian Danelaw.

Runcorn burgh was the most ancient structure on the Mersey and traces of it remained into the nineteenth century. From a description of the site made by a Mr. Moulsdale in 1819, we learn that the defences occupied an area of land about 40 metres by 30 metres on a rocky promontory which jutted out into a deep channel in the river. The landward side was protected by a ditch six metres wide and cut through the rock. Behind the ditch there was a rampart which was about two metres in height when Moulsdale made his observations. The burgh was a simple fort, hastily constructed and it probably consisted of the ditch with an embankment topped by a wooden palisade. Certainly it bore no resemblance to 'Runcorn Castle', the ornate stone citadel with turrets and battlements which is depicted on a popular postcard issued on the occasion of the thousandth anniversary of Ethelfleda's foundation.

We do not know if the burgh's defences were ever put to the test, or if they succeeded in deterring Viking longships from attempting to force the narrows of Runcorn Gap, but it is worth noting that when we look for Scandinavian placenames in our area, we find that Norse settlement east of Helsby appears to have been slight. Placename evidence of Scandinavian settlement on the Wirral peninsular is plentiful with such places as Irby, Caldy, Greasby, Whitby etc., but very few others are to be found throughout the rest of Cheshire. It is indeed possible that Ethelfelda's burghs were successful in containing Viking expansion. Whilst the strategic position of Runcorn fort is obvious, its importance was certainly overrated in a comment of 1574, which has been attributed to Sampson Erdeswicke. Writing some 660 years after the foundation of Ethelfleda's castle, Erdeswicke says, *"By West Halton uppon the river of Mersee a myle from Halton, standeth Runcorne, which in tymes past was a greate towne and had a strong castell called Runcolan which was kept with a strong garrison for the scourge of the inhabitants of Northumberland"*.

Apart from the brief contemporary comment in the Anglo-Saxon Chronicle, we know nothing of the history of Runcorn burgh. No doubt its defences were destroyed when Danish rule finally embraced Cheshire early in the eleventh century. The site then remained undisturbed until the Duke of Bridgewater carried out excavations in order to improve the navigation to his canal and the last vestige of Castle Rock disappeared when the railway bridge was being constructed in 1863. When the foundations were being built an ancient well was discovered but the railway company would not permit archaeological exploration in case it delayed work on the bridge and no artifacts were found on the site of Ethelfleda's fortress.

Runcorn burgh, together with that at Thelwall, occupied a salient position vital in the defence of Mercia's borders. The Runcorn-Thelwall link was to endure for nearly nine hundred years into Victorian times for Thelwall remained a detached township within the ancient parish of Runcorn, even though it was separated from Runcorn church by the parishes of Grappenhall and Great Budworth.

From the Anglo-Saxon Chronicle we have positive testimony that Runcorn is an ancient place. We also know that its establishment pre-dates Liverpool's foundation by nearly three hundred years and that Runcorn was already nine hundred and thirty years old when the beginnings of industrial Widnes appeared in the middle of the last century. That is all we know. Our knowledge of local events during the tenth and eleventh centuries is non-existent and we have no buildings of the period. However, on Cuerdley Marsh there are indentations in the turf which are said to be the site of a Danish encampment. These 'Danish Entrenchments' may be the only evidence of the Norsemen in our locality.

Bibliography

The general background reading for the prehistoric and Roman periods in Cheshire has been well covered in a number of Cheshire Community Council publications. These are W.J. Varley's *"Cheshire Before the Romans"* (1964); F.H. Thompson *"Roman Cheshire"* (1965); J.D. Bu'lock *"Pre-Conquest Cheshire 388 to 1066"* (1972). A most useful work for the better understanding of historical developments at a glance is *"The Historical Atlas of Cheshire"* by Dorothy Sylvester and Geoffrey Nulty, a Cheshire Community Council project of 1958. *"Man's Imprint on Cheshire"* (1975) by Oliver Bott and Rhys Williams is an essential background study for students of Cheshire history at any level. W.T. Watkin's *"Roman Cheshire"* (1886) is a major work of nineteenth century scholarship. Recently reprinted it is still very much an authoritative study which contains a number of references to this immediate district.

The Roman site on Halton Brow is discussed in R. Newstead and J.R. Droop's article "A Roman Camp at Halton, Cheshire" in the *"Liverpool Annals of Archaeology and Anthropology"*, Vol24 (1937) and also in the *Journal of the Chester Archaeological Society No.58* (1975) by A. Brown, J.B. Leaning and J.H. Little.

Historical information of the area which has been derived from placename evidence has been taken from J.M. Dodson's "The Place-Names of Cheshire" Part II. *"The English Place-Name Society"*, Vol.XLV (1970).

Information was also gleaned from J.W. Jackson "The Prehistoric Archaeology of Lancashire and Cheshire", *"Transactions of the Lancashire and Cheshire Antiquarian Society"* Vol.L (1934-5) and W. Shone *"Prehistoric Man in Cheshire"* (1911). The references to the Neolithic pottery discovered in Norton village are to be found in an article by J.P. Greene and P.R. Hough in *"Cheshire Archaeological Bulletin"* No.5 (1977).

The account of stray finds was supplied by Rhys Williams, Principal Archaeologist of the Cheshire County Planning Department from the department's records.

The reference to the foundation of Runcorn burgh is to be found it the *Anglo Saxon Chronicle*, revised translation by Dorothy Whitelock (1961) whilst a description and plan of the site can be found in G. Fowler *"A Vistor's Guide to Runcorn and its Vicinity"* (1834). The "Danish Entrenchments" on Cuerdley Marsh are illustrated in *"Old Widnes and its Neighbourhood"* (1906) by Charles Poole.

Chapter 2
Norman Rule

The Norman Conquest brought about a sudden transformation in English society. After Hastings a new aristocracy of about two hundred Norman lords inherited the country and Norman bishops replaced the native clergy. New churches and French monasteries replaced the old foundations and Norman sheriffs were appointed to govern the shires.

However, it was to be a few years before the Normans were able to take firm control over the whole country. At first they were few in number. They were thinly scattered throughout a hostile population and, after the initial shock of defeat and occupation, the Saxons began to offer resistance. During King William's absence in Normandy, a great rebellion broke out in Yorkshire and Durham followed by another in Mercia where the local English found Welsh allies to take advantage of the confused situation.

William restored his authority with a terrible vengeance by carrying out a campaign of terror across the north of England. During the 'Harrying of the North" his army ravaged the countryside laying waste crops and houses, slaughtering cattle and leaving a trail of death and destruction. The ruined survivors were scattered and their resistance was broken for ever. William then turned south to cross the Pennines and in the winter of 1069-70, he savaged Cheshire with similar ferocity. Great areas of the county were laid waste to remain desolate for years.

Historians believe that on entering Cheshire, William's avenging army divided into three or four groups. A northern arm advanced through Lymm to Halton and thrust its way across the Weaver through Frodsham to Chester looting and burning the settlements in its path. We know nothing of the fate of the English but those landowners who survived were dispossessed and the Norman grip became absolute.

After centuries of darkness about which we have such scant knowledge, the remarkable Domesday Book of 1086 illuminates the local scene to give us a brief glimpse of life in the eleventh century and then once again we are confronted by a total blank for the next hundred years. The Domesday Book was a survey intended for taxation purposes. It records people, their status and occupations, the extent of land with its use and value, together with some information concerning mills and fisheries. William required to know the value of the land when Edward the Confessor ruled the kingdom in 1066 and also its

worth in 1086, twenty years after the Conquest. By this date only about 8% of the land remained in the hands of the English.

From the Domesday Book we know that in 1066 Norton (Nortune) was held as two manors by Tokig and Uhtred. Tokig, from his name, a wealthy descendant of Norse settlers, also had four manors on the Gowy. Norton was worth sixteen shillings in 1066 but twenty years later its value had fallen to nine shillings and four pence. The Domesday entry states, *"There is land (enough) for 6 ploughs. In the demesne there is 1 plough and 2 serfs and (there are) 3 villeins with 1 plough. There is 1 fisherman and 3 acres of meadow and 4 acres of wood(land) and 2 hays … He found it waste".* Although Domesday's references to 'waste' do not necessarily meant that an area had been destroyed by William's army sixteen years previously, it is almost certain that this is what happened at Norton and the manor had recovered slowly to reach just over half its previous value by 1086. In that year Norton was held as one manor by Ansfred.

Halton (Heletune) suffered the same fate as Norton, for Domesday tells us *"The whole manor was worth 40 shillings (In the reign of King Edward the Confessor) and afterwards was waste; now what William holds is worth 50 shillings and what (his) knights hold is worth 54 shillings".*

The Saxon lord of the manor of Halton in 1066 was Orme. Twenty years later we learn that, *"There are 10 hides. Of these, 5 pay geld and the others do not. There is land (enough) for 20 ploughs. In the demesne are 2 ploughs and 4 oxmen and (there are) 4 villeins and 2 bordars and 2 priests with 5 ploughs among (them) all. There is wood(land) 1 league long and half (a league) wide. There are 2 hays … Of this land of this manor Odard holds half a hide, Geoffrey 2 hides, Aitard one and a half hides, Humphrey one and a half hides, Odard half a hide, Hardwin half a hide".* The entry for Halton further informs us, *"In the demesne there are 3 ploughs, and (there are) 12 villeins and 1 radman and 5 bordars with 5 ploughs between (them) all and 6 oxmen and half an acre of meadow and 18 acres of wood(land)".*

The term 'radman' applied to a free tenant who had his smallholding on condition he served the lord on horseback. The radman used his horses to plough, harrow and cart on the lord's lands. The bordar held his small piece of land on condition he supplied the lord with eggs and fowl. Both the radman and the bordar did work on the manor for wages. But most workers on the manor were villeins and their status was little above that of slaves. They were tied to the land but they could be dispossessed of their hovels at the whim of the lord. The villein was required to work for two or three days on the lord's estate and he had to make certain payments to the lord's steward at Easter and Michaelmas. When a villein's daughter was married or his son entered the church, a fee had to be paid.

It goes without saying that there was an enormous gulf between the peasants and the wealthy ruling class and the differences were further emphasised by the fact that the latter spoke only Norman-French.

About a mile south of Norton was the settlement of Enelelei (Eanley in Norton). Wighe held it before the Conquest and by 1086 there was half a hide and *"There is land for half a plough (team). It was and is, waste"*.

Weston (Westone) was held by Gruffyd (Grifin) before the Norman Conquest. At the time of the great survey it was held by Odard and Brihtric. There was *"woodland 1 league in length and half (a league) in width and a hay. It was worth 8 shillings (in King Edward's time) now worth 35 shillings. He found it waste"*.

Aston (Estone) was in the possession of Odard. It had previously been the domain of the Saxon, Leofric. In addition to the usual details of occupation we learn that, "There is a mill for grinding for the hall".

No reference to Runcorn appears in the Domesday Survey and it is generally assumed that the hamlet was included as part of the large Halton estate. There are two priests listed for Halton and there is a belief that one served Halton village and the other ministered Runcorn hamlet. From the Domesday Book we get a tantalising glimpse of life in the first twenty years of Norman rule. The population of the area was very small. Halton was one of only four places in Cheshire with more than fifty inhabitants recorded. When the figure is multiplied by five to allow for families the total population of Runcorn and Halton numbered perhaps two hundred and fifty men, women and children. On the same basis Weston would have about 75 whilst Norton might have had 45 persons all told.

While there is some argument about the actual dimensions of the ancient land measures used in Domesday and there is so much more we would like to know about the landscape, we learn that the area was still heavily wooded with a small population existing on scattered settlements and farming small pieces of land to provide for its livelihood. It was a poor and undeveloped region, remote and isolated from the main centres of activity and only slowly recovering from the impoverishment caused by the 'harrying' of the country in 1070.

William the Conqueror created three powerful earldoms to protect his kingdom from Welsh attacks. In order to safeguard his borders he established the earldoms of Shrewsbury, Hereford and Chester. William granted the earldom of Chester with almost viceregal powers to Gherbod the Fleming and when Gherbod returned to his continental estates, the King gave the earldom to Hugh of Avranches, also known as Hugh Lupus (the Wolf) or Hugh the Fat. It was Hugh Lupus who appointed Nigel to be the first baron of Halton. Initially, Norman Cheshire was divided into ten administrative sub-divisions called 'hundreds'. Halton and Runcorn lay within the hundred of Tunendune which later amalgamated with Bochelau hundred to form the hundred of Bucklow.

The rebellion of 1069 and the ever-present possibility of further Norse attacks, made the establishment of a secure base in the barony a matter of urgency and at 100 metres above sea level, Halton Hill afforded an excellent situation for a castle and centre for local government. Today there are no features of Norman military architecture apparent in the ruins of Halton Castle but it is almost certain that Nigel constructed a typical motte and bailey castle with wooden ramparts so that there are now no remains of the original fortification. It is surprising that Halton Castle is not mentioned in Domesday by which time it was well established as the centre of local administration.

From Domesday we learn that William FitzNigel, the second baron of Halton, held some thirty manors throughout Tunendune and Bochelau as well as other holdings in Wirral. He married the eldest daughter of Yorfrid, the baron of Widnes and as Yorfrid left no male heir, the Widnes barony became extinct and the Lancashire manors of Widnes, Appleton, Cronton and Rainhill came to William on the death of his father-in-law. William FitzNigel thus controlled both sides of Runcorn Gap and in order to protect his widespread possessions, he would require a stronghold at the river crossing. In his 'Cheshire under the Norman Earls", B.M.C Husain suggests that the baron of Halton probably built a small castle at the narrows. It is not unlikely that he found the site of Ethelfleda's burgh to be the ideal position for his new fort.

The Translation of Runcorn Priory

In 1115, William FitzNigel founded a priory of the Augustinian Order of Canons Regular at Runcorn which some historians believe was colonised from the large and wealthy Austin priory at Bridlington in Yorkshire. But the new priory was not to remain long in Runcorn, for in 1134 William FitzWilliam, the third Baron of Halton, out of pious regard for the soul of his father, gave the canons a more favourable site three miles to the east at Norton. The Charter of Norton Priory lists the various properties throughout Cheshire and the Midlands to which the canons were entitled.

"In the name of the Father, Son and Holy Ghost; I, William the son of William the son of Nigel do give and grant to the Holy Church of Mary of Norton and to the Canons Regular serving God there, the vill of Norton in free alms, with all appurtenances in wood, with forests and warren, and in plain with lands, pastures and waters, and at the request and by the advice of Roger, Bishop of Chester and by the advice of my own people I change the habitation of the said canons from Runcorn to Norton, which Norton I give and grant to the said canons in free alms and all the exchange of three carucates in Stannings and one carucate and a half in Aston, in lieu of all Runcorn except the church and four oxgangs of land and one fishery which is called Pulceope which belongs to the Church of Runcorn which church belongs to the aforesaid canons.

Also I give and grant to the aforesaid canons the mill of Halton, with a moiety of all the fisheries which belong to Halton. I also grant them and their tenants common in the woods, waters and pastures which belongs to Halton and two oxgangs of land in Halton with one dwelling there and one moiety of my whole fishery of Thelwall with one oxgang of land and the fisherman there.

Also two oxgangs in Widnesse with common of the woods and pastures belonging to Pulton for them and three dwellings in Widnesse. I also grant to them common of the woods and pastures in Cuerdley and the mill at Barrow and two parts of the demesne tithes of Sutton and likewise in Stanney and in Roby and in Stannings with one dwelling in Chester and the church of Great Budworth and the church of Dunnington in Leicestershire and the tithes of the same vill and mill and of the parish itself and Wavertoft, which is computed as half a carucate of land and the church of Raclyffe-upon-Soar in Nottingham, and the tithes of the fourth part of mills and the tithes of the three parts of the same vill, and the church of Oneshall in Nottingham and the tithes of the mills which belong to the same vill which are near to Sitella, and the tithe of the mill in Alfreton and the Church of Burtone in Lincolnshire and the same church in Pirinton in Oxfordshire."

The generosity of William FitzWilliam set an example for others to emulate and during the next four hundred years, first the Barons of Halton and later the wealthy local land-owning families, endowed the priory with gifts of money and land. In return for their liberality the benefactors expected to be buried within the priory church. The founder, however, was not to receive this privilege for William FitzWilliam died childless in Normandy sometime before 1150.

The foundation charter of Norton Priory asks for a blessing on all who support the canons, *"Whoso, therefore, shall augment or maintain this charitable foundation may he, through the benefits of Holy Church, obtain the Kingdom of heaven, but whoso shall infringe or violate them in any respect, maybe, unless he make restitution, be punished in Hell with Judas and Pilate, Dathan and Abiram".*

From their hooded black cloaks and white surplices with black cassocks beneath, the Augustinians were known as the Black Canons. They were not confined to the priory or abbey but ministered in the parish churches which had been appropriated to them.

Besides the churches at Runcorn and Great Budworth which are mentioned in the foundation charter, other Cheshire churches were eventually appropriated to Norton Priory - Norton Abbey from about 1391. These were Daresbury; Grappenhall, St Helen's at Witton, Northwich; St Oswald, Lower Peover and probably St Martin at Ashton-upon-Mersey. The Abbots of Norton also provided canons or nominated clergy to serve as priests in the chapels of ease at Aston and Halton.

The Ferry

Until fairly recent times the upper estuary of the river Mersey constituted a formidable barrier to trade and communications. However, it was possible to effect a crossing of the river by way of the ford between Hale and Weston Point, or by the one at Runcorn Gap. Even under favourable conditions both routes could be hazardous particularly the ford at the narrows. The latter way across was very dangerous and the passage was only possible for a brief period at the lowest of the tide. Nevertheless, horsemen, packhorses, men on foot and even carts hurried across the sands on neap tides in dry weather.

It has not been possible to establish the date of the foundation of the regular ferry boat service at Runcorn but, without doubt, soon after the Norman Conquest, boats would have been available for court and baronial officials, for soldiers, churchmen and others whose business required them to travel the region. In order to maintain contact with the tenants and retainers on his Lancashire estates, the Baron of Halton would require a boat, therefore an irregular ferry service must have been in operation from the time the Barony of Widnes was united with the Barony of Halton at the end of the eleventh century. Opinions as to when the permanent ferry crossing was established vary but it is generally accepted that this may have been around 1178.

The earliest charter to refer to a ferry is that by Richard de More (of Moore) which granted two bovates of land in Roncover to his son Wgoon. Besides the land, which was formerly the estate of Beatrix of Higher Roncover, Wgoon received "one toft and croft in Widnesse". He was required to maintain half the costs of the ferry with, presumably, the other half coming from passenger's tolls. "And the same Wgoon and his heirs shall find the necessaries for the passage of half the ship of Widnesse for ever for all who wish to cross there for the love of God. And the same Wgoon shall give the third part of his goods to God and the Hospital (of the Holy House of Jerusalem) at his death".

When this ancient charter came up for sale at a public auction in March 1984, the document was bought by the Borough of Halton for £200.

According to a similar charter of 1190, the annual payment to be paid to the English Brotherhood of the Knights Hospitallers for the ferry was increased from two to four shillings a year. The Hospitallers were dedicated to the care of the sick and the poor and particularly to the welfare of travellers and pilgrims. The charter of 1190 states that *"Garnier de Naplouse, grand prior of the English brotherhood of Knights Hospitallers, granted lands in Platt and elsewhere to Richard de la More and his heirs, in consideration of his paying four shillings yearly at Michaelmas, and keeping in repair on the River Mersey at Runcorn, the vessel which John, Constable of Chester, for the love of God, had formerly provided to carry across the stream those who desired it, upon condition that one third part of the chattels of Richard and his heirs in succession at the death of each were reserved to the brotherhood for the good of his soul"*.

The custom of granting and renewing charters to the operators of the ferry was carried on during the following centuries so that the service should continue and in order to deter persons from attempting to establish illegal rival ferries. At the beginning of 1366 the Black Prince, as Earl of Chester, forbade any passage of the Mersey to be made except at those places which had always been used for crossing. Anyone attempting to establish new routes was to be arrested and imprisoned in Chester Castle. For the matter to have received the attention of the prince suggests

that there was a serious problem which was probably of long standing. It would seem that adventurers were operating illegal crossings and were trying to draw custom away from the chartered Mersey ferries, the services of which were profitable and in demand.

The Medieval Parish Church of St Bertelin

Tradition has it that the first Parish Church to be dedicated to St Bertelin at Runcorn was founded in 915 by Ethelfleda and that it was situated on the site occupied by the present church of All Saints. As Ethelfleda's fortress would require the services of a small community in order to garrison and maintain it, it is reasonable to assume that the traditional view is well-founded and that a small church was built to serve the needs of the settlement. The Lady of the Mercians was a devout princess, the daughter of the fervent King Alfred and it is likely she built a modest church, probably of wood and thatch, a few hundred yards to the east of her defences. The fact that a year before coming to Runcorn, Ethelfleda had been building defences in Stafford where there is also a church dedicated to St Bertelin, lends some credence to the belief that she was the founder of Runcorn church. Of Bertelin himself we know little. He was reported to have been a Mercian prince of the ninth century. On the Norman font at Ilam church in Derbyshire, where he is buried, there are carvings which are said to be illustrations of events in his life.

So whilst we may reasonably assume the existence of an early tenth century church, there exists no documentary or archaeological evidence to substantiate the assumption. However, if we do accept the traditional belief, then it is probable that Ethelfelda's church lasted into Norman times when it was replaced by a more substantial building. Or perhaps the church of Runcorn Priory was given to the township to serve as its parish church after the canons had departed for Norton in 1134? There is so much we would like to know.

Although there is no reference to Runcorn or Runcofan and no mention of a priest or church in the Domesday Survey of 1086, we learn from another source that a church did exist at Runcorn. Nigel, the first baron of Halton, is recorded as having conferred the church at Runcorn on "Wolfrith (or Wolfaith) a priest in the days of the Conqueror". There are no remains of Norman building to be seen today but when the medieval church was being demolished in 1846, Norman capitals were found in the masonry of the old tower.

We are able to discuss with more certainty the thirteenth century Parish Church which lasted for six hundred years until its destruction in the middle of the last century. From various old drawings and paintings and from descriptions in directories as well as from details in diocesan records, we can obtain a clear picture of this building. Some nineteenth century artists' representations of the medieval church can also help us to date the various periods of building with some degree of confidence. Illustrations of the interior indicate that the oldest part to survive into Victorian times was the northern nave arcade. This shows that the church was probably built about the year 1250 in the Early English style of architecture. The nave had four pointed arches each resting on clustered columns with ornamented capitals to produce a most pleasing result. The arcade impressed Thomas Rickman, the architect who, in the early years of the last century, first categorised English ecclesiastical building styles. He wrote, "In Runcorn church there is a pier consisting of four triangular shafts with a handsome flowered capital which has altogether a very fine effect".

The chancel was small with the ceiling and roof being much lower than the main body of the church. It was square in plan and the same width as the central nave. Early Victorian illustrations show that the chancel ceiling was bridged by ponderous timbers. Four heavy rafters rested on wall plates fastened to massive tie beams which spanned the chancel. On either side of the ridge beam it seems that there were four purlins. This heavy framework must have created an impression of enduring strength and permanence. The short length of wall on the south of the chancel was pierced by three small windows each having a flat lintel. The easterly of the windows had three narrow lights whilst the others had two lights.

It is certain that the chancel was rebuilt in the fourteenth century for the large east window of three lights had tracery of the decorated period. Some of the chancel windows retained fragments of ancient painted glass until the demolition of the church in 1846.

The magnificent pre-Reformation rood screen which divided the chancel from the nave, survived the activities of sixteenth and seventeenth century religious fanatics only to be destroyed during the Victorian era of church 'restoration'. It was the principal piece of church furniture and its loss has been nothing short of a major tragedy. The elaborately carved screen had retained its rood loft and the brestsummer beam which supported the loft was intricately carved with at least four bands of decoration. In the Middle Ages the beam was a plinth bearing the figure of Christ accompanied by angels or by figures representing the Virgin and St John. The space between the rood beam and the apex of the nave roof was filled by a light frame wall which formed a plastered background to the figures.

The screen has been identified as a genuine example of the Welsh type, similar to those which still exist in churches at Llananno and Llanwnog in Powys. On each side of a wide central doorway there were four bays of delicate tracery with niches and carved bands of leaves and flowers. In the fifteenth century the screen would have been richly gilded and painted. The wanton destruction of such fine craftsmanship has long been lamented by historians and experts in church furnishings but although the screen vanished with the rest of the old church, a few fragments of it were saved to decorate the stalls of the present church. These were tracery heads salvaged from the remains of the old screen wainscot. Twenty pieces remain showing eight different designs. They have flattened ogee arches below with slightly pointed arches above. One head is particularly interesting with its circles and intertwined triangles forming ingenious patterns. The destruction of the ancient church was total and no other artifacts of the medieval period have survived.

The square west tower was a fourteenth century addition with a belfry stage either added or rebuilt in the fifteenth century. It was a low tower, embattled and having a west window of three lights with curvilinear tracery. On the south side of the tower there was a niche or ornamental recess originally intended to hold a small statue. Each of the four faces of the belfry had a window of two lights. The tower was completed with gargoyles and castellated battlements and with diagonal buttresses canopied at the offsets and which reached to the parapets.

As far as is known there exists no illustration which depicts the south side of the church as it was before the extensive alterations which were carried out in the early years of the nineteenth century. However, there is a watercolour sketch executed by the Reverend J. Allen about 1835 which shows the building from the north-east. The picture shows that the north aisle facing the river had two windows with square heads each having curvilinear tracery. Towards the west end of the north aisle there was an Early English doorway with fine deep mouldings and foliated capitals. Glynn describes the north aisle as "narrow and low" and he says that its west window was lancet-shaped. The aisle had a large east window and Allen's watercolour clearly shows its Early English intersecting "Y" tracery. The south-east corner of the chancel was supported by a deep diagonal buttress.

It was a small church. From an architect's survey made a few years before its demolition, we learn that the nave was fifty-two feet long and forty feet wide. At fifty-seven feet in height the tower was the dominant feature of the river bank for more than four centuries.

Runcorn parish churchyard did not become "an immense accumulation of upright gravestones" until the early decades of the nineteenth century. In medieval times the graveyard was a grassy plot which was much used by the parishioners when they celebrated weddings and baptisms. The churchyard was also the scene of boisterous entertainment on major feast days. It was sometimes the venue for illegal markets and the place where neighbours solemnly swore oaths to settle disputes after mass. A vicar in the reign of Queen Elizabeth I succeeded in making a profit out of God's Acre. He was upbraided by the archdeacon for using the churchyard as a smallholding in which to graze sheep.

At an unknown date the dedication of Runcorn church was changed from the pre-Norman St Bertelin to the better known St Bartholemew and later to All Saints by which it is known today. Happily, the original name has been perpetuated in the new church of St Berteline recently built at Windmill Hill.

The ancient parish of Runcorn was unusually large, with nineteen townships within its widespread boundaries. Extending roughly eleven miles from Weston Point to include Thelwall to the east and being five miles across to Dutton in the south, the parish had chapels of ease at Halton, Daresbury, Aston and Thelwall. In addition to these places, Runcorn was the mother church for the townships of Norton, Moore, Acton Grange, Higher and Lower Walton, Weston, Clifton, Stockham, Keckwick, Sutton, Newton by Daresbury, Hatton, Aston Grange and Preston-on-the-Hill.

In spite of the fact that the practice of appointing canons or monks to the livings of appropriated churches was condemned by English law in an act of 1403 which specifically ruled that, "The vicar of every church should be a secular person and not a member of a religious house, that he should be vicar perpetual and not moveable at the caprice of a monastery", the parish of Runcorn was always administered by the prior or abbot of Norton. Every vacancy to the vicarage right up to the dissolution of Norton Abbey in 1536 was filled either directly by the installation of a canon or by an appointment made by the prior or abbot.

The rights which the abbots of Norton claimed to appoint to livings was challenged in 1455, when a special episcopal commission met in Great Budworth to enquire into the vacancy there and into the rights of patronage of the church. The commissioners found that the Abbot of Norton possessed the right, by virtue of a special dispensation, to present one of the brethren of Norton whenever the vicarage

The lead seal from a papal manuscript of Pope Boniface IX (1389 - 1404) found in Runcorn Parish churchyard in 1910.

became vacant. In his article, "The Elevation of Norton Priory to the Status of a Mitred Abbey", Patrick Greene who was the archaeology officer to the Runcorn Development Corporation and the excavator of Norton Priory, puts foward the view that the churches which were served by the canons of Norton probably held papal documents which could be produced to prove ancient rights. This would explain why a lead seal, which was once attached to a papal manuscript or bulla, came to be found in Runcorn Parish churchyard in 1910. The bulla has been identified as the seal of Pope Boniface IX (1389-1404). One side of the seal has the Pope's name and on the other, two heads which represent St Peter and St Paul.

From early in the thirteenth century, papal tithes which were levied throughout Europe formed the staple income of the Papacy. In 1291, during the pontificate of Pope Nicholas IV, the annual income of Runcorn church was assessed at £20 and that of Frodsham at £24. The papal chamberlain received therefore, £2 from the vicar of Runcorn and two pounds four shillings from Frodsham church.

Although for centuries the parish church of Runcorn was the centre of worship and social activity, we know little of daily life in the parish. However, there is an interesting record of the responsibilities of the parish towards sanctuary seekers. In 1403 after a hue and cry, Robert Morysson, a felon charged with the murder of Thomas de Builde, took refuge in Runcorn Church from which he later escaped. The parish was collectively fined £8 for failing to arrest Morryson and the King's sergeant, Richard

Castell, was ordered to collect the fine which was paid in two instalments.

The size of Runcorn parish made necessary the building of 'chapels of ease' in the outlying areas for those parishioners who would be unable to attend services at the mother church because of the difficulties of travel and the distance involved. The earliest chapel provided for the inhabitants at Aston was the chapel of Poosey or Pooseye, meaning the chapel situated between the park pool and the river Weaver. It was built by Sir Thomas de Dutton in 1236. In 1329 Edward III, after confirming a royal charter of 1154 to the canons of Norton, also confirmed a gift made by Hugh, son of Hugh de Dutton, of two shillings and eight pence rent from Pulleseia and land there with a chapel. Sir Peter Leycester, the Cheshire historian, writing in 1673 states, *"Richard de Aston gave to Hugh Dutton of Dutton six bovates of land in Aston about 1230 ... These lands belong now (1673) to the demain of Dutton, wherein the Chapel of Poosey (now in decay) was situate within the parish of Runcorne, and had its name from the situation, being seated between the park-pool and the river, thence called Poosey Chapel; "Ee" or "Ey" signifies a brook in the old Saxon language"*. About 1236, the prior of Norton agreed with Hugh de Dutton to find a chaplain to officiate for ever and to keep a lamp burning during the services. Eighty years later, the Bishop of Lichfield received a complaint alleging that the prior of Norton had neglected to provide the chaplain and the lamp for Poosey chapel whereupon the bishop gave orders that the prior should furnish both.

Poosey chapel was in regular use for about four hundred years until Lord Kilmorey (died 1653) and his wife came to Dutton. They beautified the domestic chapel at Dutton Hall and kept a private chaplain with the result that all the neighbours went there for Sunday services and Poosey chapel fell into total ruin. Some parts of the old building were still standing at the end of the seventeenth century.

There is the possibility of yet another ancient chapel existing at Aston. Sir Peter Leycester's account of events is not clear when he refers to Middleton Chapel at Middleton Grange. He could be referring to Poosey chapel or to another church situated in the same area. Leycester records, *"In this Aston lieth a certain parcel of land called Middleton Grange ... here was anciently a chappel called Middleton Chappel, where the pryor and convent of Norton were bound to find a priest, in former ages, to say mass on Sundays, Wednesdays and Fridays, weekly for ever; which chappel being out of repair and service said there onely on Sundays for forty years then last past, it was complained of by Richard Aston, son of Sir Robert Aston at a visitation 3 Hen. VI 1425, and an order was made by Richard Stanley then archdeacon*

of Chester the twentieth of August 3 Hen. VI, that whereas the prior and convent of Norton, long before the same was an abbey, did covenant with the abbot of Vale-Royal, to find at their own proper cost a fit chaplain to officiate here three days a week, as aforesaid; it was ordered, that the said agreement should be kept and observed ... But these variances concerning Middleton Chappel, between Robert ,Abbot of the monastery of St Mary of Norton and Richard Aston of Aston Esquire, were composed by the mediation of Thomas Dutton, esquire and Anne his wife, Dame Isabel late wife of Sir John Carrington and Jenkin of Leycester dated tenth of November 32 Henry VI.

But after that Middleton chappel fell into decay, another chappel was erected in later ages, somewhat nearer to the hall of Aston, called Aston Chappel situate within the parish of Runcorne; and in lieu of finding a priest to officiate here by the abbot of Norton, the King (after those lands came into his hands) gave five pounds yearly rent to the maintenance here at Aston Chappel, issuing out of the lands late belonging to Norton abbey, by a decree in the court of augmentations at London dated 28th January 33 Henry VIII (1542) which decree was exemplified and confirmed 13th year of Queen Elizabeth (1571) ... which sum of five pounds is yearly paid to this day, 1671 by the King's auditor at his office in Chester".

"Poolsey" chapel is mentioned in 1609 in the inquisition of John Dutton and also in that of Thomas Dutton in 1615. Licenses authorising marriages at Poosey chapel were granted in 1624 and 1629 but after Leicester's record of 1673 there are no further references to either Middleton or Poolsey. No vestige of the chapels remains and the earliest church on the site of the present one at Aston was probably built in the first half of the sixteenth century.

Towards the end of Henry III's reign Weston village had a chapel of ease. It is known that from about 1265 the villagers were allowed to have divine service in their chapel on the understanding that the mother church in Runcorn continued to receive all the tithes. This privilege was granted to the inhabitants of Weston by the prior of Norton, Roger of Lincoln, but little more is known of the chapel which had disappeared by the late Middle Ages.

In Weston village there is the remnant of an ancient preaching or market cross. The cross was restored in 1897 to commemorate Queen Victoria's Diamond Jubilee and again in 1960 and only the plinth is now original. The age of Weston cross and the precise reason for its existence are unknown but it was probably the venue for open-air religious meetings before the Reformation.

In 1262, the prior of Norton granted permission for mass to be said in a manor house at Sutton

Weaver. Sir Geoffrey de Dutton was allowed this privilege provided the family continued to attend services at Runcorn church on major feast days and make their offerings there.

Until early in the present century there was a small medieval house known locally as 'Abbey Cottage' in Mount Pleasant, off Mersey Road in Runcorn. In a national magazine published before the first world war it was described as 'The oldest cottage in England and a landmark from time immemorial". The cottage is said to have been an occasional lodging for the mendicant friars of the Order of St Augustine who travelled the region from their house in Warrington from the last quarter of the thirteenth century until the friary was closed in 1539.

This magazine illustration from early in this century claims that the thatched "Abbey Cottage" on Mount Pleasant off Mersey Road, was "the oldest cottage in England".

Bibliography

The essential background material for this chapter has been gathered together from B.M.C. Husain's *"Cheshire Under the Norman Earls"* (1973); *"Cheshire and its Rulers"* by Brian Harris (1984); J.J. Bagley's *"The Story of Merseyside"* (1968) and from William Beamont's *"A History of Halton Castle and the Priory or Abbey of Norton"* (1973). Additional information is to be found in Charles Poole *"Old Widnes and Its Neighbourhood"* (1906) and C. Nickson, *"History of Runcorn"* (1887).

The account of the Domesday survey of this district comes from *"The Domesday Book. Cheshire"* ed. Philip Morgan (1978) and from H.C. Derby and I.S. Maxwell's *"The Domesday Geography of Northern England"* (1962). *"The Historical Atlas of Cheshire" (1958) by* Dorothy Sylvester and Geoffrey Nulty and J. Tait's "The Foundation of Charter of Runcorn Priory", *Chetham Society (1939)* provided useful information.

Other publications used include J.P. Greene *"Norton Priory"* (Handbook of the Norton Priory Trust, 1975); "The Place-Names of Cheshire" *English Place-Name Society* Vol.XLV, Part II (1970) by J.M. Dobson and G. Ormerod's *"History of the County Palatine and City of Chester"* ed. T. Helsby (1882).

For the account of the medieval church of Runcorn reference has been made to *"Runcorn Parish Church"* - Centenary Publication (1949) and *"A Visitor's Guide to the Parish Church of All Saints Runcorn"* (1978). A most useful source was "Notes on the Churches of Cheshire" by Sir Stephen Glynne, ed. Rev. J.A. Atkinson, *Chetham Soc.* (1894). Information about the original stallwork in the church at Runcorn comes from Fred H. Crossley "Concerning Certain Designs in Screens and Stallwork found in the Borderland of England and Wales" in *"The Transactions of the Lancashire and Cheshire Historic Society"* Vol.97 (1945); *"The Church Screens of Cheshire"* by Fred Crossley (1918).

Other references to Runcorn church can be found in Thomas Rickman *"An Attempt to Discriminate the Styles of Architecture in England"* (1841); *"Old Cheshire Churches"* (1947) by Raymond Richards; and "The Elevation of Norton Priory to the Status of a Mitred Abbey" by J.P. Greene, *"Transactions of the Lancashire and Cheshire Historic Society"* Vol.128 (1978).

The Chapel of Poosey is described in Leycester's *"History of Cheshire"* (1673) and in *"Cheshire Sheaf"* Vol.XXVIII (1933).

*The earliest charter of Runcorn Ferry. It bears a seal of green wax with a trefoil and the imprint
"Sigillum Ricardi de la Mor".*

(Photograph. The Borough of Halton.)

Know all (men) as well present as to come that I,
Richard de Mora, have given etc., to Wgoon my son two
bovates of land in Roncover which were of Beat(rix) on
this side of Higher Roncover, and one toft and (?) one
croft in Widnesse which John the Constable of Chester
gave to me. And the half of "la hoc" which I obtained of
William the son of DolFin. And the croft of Bickerstathe
which I had of Adam the son of Bernulf. To have and
to hold of God and of St. John the babtist and of the Holy
House of the Hospital of Jerusalem. Rendering thence
annually to God and St. John, and the Holy House of
the Hospital two shillings at the Nativity of St. Mary,
as freely and quitly as I myself have held the afordsaid
lands of the hospital. And the same Wgoon and his heirs
shall find the Necessaries for the passage of half the ship
of Widnesse for ever for all who shall wish to cross there
for the love of God. And the same Wgoon shall give the
third part of his goods to God and the hospital at his
death. These being witnesses:- Adam de Dutton, Hugh
de Dutton, his brother, Hugh Norreis, Fulk then serjeant
of Wineton, Andrew then reeve of Wineton, Orme de
Wineton, Peter de Hopw(o)de, Adam de Mora, Hulle de
Mora, and many others.

Chapter 3
The Medieval Community

Runcorn in the Middle Ages was typical of the hundreds of small communities scattered throughout the length and breadth of the county. It was a tiny, lonely hamlet in contact with similar communities in Cheshire only by way of muddy trackways which became impassable in winter. To the north the Mersey was an effective barrier to interchange between the village and the homesteads in Lancashire. Because of their isolation the inhabitants were of necessity forced to rely on their own energies and skills to produce all the food, clothing, tools, furniture and fuel they needed in order to survive.

Runcorn's only substantial stone building was the church. The hovels of the manorial peasants were flimsy structures of timber with a mud infilling between the oak frames. They were devoid of glass and chimneys and often the only source of light and air was by way of the open door. These mean dwellings had floors of pounded earth. They were roofed with thatch or turf and were heated by peat fires or from sticks gathered in the woodlands, the smoke escaping through a hole in the roof. Some cabins boasted a small fenced vegetable plot with perhaps one or two fruit trees. Not one of these houses or even a single domestic item has survived to posterity.

The land was undrained and weedy. The flocks and herds consisted of bony creatures which were susceptible to endemic animal murrain. When the crops failed after a wet summer, the resulting local famine often spelled disaster for the villagers during the following winter. Rarely was there a surplus of anything. Life expectancy was less than 40 years.

The settlements of Halton, Runcorn, Weston and Norton were small islands of arable land set in waste, marsh and woodland. The villeins had rights in the woods. They could take fallen wood for their fuel at any time, as well as 'housbote' or lesser timber with which to repair houses. The peasants were allowed to dig peat and, on the payment of a tax called pannage, they could agist pigs in the woods when acorns were plentiful. They also had rights of pasture for their cattle on the common grassland.

The manorial records of the stock on the Halton estates are extant for the years 1294 and 1305. In 1305 there were 7 oxen, 3 bulls, 50 cows, 20 steers, 35 yearlings and 10 calves. These figures represent an increase in animals of over 100% on the returns for 1294. A few peasant families kept a cow for butter, milk and cheese and also an ox

for ploughing and draught purposes. When his working days were over the ox was killed and the meat was preserved in Cheshire salt which was easily obtained. The money collected as pannage and shown in the manorial accounts for 1371 indicates that large numbers of pigs were kept in Halton and Runcorn. Pigs provided the main source of fresh meat with bacon being a staple winter food.

The traditional open field system whereby the medieval village community worked large unenclosed fields of strip allotments was certainly the pattern of agriculture in Norton village. An estate map of 1757 shows the land around the village still divided up into long narrow strip fields of about an acre and half an acre each. This field pattern of land holding had obviously been handed down little changed from the Middle Ages when each peasant farmer had a number of strip fields scattered over the open field between those of his neighbours. There were no hedges and one strip was divided from the next by a narrow grass balk. This system of strip farming was devised as a fair method of ensuring that each peasant had his share of good and poor land.

Excavations carried out at Lodge Farm in Norton village in 1977 uncovered cobbled tracks, cess pits, platform-shaped mounds indicating the collapsed remains of a couple of small cottages, as well as pottery shards dating from the thirteenth to the seventeenth century.

The Manor of Halton

From the surviving manorial accounts of Henry de Lacy, the tenth Baron of Halton, we have some insight into everyday life in our area at the end of the thirteenth century.

Henry de Lacy was one of the most prominent and powerful barons of the kingdom. He was Baron of Halton, Lord of the Honour of Clitheroe and hereditary Constable of Chester. He owned great estates in Yorkshire, Lincolnshire and elsewhere. He was a ward of Henry III and had been brought up at his court. At the early age of 6 years he married Margaret, the eldest daughter of William Longspee who was a grandson of Henry II. De Lacy's early manhood was spent in warfare under Edward I to whom he became a chief councillor and devoted friend. On March 8th 1272 de Lacy was created Earl of Lincoln and made governor of Knaresborough castle. His chief Yorkshire barony was that of Pontefract where he held his court. In 1276 de Lacy entered upon the first of many campaigns against the Welsh. A conspicuous and mighty noble, it is unlikely that de Lacy concerned himself with the barony of Halton. However, his auditors were frequent visitors to Halton and their detailed accounts of rents and monies due to the earl make interesting reading.

On 15th November 1296 two accountants, the clerics William de Noney and Thomas de Fisseburn, were at Halton to scrutinise the financial records of the barony. They collected the taxes from Halton and from Higher and Lower Runcorn due for the grazing of cattle on the earl's lands and also for the pigs feeding in his woods together with the rents from the mills and fisheries on the estate. The income from the tolls of Halton market indicates thriving business. "William de Wambwell, Receiver, renders his Compotus at Halton on 15th November, before William de Nony and Thomas de Fissburn from 30th September 1295 to 30th September 1296".

	£	s	d
Rent of Runcouer upper and lower with 6d rent of Thomas the parker as in the last compotus Nov 11th and June 24th	7	2	9½
Rent of a horsemill, this year being the first and next year it shall pay 10 shillings	0	5	0
Fishery at Runcouer 2nd February and 29th September	1	1	0
Fishery by a weir	0	1	0
Cattle agisted in Northwode	3	13	2
Pannage at Halton and Runcouer		11	6½
Tallage of bondsmen at Runcouer upper and lower	2	3	8
Toll of Halton market this year	16	11	6
Toll of beer there	0	6	9
Three foresters of Northewode for the bailiwick of the forestry	2	5	0

The earl also enjoyed considerable income from his Lancashire properties in Widnes and Appleton. The accounts inform us of two mills in Upton and we learn that the men of Runcorn crossed the river to dig peat on Widnes marsh.

Wydenesse. From the men of Runcouer for having peats	0	2	0
Rents of Wydnesse, Apeltone with breda 25th December and 24th June	8	19	1
Rent of two mills there at the same term	1	10	1

The expenses incurred for repairing store houses in the castle and the fees allowed for the manorial officials are given :

Expenses of the Manor			
Roofing and repairing houses within the castle and stalls in the market	0	15	10
Two millstones bought for the horsemill	0	7	7
Wages and robe of the parker yearly	1	12	8
Expenses of the keeper of the market this year	0	12	10
Fees of the Seneschall yearly	6	13	4
Fee of the Constable yearly	7	10	0
Carrying letters to various places	0	5	4
Removing 141½ roods of old paling and planting there 13 roods of new paling and 27 roods of hedge made round the park	0	12	10

On the 21st February 1307 the earl's accountants, William de Nony and Robert de Silkstone, arrived from Pontefract to conduct the annual reckoning with William de Heskeyth, Seneschal and his receiver, William de Wambwell at Halton Castle. The compotus or annual rendering of the accounts for 1307 is more detailed than that of 1296 and more of the manorial hamlets are listed in the returns. From the items given in the accounts we gain further insight into the everyday life of the manor. By 1307 there were four mills on the estates and the records clearly show that the lord of the manor was determined to extract as much revenue as possible in order to finance his military adventures in North Wales. One interesting item in the accounts concerns 'thistletack', a local tax of a halfpenny to be paid to the receiver for every animal which was driven over common land, a charge which became due even if one animal stopped to eat a single thistle. The earl allowed himself to indulge in charitable works for the good of his soul with a donation of £1 to the friars of Chester. Among the details in the accounts are the following items :

Compotus of the lands of Henry de Lacy, Earl of Lincoln 33 Edward I			
Rent of Haltone	5	13	9
Rent of Runcoure lower and upper 11th Nov, 24th June	7	3	10½
Thomas the parker for one cottage in Runcoure	0	0	6
Rent of 4 mills 2 nd February, 29th September	4	0	0
Fishery at Runcoure	1	0	0
A certain fishery between Haltone and Runcoure this year the first	0	6	8
A pair of gloves the rent of Thellewelle 29th Sept.	0	1	0
Thistletack of Northwode this year	1	9	10

	£	s	d
Thistletack of Runcoure, Haltone and More	. 14	..	9
Marketgelt of Haltone	. 16..		9½
Tallage of bondsmen of Halton	0	. 19	.. 2
Tallage of bondsmen of Runcoure	4	..8	..9
Tallage of bondsmen of Whitley	4	. 13	.. 4
Wild honey and wax sold	0	.. 8	.. 9
Toll of Haltone markets	17	..0	. 10
Toll of beer at said markets		.. 9	.. 2
Wydenesse. Serfs of Runcoure for having peat		.. 2	.. 0

The manorial expenses include allowances for the repair of Halton mill and for new palings around the deer park. Small amounts are allowed for market maintenance and for repairs to the store houses in the castle. It is noticeable that the salaries of the officials had not increased in the ten years since the audit of 1296. Among the items of expense are the following:

	£	s	d
Covering the hall of pleas with bords made and nails bought	0	.. 4	.. 6
Removing a hous and rebuilding it next to the grange for steers	0	.. 4	.. 0
Mowing 16 acres of meadow, spreading the grass, gathering, carrying and stacking hay	0.	. 14	.. 0
Fee of William de Heskeyth, Seneschall,	6..	13	.. 4
Robes for same	2	.. 10	.. 0
Fees and robes for the Receiver yearly	7..	10	.. 0
Fee for the porter yearly	0	..13	.. 4
Wages and stipend of the parker yearly	1..	12	.. 8
Fee of William de Midgelay, Counsel, yearly	0..	13	.. 4
Bringing money safely 3 times to Pontefract	0	.. 5	.. 0
Given to the Friars Preachers of Chester by the Earl's letter	1	..0	.. 0

During the Middle Ages Halton market was probably a weekly event with few or no full-time traders but it was a very profitable undertaking and evidence of its former site is still obvious in the village street today. The modern roads follow the same pattern as the medieval lanes along the slopes of Halton Hill and, at its junction with Holt Lane, Main Street widens considerably in order to accommodate the market stalls. Indeed, it appears that the street was specifically planned to serve as the market place for the township. Halton weekly market and the annual fair, which was held on the Nativity of Our Lady, were important sources of revenue for the Lord of the Manor who levied dues on the visiting merchants and traders. Both the market and the yearly fair lasted into the early years of the nineteenth century.

By the end of the thirteenth century Halton was a town of some consequence. The baronial castle of stone was probably complete in the middle of the previous century, but no identifiable remains of Norman building are obvious today. Although the Baron of Halton was the hereditary Constable of Chester it is doubtful if the title carried any real responsibilities, even though he held precedence over all the other barons of Cheshire by virtue of his office.

The Barony or "honour" of Halton was not a cohesive unit for it consisted of many estates scattered throughout Cheshire. The lord's demesne, that is the land which was held in the baron's own hands, included the manors of Runcorn, Halton, Moore, Newton, Preston, Cogshall near Comberbach, Higher Whitley, Appleton, Crowley near Arley and Congelton. The baron's principal retainers and men of rank held land from him. These major tenants held the manors of Weston, Clifton, Sutton, Aston, Aston Grange, Keckwick, Acton Grange, Bartington, Hatton and Little Leigh. Other retainers held the distant manors of Odd Rode near Astbury, Wallasey, Great Barrow near Chester, Shotwick, Sale, Henbury-with-Pexhall near Macclesfield, Lostock Gralam, Nether Peover, Over Knutsford, Toft, Marbury, Tabley Superior and Over Alderley.

During the Middle Ages the Baron of Halton was the principal landowner of the area but the prior and later, the Abbot of Norton, also possessed considerable holdings. Throughout the twelfth and thirteenth centuries gifts of land from patrons and benefactors greatly increased the original priory estates. The prior and convent owned mills, houses, fisheries, rights of common in the townships as well as tithes on land and on the profits of Runcorn ferry.

The Deer Park

Feudal noblemen entertained in style and to do so they appropriated vast areas of productive land for leisure activities. A particular source of much grief to the peasantry was the setting up of expensively enclosed deer-parks which were intended for the exclusive use of the lord of the manor and his hunting parties. It was a serious offence for anyone to kill the deer even if the animals escaped from the park to devastate the crops growing in small fields around the village. Heavy fines would be imposed on peasants who dared to take grass or to damage the foliage of the park. In times of food shortage caused by the unscientific husbandry of exhausted soil or when population increase exerted pressure on the limited area available for peasant farming, there was great resentment at the presence of a five hundred-acre deer-park even though it was the essential source of fuel and necessary for the feeding of the villagers' pigs.

Halton Park or Northwood spread across much of the area now occupied by the new town estates to the south and west of Halton Castle and in manorial records there are numerous references to its maintenance. We learn that in 1296 there were three foresters in Northwood and that Thomas the parker received an annual wage of one pound twelve shillings and eightpence. Thomas de Pilkington was appointed keeper at Halton on 7th April 1383 and in 1420, by which time Northwood Park was part of the royal estates, Sir Piers Dutton was styled "Parcarius de Northwoode".

Throughout the fourteenth and fifteenth centuries the park was gradually being 'assarted' or reduced by agricultural encroachment and when in 1476, an 'Official Progress' or inspection of the stewardship of the honour of Halton produced its report, the commissioners paid close attention to the situation in Northwood Park. They were dissatisfied with the standard of maintenance. The woodland had been drastically reduced, the hunting lodge needed major repairs and more seriously, vaccaries or enclosures for cows, had been established within the park and areas had been taken for the growing of crops with the result that the woodland available for the deer had been reduced so that their numbers had lessened considerably.

In the King's name the commissioners ordered that the paling around the illegal enclosures should be removed and the area restored to the deer. The report offers us a brief glimpse of the topography of fifteenth century Runcorn:

"*Northwood Park.*

The same park is VI myles aboute at the lest and in good pastur and the wodes therof, specially the tymbre, is felled and wasted soo as there is nat tymbre for palying therof if eny should be taken for the kinge's reparacions. And there is also in the same park made of newe diched aboute and a pale set upon it soo as the dere may not have thair way into hit. And also ther is a close made therin diched and part therof set with quyk set and the residue with pale soo as the dere may not resorte into hit. And the same close is sown with barly and ootys, by the which and overcharging the pasture with bestes the dere therof is destroied soo as there is almmost no dere therein.

The logge is ruynous nat repaired and specially in lakke of shyngle, and the pale aboute the park is olde and feble. Wherefore it is ordeigned that the pale about the said new frith shalbee taken up and bestowed aboute the paling of the said park where moost nede is.

It is ordeined that from hensforth noo frith ner closure shal bee made within the said park ner yet reparacions of the logge or eny other thinge, of lesse than it be doon by thadvys and oversight of the receviour there or his deputie in the office for the tyme being.

As to the herbage of the said park which Sir John Savage claymeth to have without eny thing yielding, it shalbee kept for stuff of the kinges housould on lesse it bee otherwise commaunded by the King".

The timbers of Halton Park were required from time to time for repairs to the castle and for use on the royal estates. In 1431 William Harrington, the seneschal, issued a warrant to the keeper of Northwood Park directing him to supply an oak for repairs to the roof of Farnworth church in Widnes and in 1476 it was ordered that "the mille called Appulton Mylle in Wydenesse shalbee repaired, towards which the Lord Stanley has geven ij ookes, wherof oon shall be able for a mylle post, wich ij ookes shall be had". At Halton a 6-year lease specified that the miller should maintain the windmill in everything except heavy timber and millstones. A few years before the Dissolution of Norton Abbey, Henry VIII acceded to a petition from William Merton, who was the abbot between 1510 and 1517, to allow thirty oak trees from Delamere forest to be taken for repairs to the abbey following "the misfortune of fire". The fact that the abbot had to go so far for his timber shows that the woodland of Halton Park had been greatly reduced. The canons possessed ancient rights in the park which dated almost from the foundation of the priory at Norton in the twelfth century. They had been allowed by the baron to take two deer every year at the Assumption of the Blessed Virgin Mary and they also had the right to agist their pigs on land reserved for the baron's pigs.

With population growth during the the fifteenth century, there came an increasing demand for wood for housebuilding, ship building and for charcoal for use in metal working. At the end of the century the forest laws were relaxed and the woodlands were rapidly denuded of their highly prized trees. However, enough of Northwood remained into the seventeenth century to provide James I with a day's deer hunting. In 1610 it was recorded that there were still 120 deer in the park.

Within the park there was a moated house, possibly the residence of the keeper and probably dating from the second half of the fifteenth century. The house was rebuilt and much altered over the years. Latterly it was known as Hallwood Farm, then it was modernised to become the "Tricorn" public house.

As for cultivated land, we know that even in good years the sowing rarely returned five times its seed but in Halton successful attempts had been made to increase the number of farm animals. The stock on Henry de Lacy's Halton manor more than doubled between 1296 and 1305. In his book "Essays on Medieval Agriculture", M.M. Postan refers to de Lacy as a "reforming administrator who was able to squeeze higher profits than ever before". Certainly, the administration on his estates did become more efficient and profitable and the manor began to produce a surplus of wool, meat, grain and beans for sale in the local market. From a court case heard in 1414, we learn of the variety of crops grown on the lands of the Abbot of Norton. The abbot complained that he had not been paid sixteen shillings and eight pence for the wheat, barley, oats and peas which he had sold to William Starkey of Northwich.

Cheshire was one of the few areas in England where marling was practised. Land on which marl (a mixture of lime and clay) was discovered was worth much more than land where it was not to be found. Energetic efforts were made to produce good pastures in Runcorn and Halton by marling. Almost every field in our area has a pond which is the site of a marl pit. Most were dug to increase food production "in Boney's day" — during the Napoleonic War — but some are more ancient in origin and may date from enlightened husbandry in late medieval times.

In addition to the reference to the horsemill and to the four other mills on the lands of Henry de Lacy in 1307, we have an early record of a mill at Runcorn. A document of 1134 mentions the "molendinium de Haltona quod est iuxta ecclesiam de Runcoura". Where there was a stream with a constant flow of water which could be dammed to provide a mill pond, watermills were preferred and although we have no record of a windmill at Runcorn in the Middle Ages, there is firm evidence of the existence of a watermill on the Sprinch stream in the seventeenth century. This mill, situated near to the present "Royal Hotel", was probably the site of an earlier one. The rent of "Runcorn Mill" in 1372 was £1..6..8.

The Fish Garths

Throughout the Middle Ages and for centuries later, the Mersey was a notable salmon river. The river was more important for its fisheries than for its value as a commercial waterway. Nets and weirs were preferred to barge traffic and there were clashes of interest between fishermen and watermen. The Domesday Book notes fishermen at Halton and Weston and at Aston. Early in the thirteenth century Philip de Orreby was granted fishing rights by John Lacy, the eighth Baron of

Halton. By the agreement Philip and his heirs were allowed a boat and one net within the limits of Halton. The annual rent for this concession was sixpence or a pair of spurs. Eighty years later in 1296 the rent for "the fishery at Runcoure" was £1..1..0.

The staked fish nets anchored in the river were a menace to navigation and in 1388 the Abbot of Norton was charged with making two fish garths — one called "Charity" and the other "Gracedieu" — which impeded the traffic on the river. Five years later the abbot was again in trouble for a similar offence. In 1476 the seneschal of Halton was ordered to remove all nets which hindered barge traffic in the Mersey's sailing channels. He was required to inspect the meshes of all nets to see that they were of regulation size so that they did not trap small fish. If the nets were found to be in contravention of the law, the seneschal was to destroy them. For his trouble he was entitled to the fish caught in the nets. The seneschal's orders were explicit:

"It is ordeined that the stiward of Halton shall serche the weres upon the waters of Mercy from a place called Fresshe Pole unto another place called Thelwall and see that every weer be left open soo as a bote of viij oors, every ooer of the length without the bote of viij fete, may passe through the were at the lowest of the water, and also to serche the nettes of every of the same weres and if he fynde any were straited soo as a bote with viij oors as afore is said may nat poss through, that then he breke it downe and enlarge it as afore is said. And if any nette be made contrarie to thassise werby the younge fish be destroied, that then he doo the same netts to bee brought to the castell of Halton and there dammed and brent, he taking for his labour in this behalve such fisshe as he fyndeth in every were at his serche making according to the use and custume of long tyme contynued. And this serche to begynne afore the fest of Michelmas next commying and soo yearly from tyme to tyme as the case shall require".

Salmon were highly valued and the young fish were protected by the law. A statute of 1389 specifically concerned with the Mersey states that: *"No young salmon (are to) be taken or destroyed at mills, dams and other places from the middle of April till the Nativity of St. John the Baptist and it is ordained and assented that the waters of the Mersey be put in defence as to the taking of salmon from Michaelmas Day to the Purification of Our Lady and in no other time of the year because the salmon be not seasonable in the said waters in the time aforesaid".* Water bailiffs were appointed to supervise the conservation of the fish.

In spite of strict legislation the law continued to be broken. At the Lancaster Assizes in 1498 a complaint was heard concerning the activities of Thomas Ashton of Penketh and others. It was alleged that on 4th March in Lent in 1496 they "obstructed the Mersey between Runcorne and Weryington so that the Easter boats could not go backwards and forwards to the great inconvenience of the merchants of Weryington and the surrounding district".

Besides the salmon and sea trout, the Mersey teemed with a variety of fish. Sparling, lampries and eels were plentiful and sturgeon made their way to the upper reaches to spawn. A royal fish, the King had the right to all sturgeon caught in the kingdom. Those netted within the manor of Halton had to be surrendered to the steward at the castle but it seems that on occasion the King's covetous subjects appropriated them. In 1532 Sir William Brereton, the steward of Halton, wrote to Sir William Fitzwilliam, the chancellor of the Duchy of Lancaster, complaining of the activities of Sir Piers Dutton in connection with a sturgeon caught at Weston: *"... all maner of fishes royall which have byn taken within the lordship and liberties of the sayd honor of Halton, and were used to be brought into the sayd castell of Halton to the Kinge's steward or his deputy for the Kinge's use, so it is that of late tyme, one Richard Penkethman did take one fish royall called a sturgion in the lordship of Weston, beinge within the liberties of the sayd honor of Halton, which he would have brought to the sayd castell according to custome afforsayde. Which being perseaved by one Sir Peires Dutton, Kt. entendinge to deseave and disinheret the Kinge of the sayd fish, but also of all other fishes royall hereafter to be taken in the sayd lordship with force of armes, in a royotus manner, x June, 23 yeare of our Lord the Kinge, did take away from the sayd Richard the sayd fish royall wheras the sayd Sir Peires of right hath no medlinge nor dowinge in the sayd lordship"*.

Vast shoals of herring entered the Mersey to be caught to provide a welcome addition to an otherwise dreary diet. The statue of St. Christopher, which can be seen at Norton Priory museum, dates from the fourteenth century and there is little doubt but that the statue was venerated by travellers intending to cross the dangerous Mersey. Carved into the base of the statue are some of the kinds of fish which proliferated in the river until the middle years of the nineteenth century. During the excavation of Norton Priory many oyster shells were found. This points to the fact that the Mersey estuary had shellfish beds before the pollution of its waters by industry. Mussel shells and cockle shells were also discovered at Norton.

In medieval times the upper reaches of the Mersey carried little barge traffic although Frodsham was a small port with craft bringing cargoes of grain from Ireland. In 1280 the ship tolls of Frodsham amounted to ten pounds. The Prior of Norton was engaged in trade with Ireland and an entry in the Patent Rolls for 1289 records: "There is safe conduct for the men of the Prior of Norton going to Ireland for victuals and other things".

Richard Starkey in 1354, had craft on the river and he claimed that they were used "to fish and to carry to all manner of lands being in the place of the Lord the King".

Towards the end of the fifteenth century it appears that Runcorn had begun to develop into a landing place of sufficient consequence to cause concern to the merchants of Chester. The burgesses of the city petitioned the Earl of Chester, King Edward IV, asking him to instruct the Mayor of Dublin that no goods should be landed in Cheshire except at the port of Chester. The King acceded to their petition and in 1481 the sheriff was ordered to arrest any vessels attempting to discharge cargo at Runcorn. There was one exception for in 1482, Edward Walsh obtained licence to sail his ship directly from Runcorn to Ireland.

As the jealously guarded rights of the Chester merchants were now protected by royal edict, there was no possibility of a port developing on the Mersey. Thus Runcorn was destined to remain an obscure village for centuries to come. Few persons of consequence ever found cause to visit the district but there is a belief that in 1207 King John visited Halton Castle when he is reputed to have given £5 towards the upkeep of its chapel. Edward II certainly stayed in the area. He was at Halton from the 1st to 3rd of November 1323 and on one of those days he visited Norton Priory.

The Peat Moss

Disputes concerning rights on common land were frequent occurrences and in 1476, the tenants of Runcorn and Halton were in conflict with those of Moore over grazing and peat digging on Moore Moss. In order to settle the differences between the two groups, the Council of the Duchy of Lancaster ruled that the common pasture should be divided equally by a ditch, the cost of which was to be borne by the villagers of the townships involved and Sir John Savage was ordered to see that the dispute was resolved to the satisfaction of all concerned. The council ordered that — *"the said tenauntes of Halton and Runcorne shal have oon half of the said comen pastur for their bestes, paieing xijd by the yere, and the said tenauntes of More shal have the other half therof for thair bestes, paieing xijd by the yere. And that the same comen shall be evenly departed and severed by diggying betwix thaim by the discrecion and over sight of Sir John Savage thelder and Hugh Garthsyde at the costes of both parties evenly to be borne"*.

As for rights of turbary or peat digging, the Council ordained that peat was to be taken between specified dates in the year. It was to be used for fuel by villagers but was not to be offered for sale. Rules of compensation were laid down to penalise the owners of stray animals which damaged stacks of drying turf. The council's ruling was explicit:

"the said tenauntes of Halton and Runcorne as the tenauntes of More shal have sufficient turbarie in the saide mosse for thair fewell to bee expended upon thair tenures in the said townes as thay of old tyme have used and accustumed without wast or destruccion dooing or eny sale making therof. And they shal begynne to delve and digge thair turf yerely within iij daies next after the fest of the Invencion of the Holy Cross (3rd May) and drie and carie it out the said mosse afore the thassumpcion of Our Lady (15th August), if unseasonable weder fall not, soo as they be letted therby. And every of the said tenauntes having eny bestes gooing in the said mosse and pastur betwix the said festes shal soo kepe his bestes therin that thay shal not hurt eny turf of his neighbours. And if he bee necligent in keping his bestes there wherby his neighbours turfes is destroied or hurted, that then he having such hurt doo pynne the bestes dooing him such hurt and thaim kepe in lawfull pownde unto the tyme the owner of such bestes have founde him seurite to make him amendes by thoversight and jugement of iiij or ij of thair both neighbours indifferently chosen therto".

The tenants of the townships of Halton, Runcorn, Moore and Widnes had the right, annually, to choose their own bailiffs but the Chancellor of the Duchy of Lancaster warned them that they must exercise care to select from their number only men who were competent and capable of performing the duties required of them. Failure to appoint an able man to be bailiff would bring penalties on all the tenants. *"And if they chese eny that is not sufficient that then they shall answere the Kinge of thair dueties as thay bee bownden to doo, wherunto thay bee agreed, and over that have promitted that from hensforth that every bailif chosen by thaim shal fynde seurtie to the township that he is bailif of to make his accompts to the kinge and answere him of his dueties and that thay shal at thair court of elleccion of thair baillif delivere to the stiward the names of seurties that shal bee bownden for thair bailiff to thentent that the same stiward may delivere to thauditour upon their audite".*

There were bailiffs who were less than satisfactory and reference is made to them in the official progress. *"Item John Richardson late baillif of Wydnesse is pardoned xiiis ixd ob.q. part of his arrerages because of his povertie. And as for xxs residue therof, he is committed to warde in the castell of Halton".* Another bailiff of Widnes even managed to retain some of the money that he was due to pay to the steward. The curious entry in the records leaves one wondering how Henry Delaney managed to obtain his rebate. *"Henry Delanie late baillif of Wydnesse is releissed xiis viijd ob.q. in consideration of his good service to the kinge in his office".*

After the Plague

The Black Death reached Cheshire by June 1349 and there is reason to believe that its impact was devastating. When one third or more of the inhabitants of England died in two years, the effect on the social and economic life in countless villages was incalculable. Within a few weeks of each other, the heads of the largest of Cheshire's religious houses were dead. The Abbot of St. Werburgh's, Chester, the Prioress of St. Mary's, Chester and the Prior of Norton Priory died of the disease and there is plenty of evidence to show that in thinly populated Cheshire the plague claimed many lives. Throughout England whole village populations were wiped out and in others the inhabitants fled before the scourge. Because there is a complete paucity of evidence we would not be justified in making even a tentative guess about the effects of the visitation of the plague in the Runcorn area. However, there are a number of sites which are believed to be the locations of deserted medieval villages. Of course, hamlets may have been abandoned at a later date due to changes in agricultural economy but it is worthy of note that Stockham, first mentioned in 1288 and Eanley, near Eanleywood Farm, Norton, mentioned in Domesday in 1086, are believed to be deserted medieval villages. Acton Grange, a manor which was a grange of Norton Priory and first mentioned in 1194, is also the possible site of an abandoned medieval village whilst Newton-by-Daresbury which is mentioned in twelfth century documents, was possibly a deserted medieval settlement. Without doubt, the aftermath of the plague saw many derelict holdings and a shortage of labour to till the land.

Throughout the Middle Ages the only means by which a man of humble origin could receive an education in order to reach an eminent position in society was by entering the Church. The clergy formed the literate class and they were employed by the King and his nobles as administrators in government and estate management. However, there was a price to pay before a serf could obtain his freedom to enter the Church. The young man's father was required to pay a fine to the lord of the manor before the son could become a cleric. In 1367 Thomas Castle and Richard Archer of Halton had each to pay 40 pence before their sons were permitted to enter religious life. Some local clerics even managed to enter the King's Service. In his study of social mobility in Cheshire in the late Middle Ages, M.J. Bennett has identified a group of clerics from Halton and Widnes who, in the early years of Edward III's reign, had established themselves in royal administration.

The only other way of escaping from the drudgery of labouring on the manor was to engage in military service. Cheshire archers were famous and local men were recruited to serve in the wars against the Scots, the Welsh and the French. In the spring of 1406 orders were issued throughout the county for the raising of troops to fight the Welsh rebels. Bucklow hundred was asked for 20 men at arms and 60 archers. William Harrington who was the seneschal of Halton in 1430, had served at the battle of Agincourt in 1415 and he obtained his position for his services in France. A muster roll of 1417 lists a total of 439 archers raised in Cheshire. Of this number Bucklow supplied 107 more than any other hundred. Three years later the seneschal of Halton, Sir William Stanley, was engaged in recruiting archers for Henry V's army. Sir William personally added ten recruits to the rolls.

In order to maintain English superiority on the battlefield, archery was encouraged by statute at the expense of other forms of amusement. Shooting at the butts was practised in every Cheshire village long after the bow had become an obsolete weapon. The English belief in the efficiency of the longbow persisted until late into the reign of Queen Elizabeth. The fact that gunpowder had long made the archer redundant was not recognised by the authorities who wished to foster the national pride which had been generated by the success of the bowmen in the great victories of Crecy in 1346 and Agincourt in 1415. In 1578, a hundred and sixty-three years after Agincourt, Thomas Brooke of Norton and John Dutton of Dutton were responsible for raising and equipping the local militia. Among the nondescript force of musketeers, pikemen and horsemen there were a number of archers.

Law and Order

Throughout the fourteenth and fifteenth centuries Cheshire was notorious for the frequency of break down in law and order. The county had contributed more than its share of fighting men to the armies of King Edward III and the Black Prince and on their return to England when there was a lull in campaigning in France, these hardened soldiers helped to add to Cheshire's reputation for violence and general lawlessness. To enforce law and order each hundred within the county had its Hundred Court with officials who were responsible to the Sheriff of Cheshire but, unfortunately for historians, the records of the Bucklow court have not survived. Although the law was applied in Cheshire as it was throughout the rest of England, the county had its own legal customs. One example of a legal practice particular to Cheshire was the Duke of Lancaster's claim, as Baron of Halton in 1359 to have the right, on behalf of his sergeants, to behead all thieves who were taken within the manor and who admitted their crime. According to Ormerod, a number of thieves, led by William de Huxley, broke into Halton Castle in 1319 and stole a number of small items. They were caught, tried at Chester, were found guilty and executed.

The most authoritative court in Cheshire was the County Court which was held about ten times a year. Much more dominant than the modern court which bears the same name, the County Court considered both civil and criminal actions and was presided over by the Justice of Chester who was considered to be the Earl of Chester's deputy. In 1353 Edward, the Black Prince, visited his earldom of Chester in order to ascertain the extent of public disorder in the county. The prince commissioned a "Court of Trailbaston" to clear a backlog of serious charges and the names of a number of local men appear in the court records. Sir Geoffrey Warburton, junior, was accused of assaulting John, the son of William Danyers at Halton on the Sunday within the octave of the Blessed Virgin Mary in 1351. He admitted his guilt and was fined the sum of three pounds, six shillings and eight pence. Sir Geoffrey's father, also called Geoffrey, was accused of a far more serious crime. It was claimed that Sir Geoffrey Warburton, senior, feloniously killed Ranulf Bolt at Norton on 14th September 1322. Sir Geoffrey pleaded guilty and was fined thirteen pounds six shillings and eight pence. The same amount of fine was imposed on Robert, the son of Richard Frodsham of Frodsham Bridge, who had to pay thirteen pounds six shillings and eight pence after being found guilt of raping Alice, the wife of Hugh of Frodsham Bridge in June 1340. Sir John Danyers was fined three pounds for assaulting Gilbert, the son of Richard Walton at Halton in 1352. Roger Lowe was accused of stealing pike, bream and eels worth six shillings and eight pence from Geoffrey Warburton at Sutton on September 8th, 1351. He was found not guilty.

To maintain law and order a system called Frankpledge came into being. Under this scheme the inhabitants of each village were divided into groups of ten men called tithings. The members of each tithing were bound to stand security for the others' good behaviour and the villagers were duty bound to seek out offenders under pain of collective penalty. Collective responsibility for the apprehension of wrong-doers was a means by which the authorities curbed anarchy and law breaking. Twice a year the manor court would hold a view of Frankpledge in order to see that the tithing system was being enforced. In 1359 the Duke of Lancaster as Baron of Halton claimed the right to have Halton Castle battlemented, to hold a view of Frankpledge twice a year, and to have a prison in the castle. He also claimed the right to hold a weekly market at Halton as well as two fairs a year, one — "on the four days next before Lady Day and the other on the day and the morrow of St. Catherine's Day". The Duke also claimed the stallage rent from all the pedlars who attended the market and fairs and who lived in one of the thirty-three villages within the manor. The administration of Halton fair and the weekly market was the responsibility of the steward of the Lord of the Manor. The steward presided over the Pie Powder Court so called from "pieds poudreux" (dusty footed wandering pedlars). At this court, on-the-spot justice would be administered to chapmen found guilty of fraud, short measure or unruly behaviour. The court levied fines on offenders and settled any disputes which arose.

It is a matter of regret that we have, as yet, such little information about the day-to-day activity in Halton and district even though extensive records exist in the Duchy of Lancaster archives. Charles Poole, writing in 1906, states: *"In a bundle of miscellaneous papers, 5th James I, in the Duchy office in the steward's certificate for the Honour of Halton, showing the lordship or manor Halton, together with the manors of Runcorn, Moore, Over Whitley and Cogshall in the county of Chester and the manor of Widnes with all the appurtenances in the county of Lancaster to be holden of His Majesty by copy of court-roll within the honour and fee of Halton and certifying the fines and customs of the said manors and also that the records and court rolls of the manors, were then in the castle of Halton and had been kept there from the time of King Edward the third".* When details of the Court Rolls of Halton are made available by researchers, our knowledge of the history of the district from the fourteenth century will be enormously increased.

It is known that from the middle decades of the twelfth century the Prior of Norton enjoyed the privilege of holding his own court. Even the canons were not always law abiding. In 1430 one of the brethren was accused of rape, abduction and theft.

For centuries Halton township predominated as the centre of manorial administration. The Lord of the Manor's Court Baron or Court Leet was held there. This court was the private jurisdiction of the Baron of Halton and its main business was concerned with the transfer and surrender of land, the use of common fields and waste and the recording of lord and tenant agreements. The court was also responsible for the appointment of minor officials — a hayward to look after the common land, the village swineherd and a woodward as well as the petty constable and an ale conner who tested the quality of ale sold on the manor and who was responsible for ensuring that the weights and measures used in the market were correct. The court's jury of neighbours had to see that the numerous small public offices were filled by local people either by election or by rotation. Even in medieval times the serf-farmer was aware that he had certain rights as well as responsibilities. He might not be able to override the powerful lord's steward but he attended the court and could exercise some check on tyranny by taking part in the self-government of the community even though in a minor capacity.

The Court Leet dealt with petty offences, disputes and common nuisances and, in order to standardise the penalties and fines for proven offences, it appointed two officials, called 'affeerers'. Sometimes the court was known as the Halmot and such a court was established in Farnworth in Widnes for the convenience of the Baron's Lancashire tenants who had the right to choose their own bailiff. The court was empowered to deal with civil and minor criminal cases but not cases where felony was involved. The manorial accounts of Halton for 1361 include a list of officials' salaries among whom was the "attorney of the courts" who received a yearly payment of two pounds for his services.

In the absence of effective law enforcement agencies, medieval society was prone to violence and men often took the law into their own hands. Retribution on apprehended criminals could be severe in the extreme and William Beamont recounts a number of crimes where capital punishment was administered. At Halton in 1380 William Harper killed Adam Musket for which he was tried, found guilty at Chester and brought back to Halton Castle where he was hanged. The sale of his few effects realised sixpence which was paid to the lord of the manor. Burglary was also a capital offence. Two Welshmen broke into a house in Keckwick in 1474. They stole a number of items including a sheaf of arrows. The thieves were soon apprehended and they were taken to Halton Castle. In spite of being chained the two men succeeded in escaping taking their fetters with them but they were quickly recaptured, brought for trial before Lord Stanley, the seneschal, found guilty and were hanged within the castle.

Even the clergy became embroiled in outbreaks of violence. In the Halton Rolls for 30th March 1370 there is an account of the activities of a number of servants of the Prior of Norton who, at the prior's command, entered the house of William of Keckwick in Moore and carried away his wife, Margery. The lady was taken to the priory where she was kept a prisoner until her husband had settled his debts with the prior. In 1510 Abbot William complained to the court in Halton of the conduct of a Laurence Malborn. There are no details of the alleged offence but it must have been a very serious charge for Laurence was bound over in the enormous sum of £40. At Halton Court, held on 4th October 1544, the grand inquest of sixteen persons found Sir John Holcroft guilty of assaulting Richard Gerard, the rector of Grapenhall, who suffered serious stab wounds to his arms.

The Halton halmot was held at least three times a year and much of its time was taken up in considering minor offences and petty crime. In 1499 thirty brewers, of whom twenty-six were ale wives, were fined for selling ale in unsealed measures. In 1512 Elizabeth Heath and Agnes, the wife of John Owen, appeared before the court accused of taking away poles and racks which were used to hold hay for the King's deer in Halton Park. They were found guilty and were fined.

Typical of the petty offences to appear before the Halmot of Halton is the following held before Piers Dutton in 1544 when *"inquisition was made on oath that Margaret Norland made an attack on Robert Carrington and struck him with her hand contrary to the peace and that Ellen Norland, daughter of Richard Norland, underwent the punishment of the thewe (ducking stool) lawfully"*. The fair sex seem to have monopolised this particular session of the court with other ladies being accused of rowdy behaviour: *"And that Alice Lesthwyte, widow, for entertaining other men's servants and that the wife of Oliver Whitley; Joan White, wife of William White and the wife of Richard Lightbone were common liars and scolds"*.

The law of trespass was strictly enforced against those who entered the deer park. In 1518 Thomas Aston, gentleman, was sued for trespassing in the park and two years later Thomas Butler and John Farrington were accused of trespass *"on the herbage and pannage of the park at Halton"*. The keeping of dogs was subject to strict control. In 1515 William Runcorn of Runcorn, chaplain, was penalised for keeping a hunting dog. He was charged with *"not being beneficed to XIs a year did keep a hare hound and was a common hunter"*. Presumably if the parson had a stipend of more than forty shillings a year he would have been regarded as

a superior personage and therefore exempt from prosecution.

Some villagers fell foul of the legislation which was introduced in the middle of the fourteenth century in order to avert economic collapse. The devastation caused by the Black Death in 1348 and the further eruptions of the plague in 1361 and 1368, reduced the country's population by nearly a half so that the market value of labour doubled within a couple of years. Soon craftsmen and labourers were demanding wages that were not economically feasible. By the Statute of Labourers of 1351 and by later ordinances, Parliament attempted to enforce a prices and wages freeze. However, the statutory limitation on wages was met with defiance in spite of the forty days prison sentence imposed on first offenders. At an inquiry into labour offences held before Sir Laurence de Dutton, Sheriff of Cheshire, at Halton in July 1372, the Earl of Chester's commissioner inquired into cases of "workmen and articifers who take excessive wages against the Statute". A number of weavers, spinners, shoemakers and labourers from the district were charged with profiteering. Two shoemakers living in Halton were accused of having *"sold shoes to various people in Halton and elsewhere, taking excessive profit for the same, that is at a price of sixpence a pair against the Statute of 1369 and previous years"*. Also charged with contravention of the statute was Robert, son of Ranulf de Comberbache, "wollonwebster", who *"tooke 14d from Peter de Whitelegh and a half bushel of wheat (worth 9d) for weaving seven ells of woollen cloth at Comberbache, on Monday before Christmas, 45 Edward III (22nd December 1371), and similarly from many others of the neighbourhood, against the statute"*.

Open defiance against the authorities' attempts to enforce the law was often encountered by the village constable. The jury at the Halton inquiry of 1372 was informed that "Emma, wife of Thomas Hoggessone of Coggeshull, "whelspynner", refused to appear before the constables of the township of Coggeshull, to swear to observe the statute at Coggeshull on Tuesday before the Nativity of John the Baptist". The Sheriff also heard *"That there are no stocks in the township of Marbury-next-Cumberbache in which delinquents who have offended against the statute ought to be placed because Robert de Longedon and Ellen, daughter of John de Marbury, joint owners of the township, refuse to make their part of the stocks against the statute"*.

The Statute of Labourers stipulated that in order to control wages agricultural labourers were to be hired by the year and not by the day. The Halton jury heard the "David (le Walsh) and (...) living at Whitelegh took wages of 2d a day with food from Peter de Whitelegh and others of the same

Halton Castle and village from an illustration of 1800.

township for several years, against the statute".

The chronic labour shortage with the consequent increase in wages enticed many to leave their employers to seek better paid work. There was a dearth of servants and at Halton one employer was accused of abducting his neighbour's servant. It was alleged that *"Richard de (...) abducted Cecily and took her from the service of Thomas de Marbury at Marbury-next-Comberbache against Thomas's will, on Sunday after the Translation of St. Thomas, Martyr, against the statute"*.

Among the petty offences listed in the Halton court records there is the occasional capital offence. After William Geston, a servant of the Bishop of Chester was presented at Halton accused of the murder of John Finley, a hawker of cloth, he was sent to Chester Assizes where he was found guilty. It was important that justice was seen to have been done and he was executed in Grappenhall where the crime had been committed and his body was hung in chains.

William Beamont refers to the considerable number of Halton rolls which relate to the Borough of Congelton which was within the honour of Halton and which received its first charter from Henry de Lacy in 1294. The Congelton records include a reference to "sturdy beggers" who were whipped out of town in Queen Elizabeth the First's reign. "Pay'd Rauf Stubs for taking sayd rougs to Halton Castell to be tried ... 4d" and also "Pay'd for two cords which whipped two rougs ... 1d". The court rolls contain declarations from the various townships which confirm that the stocks and whipping posts are in good order.

Much of the law breaking was trivial. George Thelewall and Hugh Raynshaw were charged with taking twenty partridges with nets in Halton in 1539. They were fined because they were in breach of the law in "not having lands and tenements to the value of XIs a year". Robert Bold and Thomas Heyper were presented at Halton for "keeping dice in the house". A man was fined for uttering seditious words against Mary Tudor in 1555. The queen was unpopular and there is no doubt but that he was only expressing the general opinion held by most of his neighbours.

The Hundred Years War and the Wars of the Roses bred habits of violence in the country and the prison at Halton Castle was kept in good repair. In 1421 six workmen are recorded as being employed at sixpence each per day in making a prison under the Earl's chamber and two years later a man was paid the same wage for repairing the base of the round tower and the sally tower and in making good certain defects in the castle chapel. Major works were carried out at the castle between 1450 and 1457 in the reign of Henry VI when a new gate tower was erected at the main entrance at a cost of £347. Although it seems that the castle was of sufficient importance for the building work to be supervised by John Heley who was the King's master mason in Lancashire, there is no evidence that it played any role in the Wars of the Roses. Halton Castle had no strategic position. It did not command a main highway being simply an obscure fortress which was kept in good order because of the general lawlessness prevalent during the reigns of Henry VI, Edward IV and Richard III.

During frequent conflicts of the fifteenth century, local men were engaged in fighting for the King not only in France but also in the many battles which took place on English soil. Henry IV relied heavily upon the expertise of Cheshire archers and many were recruited from the north of the county to serve in the English army which was trying to contain Owen Glendower, the Welsh chieftain, who was conducting a guerilla war against the English border counties. When Glendower faced Henry IV in a set battle at Shrewsbury in 1403 he suffered a defeat. However, there were many casualties on the English side. Among the dead were Richard Hey, Thomas de Newhall and John Carre, three of the King's tenants from Whitley. Because the three men had died fighting for the King their wives were given immediate right to their lands. For some years skirmishing continued along the Welsh border and in the spring of 1406 Bucklow hundred was obliged to provide eighty men to serve against the rebellious Welsh. In 1400 local men were serving in Henry IV's army in Scotland. In this campaign Bucklow supplied 103 archers and among their leaders Peter de Dutton, Thomas Danyers and John Savage each led a contingent of twelve archers.

Local men were later involved in the Wars of the Roses and the Cheshire gentry and their followers were strongly represented at the battle of Bloreheath which was fought in Staffordshire in 1459. Amongst the Lancastrian supporters killed were Sir Thomas Dutton, his son, Peter, and his brother, John. Sir Richard Aston, who was the seneschal of Halton from 1397 to 1401 served with the King's army in France. He was in Calais when tragedy overtook his family. In a letter which was read in Halton court Sir Richard stated that when he returned to his house at Ringey he found that *"the plague had carried off his wife and all his little ones"*.

Returning soldiers were only too ready to find employment by joining feuding families in the turbulent society that was fifteenth century Cheshire. In 1419 a long standing dispute between the Dutton and the Atherton families was settled. Sir Peter Dutton and his men had raided Sir William Atherton's Lancashire estates taking forty oxen and cows and they had assaulted his servants. Atherton's retribution was swift and he raided Dutton property seizing his enemy's horses with their saddles. We do not know how long the peace lasted but the coalescence of rival groupings among the gentry of the county helped to fuel the malevolence which was manifest at the start of the Wars of the Roses. It was a period of instability and violence. Marauding companies of armed men roamed the countryside. Prudence demanded that the defences of Halton Castle should be kept in good repair and that the isolated house of the Keeper of Halton Park at Hallwood should be surrounded by a moat.

From the reign of William the Conqueror Cheshire gradually assumed a considerable degree of autonomy and by the beginning of the fourteenth century the county was almost independent of royal control. Indeed the Crown held no land within the county. The Earldom of Chester had been created by William I as a buffer against incursions by the Welsh and over the years the Earl of Chester came to be regarded as a prince who ruled over territory which was not subordinate to England or Wales. The earl granted charters to his tenants, the county was not represented in Parliament and it did not contribute to national taxation. In the early fourteenth century the terms "Palatinate of Chester" and "County Palatine" came into common use. These titles signify a county of special status which enjoyed almost complete independence from the rest of the kingdom. A hundred years later, many of the Cheshire gentry had begun to assert that William I had granted Hugh Lupus a special status for the Earldom which had amounted to the creation of a separate realm. Even though in 1399 the Barony of Halton became the property of the monarch, the Duchy of Lancaster still retained its own administration from the one controlling the other Crown possessions.

The royal policy of exercising control over sensitive areas near the Welsh border by delegating unlimited power to "men of Worship" began to change in Tudor times. The new thinking was towards a united kingdom and the notion of powerful potentates, usually acting in their own interests when controlling large parts of the country, could no longer be tolerated. By 1532 William Brereton of Malpas had become an obstacle to progress and national unity. It was held that in Cheshire Brereton *"hadd all the holle rewl and governaunce under owr sovereigne Lord the Kinge's grace"*. Certainly Brereton was the greatest

royal servant in Cheshire and North Wales. Among his Crown offices and grants was the stewardship of Halton awarded him for life in 1524. At Michaelmas 1532 he was appointed Keeper of Halton Park. He was Constable of Chester Castle, Sheriff of Flint, Sheriff of Merioneth, Ranger of Delamere Forest and Chamberlain of Chester. He had the rent of the Menai ferries and he possessed the manor of Lesnes in Kent.

Sir William Brereton was born in 1490. His father was Sir Randle Brereton the Chamberlain of Cheshire and his mother was Eleanor, the daughter of Piers Dutton of Dutton and Halton. William Brereton entered royal service to become a groom of the King's chamber by 1521 and three years later he was a groom of the Privy Chamber. He rose rapidly in royal favour and by 1536 he had acquired no less than thirty-six Crown offices and grants. Perhaps the most profitable of Brereton's acquisitions came from his connection with the Savage family of Clifton. When the irresponsible behaviour of Sir John Savage's son and grandson had resulted in the bankruptcy of the family fortunes, the Clifton estates had to be temporarily surrendered to the Crown. Brereton obtained the lease and in 1529 he secured the wardship of the heir when he married Elizabeth, the grandson's widow. Lady Savage not only had status in Cheshire, she was also the daughter of the Earl of Worcester who was cousin to Henry VIII. Through his marriage Brereton was to have control of the Savage fortunes until 1547.

By 1536 Sir William Brereton's circumstances were at their most favourable but, unfortunately, he was one of the courtiers who rallied to the support of Anne Boleyn when the King had begun to transfer his attention to Jane Seymour. Thomas Cromwell brought about the downfall of the queen by accusing her of adultery with Brereton and others. This pretext led to Sir William's execution for high treason on Tower Hill two days before the queen was beheaded in May 1536. With Brereton's death the Crown made sure that immense power should never again be allowed to accumulate in the hands of one man and Brereton's offices were divided among many.

Power on the scale that Brereton enjoyed made him enemies within Cheshire. There was enmity of long standing between the Duttons and the Breretons. In 1504 Sir Randle Brereton had supported the Abbot of St. Werburgh's, Chester, in his dispute with Sir Piers Dutton and as a result of the quarrel, Sir Piers had been imprisoned in Chester Castle. After William Brereton's execution in 1536 Dutton's main rival for power was another William Brereton, the Deputy-

Chamberlain of Cheshire. At the Dissolution of the Monasteries the two men were among the commissioners charged with closing the religious houses in the county. Their inability to co-operate in the aftermath of events following the closure of Norton Abbey in 1536 probably saved the lives of the abbot and a number of his canons who were accused of treason.

The social advancement of a number of local families became more noticeable during the Tudor period. The "men of substance" of the reign of Henry IV were followed by descendants who were pushing to become powerful landed gentry. War often provided the means whereby a man and his family could climb the social ladder. In 1544 Henry VIII tried to force the union of England and Scotland by sending an army commanded by his brother-in-law to invade Scotland. The English army captured and sacked Edinburgh and a number of Cheshire men received honours for their services in the field. Among those to be dubbed knight was Edmund Savage and William Brereton and Hugh Dutton were made esquires.

At the Reformation a new family, the Brookes, came into the area. Richard Brooke esquire, of Leighton near Nantwich, former Knight of the Hospitallers of Jerusalem of Rhodes and Malta and the purchaser of Norton Abbey, was released from his vows and married Christian Carew, the daughter of John Carew of Haccomb in Devonshire. Richard Brooke was Sheriff of Cheshire in 1563 and his son, Thomas Brooke, esquire, was Sheriff in 1578 and 1592.

By the middle years of the sixteenth century three influential families of great wealth controlled the land between the Mersey and the Weaver. The Duttons, the Savages or the Brookes also held the prestigious office of seneschal of Halton on a number of occasions in the reign of Elizabeth I.

The Fifteen Barons

Our reference libraries contain numerous accounts of the lives of the fifteen barons of Halton. These narratives vary in size from William Beamont's lengthy chronicle in his "History of Halton Castle and the Priory or Abbey of Norton" to the single information sheet compiled by the Information Service of Halton Borough Council. At some future date when the records of the Duchy of Lancaster have been studied in detail, a great deal more will be added to the biographies of the barons of Halton but until new findings are at hand there is no point in attempting to enlarge on what is already in print. It is sufficient to recount some of the main

events in a baronial line which lasted from about 1070 to 1412.

Reference has already been made to Nigel, the first baron and to his son William FitzNigel who founded Runcorn Priory. The third baron, William FitzWilliam, removed his father's Runcorn foundation to a more favourable site at Norton. He died childless in 1150 and was succeeded by Eustace FitzJohn who married for his second wife, the third baron's sister. Eustace's first wife had also been an heiress and he, like many of the other barons of Halton acquired lands and titles by marrying well. By his first marriage, he had added the baronies of Malton and Alnwick to his original inheritance of Knaresborough. He died fighting the Welsh in 1157. Richard FitzEustace, son of the fourth baron by his second wife, married into the rich and influential de Lacy family and in doing so enriched the barony through a favourable marriage settlement. His son John FitzRichard, the sixth baron, was a patron of science who maintained an astronomer at Halton Castle. The astronomer, William, wrote a book on the planets in 1184. He was probably a canon of Norton Priory. It is likely that John FitzRichard established the ferry at Runcorn. He also founded the Cistercian monastery at Stanlow. John served Henry II in the newly conquered territory in Ireland. He went on the third crusade with King Richard the Lionheart and died at the siege of Tyre in 1190.

Roger, the son of John FitzRichard became the seventh Baron of Halton and he adopted the prestigious de Lacy surname. A renowned soldier, Roger was nicknamed "Hell" Lacy because of his military daring. It is asserted that he gathered together the minstrels, beggars and idlers at the Chester fair and led them to the relief of Rhuddlan castle where the Welsh were besieging the Earl of Chester. When they observed what appeared to be a formidable force approaching, the Welsh army withdrew. For his daring the Earl granted Roger the right to licence all minstrels and beggars in the county of Chester.

Roger de Lacy was an absentee baron. In 1192 he was in the Holy Lane with Richard I and on his return to Europe he served King John in his unsuccessful attempt to thwart the French conquest of Normandy. It was during his service in France that Roger became a prisoner of war but such was his reputation for valour, the King of France, Philip Augustus, decreed that he should not be kept a close prisoner. Although King John had reason to mistrust Roger de Lacy he nevertheless paid the ransom but after Roger's return to his castle at Pontefract the King detained his son as a hostage. Roger de Lacy died in 1211 and was buried in the abbey founded by his father at Stanlow.

The eighth Baron of Halton was John de Lacy who, like his father, took the side of those barons who opposed the King. John de Lacy joined the alliance of barons in order to prevent the King imposing crippling taxation and tyrannical laws. He was one of those entrusted with the duty of seeing that King John kept the agreements he made when he signed Magna Carta at Runnymede in 1215. John de Lacy married the niece of Ranulph, Earl of Chester who died without male issue in 1217 and whose titles, including the Earldom of Lincoln, passed to John on the death of his father-in-law. From this time onwards the Halton possessions became less important to the family because they now had richer estates elsewhere. Among the new lands which came into de Lacy hands was the manor and the castle of Bolingbroke. John de Lacy died in 1240 and was buried at Stanlow.

Of Edmund de Lacy, the ninth baron there is little to record. He was educated at Court and was probably a rare visitor to Halton. Edmund died in 1258 and was succeeded by his son Henry. As noted elsewhere, Henry de Lacy became chief councillor to King Edward I and was given several important commissions including one to reform the law. When the King was engaged in military adventures against the Scots, Henry de Lacy was appointed Protector of the Realm and as such he held the rank immediately below that of the Prince of Wales. Because he was often engaged on matters of national importance it is not likely that the tenth baron made frequent visits to his Halton estates. Henry experienced great sorrow through the tragic deaths of his two sons. One was drowned when he fell into the well at Denbigh Castle and the other died when he fell from the roof at Pontefract Castle.

Henry de Lacy's daughter, Alice, married Thomas, Earl of Lancaster and cousin of the King. Henry de Lacy died at his London house, Lincoln's Inn, now one of the Inns of Court and was buried in old St. Paul's Cathedral.

It was during the time that Henry de Lacy was Baron of Halton that disaster occurred at Stanlow Abbey. In 1279 the Mersey flooded the claustral buildings and in 1287, during a fierce storm, the great tower collapsed and a fire destroyed part of the abbey. Situated near the cold Mersey marshes, Stanlow was an inhospitable situation and the monks appealed to the Pope to permit the refounding of the house on a better site. With the Pope's consent and the agreement of King Edward I and Henry de Lacy, the Cistercians moved their monastery to Whalley near Clitheroe where "the glebe is

warm, fertile and pleasant". The Whalley site was given to the monks by Henry de Lacy but Stanlow was not completely abandoned for a small "cell" continued to be maintained there up to the Reformation.

Thomas, Earl of Lancaster, the son-in-law of Henry de Lacy and the eleventh Baron of Halton, took up arms against the lazy and incompetent King Edward II in 1322. Proud and stupid, Thomas led the baronial opposition to the rule of the King and his corrupt advisors. The rebellion did not last long and Thomas was forced to flee from Tutbury Castle across a river where his money chest fell into the water and was lost. Thomas surrendered on the following day and he was imprisoned in his own castle at Pontefract. Six days later, after a quick trial, he was beheaded and his estates were forfeit to the Crown. Five hundred years after these events Thomas of Lancaster's treasure was dredged up during a river widening scheme.

Soon after the execution of the Earl of Lancaster a cult of martyrdom began. This veneration of "St. Thomas of Lancaster" was spread by monks who had profited from their friendship with the late Earl. The King issued a proclamation denouncing the so-called miracles said to have been performed by the dead traitor and he made visits to a number of religious houses in north-west England to see that his edict was obeyed. Norton Priory was one of the houses visited on the Royal Progress.

The twelfth Baron of Halton is believed to have been Sir William Glinton, a distinguished knight who had rendered notable service in France. Sir William may have held the honour as a non-hereditary arrangement, or he may have held it during the lifetime of Lady Alice, widow of the eleventh baron. Henry of Lancaster, the nephew of Thomas eventually secured the family estates to become the thirteenth Baron of Halton. He was one of the first Knights of the Order of the Garter and he was the first subject to be accorded a dukedom when he was created Duke of Lancaster. The barony of Halton formed an insignificant part of his lands. Henry served the King in France and died of plague in 1361.

John of Gaunt (named after Ghent where he was born) married Blanche, the heiress of the thirteenth baron, to become the next Baron of Halton. He was the third surviving son of King Edward III and during the infancy of King Richard II he was appointed Regent. John of Gaunt was a patron of the reformer Wycliffe and a friend of Chaucer. "Time-honoured Lancaster" is believed to have used Halton Castle as an occasional hunting lodge and also to have improved its fortifications. King Richard granted his uncle the office of Constable of Chester, thus this post and the barony of Halton were once more held by the same man. In 1398 John of Gaunt's eldest son was banished from England by the King. This and subsequent events, form the plot of Shakespeare's "Richard II". In response to his uncle's pleading, Henry Bolingbroke's term of banishment was reduced from ten years to six but when John of Gaunt died Richard confiscated Bolingbroke's inheritance and announced that his banishment was for life.

Henry Bolingbroke became the fifteenth and last Baron of Halton. His return from France to claim his paternal estates caused the whole country to rally round him. The Lords and Commons had had enough of Richard's erratic and despotic rule and he was deposed. Henry Bolingbroke, Duke of Lancaster, the first King of the House of Lancaster ascended the throne of England as King Henry IV in 1399 and his twelve-year old son was immediately proclaimed Prince of Wales, Duke of Lancaster and Earl of Chester. By a charter of 1399, it was directed that the Duchy should belong to the King but that it should be administered separately from the other possessions of the Crown. Today the Duchy of Lancaster with its properties and revenue are in the personal ownership of the monarch and it is distinct from the Crown Lands. Since the days of Henry Bolingbroke the title of Duke of Lancaster has never been bestowed upon a subject and to this day the ruins of Halton Castle form part of the Queen's Lancastrian inheritance.

Halton Castle. Nearly half the masonry shown in the picture has fallen since the photograph was taken in 1900.

Bibliography

The information in this chapter concerning the accounts of the Manor of Halton in the years 1296 and 1307 is taken from "The Compoti of the Lancashire and Cheshire Manors XXIV and XXII Edward I" by the Rev. P.A.Lyons, a *Chetham Society* publication of 1884. The Manor of Halton is also considered in "An Official Progress through Lancashire and Cheshire 1476" by R.A. Myers in the *Transactions of the Lancashire and Cheshire Historic Society* Vol. 115 (1964). Reference has also been made to *"An Account of the Rolls of the Honour of Halton"* (1879) by William Beamont.

Cheshire histories used in this chapter include *"Cheshire under the Three Edwards"* (1966) by H.T. Hewitt; *"Cheshire in the Later Middle Ages"* (1970) by J.T. Driver and *"History of the County Palatinate and City of Chester"* (1882) by G. Ormerod (ed. T. Helsby). Other sources include "The Earldom and Palatinate of Chester" by Geoffrey Barraclough to be found in the *"Transaction of the Lancashire and Cheshire Historic Society"* Vol. 103 (1952) and *"Medieval Cheshire"* (1929) by H. Hewitt.

The general background reading includes *"The Black Death"* (1969) by Philip Ziegler; J.J. Bagley's *"The Story of Merseyside"* (1968) and William Beamont's *"A History of Halton Castle and the Priory or Abbey of Norton"* (1873). Reference to the local Cheshire landscape in the medieval period can be found in two articles by Dorothy Silvester, "The Open Fields of Cheshire" in the *"Transactions of the Lancashire and Cheshire Historic Society"* Vol. 108 (1956) and "The Manor and the Cheshire Landscape" Vol. 70 (1960) of the *"Transactions of the Lancashire and Cheshire Antiquarian Society"*.

References to this immediate locality are to be found in "Early Warrington Fisheries" (1929) by G.A. Dunlop in the *Proceeding of the Warrington Literary and Philosophical Society;* "Letters and Accounts of William Brereton of Malpas" by E.W. Ives, *Record Society of Lancashire and Cheshire,* Vol. CXVI (1976); "Calendar of Cheshire Trailbaston Proceedings" by Paul Booth, *Cheshire History* Nos. 12, 13, 14 (1983, 1984); "Muster Rolls 1417" *Cheshire Sheaf,* New Series, Vol. 6 (1906) and *Cheshire Sheaf* (1914).

A description and plan of Hallwood by J.P. Greene is to be found in Cheshire Archaeological Bulletin No. 3 (1975) and *"Halton Castle"* (1981), by A. Whimperley gives an impression of life in medieval Halton. Social life in the Middle Ages in Cheshire is explored in "Sources and Problems in the Study of Social Mobility" by M.J. Bennet in the *Transaction of the Lancashire and Cheshire Historic Society,* Vol. 128 (1979) and in *"Cheshire and Its Rulers"* (1984) by Brian Harris. After exhausting Beamont the account of the Barons of Halton has been compiled from *"The Barons of Halton"*, a booklet issued by the Information Service of the Halton Borough Council.

For providing the details of the 1372 Inquiry into Labour Offences against the Statute of Labourers the author is indebted to Mr. P.H.W. Booth who supplied the transcriptions from his own research findings.

In 1986 archaeological excavations directed by Robina McNeil were undertaken at Halton Castle. Miss McNeil's well illustrated report, "Halton Castle. A Visual Treasure" (1987) produced for the *North West Archaeological Trust,* includes notes on the historical background to the castle together with plans and an account of the various periods of building.

*The Norman doorway at Norton Priory, erected about 1180,
is the finest to survive in Cheshire.*

Chapter 4
Norton Priory

The history of Norton Priory and Abbey is best discovered by a visit to the splendid museum of monastic life which houses many of the artefacts discovered since 1971. In that year Dr Patrick Greene began the archaeological dig and his excavations together with his research into archives has provided us with much information about the abbey at Norton. The present work does not attempt to present either an exhaustive account of the Priory's history or a lengthy narrative of the discoveries made during the excavations. Much of what follows is a synopsis based to a large extent upon Dr Greene's articles and reports.

When the Augustinian canons left Runcorn in 1134 the original endowments were transferred to the new foundation at Norton. By the original gift of William FitzNigel in 1115, the prior and brethren of Runcorn Priory had been endowed with properties throughout Cheshire, Lancashire, Nottingham, Lincolnshire and Oxfordshire. In our region the priory owned the mill at Runcorn, half the fisheries at Halton and half the fishery at Thelwall, two bovates of land and a house at Halton, two bovates of land in Widnes, a house in Chester and the mill at Great Barrow east of Chester. The prior had rights of common in Appleton and Cuerdley in Widnes. He was entitled to two thirds of the demesne tithes of Barrow, two thirds of the demesne tithes at Raby near Stanney on Wirral, two thirds of the tithes at Guilden Sutton and two thirds of those at Staining. The gifts of William FitzNigel to Runcorn Priory included lands at Tarbock and Bold, at Aston, Budworth, Preston-on-the-Hill and Frodsham. The church at Great Budworth was a valuable asset and further afield, the church at Castle Donington in Leicestershire together with the mill there and some ploughland, also the church at Ratcliffe upon Soar, Nottinghamshire with the fourth part of the mill there, were part of William FitzNigel's gift. In addition the canons had the churches at Burton upon Stather in Lincolnshire; Kneesall in Nottinghamshire and Pirton in Oxfordshire, all given by William in 1115. Later in the century further endowments added a house in Derby, a salt house in Northwich, land and tenements in Northgate Street in Chester, the church of St Michael in Chester as well as property in Warrington and land at Comberbach, Lach Dennis, Barnton and Rostherne. By 1195 Norton Priory had eight churches, five houses, the tithes of at least eight mills and rights of common in four townships as well as a tenth of the profits of Runcorn Ferry. The prior also supplied the chaplain to the Constableship of Chester and also the chaplain to the Baron of Halton.

During the late twelfth and early thirteenth centuries the Barons of Halton and their principal retainers were the main benefactors of Norton Priory and during this time there was much building with the size of the house increasing considerably. It is possible that during this period the community doubled with twice as many canons being accommodated in the enlarged claustral buildings. However, from about 1200 there was a falling off in the donations made to the priory. This was due to the fact that Stanlow Abbey had assumed a more important role in the religious life of the region and the Barons of Halton transferred their generosity to Stanlow. As far as is known only two members of the baronial family of Halton were buried at Norton. According to Professor Barraclough one was Richard, the brother of the seventh baron who died of leprosy in 1211 and the other was a Lady Alice of Halton.

The Dutton family of Dutton had been associated with the priory since its beginnings in Runcorn and as the patronage of the barons of Halton in Norton Priory declined, the Duttons assumed a more important role in the fortunes of the house. The Duttons were the most notable tenants of the Constable of Chester and they were descended from Odard who, in the time of the Conqueror, had held his original holding in Dutton from the Earl of Chester and his other holdings at Halton, Aston, Weston and Whitley of the Baron of Halton. There were two branches of the family of Dutton, one living in Dutton hamlet and the other at Sutton Weaver. In the thirteenth century Thomas de Dutton built the chapel of ease at Poolsey in Aston and he provided a chaplain from Norton to conduct the services there. The Duttons also had their own burial chapel at the priory and in three wills of family members, burial at Norton is specified. In 1392 Lawrence Dutton left his body to be buried at Norton which had been raised to the status of an abbey twelve months before his death. To the abbot and convent of Norton, Lawrence left his black horse as a heriot or funeral present and to the poor he left ten marks, with thirty pounds to the chaplains who would pray for the repose of his soul in the church at Great Budworth and in the family chapel at Norton. One of the Duttons of the Sutton Weaver branch moved to Warburton and adopted the name of the place as his surname and in 1448 we find Sir Geoffrey Warburton leaving instructions that his body was to be buried at Norton Abbey between the high chancel and the chapel of the Blessed Virgin Mary. Geoffrey left a hundred shillings to the chaplain to pray for his soul and the abbot was to have his best horse. A few years ago it was discovered that within the brick interior of Sutton Hall Farm at Sutton Weaver there are the roof timbers of a large medieval timber-framed house and there is little doubt that the farm house was formerly the manor house of the Sutton branch of the Dutton family.

The Aston family of Aston were also represented among the benefactors of Norton Priory and their principal gift was that donated by Richard FitzGilbert de Aston who gave "all his land in Hendeley with all its appurtenances" to the priory in the early years of the thirteenth century. Hendeley was the settlement of Eanley which was situated south of Norton village and which was mentioned in the Domesday Book.

When a parish church was granted to a religious house the abbot or prior and the convent not only acquired the right to appoint incumbents but they also gained the property and the land which had been accumulated by the church. Such a church was said to be "appropriated" to the abbey or priory and as the abbot became responsible for the religious welfare of the parish he appointed the clergy to the parish. We know that canons from Norton were appointed at Great Budworth on three occasions during the fourteenth century and on two in the fifteenth. Every appointment at Runcorn for over four hundred years was made by the head of Norton Priory. In 1331 it is recorded that "Peover Chapel in the Parish of Great Budworth, appropriated to the prior and convent of Norton is to have a font". Norton canons were presented to Pirton and in 1210 Canon Richard was presented to the church of Burton upon Stather as chaplain. Grappenhall had Norton canons at least from 1302. Norton Priory does not appear to have fully appropriated the church of Ratcliffe upon Soar in Nottinghamshire and in 1357 the prior asked for permission to sell the avowson of Ratcliffe in order to settle heavy debts at Norton. This was granted and the link between the prior and the church was severed. Similarly the church at Kneesall in Nottinghamshire does not appear to have been fully appropriated and it was disposed of at an unknown date. Five appropriated churches were held by Norton Abbey up to the Dissolution of the Monasteries. They were Runcorn, Great Budworth, Donington, Burton upon Stather and Pirton.

The wall arcade. Norman architecture at Norton Priory

The archaeological excavations have uncovered at Norton a major monastic foundation which had undergone much rebuilding and expansion over four hundred years. The original foundation was probably designed to accommodate twelve canons and the prior but at the end of the twelfth century the priory underwent considerable rebuilding. The church was lengthened and a new and larger chapter house was built. A large chapel was added at the east end of the church. This chapel may have housed the Holy Cross of Norton which was believed to have the power to cure the blind and the dumb. About 1200 the west front of the priory church was enlarged and a bell tower raised about the same time. Guest quarters were also constructed. It seems obvious that the building work became necessary because of the increase in the number of canons. In 1236 a disastrous fire destroyed the church and cloisters but rebuilding is believed to have begun immediately. Another catastrophe occurred in 1332 when exceptionally high tides on the river flooded much of the priory estate and inundated reclaimed land in Norton and Astmoor. From documentary evidence it is known that the canons were responsible for building embankments on the Mersey marshes. The excavations have also revealed that they created a system of moats which surrounded the monastic buildings on the south, east and north sides with a mill pool and fish ponds to the west. The moats were about ten metres wide and two metres in depth. When in 1391 Norton Priory was raised to the status of a mitred abbey, extensive new living quarters were built for the abbot and a tower was erected to the west range. Some indication of the wealth of the house can be ascertained from the fact that the workmanship was always of the highest quality. An examination of the surviving masonry shows that the best master craftsmen were employed in every period of construction. It has been estimated that some forty thousand floor tiles were used in the abbey church. These were made by peripatetic tile makers who built their kiln on site using the local clay. The excavations of 1971 uncovered the largest area of mosaic tile floor to be found on any site in Britain. By the early years of the sixteenth century, Norton Abbey was the most conspicuous array of buildings in north Cheshire. The claustral buildings exhibited an amalgam of architectural styles dating from the Romanesque of the Norman period to the perpendicular style of the fifteenth century.

However, from the beginning of the fifteenth century the abbey began to meet severe financial difficulties due to the costly maintenance and repair of the extensive range of buildings and in 1427 there was a recurrence of the disastrous floods which had caused such damage a hundred years before.

In the century before its closure the financial state of Norton Abbey was precarious due to mismanagement of funds and to the fact that the gifts from benefactors were not nearly so munificent as they had been in the previous centuries. The abbey buildings and the church fell into serious disrepair and the number of canons was reduced. At the time of its elevation to an abbey in 1391 there were fifteen canons including the prior at Norton. By 1518, in spite of the determined efforts by the abbot to recruit a full complement of twelve brethren, there were only seven canons and the abbot and the size of the community remained unchanged up to the dissolution in 1536.

If the report of the Bishop of Lichfield after the visitation in 1516 is correct, the prestige of the abbey was high with no evidence of untoward conduct by the canons or laxity in the observation of the Rule of St Augustine. At a visitation all brethren were obliged to answer all questions put to them and they were duty bound to report any irregularity or failure on the part of the canons or the abbot. William Merton, the abbot; William Hardware, prior; Roger Haghton, sacrist; William Chester, precentor; Richard Roo, the kitchener; Henry Sutton, the infirmarian and Hugh Smith, the almoner, were interviewed and nothing was reported amiss. Everything appeared in good order; *"Brother William Hardware, prior, says he knows nothing worthy of reformation and he praises the abbot in administrations and in religion even more; all the brothers live in continence, they have no accounts nor inventory but however everything is kept in good order as far as he knows"*. The abbot declared that he had no problems and that everything was well regulated, *"Brother William Mereton, abbot of the same, says it is not burdened to anybody, he returns and causes to be returned an annual account from all the brothers who hold office, nothing has been given away under the common seal; he has an inventory of all moveable goods, the brothers live continently and are subject to discipline, silence is well observed and the essentials of religious observance are carefully preserved"*. Much the same kind of report was made after the visitation of 1521 but the judgement of the King's Commissioners in 1536 was one of denunciation, with charges of scandalous living, worldliness and opportunism being directed at the canons.

At the Dissolution of the Monasteries all the lands and properties of the country's religious houses comprising nearly one quarter of all the land in the kingdom, passed into the ownership of the Crown. In 1535 a commission ascertained the income of all religious foundations and its findings were entered in "Valor Ecclesiasticus" -

a detailed register of the wealth of every religious house. By an Act of Parliament of the following year, all abbeys, priories and nunneries whose total income was less than £200 per year, or those institutions which had under twelve members of a religious order, were to be dissolved and their estates and possessions were to be surrendered to the Crown. It was alleged that these "lesser monasteries" were ill-governed and that they were often houses of depravity and criminal activity with their inmates more interested in extortion and luxurious living than in religious observance. The King's commissioners who inspected the monasteries in 1535 were often dishonest in producing reports that were both virulent and manifestly exaggerated. Their statements were contrived to bring about the early transfer of ecclesiastical property into lay hands and their observations were often distortions of the truth.

The first moves to close Norton Abbey began with its financial assessment in "Valor Ecclesiasticus" where the house was undervalued in order that it could be dissolved as a minor monastery. The abbey of Norton was stated to have an annual income of £258 per year but this was reduced to £180 when expenses and pensions were paid. It was thus classed among the smaller houses and marked for early closure. At the same time, a campaign of vilification was directed at the canons. Doctor Layton and Doctor Legh asserted that four of the canons were guilty of debauched conduct. It was reported that Thomas Fletcher, a canon of Norton and also vicar of Runcorn had ten or twelve children by an Agnes Habram. William Hardware, the vicar of Great Budworth and also a canon, was alleged to have kept Margaret Kynderdale, a single woman, in his house and that he had fathered several children by her.

By far the greatest menace to the abbey and convent of Norton was Sir Piers Dutton, the Sheriff of Cheshire who was, according to his rival Sir William Brereton, the deputy-chamberlain of Chester, so powerful "that he can do as he likes in this county". Dutton's estate bordered that of Norton Priory and he hoped to obtain abbey lands from the Crown after their confiscation. In 1535 Dutton plotted to bring down Brereton with eight of his party as well as the abbot by falsely accusing them of issuing counterfeit coins. In order to achieve his purpose, Dutton planned to use a Piers Felday who had already forfeited his life by making false currency. Felday was promised a pardon if he would become a Crown witness and accuse Brereton and the abbot of coining. Two servants of Abbot Birkenhead, Thomas Holfe and Robert Jannyns, were already imprisoned in the Tower

of London accused of attempting to pass false coin in Staffordshire and it was held that Holfe had only been taken into the abbot's service because he had previously been employed in the Royal Mint. The abbot was taken before the King's Council in London but Felday proved to be an unconvincing witness and the charge against the abbot of complicity in false coining was dismissed and he was released. Felday however fell into the hands of Sir William Brereton to whom he made a declaration about Dutton's plot and the methods used by him to implicate Brereton. The full details of Dutton's machinations were sent to Thomas Cromwell, the Lord Privy Seal, on 8th June 1537. While Felday lived he was a threat to Dutton but the coiner was abducted from Brereton's custody at Chester by Dutton's servants. In early August Felday was executed. On the scaffold he would not name the instigator of the plot because he did not desire to "set debate among the gentlemen of the shire". He said to the crowd who had come to see him die, "Never trust to knight, esquire or gentleman for I was fair promised, howbeit it is an old saying, fair words make fools fain". Felday went on to say that there were three sets of coin moulds in the county in the ownership of some of those who were listening to him. Before he could say more, Dutton's men pushed him off the ladder. There was nothing more that Brereton could do except complain to Cromwell demanding that he do something to curb Dutton's misuse of power in the county.

The final events in the four hundred year history of Norton Priory and Abbey took place in 1536 amid scenes of high drama. On the 11th October the royal commissioners, Combes and Bolles, arrived at Norton Abbey to appropriate the valuables for the Crown. They had gathered together "such jewels and other stuff" as the canons possessed when they were menaced by a crowd of some three hundred local people. Fearing for their lives, the commissioners locked themselves in a tower but they succeeded in sending a letter to Sir Piers Dutton who received the message about nine o'clock at night. In the meantime the abbot had given the crowd an ox to roast, whether to pacify or distract them, or to reward them for their support has never been determined. Dutton and his men arrived suddenly to find fires lit inside and outside the abbey gates but, in spite of having the element of surprise, the sheriff did not capture any of the demonstrators who, knowing the ground, quickly escaped through the fish ponds under cover of darkness. Dutton arrested the abbot and four canons and took them first to Halton Castle and then to prison in Chester. Having restored order and secured the release of Combes and Bolles,

Dutton reported his account of events to the King.

On October 19th Henry VIII jointly addressed a letter to Sir Piers Dutton and Sir William Brereton, his principal officers in the county, stating that if indeed the abbot and his canons had behaved as Dutton had alleged then they were to be immediately hanged as traitors. But it seems that Brereton adopted a strategy of non-co-operation with Dutton over the matter and the lives of the canons were spared until the two men could meet to hold an enquiry into the truth of the matter. However, developments favoured the prisoners when the Earl of Derby wrote to Dutton telling him that he could not move against the canons because the political atmosphere had changed. After a rising in favour of the monks in Yorkshire known as the "Pilgrimage of Grace" was suppressed with great severity, some leniency towards those guilty of non-compliance and transgression over religious issues was being considered. There was much popular support for the canons of Norton. It seems that they were fair employers and good landlords. Sir William Brereton was hesitant about taking action against the abbot and support for the canons' cause came from Sir Thomas Boteler, the lord of Warrington who wrote to Cromwell declaring that he thought the abbot and his canons were innocent of treason. Boteler said that, "The common fame of the county imputes no fault to them". No doubt there were others who also doubted Dutton's account of events and who made representations on the canons' behalf for, within a few weeks, the abbot and his brethren were released after having given sureties.

Norton Abbey was immediately made inhospitable. The roof lead, bell metal and any other valuable materials were confiscated for the King's use and for nine years the abbey lay empty and derelict. In 1545 Richard Brooke Esquire of Leighton in the hundred of Nantwich and a vice-admiral of England, contracted to buy the manor of Norton including the abbey buildings and appurtenances from the Crown. He was granted fee simple to acquire Norton, Stockham, Acton Grange and Aston Grange in Cheshire and Cuerdley in Lancashire. Brooke adapted the abbot's quarters to make his residence. The remaining buildings and the church were demolished over the years to be sold for building stone. Tradition has it that the linenfold panelling in Weaverham church came from Norton Abbey as did the medieval stallwork in the church of Great Budworth. Richard Brooke had paid the huge sum of £1,500 for the abbey and its lands and it is certain that he made efforts to recoup some of his outlay by selling his

unwanted assets but it is extremely unlikely that the popular story that he sold the abbey roof to the church of St Helen in Witton, Northwich has any foundation in fact. In the church of St Oswald, Lower Peover, there is a massive dug-out chest of oak roughly hewn and bound with iron. It was used for the safe keeping of vestments, plate and books. The chest came from Norton Priory in 1269 when a canon came to officiate as the priest of Lower Peover.

Of the brethren of Norton we have a little knowledge. After the Dissolution of the abbey Thomas Birkenhead, the Abbot, was awarded a pension of £24 a year and was given a dispensation to become a secular priest. Fortune favoured the abbot for, under the will of a man from Middlesex, Birkenhead received a house and garden in Astmoor. Canons William Hardware and Henry Barnes were given dispensations and became secular priests as did John Penketh and Thomas Fletcher. Richard Wright, canon of Norton and vicar of Burton on Stather, retained his living as a secular priest. James Pate and Richard Walton were dispensed from their vows. The charges of licentious conduct which had been made against William Hardware, Vicar of Great Budworth and Thomas Fletcher, the vicar of Runcorn in 1535 did not prevent them from continuing their work in their parishes after the Dissolution of Norton. On the tower of the church at Great Budworth can still be seen the arms of Norton Priory carved in the stone.

The patronage and the right of presentation at the churches of Runcorn and Great Budworth which belonged to Norton Abbey, together with the tithes of both churches, were granted to Christ Church College, Oxford. After the sale of the abbey, the rectory of Runcorn was leased to Richard Brooke Esquire by Christ Church and Richard's descendants were to enjoy the great tithes of the parish of Runcorn for centuries to come.

The Brookes gradually converted the former abbots' lodgings into a Tudor house which was to serve the family for over a hundred and eighty years. About 1730 the Tudor building was demolished and it was replaced by a Georgian country house which was extensively remodelled in 1790. Further changes were made in 1868 when a large entrance porch was added to the front of the house. By this time industry was beginning to appear at the boundary of the estate and soon the house went the way of so many other country houses. By the early years of the twentieth century Norton Priory mansion was inconvenient and out-moded. It lacked mains services and its upkeep was enormously expensive. In 1921 the Brooke family left the district and, after standing empty for seven years, the house was demolished, its rubble being used as hard core in the foundations of a new chemical works. But not everything was pulled down for Sir Richard made provision for the retention of the ancient cellarer's undercroft which was roofed over with a capping of concrete. This roof lasted to protect the old masonry until restoration work could be carried out when Norton Priory Museum was created in the 1970s.

After being in the possession of his family for over four hundred and twenty years, Sir Richard Brooke gave Norton Priory in trust for the benefit of the public in 1966.

The fourteenth century statue of St. Christopher at the Norton Priory Museum.

This dug-out chest for the safekeeping of vestments, plate and books is to be seen in St. Oswald's Church, Lower Peover. It came from Norton Priory in 1269.

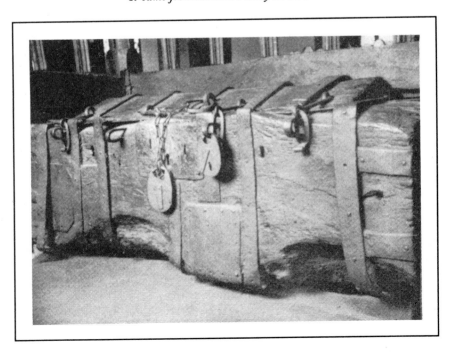

Norton Priory. The mansion house which replaced the Tudor building about 1730.

Bibliography

Until recently there was little in print concerning the history of Norton Abbey and this chapter relies heavily upon the researches of Dr J.P. Greene, the excavator of the abbey. Among his articles concerning the abbey at Norton are the following:

Greene J.P. "Norton Priory" (Handbook)
Norton Priory Museum (1975)

Greene J.P. "Roots for Runcorn", *Cheshire Life*, May 1975.

Greene J.P. "The Elevation of Norton Priory to the Status of a Mitred Abbey", *"Transactions of the Lancashire and Cheshire Historic Society"*, Vol.128 (1978).

Greene J.P. "Norton Priory. An Archaeological Examination of the Priory, Its Hinterland and Its Economic Links". Unpublished Ph.D. thesis, University of Leeds (1984).

In addition to material from the works of William Beamont and George Ormerod, information was obtained from *"Valor Ecclesiasticus"* ed. J. Caley and J. Hunter, Record Commission (1810-1834) and also from *"English Medieaval Monasteries 1066-1540"* by Roy Midmer (1979). There is an account of the dissolution of Norton Abbey in *Cheshire Round* (1 and 2 of 1962) by G. Chesters and also a reference to the closure in "Letters and Accounts of William Brereton of Malpas" by E.W. Ives, *Record Society of Lancashire and Cheshire*, Vol. CXVI (1976).

Transcriptions of the Bishop's Visitations to Norton Abbey in 1516 and 1521 were provided from the records of the diocese of Lichfield by Michael Cooke, archivist of the University of Liverpool.

The rivalry between Brereton and Dutton and the account of the disturbance at the closing of Norton Priory are well described in *"Policy and Police. The Enforcement of the Reformation in the Age of Thomas Cromwell"* (1972) by G.R. Elton.

An essential source of information on medieval religious matters with an account of Norton Priory is that to be found in Volume III of the *Victoria County History of Cheshire* ed. Brian Harris (1980).

Chapter 5
Matters of Religion

From the few surviving fragments of information still in existence we have but brief glimpses of Tudor Runcorn during the Reformation period of transition from Catholicism to Protestantism. Henry VIII as Supreme Head of the Church, proceeded to reform the religion of his kingdom and there were many changes made in religious practice. All over the country statues were taken down and new forms of prayer in English were introduced. During King Edward VI's brief reign the Reformation saw the strengthening of the Protestant Church of England but when Edward died in 1553 his half sister, Mary, a fervent Catholic, became queen. Mary immediately began to bring about a reunion with Rome with the restoration of the old faith and the Latin mass.

It would appear that the vicar and churchwardens at Runcorn were slow or reluctant to change back to the old practices and at the bishop's visitation in 1557 they received a reprimand for not conforming with the law. They were also threatened with penalties if they did not carry out repairs to the chancel. *"Roncorne. The Bishop of Chester's Visitation for the year 1557. Against John Mayre the vicar there — to communicate with the Lord Bishop. Against the churchwardens there — they have not the image of Christ, (carent imagine Christi) the books and other vestments. They are to amend all before the Feast of All Saints under pain of XX shillings and under pain of sequestration of fruits if the chancel is not repaired".*

Robert Dobbs who was the vicar of Runcorn in 1592 was accused of neglecting his duties. It was alleged *"The vicarage house (is) ruinated and (he) doth not catechise: (he is) not residente at Runcorne ... he abuseth the churchyard and porch with sheep".* Vicar Dobbs was one of the many vicars who would be disheartened by the dilapidation and decay of church or vicarage. For centuries the need for major repairs to both would draw heavily upon the parish coffers and on the resourcefulness of the incumbent.

Mr. Dobbs was also responsible for the administration of Daresbury Chapel and at the bishop's visitation of 1592 he was called to account for the shortcomings there : *"Daresburie Chappel. Against the vicar there. The chapell hath bene destitute of a curate manie times and the vicar doth not catechise but once in Lent last".*

In 1587, when the possibility of a Spanish invasion looked certain, the loyalty of local Catholics came under deep suspicion. They were regarded as a potential enemy within the country and they were subjected to sudden searches for hidden arms. Catholics were liable to arrest if it was suspected that they were any less patriotic than their Protestant neighbours. In June 1588 Lord Strange, the Acting Lieutenant for Lancashire and Cheshire, issued instructions to his Justices of the Peace commanding them to arrest all rumour-mongers and those whose loyalty was in doubt. The Justices were to *"take all idle and vagrant persons within their townships and hamlets and to take and examine all News and Tale Carriers and other insolent persons that should raise any rumours among the Common People".*

In order to counter serious public disorder or insurrection, Commissions of Array and later, Commissions of Lieutenancy, possessed the power to raise defence forces of men-at-arms. The muster of these poorly armed and untrained companies was financed at the expense of the parish and by demands levied on the gentry. The menance from Spain made necessary an attempt to standardise the arms and equipment of the local militia and from "A booke conteyninge the numbre and names of all the knights, esquires and gentlemen with freeholders with their horses, armour and other furnyture" the following list of October 1587 illustrates the demands made on the local gentry :

"Sir John Savage of Clifton, Kt:
Two dimilance (armour for cavalry)
xviii lighte horse (lancers)
xxxv corslette (foot soldier's chest armour)
fiftie calyvers furnished (matchlock handguns)

Thomas Brooke Esq. of Norton:
One dimilance
Three corslette
Three Allmain Ryvette (light armour for footmen)
Three archers
Two calyvers furnished"

John Dutton Esquire of Dutton was required to provide the same number of men and weapons as Thomas Brooke and Robert Janion of Norton had "to furnish one cote of plate". On the 9th of April 1588, Thomas Brooke and John Dutton each contributed £25 towards the defence of the country.

When the Spanish invasion appeared imminent, huge piles of wood and combustible materials were carried to hill tops throughout the country ready to be set alight to warn of the enemy's approach. Lord Strange ordered constant watch and guard at every beacon in Lancashire and

Cheshire and on the night of 30th July 1588, the sky was red with warning fires. In a couple of hours the news of the coming of the Armada had travelled from one beacon to another from the English Channel to the Scottish border. The beacon on Frodsham Hill alerted the watch on Runcorn Hill and the fires were seen by the men guarding the beacon at Rivington Pike near Wigan. To the east, fires could be seen in the Pennines. Within a week came victory and the emergency was over. The defence precautions were relaxed and thanksgiving services were held in all the churches and chapels in the kingdom.

The long and costly war with Spain required a regular imposition of direct taxation and the demands made in 1593 aroused some complaint in the county. In that year Thomas Brooke of Norton and Peter Warburton were appointed as commissioners to collect the subsidy or tax on land and moveable goods from the better off in the Hundred of Bucklow. The subsidy was levied at the rate of sixteen pence in the pound on lands and a shilling in the pound on moveables. In Runcorn township Thomas Muskett, Robert Parker and Prudentia Lydiate were taxed on moveable goods and in Halton, Thomas Brooke, Robert Cheshire and Richard Okell had to pay the subsidy on their lands. In order to finance the war against the Spaniards occupying the Low Countries, a levy was imposed on the Cheshire gentry in August 1597. The tax raised £1,675 of which Thomas Brooke contributed £25.

The Recusants

Even though attendance at the Sunday service at the parish church was legally compulsory, there were many Catholics in Lancashire and Cheshire who refused to attend. These refusers or "recusants" were not harshly treated until the Pope excommunicated Queen Elizabeth in 1570.

Bishop Downham of Chester was easy-going and tolerant but his successor, Bishop William Chaderton, took firm action against the recusants who came to be regarded as potential traitors as the threat from Catholic Spain grew in the 1580s. On July 3rd, 1580, the authorities of the diocese of Chester received instructions from the Privy Council ordering them to impose heavier penalties on those who refused to attend the parish church services. Halton Castle was the first prison in the county to be prepared to hold the most obstinate of the recusants. The letter from the Privy Council demanded that the recusants should be isolated from other prisoners "since heretofore such as have bene committed to your ordinarie prisons have growne ... to be more obstinate". Sir John Savage of Clifton, the Constable and Seneschal of the castle, was appointed custodian of "such as bee notorious recusantes within the counties of Lancaster, Chester and North Wales". The prisoners were to be "committed there to remaine togither and be kept from the infecting of others that are well-disposed subjects and obedient to her Highness' lawes".

One old Marian priest was still active twenty-three years into Elizabeth's reign. In the autumn of 1581 it was reported that "Sir Richard Bannister, an old priest, is receipted at the house of one, Carter, nere Runcorne Boate". He may have continued his work until he died, for there is no record of him being captured and imprisoned. The Victoria County History of Cheshire also has a reference to a priest officiating in the Runcorn district in 1586.

Recusancy in the Elizabethan period was much weaker in Cheshire than it was in Lancashire and only about two hundred Roman Catholics have been identified in the county with any degree of certainty. A number of young men left Cheshire for Catholic Seminaries abroad but none appear to have returned to work in their native county. Edmund Campion, the first of the English Jesuit martyrs, is believed to have stayed at Hatton on a journey through Cheshire in 1581. One or two local people were suspected of being Catholic sympathisers. The Bishop's visitation in 1592 charged Matilda, the wife of Richard Kelsall; Thomassin, wife of William Haward and Ellen Haward of being "favourers of the Romish church". All three were ordered to appear before a council to explain their beliefs.

During a major anti-Catholic persecution drive in 1640 it was found that Runcorn was one of two parishes in the county where recusants were to be found in significant numbers. A census of parishioners who were obliged to attend Sunday service at Runcorn church revealed that refusers were present among the aristocracy and the poor. The Vicar of Runcorn, Hugh Burrows, submitted the following list of recusants to the bishop :

"A trew Presentment made by the Churchwardens of the Names of all Recusantes within the Parish of Runckhorne (leavinge the chappels to themselves) to our best knowledge

John Earle Rivers and his Countiss. Henry Savage et Uxor, Mrs. Colvet, Niccolas Morley, Mrs. Volcar, Margaret Ford, William Blag, Dorothy Ethead, Margaret Enterley, Elizabeth Heward, Edmund Potter, Edward Wicktin, William Thornburgh et uxor, Margaret Ley and A servant man of Mr. Thornburgh whose name we cannot come to knowledge of, William Southworth and Prudence Ince".

Hugh Burroughs	Vicar
Robt. Jackson	Churchwarden

Richard Madder   Churchwarden
12th January 1640

Pre-occupation with religious issues was the dominant feature in sixteenth and seventeenth century England and the divisions between the various sects grew wider as the Civil War approached. Appeals for help from persecuted Protestant brethren far away were met with a sympathetic response. When the Protestant Rhenish Palatinate was attacked by Catholic Austria, the clergy of Cheshire were expected to contribute "loans". Frederick, the Elector of the Palatinate was James I's son-in-law and two loans were demanded. In diocesan records are the following details :

"First loan of the Clergy of the Diocese of Chester, 1620, for the use of the Count-Palatine of Rhine, the King's son-in-law

Mr. Dobs, vicar of Runcorne .... £0 .. 6 .. 8

Two years later there is another compulsory levy.

"Contributions from the Clergy of the Diocese of Chester 1622 towards the recovery of the Palatinate."

Vicar of Runcorn Mr. Burrowes .... £1 . 18 .. 4
Schoolmaster of Halton
Mr. Piggott .... 0 .. 6 .. 8

The Reverend Hugh Burrows was presented to the vicarage of Runcorn on June 28th 1621 and immediately problems more pressing than recusancy began to occupy the new vicar's mind as taxation demands increased in the years leading up to the Civil War. His contribution to an unspecified demand is recorded in the diocesan accounts for 1624 :

"A subsidy from the Clergy of the Diocese of Chester

Vicar of Runcorne.
Hugh Burrowes .... £1 . 16 .. 4"

Mr Burrows is also listed in 1634 when he gave a donation of five shillings to the Cheshire Clergy's Fund for repairs to old St Paul's Cathedral in London. In the reign of Charles I frequent and swingeing demands for money were made and when the bankrupt King raised taxes by illegal methods, the indignation of his subjects reached the level of revolt. The levy of Ship Money was a necessary expedient urgently needed to finance the reconstruction of the Royal Navy which had been allowed to run down to a dangerous condition. Nevertheless, this tax was a particular source of resentment. It was raised without Parliamentary sanction and was condemned by the public to become a major factor in precipitating the Civil War. The inhabitants of Cheshire had to bear their share of the heavy taxation. The Bishop of Chester ordered two clergymen from each deanery to collect the Ship Money. Vicar Burrows of Runcorn and Vicar Osley of Frodsham were designated collectors for the Frodsham deanery. The entry in the records is as follows :

"The First Ship Money of the Clergy of the County of Chester 1635. The sum for a ship for the defence of the kingdom imposed on Cheshire was £3500 whereof the City of Chester was charged with £300. The clergy of the city and county with £200 and the layte of Cheshire with £3000. "

Ffradsam Deanery

Vicar of Runcorne
  Hugh Burrowes .... £1 . 16 .. 0
Curate of Halton
  Jo. King .... £2 .. 0 .. 0
Curate of Daresbury ....
  Edward Williams .... £0 .. 5 .. 0
Curate of Aston
  Robt. Marton .... £0 .. 5 .. 0

The fact that the curate of Halton paid more than his vicar is surprising but in a second Ship Money collection in 1636 Mr Burrows was required to pay another sixteen shillings and ten pence.

The Scottish revolt of 1638-40 found the King once more pressed for money to pay his troops. Again the clergy of Cheshire had to make a compulsory contribution and Mr Burrows was required to find a sizeable sum. His donation is recorded in *"Contributions of the Clergy of the Diocese of Chester in Aid of the war against the Scotch 1639"*

"Vicar of Runcorne
Hugh Burrowes .... £2 .. 0 .. 0

Mr Burrows had other expenses to meet with the vicarage house always in need of repair. In 1622 the vicar wrote a letter to a Thomas Grimsditch in which he mentioned the poor condition of the manse. *"The vicarage dilapidations require new thatch, thirteen score yards of courtyard wall, a wainhouse, stable, barn and roof lats and 500 nails for the house, a new door into the yard, a new door on the greate chambre, a new kitchen door and a new street door"*.

Hugh Burrows was succeeded in 1648 by Ephraim Elcock. Pastor Elcock was one of the Presbyterian ministers who signed the Cheshire Attestation of 1648 which called for the establishment of a national church. Mr. Elcock was the minister at Runcorn until about 1657 when he was succeeded by William Finmore, an ardent Royalist. The exact date of Mr. Finmore's induction at Runcorn is not known and it is difficult to reconcile the presentation of so fervent a Royalist to an ecclesiastical living during the period of Parliamentarian rule.

Vicar Finmore's sympathy for the Royalist cause was soon recognised and a short time after his taking up his appointment in Runcorn he was dismissed from the living. In 1659 he joined Sir George Booth in his futile rebellion against the Commonwealth and was captured at the battle of Winnington Bridge and imprisoned in Chester. After Mr. Finmore's eviction from the parish of Runcorn Mr. Thomas Breck was appointed minister, a post he held until 24th August 1662 when, with many other non-conformist clergy, he refused to accept episcopal ordination and was ejected. Mr. Finmore was then restored to his vicarage.

William Finmore M.A. was born in Hincksley in Berkshire in 1622 and he first showed his loyalty to the King as a young man of twenty-one. He admired Colonel Gage who led the King's army to relieve Basing House near Basingstoke in 1644. When Sir Henry Gage, then Governor of Oxford, was killed in action the following year, Finmore composed an inspiring poem which began :

"Drums, beat an onset; let the rebels feel
How sharp our grief is by our sharper steel."

The young Finmore went to Christ Church, Oxford in 1642 and stayed to become a tutor at his college in 1649 before moving to Runcorn about eight years later.

Shortly after the Restoration of King Charles II, William Finmore, on the strength of his pronounced loyalty to the monarch, made application for one of the vacant fellowships at the Collegiate Church in Manchester. He was unsuccessful in his application and in 1662 he submitted a claim to the King for the position of King's Preacher in the County Palatine of Lancaster, one of four posts originally appointed by King James I at a stipend of £200 a year. Mr. Finmore's petition stated that he had been nominated by Henry Ferne who had been appointed Bishop of Chester but who died before he took possession of the see in 1662. Unfortunately for Mr. Finmore his plea was declared void by reason of the vacancy in the see of Chester and another applicant procured the post of King's Preacher.

Later in the year Mr. Finmore was restored to the vicarage of Runcorn which is in the patronage of his college, Christ Church. William Finmore had official connection with the Diocese of Chester as early as July 1664 when he was collated prebendary of the sixth stall in succession to Dr. Thomas Mallory. On November 6th 1666, he was

appointed Archdeacon of Chester. Archdeacon Finmore died on April 7th 1686 and was buried in the north aisle of St Mary's Chapel of the cathedral where there is a tablet to his memory.

Vicar Finmore had a number of disputes with his parishioners. In 1662 he had taken Thomas Salton to the Consistory Court for non-payment of the tithe of a "wind and corn mill driven by water". He was also involved in a quarrel with a more formidable adversary in the person of Sir Richard Brooke of Norton Priory. In 1665 and again ten years later, the vicar went to the Consistory Court at Chester in order to obtain Sir Richard's "share of repairs" to Runcorn church.

There was another dispute which remained the subject of contention for centuries. The township of Thelwall was situated within the parochial chapelry of Daresbury and both were within the ancient parish of Runcorn. The congregations of Halton, Daresbury, Aston and Thelwall were obliged to contribute towards the upkeep of the parish church at Runcorn - an obligation which they met with ill-grace. In 1663, there was a suit pending between Peter Dunbabin and Richard Eaton, the churchwardens of Daresbury and Peter Drinkwater and Robert Leigh on behalf of themselves and other inhabitants of Thelwall, respecting a contribution claimed from the latter towards the repair of Daresbury and Runcorn churches.

Peter and Robert alleged that neither they nor any of the inhabitants of Thelwall had "from time whereof the memory of man, had any pews, seats, formes or kneelings in the church of Daresbury nor had christened their children, received the Sacrament of the Lord's Supper or buried their dead therein or thereat". The churchwardens at Daresbury wrote the following to Thomas Boulde, churchwarden at Thelwall.

"Whereas it was condescended unto and agreed by ye Gent. and Churchwardens with other inhabitants of the parochial chappelry of Daresbury at a generall meeting, March 13th 1662, that there should bee forthwith six assessments gathered throughout ye said chappelry, ffowre whereof towards repaire of such part of Runcorn church as ye chappelry stands liable to pay and two assessments to ye use of ye poore and impotent inhabitinge within ye said chappelry. These are to require you to collect and gather ye ffowre assessments throughout your township of Thellwall. The same amounting to ye sum of £2 . 10 .. 8, pay over to mee at my house in Newton upon ye 16th day of this instant."

Aprill 2nd Ann. Dom. 1663

Included with the demand was a list of names of Thelwall people who were required to subscribe to the assessment. The reply from the Thelwall churchwardens was not long in coming :

"Neighbours you have sent to this towne a paper whereby you require fower assessments from the persons herein named, for our share for the repaire of Runkhorne church, wherof wee have retorned you a copy, and as we think you require two assessments for the poore, but you have named in your paper such persons as are not known to us nor any such in our towne, and wee believe it is some old coppy neere one hundred yeares old, because you name one, Sir Robert, who wee have heard and believe, was reader at our chappell before wee were borne, and such as are in our towne, you have charged some too much and others too little accordinge to the lands they now hold. Therefore this money cannot bee now gathered. Wee shall meet you where reason will be heard and right will bee done us."

Thomas Chesshyre, gentleman, of Hallwood was called upon to give evidence on behalf of the Vicar of Runcorn. He said that there had always been an ancient link between Runcorn Church and Thelwall and that former vicar, Mr Hugh Burrows, went every year for thirty years to preach and administer the Sacrament at Easter in every chapel in his parish. Thomas declared that on one occasion he had accompanied Mr Burrows to Thelwall Chapel and heard him preach there.

After much litigation an agreement was reached by which the churchwardens of Daresbury bound themselves to accept the sum of twenty-four shillings yearly from the inhabitants of Thelwall in discharge of all future contributions to the repairs of either the mother church or the parochial chapel of Daresbury. This payment was paid every year for more than two centuries until Thelwall was formed into an independent parish in 1870.

The Quakers and the Church Tithes

Shortly after his presentation at Runcorn there arose another, more urgent problem which demanded the attention of Mr. Finmore. To the concern of the church authorities the Quakers, or Society of Friends, began "to spread mightily" in Cheshire. When George Fox, the Society's founder visited Frandley, near Great Budworth in 1657, he attracted a crowd of three thousand people. The Conventicle Act of 1664 made prison and transportation the punishment for those caught taking part in dissenting worship, yet in spite of insult, persecution and imprisonment the Friends increased in number. Before long the bishop was informed that: "In Runcorn (as is famed and reported) there is a meeting of Quakers at Widow Copock's house in

Norton" and among "certaine persons called Quakers or church absenters" in 1662, were John and Margery Sharpus of Weston. Seven years later when it was obvious that the Friends were firmly established in the district, the Bishop received the information that, "Frodsham has a conventicle of Quakers and Runcorne has the like". The Quakers did not feel any obligation to the established church and they positively refused to make any tithe payment. The Friends even appointed an official whose duty it was to travel the district to "inspect Friend's clearness with respect to tithes". In other words the official was to insist on non-payment.

Obstinate Quakers suffered greatly because of their pertinacity. Their crops, animals and household goods were seized and then sold to satisfy the tithe requirement. Among Quaker records is the following account of the afflictions of the Friends in Runcorn in 1657 during the Protectorate.

"A Relation of the Suffering of Friends in Cheshire because that for conscience sake they could not pay tithes and other things.

Runkorn Parish. William Finmore, Priest.*

Henry Burtonwood for tythe of the value of five shillings had taken from him one cow worth £2 13s 4d for the use of the said priest abovesaid.

At another time Henry Burtonwood for tythe-corn of the value of £2 1s 1d had taken from him two cows and one heifer stirk which were sold for about seven pounds for the use of the priest Finmore abovesaid.

John Burtonwood for tythe-wool and lambs of the value of eight shillings and three pence had taken from him two young beasts which they sold for £1 5s 0d.

Thomas Boulton, for tythe-corn of the value of thirteen shillings had taken from him corn worth five pound for the use of Henry Brooke.

Sisly Cleaton had taken from her one Warming-Pan worth six shilling for tythe-flax and she had none being sued at law and cast by a false Oath for the use of Collonel Brooke.

Widow Royle for tythe-corn of the value of £1 3s 0d had taken from her for the use of Coll. Henry Brooke. And likewise taken from her one load of beans, nothing being demanded and likewise she had one Bed Hilling taken for tythe for Coll. Brooke".

By 1676 the Quakers were holding men's meetings every week in Norton. The Friends were harmless and posed no threat to the authorities but because they challenged the social order of the times their lives were made miserable by constant harassment.

For the next two centuries the Quakers continued to refuse to pay the tithes. In the first half of the eighteenth century the Hough family of Sutton suffered every year on account of tenacious adherence to religious principle. John Hough had flax and hemp sequestrated in 1712 and twenty-nine years later he suffered heavy loss when corn to the value of £6 was taken for non-payment of tithes.

The Toleration Act of 1689 gave freedom of worship to Protestant dissenters and in the rural areas of north Cheshire the Quakers attracted many converts. Although the Friends had been meeting in Norton since the 1660s, the record of their meetings survives only from 1748. By then it was reported that the meetings were not as well attended as they had been in the early years and one curious entry in 1750 states that "Love and unity in general is pretty well kept up but not so well as particularly" (sic).

The Society of Friends had its own local burial grounds. Elizabeth Boulton who died in 1754 aged 20 was buried at Over Whitely and Sarah Hough, who died in 1776 aged 86 was "buried in the Friends' burial ground in Newton by the forest". Young people intending to marry had first to declare their intention at the preparatory meeting. At the men's meeting in August 1778 *"Joseph Taylor and Mary Dunbavand laying before us their intention of taking each other in marriage and he, producing a certificate of his parent's consent and her parent being present, gave his consent, they have liberty to lay it before our monthly meeting"*.

By the middle of the eighteenth century the local Quaker community was prosperous. Indeed, the Friends had difficulty in finding poor brethren on whom to bestow charity. In 1779 they sent a subscription "towards the relief of poor Friends in America" and twenty-one guineas to the Quaker boarding school at Ackworth in Yorkshire. About this time a wealthy Friend, John Hough, left a legacy to the Quakers of Norton which was invested in land the rent from which was used for charitable purposes.

At Norton by 1780 there was a serious falling away in attendance and it was reported that "meetings have been kept up but are slenderly attended on weekdays". Another meeting house had been built at Sutton by Frodsham in 1733 and Friends from various parts of the country were welcomed at the meetings. Quakers from Cumberland, Devonshire and Wiltshire "had meetings at Sutton to the Friends' satisfaction". Both Norton and Sutton declined in the last years of the century and they were both closed by 1794.

There were others who suffered for their allegiance to a dissenting sect. The elaborate lies of Titus Oates and the "Popish plot" of 1678 were, for a time, believed by most people and innocent Catholics were the victims of a cruel persecution. Following the accusations, the Justices of the City of Chester and the county were ordered to seek out the Papists and jail their leaders. Amongst those unjustly imprisoned was John Savage of Clifton. The Toleration Act of 1689 did not extend to Catholics who were under suspicion for their alleged Jacobite sympathies. Fortunately for them, the laws were never fully implemented and life was endurable for the few Catholic families living in the district. In 1717 Bishop Francis Gastrell was informed that in the Frodsham deanery of which Runcorn parish was a part, there were thirty-nine Papist families and it was reported that Catholic worship was taking place in a farmhouse at Dutton Lodge in Little Leigh.

There were some who were, apparently, untouched by the bigotry and bitterness of the times. In Runcorn parish church there is a memorial tablet with an inscription which probably commemorates the wives of two incumbents.

> *Between these pillars*
> *the bodies of two devout women*
> * rest in hope.*
> *Phillipa Finmore of Oxford*
> *deceased August 3rd 1672 and*
> *Ann Breck of Wyral, January 30th 1671-2*
> *both good wives, good neighbours,*
> *good subjects, good Christians*
> *Most intimate in their lives*
> *and in the grave they were not divided.*

The macabre monument with its skeletons, hourglasses, skulls and gravedigger's spades commemorates Phillipa, the first wife of Mr. Finmore, whilst Ann Breck was almost certainly the wife of Thomas Breck, the Presbyterian minister, who was ejected in 1662. It seems that the two women became close friends in spite of their husbands' strongly held diverging views on religion.

In the diary of Thomas Cartwright, Bishop of Chester there is a strange reference to Mary, Mr. Finmore's second wife. On the 5th October 1687, over a year after the death of Archdeacon Finmore, the bishop noted, *"Mrs. Finmore was with me to demand payment of her husband's salary as Archdeacon, because she supplied the place till Michaelmas in preaching"*.

Parsons and People

Archdeacon Finmore was followed as Vicar of Runcorn by his son-in-law, Robert Chesshyre

M.A. who was the brother of Sir John Chesshyre of Hallwood. Vicar Chesshyre has the distinction of being the longest serving vicar of Runcorn. He was minister for fifty-three years till his death in 1739.

Mr. Chesshyre and his churchwardens compiled a detailed survey of the lands and properties of the vicarage of Runcorn in July 1696. This survey or 'glebe terrier' shows that a typical medieval pattern of scattered holdings still existed in seventeenth century Runcorn but the terrier also indicates that the land was gradually being consolidated into larger units by exchange deals mutually agreed between neighbours. The vicar, like so many of his calling, farmed extensively and perhaps the most interesting feature of the terrier is the information it gives concerning land use. Many of the place names are familiar to us. For example Muckland Lane is now Moughland Lane but gone out of use is "Dobhill" — the name suggest the site of a clay pit for daub.

When drawing up his terrier the vicar made sure that the parochial lands were precisely defined in order that the rights of church property should be beyond challenge. Also carefully listed are the tithes due to the vicar and the charges and fees due to him for officiating at christenings, marriages and burials. The vicar's rights to pasture and peat on the common land are stated and the terrier gives us an informative account of the vicarage house which occupied the site of the modern vicarage in Highlands Road. Although the glebe terrier is concerned solely with church property and benefices it does, nevertheless, provide an illuminating description of Higher and Lower Runcorn at the end of the seventeenth century and it is worthy of quotation in full.

A Full and TRUE TERRIER, of the

Glebe Land, Tithes, and Rights,

Due or belonging to the Vicarage of Runcorn,

in the County of Chester;

Exhibited by the Vicar and Churchwardens, of the Parish of Runcorn aforesaid, into the Registry of the Bishop of Chester, the Twentieth day of September, in the Year of Our Lord, 1696; in pursuance of Articles and Instructions, given in charge, in this behalf, at the Visitation at Chester, held the Second Day of July last past.

Imprimis   The vicarage house, consisting of six bays of building; together with a new addition for a granary.

ITEM   A stable, one bay; a cowhouse, one bay; a barn, five bays; a swine-coat, a round stone pidgeon-house.

ITEM   One orchard, one garden, one large fold, and a croft adjoining; containing in the whole, half an acre or thereabouts; abutting on the backside, in the possession of William Runcorn, tailor, on the south; and bound on every other side by the Town Lane.

ITEM   Two closes of arable land, in Runcorn, called the Britches, containing seven acres or thereabouts; abutting south-east on Runcorn common; on the north, on the close of Thomas Parker's, called the Britches; on the south-west, on the land of Robert Gregg, called the Britches; and on the several lands of John Musket, called Heath's Acres; Widow Jackson, called the Jackson's Acres; Margaret Fletcher, called the Fletcher's Acres; of John Berkenhead, called Berkenhead's Acres; Widow Bulkeley, called Bulkeley's Acres; and a certain little lane leading from toward Weston, to the said last mentioned closes.

ITEM   One parcel of arable land, lying in the open Town Field, containing by estimation, three quarters of an acre of ground; bounded by the way called the Great Green Way, on the south-east; on the north-west, by the lands of Robert Cheshire; one quarter whereof next adjoining the said way, was formerly exchanged for the like quantity of land, lying in a close called the New Hey, parcel of a tenement or estate called Dobhill-Row, in the possession of Mary Finmore, widow, or her assigns.

ITEM   One parcel of arable land, lying in the same Town Field, under a close called the Nancroft, containing thirty perches or thereabouts; bounded on the south-east and north-west, by the lands of Thomas Cooper.

ITEM   One parcel of arable land, situate, lying, and being in a certain place, called the Dale, in Runcorn aforesaid, containing twenty perches, or thereabouts; bounded by the lands of John Musket, on the south; and on the north, by the lands of Thomas Cooper.

ITEM   One other parcel of arable land, lying in the Dale aforesaid, containing one quarter of an acre, and seventy perches; bounded on the south, by the lands of Margaret Fletcher; and on the north, by the lands of Thomas Cooper.

ITEM   One parcel of arable land, lying in the Muckland; part of it lying above, and part in a right line below the lane called Muckland Lane; containing one quarter of an acre, and seventy perches; bounded by the lands of Thomas Parker,

ITEM on the north; and of Daniel Carrington on the south.

ITEM One other parcel of grass ground, lying on the Woodward-Hill, alias Wudden-Hill, containing by estimation, one half acre of land; bounded by the lands of the said Mary Finmore, on the south; and of Thomas Tarbock, on the north.

ITEM One other parcel of grass ground lying on the Woodward-Hill, alias Wudden-Hill aforesaid, containing by estimation, one quarter of an acre; bounded by the lands of the said Mary Finmore, on the north; and of Richard Denton on the south.

ITEM One parcel of grass ground, lying in the Higher Hurst, containing one quarter of an acre; and another parcel directly below the said last mentioned; those lying in the Lower Hurst, containing by estimation, twenty perches or thereabouts; both bounded by the lands of Joseph Janion on the east; and of William Runcorn, on the west.

ITEM One parcel of meadow or grass ground, commonly called the Acres' Hey, containing by estimation, two acres and upwards; bounded by the lands of Nathaniel Cooper, on the north and south; and by the Town Field on the east; and by the lands of John Musket, called the Long Ridding, on the west.

ITEM One close of pasture land, called the Can, containing by estimation, two acres or thereabouts; bounded north, by the lands of Bartholemew Adshead; on the south, by the lands of Robert Grice.

ITEM Two parcels of pasture ground, called the Delves, containing by estimation, two acres, and a quarter, or thereabouts; bounded on the south-west, by the lands of Earl Rivers, in the possession of John Alcock, and Richard Denton; on the west, by the Town Field; on the north, by Thomas Cawley's Woodward-Hill Hey; on the east, by Heath Delf, and Fletcher's Carr.

ITEM One parcel of meadow ground, called the Barn Flatt, containing by estimation, three quarters of an acre, or thereabouts; bounded by the lands of Earl Rivers, in possession of Richard Denton, on the south; on the north, by the lands of Robert Cheshire; on the west, by the Common Lane; on the east, by the Town Field.

ITEM Common of pasture and turbary, in and upon, Runcorn hills and heath, for all cattle, at all times of the year.

ITEM The church-yard, bounded by the river Mersey on the north, two lanes on the west and south, and the lands of Nathaniel Cooper on the east. No seat in the church appropriated to the family of the Vicar.

ITEM In and through Upper and Lower Runcorn, Easter offering, (to wit.) for every couple threepence; for every widower or widow, on penny-halfpenny: for every other person above the age of sixteen years, one penny. Tithe calves, (to wit.) for every calf, fourpence. Wool and lamb, hemp and flax, in kind: and of John Muskett, two shillings yearly, for his windmill and water-mill, in Lower Runcorn.

ITEM In and through all the township of Weston, all, and all manner of tithes of corn, grain, hay, hemp and flax, cows, calves, colts, bees, smoke-penny, wool and lamb, pigs, geese, fish in the rivers Mersey and Weaver, within Weston, (to wit.) the fish of one whole tide, every Sunday: the customary tithe of eggs, (to wit.) six eggs for every plough, and three for every half plough; fourpence for every tradesman as a personalty: the mortuaries according to the statute.

ITEM In Clifton, thirteen shillings and fourpence yearly, for Easter dues: six shillings and eightpence for tithe of hay, yearly: and an horse grass yearly in the park, for all the year, in lieu of other tithes, duties and rights, in Clifton.

ITEM Wool and lamb, in and through all the parish, except Clifton and the demesnes of Sir Richard Brooke, in Norton: also, hemp and flax, except in the townships of Sutton, Aston, Keckwick, Aston-Grange, Norton, Stockham, Moss-Side, Halton, Walton, and Thelwall.

ITEM In Sutton, from Sir Peter Warburton, Bart. a customary yearly rate of three shillings and fourpence, in lieu, of hemp and flax: for Easter offering from him, five shillings per annum: and for tithe of his mills, two shilling yearly: and throughout the residue of the township of Sutton, Easter offering and tithe of calves, as above is said of Runcorn.

ITEM In Aston and Keckwick, from Sir Willoughby Aston, Bart. for Easter dues, seventeen shillings yearly: six shillings and eightpence yearly, in lieu of all tithes of hemp and flax there; for the tithe of his two mills in Aston, four shillings, (to wit.) two shillings per mill yearly; and through the residue of the said town of Aston Easter offering, and tithe of calves, as above is said of Runcorn.

ITEM In Acton-Grange, Norton, Stockham, and Moss-Side from Sir Richard Brooke, Bart. a yearly customary rate of six shillings and eightpence, in lieu of tithe of hemp and flax; and Easter offering, and tithe calves, throughout the residue of the said township or places, as is aforesaid of Runcorn.

ITEM In Halton and Walton, from Mr John Brooke, of Hawarden, a customary yearly rate or payment of eight shillings, in lieu and discharge of all tithes of hemp and flax, within those townships or places.

ITEM   From Richard Wood of Halton, one shilling yearly, for and in discharge of the tithe of his water corn mill, in Halton.

ITEM   From the widow, guardian, or trustees of the heir of Peter Brooke, late of Meyre-Hall Esq. deceased, two shillings yearly, for his water corn mill, in Walton.

ITEM   In Thelwall, from the widow, guardian, or trustees of the heir of the said Peter Brooke, the yearly customary rate or payment of two shillings, in lieu and discharge of the tithe of hemp and flax within that township.

ITEM   In Acton-Grange, from John Dunbabin, one shilling in discharge of the tithe of his water corn mill there.

ITEM   From John Sutton, the yearly sum of two shillings, in discharge of his water corn mill, at the common side, within Daresbury.

All other tithes throughout the residue of the parish are generally reputed to belong to Christ Church, in Oxford, and are received by their several farmers or lessees.

ROBERT CHESHIRE,	Vicar.
THOMAS DAVENPORT	
WILLIAM SUDLOW	Churchwardens.

Vicar Chesshyre kept careful account of the tithe payments that were due to him. He visited the gentry and yeomen and noted their payment in his pocket book. "25 March 1725. The rents and sums paid by several gentlemen in the Parish of Runcorn to the vicar".

	£	s	d
Lord Barrymore. Easter dues of Clifton	0	13	4
Tithe hay of Clifton		6	8
Horse grass the whole year I value at	2	10	0
Sir Thomas Aston. Easter dues for Aston Hall		17	0
Sir Thomas Brooke. Per annum		6	8
Sir George Warburton. Easter dues for Sutton		5	8
Tithe, hemp and flax of Aston and mills		10	8
Robert Cooper for Runcorn Mills		2	0
Richard Woods for Halton Mills		2	0
George Dunbabin for Grange Mills		1	0
Mr Brooke of Mere Hall for tythe, flax, Thelwell and Walton Mill yearly		4	0
John Sutton of the Commonside for Mills		2	0

As previously noted, the churchwardens and the curates of the chapelries at Halton, Aston, Thelwall and Daresbury were obliged to contribute a fixed proportion of the costs of the repair and maintenance of the mother church in Runcorn but they did so unwillingly for the chapels were ancient buildings and they were often in need of urgent restoration so that there was never any money to spare for Runcorn church. By the beginning of the eighteenth century a desperate situation had developed at Aston. In 1736 it was reported that the collapse of the chapel was imminent. A report stated that Aston Chapel *"is a very antient piece of Building and chiefly built of timber, by length of time very much out of repair and the roof and walls thereof very much sunk and bulged out. It has now become necessary to take the said chapel wholly down and rebuild it with stone and proper material"*. However, the Aston wardens complained that they could not find the funds because they had "constantly to pay church leys for the repairs to Runcorne church".

There were frequent disputes between the churchwardens at Runcorn and those at Daresbury over monies demanded by the Runcorn wardens. The parishioners attending Daresbury chapel were required to find one third of the costs of repairs to Runcorn church and its churchyard wall, gates and stile. In addition they paid a third of the costs of maintaining the bells as well as contributing towards the cost of cleaning the church. The Daresbury congregation even paid a share of the bill for the communion bread and the wine used in the services at Runcorn. These and other dues had been levied since time immemorial and they were a source of friction to the wardens of both churches. In 1778 Mr. Heron, of Daresbury proposed the drawing up of a document which would set out Daresbury's liabilities and so clarify the situation once and for all but it was to be another hundred years before the disputes were finally settled with the separation of Daresbury from the parish of Runcorn.

Vicar Chesshyre's long incumbency at Runcorn ended in 1739. He was 86 years old when he died. In his late seventies he had supervised the building of Sir John Chesshyre's library in Halton and at the time of his death he was actively engaged in attending to its furnishing. In his will Mr. Chesshyre left money to the poor of Runcorn with the yearly interest on £20 to the repair of the church.

John Free D.D. was instituted Vicar of Runcorn on February 26th 1739. A scholar and pro-proctor of Oxford, Dr. Free was so impressed by the scenery in his new parish that he was moved to carve a Latin inscription on a ledge of rock above Weston Point which expressed his admiration of the beauty of the district. This tribute remained readable for many years afterwards. Dr. Free published "An Essay Towards an History of the English Tongue" in 1749 and a volume of his poems in 1756.

Soon after his induction the vicar was forced to give immediate attention to the south aisle of the church which was in a serious state of decay and in 1740 the aisle was rebuilt in brick. The new work did nothing to enhance the appearance of the church and the decision to use brick instead of using the local sandstone to match the original structure, was probably made because of the shortage of finance and the need for a quick solution to an urgent problem.

Dr. Free was Vicar of Runcorn for seventeen years leaving to take a living in East Coker, Somerset in 1756. No doubt the isolation of Runcorn and the problems of an unworthy house and a church in constant need of repair helped him to make up his mind to seek another parish. Dr. John Free died in London in 1791.

A local man, Thomas Alcock M.A. succeeded Dr. Free in 1756. Born in Aston in 1709, vicar Alcock was the third son of David Alcock and his wife, Mary (nee Breck). Educated at Warrington School and at Oxford, he was destined to serve Runcorn parish for 42 years. On taking up residence the vicar, like his predecessor, was confronted by the necessity for major repairs to church property. The ancient vicarage needed attention and in a glebe terrier of 1778 we learn that Mr Alcock had to rebuild the walls of his house. He describes the vicarage as *"consisting of a parlour, a hall, pantry, cellar, two small bedchambers, a servants' hall and a kitchen. The walls are of stone, a great part of them rebuilt by the present vicar. The covering is thatch. There are four chambers upstairs besides rooms over the kitchen for the servants. The last were added by the present vicar. There is a garner or cheeseroom over the backroom"*. Vicar Alcock also had to attend to other buildings and in his report he says that, *"The old pigeon house was all in ruins and has been taken down and a new one built"*.

The glebe terrier lists the vicar's entitlements: *"In and through Higher and Lower Runcorn the Easter offering to witt; for every couple three pence, for every widow and widower one penny-halfpenny, every other person above the age of sixteen years, one penny. In and through the township of Weston all manner of tithe of corn, grain, hemp, hay, flax, cows, calves, bees, colts, smoak penny, wool and lamb, pigs, geese, fruits, potatoes, the customary tithe of eggs for every plough and the fish of one whole tide every Sunday"*. For the discharge of all tithes due on various water corn mills within the parish the vicar received a shilling a year from the miller at Hatton and two shillings annually from the owners of water mills at Daresbury and Walton.

Vicar Alcock did not find the austere conditions of his Runcorn living to his liking. He was a pluralist in that he also held the vicarage of St. Budeaux near Plymouth. He much preferred his Devon vicarage and he was absent from Cheshire for much of his incumbency. He appointed a succession of curates to attend to his duties at Runcorn and although it may not be true to say that he completely neglected the parish, Mr. Alcock left little mark hereabouts during his forty-two years as vicar. He was however, generous to the poor and by all accounts he was a brilliant preacher. The vicar was fond of farming and on the occasion of his marriage to Maria Harwood he became entitled to considerable land and property. Mr. Alcock's wife died in 1777 and he married again at the age of 78. He received an additional fortune under the will of his celebrated brother, Dr. Nathan Alcock, the eminent physician, who died in 1779. Vicar Alcock died in 1798 leaving £20,000 in 3% consols as well as land and property in Runcorn. To the poor of Runcorn he left "Six pounds to be laid out in buns, bread and potatoes to be distributed on the day of my funeral". He also left land with a yearly income of £2 .. 15 .. 0 to the poor; £2 for the master of Halton school and £3 for the promotion of psalmody in Runcorn church. The property of Mr Alcock passed by descent to the Orred and Johnson families.

A marble tablet in the parish church commemorates Nathan Alcock and a short biography composed by his brother gives an account of Dr. Alcock's career. Nathan was the second son of David and Mary Alcock of Aston and after attending a local school he studied medicine at Edinburgh and at Leyden in Holland where he remained several years to take his doctor's degree in 1737. Returning to England in 1738, Dr. Alcock became Praelector in chemistry and anatomy at Oxford. He was awarded a doctor's degree in physics in 1748 and became a Fellow of the College of Physicians six years later. He also became a Fellow of the Royal Society. He achieved all this, his brother tells us, even though *"he had no fortune, no friends and he bore himself up against all opposition"*. We are told that Dr. Alcock's university lectures were crowded with students and that he *"was remarkably sagacious in discerning the nature and seat of diseases and equally successful in curing them"*.

Ill-health forced Dr. Alcock to retire from Oxford and he returned to live in Runcorn but even in retirement his services were in demand. We are told that his assistance was sought "by all the principal families in his own and neighbouring counties". The good doctor died in 1779 and was buried in a lead coffin enclosed in an oak one near his own pew in Runcorn Parish Church according to his own directions.

The Reverend William Keyt M.A. who succeeded Mr. Alcock as vicar in 1799 has been described as the first of the modern-style vicars. Unlike his predecessor, Mr. Keyt was to devote all his energies to the Parish of Runcorn. His memorial makes much of the fact that "he had an uninterrupted residence of sixteen years". However, it cannot be said that his first impressions of his new parish were favourable. He was dismayed at the neglected appearance of the ancient vicarage and in June 1800 a few months after his appointment he wrote to the bishop outlining the problems and proposing solutions: *"The parsonage house belonging to the vicarage being very old and inconvenient and the roof, walls and other parts thereof being much decayed your petitioner caused the roof to be taken off with the intention of raising the same and thereby making the house more convenient but the walls were found to be so much decayed as to be unsufficient to bear a new roof and the said house incapable of repair so as to be put into a convenient and suitable state fit for the inhabitance of the Vicar of Runcorn".*

A few months earlier the vicar had been allowed £205 towards the costs of repairing the house and outbuildings but now he proposed a clean sweep with the demolition of all the old buildings and their replacement by a new parsonage. He wrote: *"There is a large barn belonging to the said vicarage containing in length 120 feet and breadth 22 feet, and also a large stable thirty feet by ten feet which is very inconveniently situated and much too large for the necessary use and accommodation of the said vicarage. The said petitioner is desirous to take down the said parsonage house, barn, stable and other buildings and to erect a new parsonage house on the site of the old house and on glebe land adjoining and a new barn and stable at a convenient distance therefrom".* In order to raise money for the new building Mr Keyt decided to realise on the assets on church land but wherever he looked he found ruin and decay. He wrote, *"There are now, upon Glebe Land, fifty oak trees which are in a decaying state. They have a value of £67".*

The bishop duly appointed Thomas Brooke, John Orred and Peter Heron to act as commissioners to investigate the vicar's assertions and, as a result of their report, the old vicarage was demolished and a new one built. Even so, Mr. Keyt had to meet some of the costs from his own slender resources and consequently the new work was not as well built as it should have been.

It was during Vicar Keyt's incumbency that major structural alterations were made to the ancient fabric of the medieval church when a commission reported on plans to enlarge the church and the galleries. In 1801 it was stated that the parish church "was too small to conveniently contain the inhabitants of the parish. Many families are in want of convenient pews or seats". The vestry resolved to carry out the following rebuilding: *"The south wall is to be taken down and extended to a distance of about nine feet from the old foundations. That the wall on the south side be raised to a height of thirty feet and a gallery with pews added. To the eastward new work extends fifty-two feet in length and eighteen feet in breadth with a staircase and also to make a row of pews the length of the gallery underneath it.*

And also a gallery at the west end of the church to join the said intended gallery to extend in length twenty feet and in breadth fourteen feet and that all the said pews or seats when so erected to be sold by public auction to such inhabitants of the said parish who would pay the greatest price for them and that the money arising from the sale should be applied to expences of the said intended alterations and improvement and that all persons having right of burial there shall still enjoy the same rights and that pews in this area to be constructed as to be easily moved and that such gravestones and bodies in the way of the said alterations be removed and the said bodies reinterred and the stones replaced with as much decency as possible. No new graves at any time to be made within the said space".

A chart of the pews on the ground floor and in the galleries was drawn and sent to the Vicar-General and John Orred, James Adam, Thomas Sothern, William Pennington, William Wright, Samuel Wylde and Mr Keyt were appointed commissioners to see that the resolution of the vestry was carried out.

Although the new features may have provided some temporary alleviation of the problem of accommodating the increasing congregation, aesthetically they were a disaster. Where formerly there had been ancient gothic windows there were now round-headed windows of the type usually to be found in the nonconformist chapels built in the Regency period. Further more the new building work was of poor quality. It was to last for only forty-four years until the demolition of the church in 1846 when it was discovered that, *"on being taken down, the strength of the structure was found to be in an inverse ratio to the period of alteration. The enlargement not fifty years standing being the most faulty".* At the same time as these alterations were made the floor of the nave was raised level with that of the chancel.

Long before the development of the state system of elementary education its voluntary provision was championed by Mr. Keyt who established the Parish or National School in 1811. The oldest in Runcorn, the Parish School was supported entirely by subscriptions from the parishioners. It was originally conducted on the "Monitorial System" whereby the teacher taught the older children to instruct the younger ones. By this method the teacher would impart knowledge to say, ten child monitors each of whom would then be responsible for the instruction of ten pupils. Thus it was possible for one master to teach the basic subjects to a hundred scholars. Harsh economic circumstances also demanded that inexpensive apparatus should be used. At first exercise books and writing slates could not be afforded. Instead there was a long narrow table in the form of a shallow trough filled with fine sand which was smoothed over with a ruler and the children wrote on it with their fingers. This primitive device was very useful but it made the school so dirty that it was abandoned to be replaced by writing slates.

Mr. Keyt died on March 9th 1816 aged 48 years. His marble monument describes him as *"a zealous and impressive minister, a polished scholar, the Sufferer's advocate, the disinterested patriot and the Poor Man's Friend. He was a man adorned by the Author of all Excellence with distinguished talents and peculiar worth".*

Vicar Keyt had contributed much to the spiritual and temporal welfare of his parishioners and his death aroused a genuine feeling of loss throughout the town. His gravestone in the parish churchyard has a verse which conveys something of the genuine affection and indebtedness the parishioners felt towards their late minister.

> The villager with aching breast
> and sorrow in his tearful eye
> Exclaims "The friend is here at rest,
> Who taught me how to live and die.
> This lesson to my son I'll teach
> They to their sons this lesson give
> And my departed pastor preach
> To those who shall hereafter live.

Canon Alfred Maitland Wood and a parishioner in the gardens of Vicar Keyt's Georgian vicarage at the turn of the century.

Bibliography

The relationship between Catholics and the authorities in Tudor Cheshire has been explored by K.R. Wark in his book *"Elizabethan Recusancy in Cheshire"* (1971). Specific references to recusancy in the Halton and Runcorn area can be found in "Cheshire Quarter Sessions 1559-1760" of the *Record Society of Lancashire and Cheshire* Vol. 95 (1940) and in *"The Bishop of Chester's Visitation Book 1592"* by W.F. Irvine in the *Journal of the Architectural, Archaeological and Historic Society for the County and City of Chester and North Wales.* Vol. V part IV (1895). Some information on local recusancy is also to be found in an article recording the Bishop of Chester's Visitation at Runcorn in 1557 in *Cheshire Sheaf* 1896; in the *Victoria County History of Cheshire*, Vol. III and in "Returns of Recusants and Nonconformists 1669" *Cheshire Sheaf* Vol. 58 (1963).

The Subsidy Roll of Bucklow Hundred in 1593 is printed in *Cheshire Sheaf* 1925 and "Loans, Contributions, Subsidies and Ship Money paid by the Clergy of the Diocese of Chester" appears in "Miscellanies", G.T. Bridgeman (Ed.) of the *Record Society of Lancashire and Cheshire* Vol. 12 (1885).

Non conformity in seventeenth century Cheshire has been presented by J. Howard Hodson in *"Cheshire 1660-1780" "Restoration to Industrial Revolution"* (1978) and by W. Urwick *"Non-conformity in Cheshire"* (1864). The information concerning Archdeacon Finmore has been taken from *Cheshire Sheaf* August 1898; *Cheshire Archaeological Society* Vol. 40 (1953) and from the Consistory Court Records, EDC 106 (1662) and EDC 11 (1669) at the County Record Office, Chester. See also F.J. Powicke *"A History of the Cheshire County Union of Congregational Churches"* (1907).

The activities and tribulations of the Society of Friends in Cheshire can be seen in the minutes of their monthly meetings. The records of the Norton (later Sutton) Mens' meetings are deposited at the County Record Office, Chester. They date from 1748 to 1793. The suffering of local Quakers due to sequestration because of non-payment of tithes has been taken from an article by F. Sanders "The Quakers in Chester Under the Protectorate 1657" in the *Journal of the Architectural Archaeological and Historical Society for the County and City of Chester and North Wales.* New Series Vol. XIV (1908) and *Cheshire Sheaf*, March 1963.

The dispute between the chapelries of Thelwall and Daresbury is recorded in *"Chronicles of Thelwall"* (1845) by W. Nicholson, also in *"Old Cheshire Churches"* (1947) by Raymond Richards and in Charles Nickson's *"History of Runcorn"* (1887).

The glebe terrier recording the properties and entitlements of the vicar of Runcorn at the end of the seventeenth century is printed and it is to be found among the documents relating to *Dues and Fees Payable at Runcorn Church* (1819) which are in the local history collection at the library, shopping City, Runcorn.

A biography of Dr. Nathan Alcock written by his brother, the Vicar of Runcorn, is deposited in the local history collection at Runcorn library. There is also a copy of the Reverend Thomas Alcock's will at the library. The description of Runcorn Parish Church and the vicarage house in the eighteenth century has been gleaned from the following documents in the Cheshire County Record Office: Terrier EDV 8 75/3 (1778); EDP 234/11 and EDP 234/6 (1801). Consistory Court Records, EDC 5/25 and EDC 5/111.

The details of Mr Chesshyre's records of his tithe receipts are taken from the parish records of All Saints Church, Runcorn.

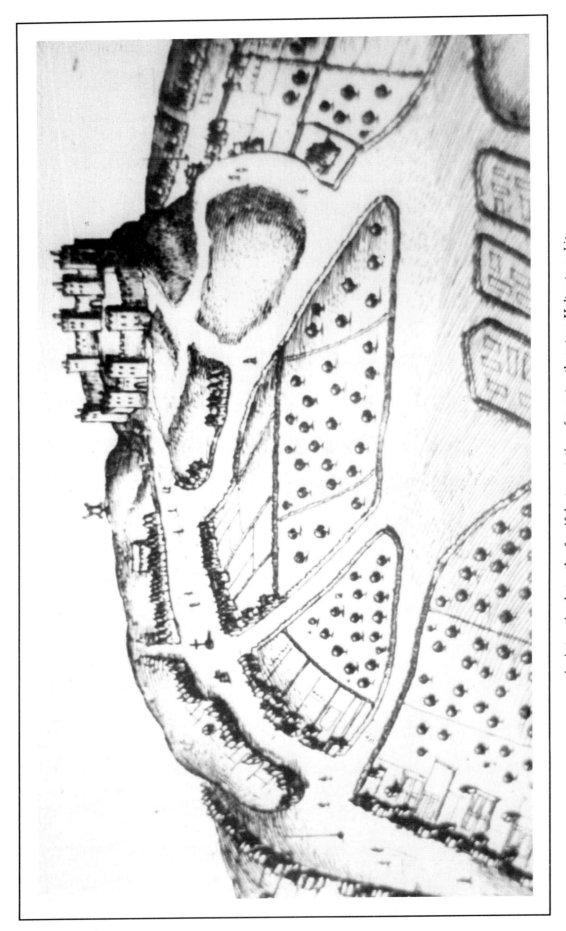

An interesting but rather fanciful representation of seventeenth century Halton township.
This well-known picture is of doubtful value as a source of historical information.

Chapter 6
The Civil War

The Civil War saw some fierce fighting in the south of the county at the siege of Nantwich and also at the siege of Chester followed by the battle of Rowton Moor in 1645. In our locality there was some sharp fighting at Warrington with some minor skirmishes at Stockton Heath, Halton and Norton Priory and throughout the war there was much coming and going with troops passing through the area en route to the main battle zones.

In the first years of the conflict small parties of Royalist and Parliamentarian soldiers were commanded by officers who were neighbours and the troops on both sides were often levied from the same districts. Consequently there was little bitterness and often politeness and consideration were afforded a defeated enemy. Both armies were composed of awkward amateurs completely devoid of the skills of warfare and the early clashes were often hesitant and indecisive. As the war progressed however, its character became savage and soon both sides acquired military adroitness equal to that of any professional army in Europe.

A man's religious beliefs usually decided his allegiance to King or Parliament. The Brookes of Norton were inclined to nonconformity and they were the first family in north Cheshire to declare for Parliament in spite of the proximity to Norton Priory of Earl River's Royalist garrison at Halton Castle. Towards the end of 1642 Henry Brooke began to take measures to defend his house. A few weeks later his precautions proved adequate and his small force of servants and tenants was able to repel a sudden Royalist attack. The following account taken from a contemporary Parliamentarian writer is given in Ormerod's history. It shows something of the bungling and incompetance associated with the war's early exchanges.

1643 February

"One place above others hath been extremely assaulted, Mr. Brooke's of Norton, a near neighbour of Earl Rivers, against wch they brought their cannon, with many horse and foot and fell to batter it on a Sabbath day. Mr. Brooke had eighty men in the house, we were careful he should lack no powder; with all other things Master Brooke furnisht them fully. A man upon his tower with a flag in his hand, cryde them ayme while they discharged their cannon saying, "Wide my lord, on the right hand, now wide two yards to the left; two yards over my lord". He made them swell with anger when they could not endanger the house, for they only wounded one man, lost sixteen of their own and the

cannonier; then in devilish rage they burnt a barne and corne worth, as it is valued £1000, set fire to another, but more execution was made on the man that attempted it for he was blinded in firing the barne, and so was found wandering in the fields and confest he had £5 given him for his service. After this they plundered Mr. Brooke's tenants and returned home with shame and the hatred of all the country".

Henry Brooke's successful action was most praiseworthy for he could not expect reinforcements. The nearest Parliamentarian forces were engaged at Nantwich and the commander there regarded the action at Norton Priory as a ruse by the Royalists to draw away some of his garrison to Brooke's aid in order that they could be overwhelmed by larger Royalist forces. The contemporary account continues: *"To this worthy man's rescue we could not go because the march (from Nantwich) was full of hazard and we thought their aim was to tire us out upon that service which they might put us every day, by reason of Halton castle in their possession and but halfe a mile from Norton".*

At Rocksavage the arch-Royalist, Lord Rivers, made early preparations for war. On 17th. September 1642 it was reported that, "Earl Rivers hath five pieces of Ordnance, ten barrels of gunpowder and sixty bullets landed at Frodsham". It is unlikely that the guns were used in local actions for Lord Rivers soon left the county with a strong contingent of troops to command a regiment at Edgehill, the first battle of the Civil War.

The bridge over the River Weaver at Frodsham was vital for the movement of troops throughout the area and both sides made determined efforts to secure it. In a letter to Prince Rupert, Lord Byron recounts his unsuccessful attempt to open the road from Chester to Warrington. *"Yesterday I sent my own regiment of foot to Frodsham with the intention to have kept the bridge but the enemy appeared there so strong that after a little skirmish, wherein some men were lost on each side, we were forced to quit that town and to quarter on two hills on this side of the bridge, the rebels having cast up a work on the other side which we were not strong enough to beat them out of".*

From the beginning of hostilities Frodsham Bridge suffered considerable damage with sections being removed so as to halt the progress of Royalist forces. As late as 1652 the bridge was still in need of satisfactory repair and crossing the Weaver could be a dangerous undertaking. The dangers were probably exaggerated by the Frodsham inhabitants who in 1652, petitioned the Justices in Quarter Sessions pleading for its repair. They alleged, *"Part of the bridge hath several times been pulled down to occasion the stop of ye enemies to march; that ye battlements of ye said bridge lies down endangering by drowning of several passengers and their cattel going betwixt the two markets. Many having in a tempest being necessitated to crepe over the bridge on their hands and knees for feare of beeing blown into ye water, and notwithstanding former references of Sessions, there is little or no relief"*.

At the outbreak of hostilities Halton Castle was garrisoned by the Royalists under the command of a Captain Walter Primrose. It is likely that the defences were in a state of serious disrepair long before the war began. Although it occupied a commanding position the castle was hardly an impregnable fortress. For instance, it had none of the massive defensive features associated with the great castles built in Wales during the reign of Edward I. At Halton the presence of many large fourteenth and fifteenth century windows and the slender curtain wall made serious defence against a determined enemy a very difficult task. Over the years the castle had become more a secure residence and centre of administration than a military stronghold and the idea that it could be prepared to withstand a prolonged siege would be out of the question. It is more likely that the castle served as a headquarters and barracks for local Royalist companies. Nevertheless, the castle was invested by Parliamentarian forces under the overall command of Sir William Brereton. According to one account the ensuing siege lasted for some weeks but regrettably, there appears to be no record of events leading up to the surrender on July 22nd., 1643. There may have been some fighting but it is also possible that the garrison simply remained enclosed until the defenders saw that their position was hopeless and they capitulated when Brereton gained the upper hand throughout Cheshire to leave them isolated. Parliamentarian troops then took possession of the castle and held it until powerful forces under the command of Prince Rupert approached the region. Brereton was forced to abandon it to the Royalists under the command of a Colonel Fenwick.

Although the Civil War was the most dramatic episode in the history of Halton Castle, details of its role during the struggle are tantalizingly few. As the fortunes of the Royalists declined they withdrew from Halton and for the second time a Parliamentarian garrison occupied the castle. In 1644 the sequestrators of the Royalist supporters' estates in the hundreds of Bucklow and Eddisbury were instructed to pay a weekly sum of £9 to maintain the garrison at Halton. Then, according to Beamont, a "Council of War"

held at Warrington in 1646 decided that the castles at Halton and Beeston should be slighted. Beamont assumes that the defences were then thrown down and the castle thus rendered useless for future military operations. Colonel Henry Brooke bought the manor and castle of Halton from the sequestrators and held them for ten years until the Restoration when they reverted back to the Duchy of Lancaster.

The Runcorn area had some strategic importance during the conflict. To the west of Warrington bridge the only passable route across the Mersey was by way of Hale Ford when, for a brief period at low water, it was possible for troops and their carts to make a hurried crossing from one side to the other. Because there was frequent military activity in Lancashire and Cheshire, Hale Ford was in constant use throughout the Civil War. When Bolton fell to the Royalists in 1643 the victors turned their attention to Liverpool. They had with them a number of prisoners whom they forced across the river. The incident is related in "A Discourse on the Warr in Lancashire".

"The prisoners were carried along being tied two and two together and forced over Liverpool water at Halesford, when it was too deep almost for horses to go. They must wade over either in their clothes or putting them off carry them upon their necks (it was supposed they intended to drown them). And this was remarkable. There was an old man, a prisoner, considering their intention to be so hard-hearted and cruel towards them, encouraged his fellows, exhorting them to be of good cheer and fear not, though they think to drown us yet they must not — God is stronger than the devil. Now the prisoners had special care one of another, keeping close together to support one another, if any were weak and in danger in the water, so that with God's power they all got through with less danger than the horsemen".

The river between Hale and Weston is about a mile wide and even at the lowest of the tide the way across is dangerous and because of the slimy nature of the permanent channel, it is difficult to believe that heavily laden carts and cannon could have been hauled over. In June 1644 Parliamentarian troops attempting to cross Hale Ford on their way to reinforce their garrison at Liverpool were captured by the Royalists and in May 1645 Sir William Brereton wrote to his commanders at Warrington warning them that Prince Rupert and Prince Maurice had reached Whitchurch on their way to attack Liverpool. Brereton was pleased that his officers had had the foresight to build earthworks to protect the strategic crossings at Runcorn Gap and Hale Ford. He observed *"Gentlemen, I am very glad that you have so good course to secure Hale Ford and Ronchorne wch I conseive must by by casting up some sconces yt I belive may doe"*. After his defeat at the battle of Marston Moor Prince Rupert fled the battlefield with the remnants of his cavalry "into Lancashire … and so to Liverpool water, through Hales Ford or the ferry and to Chester he went".

No county of its size saw more fighting and destruction than Cheshire did and no doubt the conflict took its toll in dead amongst those villagers of Halton and Runcorn who enlisted to serve Parliament or King in pitched battles and skirmishes all over England. We have no record listing local casualties but at the church of St. Mary-on-the-Hill in Chester is the grave of Captain Cheshire of Halton who was buried in St. Katherine's aisle in the church on 30th October 1646.

When Parliamentarian forces had established their military control in the region one of their first acts was to set up a sequestration committee with the result that the lot of those who still adhered to the royal cause was often made pitiable. By 1644 the "delinquents" who persisted in their loyalty to the King, together with the known Papists, were liable to have their property and estates seized by the sequestration committee. The sequestrators were empowered to confiscate and sell lands and to collect rents from the tenants of former owners. From 1645 those Royalists who paid a fine proportionate to the value of their estates were allowed to repossess their property. A number of the local gentry suffered considerable loss. Earl Rivers was compounded with Parliament for £1,100 which he had to pay for the release of his Bucklow estate and lands which had been rented out to others. Elizabeth, Dowager Countess Rivers, was compounded for £100; Thomas Chesshyre, gentleman of Hallwood for £100; Richard Heath, gentleman of Weston, for £138 and Thomas Cooper of Runcorn was fined £80 before he could repossess his property.

Even hamlets far from the scene of battle suffered from the attentions of 'friendly' companies of armed men who were passing through the district. Cattle and horses were taken as well as animal feed and grain. The tiny village of Lower Whitley experienced acute hardship and the costs of requisition in two years amounted to £372. Inevitably, there were cases of theft. Widow Ryder of Dutton complained that she lost oats, shoes and stockings to Sir Thomas Fairfax's soldiers. Troops plundered for want of pay. Leycester gives an account of wanton destruction in the church at Great Budworth: *"In the church yet is the case of a fair organ. These organs (as tradition hath it) came from Norton bought after the dissolution of the priory and were in good order, till the pipes thereof were taken out and spoiled by Parliament soldiers in the late war 1647 — which some Scotchmen among them called — Whistles in a Box".*

In 1659 an attempt was made by a number of Cheshire gentry to return Charles II to his throne. From his exile in Holland Charles promised that he would pardon those rebels who were prepared to change sides and declare their loyalty to him. He stated that he was ready to reward any Parliamentarian who performed meritorious service in helping to recover his throne. Weary of harsh military rule, years of shortages, disorder and depression in trade, the country now experienced great pressure for the restoration of the old monarchy as the solution of its ills.

Sir George Booth, of Dunham Massey, a rich Presbyterian who had fought on the side of Parliament in the early years of the war, collected a force of Royalists on Rowton Moor and took possession of Chester. He did not succeed in capturing Chester castle and when General Lambert approached the city Booth withdrew his army in the direction of Northwich. The two armies met at Winnington Bridge. Booth had about 5,000 men and Lambert slightly less. The resulting clash ended with thirty of Booth's men killed and his force scattered in all directions. Lambert restrained his men from inflicting further execution among Booth's ill-trained infantry. Three hundred Royalists were captured and taken to prison in Chester. Among the prisoners was Colonel Henry Brooke of Norton Priory. Colonel Brooke had been a staunch supporter of Parliament. In 1644 and for three successive years afterwards, Parliament had appointed him Sheriff of Cheshire and he was one of the Parliamentarian commissioners for raising the general contribution tax to carry on the war in the county. Brooke had brought his militia to Winnington Bridge. No doubt in its ranks there were men who, sixteen years previously, had fought so valiantly against the Royalists at the siege of Norton Priory. Two years after the restoration of Charles II Henry Brooke was made a baronet. He died in 1664. Two clergymen were captured at Winnington. One was Mr. Finmore, "the Minister at Runkhorne".

The news of the restoration of Charles II was ecstatically received everywhere. Church bells, bonfires, maypoles, drums and thanksgiving services greeted the news. Loyal addresses and messages of congratulations were sent to the King. The declaration of loyalty and congratulation from "the Nobilitie and Gentrie of Lancashire and Cheshire" included the name of Richard Brooke who had been the first to declare for Parliament in North Cheshire in 1642.

The restoration of the King did not bring an end to the acrimony engendered during the years of strife and partisan feeling took many years to dissipate. There were some local men who were unwise in expressing republican sympathies. Many "disaffected persons" were brought to trial at Chester accused of uttering seditious and treasonable words against the new King. John Burrows of Stockham was alleged to have said that *"the Scots would have no bishops and then we should have no King"*. John Pennington of Aston, yeoman, was indiscreet in voicing his opinion that he *"hoped the young King's head would come to the block as well as his father's"* whilst Richard Harper of Aston declared: *"I have been a Roundhead and I will be a Roundhead all the days of my life and unless the King minds his manners we will have the other bout with him"*. The vicar, two churchwardens and a gentleman of Dutton gave evidence on Harper's behalf saying that *"he was never reputed any fanatique or sectary"* but was drunk at the time of the alleged offence. However, all three were found guilty and ordered to be set in the pillory with notices proclaiming their offences fastened to their clothing. They were then stripped half-naked and whipped out of town *"till the blood follow"*. The three men were then imprisoned in Chester castle until the fines imposed on them were paid.

The end of the Civil War saw the church of Halton in ruins. Situated just below the castle walls, the chapel was a plain, square building with a bellcote on its eastern gable. It had suffered either much desecration or bombardment to become devastated by the end of the war. Shortly after the cessation of hostilities Leycester reported, *"In this town of Halton was formerly a Chappel of Ease within the Parish of Runcorne, situated near the castel, as I well remember the same in 1625, but is now in total decay"*. The derelict condition of Halton chapel was such that its repair was beyond the financial means of its congregation and the curate and wardens petitioned the bishop asking him to make an appeal to all the pious and charitable Christians in the diocese for funds to complete the rebuilding. The bishop agreed to use his influence and in his appeal he said, *"There was theretofore a comely chapel in Halton wherein the petitioners and their forefathers had worshipped and enjoyed the benefits of divine service when such chapel standing by the castle was by the soldiers demolished and totally destroyed. Since this sad misfortune the petitioners are compelled to offer up their devotions in the schoolhouse. They have collected £80 to build up the walls of the chapel and they have most of the timber for the roof but want £60 to complete the work"*. The petition to the bishop was signed by Willoughby Aston, Elizabeth Savage, Richard Brooke and Thomas Woodfall, the curate of Halton.

The response to the bishop's diocosan appeal provided the funds necessary to complete the work. Among the congregations to contribute was that of Baddiley church in south Cheshire. In the church records is the following for May 25th 1666:

"To the repairs of Halton Chappell ... £0 .. 6 .. 6".

The rebuilt chapel at Halton lasted for another two hundred years when it was reported at the Easter vestry meeting in 1847 that the roof was in need of major repair. Four years later the decay to the fabric had advanced so much that a new church became necessary. Sir Richard Brooke undertook to bear the costs of a new church and plans were prepared by Mr. George Gilbert Scott. The church of St. Mary at Halton was consecrated on November 12th 1852 and it provides a most striking silhouette which can be seen for many miles across the flat Cheshire countryside.

The ancient chapel at Aston had also suffered damage in the conflict and it was reported that the building had been "much defaced in the late Civil War". The chancel was enlarged in 1697 and the reconstruction of the nave using Runcorn stone took place between 1736 and 1740.

The long period of Civil War and Parliamentary rule brought lasting changes on Crown estates and on those of the Royalist nobility. Roundhead control had meant the sweeping away of many of the ancient rights and privileges previously enjoyed by the gentry. For instance, the deer parks were thrown open to soldiers and peasants who tasted venison for the first time in their lives and after the Restoration of Charles II the parks were never fully restored or effectively governed.

The keeper of Halton Park had problems with trespassers who were reluctant to surrender the freedom to which they had become accustomed during the Interregnum. At the Quarter Sessions held at Chester in 1682 the keeper gave evidence against two violent intruders: *"John Chaddock of Halton, keeper, saieth that he found Peter Broxton and Thomas Broxton of Runcorn gathering acorns in the park ... and this examinate wished them to go their way and come there no more and so riding round the park he found them there again. This examinate alighting from his horse to take their bags, they ran away ... this examinate overtaking them, offered to take their bags and they took hold of him by the hair of his head and pulled him down to the ground and said they would be killed before he should have their acorns"*.

The few brief contemporary references to seventeenth century Runcorn and its environs tell us little but Sir Peter Leycester writing in 1673 gives some information about Halton and its castle: *"Halton Castle. Every fourteen days on a Saturday is a court kept for all matters done within a certaine circuit thereof, it hath also a prison for thieves*

*An early eighteenth century illustration of the ruins of Halton Castle.
The gatehouse remained in use as a courtroom and prison until 1737.*

and felons taken within the said precinct which are at every sessions presented at Chester. Also once a year at Michaelmas His Majesty's officers of the Duchy of Lancaster as auditors, attornies and receivers come and lie certaine days in the said castle and there keep a law day. It hath a small market every Saturday and once a year on the nativity of Our Lady, a fair". From another source it was reported that "there was noe minister (at Halton) in 1675" but in 1715 Thomas Woodfall (who was probably the same Thomas Woodfall who was chaplain at Aston in 1681) was chaplain or curate for both Aston and Halton.

Local Society in the Seventeenth Century

Few local families were well-to-do in the early seventeenth century, the majority existing on labourer's wages of something like six shillings a week. However, most families had some rights on the common and they usually possessed a sizeable garden in which to keep a pig and a few hens and home grown vegetables and fruit provided a small addition to the diet. Worse off were the cottagers and paupers. The former attempted to be independent of wages and survived on the produce of the small field attached to the cottage but the paupers were helpless. They depended upon a pittance from the parish charity. Often they encroached upon common land to build hovels from which they were ejected by force. Theirs was a life of misery, hunger and degradation.

The gulf between the rich and the poor was enormous. The majority of folk were not able to leave much to their children. Indeed, very few labourers left wills though some smallholders or "freeholders of the lesser sort" did and a study of their wills with the accompanying probate inventories, can do much to throw light on the social and economic conditions prevailing at the time.

The probate inventory is a list of all the deceased's effects in which the value of every item was assessed by two or more reputable neighbours. The inventories, usually written in tortuous handwriting with the unorthodox spelling of untutored appraisers, present vivid testimony concerning trades and professions, affluence and life style. From an examination of about a dozen probate inventories of yeomen residing in Runcorn and Halton in the early seventeenth century, we get some view of the standard of living of the "middling sort". John Bore of Weston, who died in 1617, was an example of a comfortably-off yeoman. The inventory of his "goods and cattells' include the

following livestock and produce of the land:

	£	s	d
One yoake of oxen	9	0	0
Sixe kine	18	0	0
three calves	3	0	0
One horse and one mare	8	0	0
fower swine	1	13	4
twelve sheepe and five yonge lambes	2	8	0
tenn hens and one cocke		5	0
one goose		2	0
grase and hay for fodder	1	0	0
corne, barley and beanes	13	6	8
wheate and rye growing in ye ground	3	0	0
beefe, bacon, tallow and grease	2	3	4

Every item of the late John Bore's household goods is listed together with an estimation of its value. He had "six brassen potts" worth £4; "brassen pans" (£1); pewter (£1 .. 10 .. 0) "three oulde spinninge wheeles" (4 shillings) "muggs and drinkinge cuppes" (4 shillings). His "tables, bordes, formes and dishborde" were collectively worth one pound and the "cheers and stooles" were estimated at four shillings. The house had little else in the way of furnishings but it did boast an expensive bed. The wealthy could afford the luxury of a featherbed and John's bedding was assessed at £9 .. 6 .. 8 with "linnen" at five shillings. It was not a comfortable dwelling although the inventory gives "seven cushens" and "one iron grate with two spitts".

The necessary "husbandrieware" for use on the land includes "sickles and stone troughes" together with "instruments of iron as one chene and hammer and other iron stuffe". There were "sacks, winnowing sheets and twill sheetes", "hempe seed, flaxe and wooll". The "plows, wains and harrowes" were thought to be worth three pounds whilst "his apparrel" was valued at thirty shillings. When the appraisers, Richard Heath, John Fletcher, Thomas Norman and John Jackson had completed their work they found that their departed neighbour's assets amounted to £92 .. 2 .. 8. It seems a small amount but a labourer was fortunate if he could find enough work to earn him fifteen pounds a year.

Apart from the "cushens" there were no other items of comfort. No carpets, curtains, no mention of books, no musical instruments and yet John Bore, husbandman, was fortunate in being able to afford a lifestyle which was the envy of most of his neighbours.

Thomas Mason, a Halton farmer who died in 1635 was quite a wealthy man. His household goods included such luxury items as "sixe silver spoones" worth two pounds two shillings, "twentie pewter dishes", "one pewter bottel", carpets valued at the modest figure of nine shillings and sixpence and five "quishions" (cushions). Beds and bedding represented a high proportion of the total value of the furnishings. Some beds were decorated with curtains and valances of expensive material. In fact the "bedding and hangings" at seven pounds twelve shillings were assessed higher than any other household article. As the appraisers went from one bedchamber to another they listed a number of "trucklebeds". These were simple wooden beds mounted on wheels which were usually pushed out of sight below the high standing beds during the day. The trucklebeds would be used by Thomas Mason's servants and farm labourers who lived in the house.

Thomas was literate and his books commanded the next highest valuation at £5. He had "windowe hangings", "sixe candlesticks" and linen valued at four pounds thirteen shillings and four pence. Without doubt farmer Mason had a large house with an extended household of family and servants. There were no less than nine beds (three persons to a bed was common practice at the time); ten tables of various kinds, eight forms and at least seven stools and six chairs. The kitchen with its large open fireplace had a variety of iron utensils for cooking; "two paire of pothookes", "one cresset", "three paire of tongues", "one gridyron and two dripping panns", "one tostinyron", "two chafing dishes" (portable iron stoves), "three skellets", "two kettles", "one mortar and one pestell", "one fire shovell". Other items include "one cheese presse", "brasse potts and brasse panns", wooden treen dishes and one "mugg of salt" which was worth nine pence. Thomas Mason dressed well. His "wearing aparrell" was assessed as being worth seven pounds thirteen shillings and four pence.

By way of contrast the complete household effects of Joan Smith, a cooper's widow, of Runcorn who died in 1649 were valued at only eight pounds seven shillings and sixpence. Her flockbed of rags and wool clippings with its pillows, bolsters and "caddow" (woollen coverlet) were altogether worth only one pound ten shillings. The furniture must have been old or primitive for it was apparently worth very little. Four chests at eight shillings with "bedstockes, chears, dishborde and other like stuffe" were assessed at only thirteen shillings and four pence. Joan's clothes appraised at two pounds were the most valuable of all her possessions. Inexplicably, every item appears to have been grossly undervalued and it is a mystery how a poor cooper's widow with effects worth only eight pounds seven shillings and sixpence should have

debtors who owed her a great deal of money. John Runcorne is listed as owing £15, George Alcock owed her £17 and Elizabeth Berch £1.

By modern standards the everyday diet of even the well-off was monotonous and deficient. The inventories show that cheese, bacon, butter, peas and beans were stored in quantity. Bread with bacon and eggs or mutton must often have provided the main meal of the day. In the pantry of William King, chaplain, of Halton who died in 1649, there were baskets of "onions and garlick" valued at five shillings. Mr. King also possessed a gun — "a fyrelocke", worth eight shillings. No doubt this was a fowling-piece which the chaplain used to shoot birds in the woods and marshes in order to supplement his family's diet.

Because of the high cost of transporting it, coal was too expensive a fuel for the poor. They had to be content with fires of peat and fallen timber, but the yeoman could afford the luxury of a coal fire. Richard Ryder of Runcorn, in 1640, had "coales" to the value of one pound six shillings and eight pence, and Richard Cooper of Weston, who died in 1641 had a similar quantity. William King (1649) had "turfs, coles and other ffewell" to the value of a pound.

Spinning wheels were to be found in every household and most of the farmers had "hempe and flaxe" or hemp seed in the list of their effects. John Houghton of Halton, who died in 1602 had "two cow hydes tanned". Almost every inventory has "treen", that is wooden tableware, as well as a few items of pewter. "Muggs and earthenware" are frequently found, but rarely does one find articles of silver tableware.

The local aristocracy enjoyed a quality of life which was far removed from that of their humble neighbours.

Sir John Savage, baronet, died in 1615 a very wealthy man. In addition to his Rocksavage estate he had a house in London as well as other properties in Chester. From an examination of the household inventory of Rocksavage which was compiled in 1615, it is reasonable to assume that Sir John preferred to live much of his time in one of his town houses, for conspicuous by their absence from the inventory, are the luxury items that one would expect to find among the effects of such a prominent man. However, because Rocksavage formed but a proportion of Sir John's assets, it was probably sparsely furnished and lacking extravagance. To ascertain his true opulence, the separate inventories for his other households would need to be examined.

At Rocksavage there was no deliberate display of wealth, so typical of the houses of the gentry of the time. No mention is made of jewellery, expensive clothes, clocks, musical instruments, books, expensive tableware or glass. The inventory lists few items of silver or tapestry. The wine barrels were empty, the kitchen ill-equipped, and there is no record of any store of food. Beds apart, most of the bedrooms were austere.

Six local men began the task of appraising the late Sir John's "goodes and cattells" by estimating the value of the livestock. Thomas Chesshyre, John Malbone, John Houghton, John Wilkinson, Lawrence Smith and Edward Hargreave priced the cattle and horses, which were the most valuable of all the chattels. Among the eighteen "Horses, geldinges, mares and coults", five animals were highly prized; "Baye Rigbye in the stable" was valued at £13 .. 6s .. 8d, "the yonge graye mare" at £8, "Baye Taylor" also at £8. and the "two coch geldinges" were assessed at £13 .. 6s .. 8d. "Nyne oxen for draught at £4 .. 10s .. 0d a peece" with "fatt cattell" at £16, and seven "fatt cowes" at £3 .. 3s .. 4d each, were other major items. "Carves for the dayry in the marshe and one bull at £3 a peece" totalled £54. There were other cattle together with "sixteene swyne" at six shillings and eight pence each and "nyne swyne of the younger sort" at three shillings each. The numbers of livestock is about what one would expect to find on a large estate, and yet there is no mention of hens and geese, which must have been kept in quantity.

The exterior of the house was impressive, but the interior furnishings do not convey the same degree of affluence. Many of the bedrooms are described by their position or by their decoration, whilst others are named after related families. In one or two cases it is possible to identify the occupier of a bedroom. There was a "Red chamber", a "Whyte chamber", a "Wainscott chamber", "East chamber", Darbye chamber", "Chomley chamber", "Brereton chamber", "Cotgrave chamber" and a "Bukley chamber". Other bedrooms include "Mr. John Savage's chamber" and "Miss Elizabeth Savage's chamber". Some rooms must have been occupied by servants and staff such as "the clarke's (chaplain's) chamber", "George Baynam's chamber" and the "chamber in the gatehouse".

The main bedrooms were comfortable and well furnished, one or two with expensive hangings. The Derby chamber is described as follows:

"In Derbyechamber"

	£	s	d
"One bedstyd one matt one matterys"	1..	10	.. 0

	£	s	d
"One fetherbed one boulster two pillowes"	7.. 00	.. 0
"One silke coveringe quilted"	2.. 00	.. 0
"Two blanketts and two fustians"	1.. 16	.. 8
"One cubborde with one coveringe"	1.. 00	.. 0
"One velvet cheare one velvet quisson ..	4.. 00	.. 0
"One other quisson and two low stooles"		
"Curtaines and coveringes over the bed and hanginges at the bed head with the fringe about the bed"	6.. 00	.. 0
"Five peeres of hanginges"	24.. 00	.. 0

Provision for sanitation was limited to close stools and chamber pots. These must have been provided for every bedroom, but they were ignored by the appraisers, probably because they were of little value. In the "Chomley chamber" however, there is note of "two close stools and one which is pewter".

Good beds and bedding were testimony of the prosperity of personages of rank and they represented a high proportion of the value of the household furnishings. At Rocksavage there were twenty-two "fetherbeds". The only bed of inferior quality was that in the old manor house, which had been vacated by the family in 1568. The valuers recorded, "In the webster's (bailiff's) chamber in the olde house. One bedstyd and one old woll bed one boultser two old coverletts one blankett".

Table linen and bed linen were plentifully supplied. The closets and the twenty-five "trunckes" and "greate chests" were full of table cloths, cupboard cloths, towels, napkins, blankets and coverlets. In all there were thirty-two pairs of coarse sheets, two pairs of fine sheets, two pairs of "Hollande sheets" and one pair of flax sheets. Other items included three feather bed ticks, twenty-four table cloths, five coarse table cloths, eight cupboard cloths and eight dozen napkins besides quantities of wool, canvas, and "two coverletts of my Lady's own making". Among the more expensive items were "one cushin cloth wrought in silke", "one sheet bagge ombrodered with gould" together with one "loking glasse" and "foure great board cloths for the hall".

Sometimes warming-pans were mentioned as well as "bellowes", "tonges" and "fyre shovels". Miscellaneous articles in the bedrooms include candlesticks, "pewter of divers sorts", "one small peece of plate in a silver box", "one pewter flagon", and "one ayron (iron) grate".

In the summer of 1615 the nursery was being used as a lumber room. There were trunks of table linen, "wolle in basketts" and a "pewter sisterne" containing pewter dishes and "three mills of pewter". Most of the expensive household fittings were stored in "My Lady's chamber". Curtains, expensive hangings, small glassware, together with "three lytell boxes" containing "tryfles" valued at one pound ten shillings, and two sums of money totalling eight pounds two shillings and ten pence, were packed in large chests with the only clothes listed in the inventory — the costly "jerken, doblett and breeches" appraised at £10.

On the ground floor, the "dyninge chamber" was the centre of the living accommodation. Perhaps the most striking features of the room were "seaven peers of hanginges of Arras". These were rich tapestries in which figures and scenes were woven in colour and they were placed round the walls. The tapestries were appraised at the considerable sum of £50. A large table, six chairs and twelve stools of various sizes completed the furnishings of the room. In the "gallerye" the appraisers recorded an unstated number of pictures. These were probably the family portraits, for they were not valued in the inventory.

The kitchen seems to have been almost devoid of cooking utensils. "one frying panne", "two brasse potts", "one brasse morter", "one fleshe forke", "fyre shovell", "two dozen of pewter", and "two barrs of ayron" were the only items to be valued. Similarly the buttery, pantry and the cellar were empty. They contained "seven hoggesheads", "nyne barrels", "two halfe tubbs", "two bread bynnes", a table and frame and four candlesticks, all of which were valued at a few shillings each.

The bake house was empty, save for "one ark to put flower in", two sacks, one pan and two wheat measures. The "brue house" had accumulated old beds and bedding removed from the house. They were thrown together with a couple of barrels, three brewing combs and a bucket. The garner, or granary, held small quantities of wheat, rye, and barley, whilst the larder had three old barrels and twelve pewter dishes. The only items in "the wett larder" were a tub and an old hogshead. Together with old furniture stored in "the wardrupp" (wardrobe room), were "two bybles" and one "statute booke" valued at £1 .. 6s .. 8d.

More old beds were to be found in the stables with "three saddles with their furniture" and in a workhouse were three red curtains, "one red tester which belongeth to the red chamber, seavene old quissions, two stoles and one old canopy top". In the "wayne house" (carthouse) were "one muckinge-tumbrell, two cart bodys and a peer of old broken wheeles". Another outhouse contained Sir John's coach valued at ten pounds, as well as two ploughs, two harrows, three chains, an axe and a hedging bill. In "the wynde mylne" (windmill) there were six picks,

one ark (a bin for flour) and some rope. The "corne growinge in the mylne field, otes and barley upon the ground by estimation" was valued as being worth twenty-six pounds.

The late Sir John's Rocksavage possessions were assessed as being worth £625 .. 4s .. 10d. — not a large sum of money for such a dignitary.

Within two years of Sir John's death, his son Sir Thomas, entertained King James I and his entourage on their "Royal Progress". Such a visit was a great honour for the gratified host but the enormous costs involved could mean financial disaster, even though the royal visit lasted only one night. Small wonder that the rapacious Sir Thomas squeezed the last penny out of his tenants. He would need all the money he could lay his hands on in order to make his Rocksavage house worthy of his royal visitor. For the great occasion there would be an extravagant display of opulence. Every room would be in excellent order. Rocksavage would be filled with rich furnishings and silverware. The beer barrels and wine casks would be full. Hundreds of fowl and vast quantities of beef would be roasted in the well-equipped kitchen. Sir Thomas's servants would be adorned in new livery and every effort would be made to surpass the hospitality of the royal party's previous hosts. The great house would never again see such splendour.

At the top of society were the Savages of Clifton, the Brookes of Norton and the Duttons of Dutton. These three families dominated the local community, with the Savages looking towards Frodsham for their rents whilst the Brookes had extensive holdings in Norton, Stockham, Halton and Moore. The Duttons were the greatest of all the county's landowners. At one time they held 37,000 acres in Cheshire alone.

On March 26th. 1632, two weeks before his death, Sir Richard Brooke made his will. To John Brooke, one of the younger sons, he left twenty pounds a year for life and to each of his daughters, Elizabeth, Martha, Dorothy, Mary and Christian he also bequeathed twenty pounds a year for life. By several deeds he assured annuities (the sums not stated) to his three younger sons, Thomas , Richard and George Brooke, gentlemen. The eldest son, Henry, inherited Norton Priory with its lands and properties. The extent of Henry Brooke's inheritance is conveyed in the Inquisition Post Mortem which was the customary legal enquiry into possession and succession before transfer to the heir could take place. The late Sir Richard's estate was itemised as follows:

"At Norton a capital messuage (a large house) in Norton called the Hall of Norton and three other messuages (houses), a water mill, a windmill, a

dovecote, 150 acres of wood, 50 acres of moor, 60 acres of marsh in Norton. The whole manor of Norton with Stockham and of 20 messuages, 20 gardens, 500 acres of land, 100 acres of meadow, 500 acres of pasture, 40 acres of wood, 40 acres of moor, 40 acres of furze and heath in Norton with Stockham and of three fisheries in the waters of Mercie. The whole manor of Aston Grange and of 9 messuages, 200 acres of land, 20 acres of wood, 40 acres of moor and marsh at Aston Grange and of moiety (part of) a messuage and 6 acres of land in Aston, a messuage in Moore late in the tenure of William Horton and 2 acres of land 2 acres of meadow and 2 acres of pasture in Moore and the whole manor of Acton Grange and of 14 messuages, 200 acres of land, 50 acres of meadow, 200 acres of pasture, 40 acres of wood and 50 acres of moor and marsh in Acton Grange. All the manor of Kaverdly alias Curedley (Lancashire) and of 20 messuages, 20 gardens, 200 acres of land, 100 acres of meadow, 200 acres of pasture and 140 acres of moor and marsh in Curedley".

The manor of Weston was in the hands of the Dutton family for nearly six hundred years from the days of William the Conqueror until the line died out in 1665. Lady Eleanor, the only child of Thomas Dutton, married Gilbert Gerard of Gerard's-Bromley in Staffordshire when she was thirteen years old in 1609. Five years later she inherited her father's lands including the manor of Weston. Lady Eleanor died in 1665 and the family line became extinct. The Dutton lands and properties then passed into the ownership of Dutton Gerard.

Although it is not possible to obtain precise information about the size of the local population in the seventeenth century we can, by using certain ecclesiastical and tax returns, make reasonable estimates of the number of inhabitants in the various townships. The hearth tax returns for Runcorn, Halton and Norton for 1664 list all the heads of households who were liable to pay the tax of two shillings a year for every hearth and stove in their dwellings and also those who were exempt from payment because of their poverty. From the hearth tax returns we can calculate the population of Runcorn township to be approximately 305 persons, Halton about 380, Weston 120 and Stockham perhaps 30 inhabitants altogether. It can be seen that poverty was widespread in Runcorn township for only nineteen of the sixty-eight households were liable to pay the tax. In Norton township in 1664, twenty-four heads of households were required to pay the hearth tax and eighteen were exempt. Few people in Weston township were on parish relief for only three households out of twenty-seven were exempt from paying the tax. There were no poor in Stockham for the heads of all seven households had to pay. Sir Henry Brooke's Norton Priory mansion was the largest inhabited

The Elizabethan "Seneschal's House" in Main Street, Halton.

The "Old Hall" in High Street was demolished to make way for the Salvation Army's Citadel in 1883. The site is now the Trustee Savings Bank.

house in Runcorn, Halton and Norton with twenty-four hearths. Margaret Coppocke, Richard Jennings and John Fletcher all of Norton possessed sizable residences for each had to pay for four hearths. In Runcorn township only John Muskett and Thomas Parker paid for more than one hearth. Both lived in houses with two fireplaces.

Very few of the houses of the time have lasted until today although there are one or two stonebuilt Jacobean houses remaining in Halton and in Weston village. Perhaps the best known local building of historic interest is an Elizabethan house, the so-called "Seneschal's House" at the top of Halton Brow which dates from 1598. The Old Hall in Weston village was built in 1607 and the Manor Farmhouse, also in Weston, was probably built twenty years later. Another Old Hall, the one on Halton Common is interesting in that although it is dated 1693 it is built in an architectural style which was popular half a century before. In Halton Main Street there are a couple of houses of the seventeenth century, the Village Farmhouse and Rock Farmhouse and in Spark Lane and in Summer Lane there are cottages of the same period. Opposite the War Memorial in Runcorn there is a stone-built house which is dated 1691. Almost all the timber-framed wattle and daub

houses have gone. Two remain very much altered in Halton village and there a couple left in Sutton Weaver.

Rocksavage, the great house of the Savage family at Clifton and the Brooke's mansion of Norton Priory no longer exist but the hall of the Dutton family improbably survives in a Sussex village. The story of its rescue and removal to the south of England is a remarkable one. In 1930 Mr. John Dewar of the whisky distilling family inherited "Homestall", a couple of very old cottages which his uncle had made into one house at East Grinstead in Sussex. When visiting Cheshire Mr. Dewar saw Dutton Hall which had been used as a farmhouse for many years. Only the east side of the original quadrangle and Sir Piers Dutton's great hall remained and they were becoming derelict. Mr. Dewar bought Dutton Hall with the intention of building it on to the East Grinstead house. Under the supervision of building experts, Dutton Hall was carefully taken down, the stones and timbers were numbered and transported to Sussex there to be re-erected and by 1933 the stately house of "Dutton Homestall" was complete.

During the work of removal of Dutton, the great hall was stripped of its ceiling and this revealed massive oak frames with fine moulded shafts. Within the roof was a minstrel's gallery. The

Seventeenth century timber framed cottages in Main Street, Halton.

The restored village cross and the Old Hall, Weston.

great door of the hall with its mullions and studs of iron and the six shields bearing the arms of the Dutton and Hatton families together with the ancient porch stand today exactly as they did in Cheshire as does the solar leading directly from the great hall. The building is now used as a boys' preparatory school.

Education was valued in seventeenth century Runcorn and Halton even though both rural communities lacked the varied cultural and economic activity found in large towns. The earliest reference to education in this locality is that found by Dr. J. Philip Dodd in his researches into Cheshire wills which were proved between 1570 and 1620. Dr. Dodd discovered that Richard Rider who died in 1600 left £10 so that *"an honest, discreet, learned and able schoolmaster should for ever after be kept to teach grammar for the better education of the children of Daresbury, Preston, Newton, Keckwick, Hatton, Acton Grange, Over Walton and Nether Walton".*

In his study "Restoration to Industrial Revolution" J. Howard Hodson states that the last of the old Cheshire grammar schools to be established was that which was founded at Halton about 1725. However, it is certain that a school existed there long before that date. In 1622 the schoolmaster of Halton, Mr. Piggott, is on record as having contributed money to a fund for the recovery of the Rhine province and in the will of

John King, curate of Halton who died in 1635 is a bequest "to the poore and schoole of Halton £6 yearly for ever". At least one boy from Halton school succeeded in attaining higher education. In 1633 after four years under Mr. Percivall at Halton, John Janion, son of Thomas Janion of Preston-on-the-Hill, was admitted to Gonville and Caius College, Cambridge. Three years later he contracted plague and died in college. He is buried in St. Michael's Church, Cambridge.

Weston village had a private school opened by William Liptrott in 1642. Mr. Liptrott had previous experience as a teacher in Witton in Chester grammar schools. His Weston establishment was very successful, the pupils being mainly the sons of local gentlemen, yeomen and tradesmen. Mr. Liptrott's reputation extended beyond the immediate locality for a number of his pupils travelled some distance for their schooling with one or two coming from Wirral to take lodgings in Weston village. William Liptrott died a wealthy man in 1688 and the inscription on his brass in the old parish church bore testimony to his skill, *"William Liptrott formerly the very industrious and hence successful schoolmaster of Weston. Which department during 46 years discharging with admirable facility and with incredible alacrity, his profession forming his chief delight, he tranquilly advanced in years. He died not yet unequal to his task, 18th May 1688 aged 68 years".*

Perhaps Mr. Liptrott influenced Nathaniel Cooper of Runcorn into becoming a schoolmaster. When, in 1697 the master of Frodsham Grammar School was ejected for ill-treating his pupils, Mr. Cooper was elected to succeed him. Unfortunately the new master's first months in his post were made difficult for him by the relatives of the former master who vehemently opposed his dismissal.

As previously noted, Halton school was an ancient foundation which was in existence in the early years of the seventeenth century. By 1760 it was described as "a free grammar school to which all parishioners have a right to send their children". However, by 1778 the school was labouring under the handicap of having a master who was "old, very deaf and utterly incapable of doing his duty — though a deputy has recently been appointed". Ten years later the school had recovered its prestige under the guidance of the new master . Recalling his education at Halton where he was a pupil between 1788 and 1791, Charles Hulbert wrote … "It was a flourishing establishment numbering between its walls two hundred scholars, the greater proportion of whom paid for their education". Hulbert acknowledges his indebtedness *"to the instruction of Mr. Buckley afterwards the Revered J. Buckley, master of the school on the Edge endowed for the free teaching of youth to read only, the writer is indebted to Mr. Buckley … a worthy man and a profound scholar"*. Mr. Hulbert believed that the master was a very able teacher because he *"had the honour of giving private lessons to the present excellent Sir Richard Brooke Bt. of Norton Priory"*.

It was the tradition for the few young men from Runcorn who succeeded to higher education that they should enter Brazenose College, Oxford. This college was instituted in order to increase the opportunity of university education for students from Lancashire and north-west England. The co-founder of Brazenose was Bishop William Smyth who was born at Peel House in Widnes about 1460. He became Bishop of London in 1495 and with Sir Richard Sutton, founded Brazenose in 1508. We know that nine local men were admitted to Brazenose between 1706 and 1795. These were Thomas Daniel 1706, Richard Brooke 1708, Richard Legh 1721, Thomas Alcock 1727, Thomas Burroughs 1753, George Okell 1782, William Heron 1785, John Starkey 1787 and John Orred 1795. In addition to these, James Thomason entered Wadham College in 1727 and Nathan Alcock was admitted to Jesus College in 1735.

Of the day-to-day social life of lowly folk in the townships of Weston, Halton and Runcorn in the seventeenth century we know little and it is only when villagers' names appear briefly in court records where they are accused of breaking the law that we get fleeting glimpses of their activities. The transgressions are similar to the minor offences reported in our local newspapers today. However, one case which was heard in the Chester diocese Consistory Court in 1616 was an allegation of witchcraft. Margaret Brooke of Runcorn complained that her neighbour, Mary Houghton, had accused her of placing a spell on the churning of milk. Mary was alleged to have stated several times in the hearing of others, "Thou art a witch and thou has bewitched the chirninge of milke at the house of John Pickarne of Walford". Mrs Brooke demanded an end to the defamation of her character. In another case Ann Hough took her husband, Thomas, before the Consistory Court in 1630 accusing him of drunkenness and beating her so severely that her arms, legs and thighs were black and blue. John Fletcher in 1638 accused Ellen Webster of calling him "a damned faced Fletcher" and in 1672 Richard Heath accused Elizabeth Heath, widow, of slander in that she said that he had bought poison with which to kill her. Randle Burton and John Cartwright were in trouble in 1669 accused by the vicar of Runcorn of erecting a pulpit in Aston church and of "intruding John Witter, a dissenter, to be minister not communicating".

Justice was dispensed in the court which convened in the gatehouse of Halton Castle. The building was in poor condition in 1736 when a commission was empowered to *"look into the state of the Court House and Gaol and see if it ought to be built elsewhere on a more proper site and to seek Estimates"*. The commissioners reported that the gatehouse was ruinous and beyond repair and they recommended that the new courthouse should be built on the site of the old one. The stones of the old gatehouse were reused in the construction of the new building. The Duchy of Lancaster courthouse is now the "Castle Hotel". The first floor contains the courtroom and the prisoners were once held in what are now the cellars of the public house. A marble tablet commemorates the completion of the work. *"December 7th. 1737. At a court of revenue held for the Duchy of Lancaster before the Right Honourable George, Earl of Cholmondeley, Chancellor of the same court, it was ordered by them that £500 be forthwith raised and paid for the rebuilding of this Court Room, Gaol and Courtyard. Commissioners to survey the same, L.S. Cotton, I. Lee, H. Leigh, R. Leicester, P. Davenport and W. Tongue Esqs., The Honble. James Cholmondeley, Lord of this Manor, I. Pickering Esq., Steward; W. Middlehurst, Deputy; H. Shipton, I. Orme, Undertakers finished Nov. 1738"*.

Although Runcorn was an isolated community throughout the Tudor and the Stuart periods, there was, nevertheless, recurrent change in the

Old cottage on The Green., off the Underway in Halton Village.

The "Castle Hotel" formerly the courthouse at Halton built in 1738.

composition of its population. During the seventeenth century (and indeed long before then) there was a high level of personal mobility in rural Cheshire. In spite of the Elizabethan statutes restraining movement and vagrancy and the Settlement Law of 1662, young people travelled considerable distances looking for work or marriage partners. Because of the limited number of eligible partners in small communities, inter-village marriages were common and the parish registers indicate a continuous migration of young folk. The first baptismal entry in the Runcorn register is that of Richard Runcorn who was baptised in 1558. Obviously, Richard was the son of a man whose family was indigenous to the hamlet. The first marriage entry, however, suggests that the bridegroom came from a family with origins outside the county for, on 14th. April 1558, Hugo Wasshington married Alice Glover in the parish church. People from the countryside were always attracted to the towns and the registers of Chester cathedral contain the names of many Halton and Runcorn folk who were married there.

For everyone, rich and poor alike, there was the terror of plague. In the north-west of England there were a number of destructive plague visitations resulting in heavy mortality. Between 1557 and 1559, during a period of bad harvests, a lethal outbreak of famine–pestilence amounted to a major disaster. Again in 1623-24 there was an epidemic on a national scale. The thinly populated parish of Runcorn did not escape the infection. The registers of All Saints were commenced in 1558, a plague year, when sixty burials, fourteen baptisms and eleven marriages were recorded. The death rate was high the following year with forty deaths and twenty-two baptisms. Six years later, after the passing of the visitation, the registers show that the population was recovering with thirty-five baptisms and sixteen deaths.

Wet summers resulting in poor harvests together with the virulent attack of plague in 1622 and 1623, culminated in widespread poverty and vagrancy. Deaths from starvation and disease reached catastrophic levels. Hungry villagers from Halton and Runcorn and the surrounding districts invaded the estates of the gentry beseeching food and alms. The great plague took a heavy toll of those who, weakened by hunger, defied the vagrancy laws to seek food and a livelihood in another part of the country.

Only with the coming of winter did the scourge

of plague abate. The physicians of the time knew nothing of its causes or of any way to contain it. We know that even the poor village of Runcorn had a physician for there exists a document from 1640 which tells us that Lord Meath in Ireland nominated John Jackson as being a suitable person for the position of surgeon to the parish of Runcorn.

The passing of the centuries made little change to life in Runcorn. It was described as "a poore hamlet" by John Leland in 1540 and over a hundred years later is was still a place of no consequence. In his "Vale Royal of England" which was written in 1656, Daniel King dismisses the village in a couple of words. He said that there was "nothing but a fair church, a parsonage and a few scattered tenements".

Rocksavage

Until a few years ago there could be seen at Clifton a tall pinnacle of ancient wall which was all that was left of Rocksavage, the great house of the Savage family. Now that this fragment has fallen, the only remaining evidence of the mansion is a section of the retaining wall which once formed the boundary of the garden.

The story of Clifton or Rocksavage as it became known in the sixteenth century, began about a hundred years after the Norman Conquest when the hamlet of Clifton was in the possession of Geoffrey of Dutton. When this particular branch of the Dutton family failed, the two daughters of Sir Roger de Cheadle became co-heiresses and Clemence, the elder daughter, took Clifton as part of her inheritance. Clemence married Raufe de Baggiley and their daughter Isobel, married Sir Thomas Danyers of Bradley and Appleton. Sir Thomas was to distinguish himself at the Battle of Crecy in 1346. At a critical stage in the battle he went to the aid of the Black Prince when the prince became dismounted and when it looked as though his escort would be overwhelmed by an onrush of French cavalry. Sir Thomas rescued the royal standard and then engaged in the defence of the breach until the prince had remounted and help had arrived. The prince rewarded Sir Thomas with an annuity of forty marks payable from the income of the prince's manor of Frodsham. Sir Thomas Danyers' descendants had the gift commuted to a grant of land near Macclesfield.

Sir Thomas and Lady Isobel had a daughter, Margaret, who married John Savage of Scarcliffe in Derbyshire in 1375. For her dowry Margaret received her mother's lands and the young couple lived in the old hall at Clifton which was probably built for them.

As the Savage family was connected with the Stanleys, the influential Derby family, it was not long before John received favours from the Crown. He was appointed bailiff of the Royal Forest of Macclesfield and although the family continued to reside at Clifton they formed close ties with Macclesfield and the parish church there became the Savage family burial place.

John Savage was buried at Macclesfield in 1386. He was succeeded by his son, also called John, who served Henry V with distinction at the battle of Agincourt in 1415. For his services to the King, John Savage was knighted. He died in 1450 to be followed by his son — another John. This third John Savage married the daughter of Sir William Brereton and when he died in 1463 he was succeeded by yet another John Savage.

The fourth John Savage devoted his life to public service. He was mayor of Chester, held offices connected with the Royal Manor and Forest of Macclesfield and was made a trustee of the Duchy of Lancaster by Henry VII. Sir John had the unique distinction of having his nine sons admitted as freemen of the city of Chester during one ceremony. Sir John died in 1495 and was buried in the family chapel in Macclesfield church. The chapel had been built by Thomas, the second of the nine sons who entered the church to become Bishop of Rochester then Bishop of London and eventually Archbishop of York. He was buried in York Minster but his heart was interred under the altar of his chapel in Macclesfield.

The archbishop's elder brother was a soldier who did not live long enough to inherit his father's estate. He had fought for Henry Tudor at the battle of Bosworth and he was rewarded by the grant of estates in various parts of the country. Later he was to command part of the English army at the siege of Boulogne. Here he was killed by an arrow fired from the walls. His body was returned to England to be buried at Macclesfield. His son, the sixth Sir John, was also a soldier of renown. He raised bowmen in this locality and in the Macclesfield area and marched them to meet the invading Scots in 1513. At the battle of Flodden the Cheshire archers played a major part in the English victory but so many Macclesfield commoners and gentlemen were killed in the battle that not enough of the substantial burgesses of the town were left to form a corporation.

Sir John and his eldest son, also called John, fell from favour in 1520 when they killed a man called Pauncefote in a brawl. Both father and son were arrested and imprisoned in the Tower of London probably to await execution. However, the Savages had powerful friends and Cardinal

Wolsey and the Earl of Warwick who was a near relative, exerted their considerable influence on behalf of the prisoners. Both were released on payment of a heavy fine but they were forbidden to entire Cheshire or Worcestershire without the King's consent. Sir John died without ever seeing his Clifton estates again. In 1527 the seventh Sir John succeeded his father and although he was released from his sentence of banishment he never returned to Clifton. He died in North Wales in July 1528 leaving an infant son aged three as his heir.

The eighth John Savage progressed quickly to attain high office and while he was still in his twenties he was appointed High Sherriff of Cheshire, an office he was to hold with distinction on seven occasions — a unique achievement. Sir John was also appointed seneschal of the Honour and castle of Halton by Queen Mary and he was reappointed to the position by Queen Elizabeth on her accession to the throne in 1558. In 1585 and 1588 Sir John was appointed one of the two Members of Parliament for Cheshire and on three occasions he was Mayor of Chester. Sir John also maintained his family's close connection with Macclesfield and for some years he was the High Steward of the borough.

Because the old family home at Clifton was not now impressive enough for a man of such eminence, Sir John planned a new house which became known as Rocksavage probably because of its rocky situation. By 1568 the great Elizabethan building was complete and the old hall was relegated to become a granary and outbuildings. Rocksavage was very similar in appearance to Brereton Hall which is near Congleton and almost certainly the latter was modelled on Rocksavage. (Sir William Brereton knew the house at Clifton for he married Margaret, the daughter of Sir John Savage). The splendid front of Rocksavage had two great octagonal towers surmounted with domes and bridged by a castellated wall to form an imposing entrance. It was a vast building, four bays in depth and the second largest house in Cheshire, only Cholmondeley Hall was larger. In the hearth tax returns for 1674 Rocksavage is listed as having fifty hearths. Originally the house stood in formal, geometrical Elizabethan gardens and it was sited so as to command views across the River Weaver towards Frodsham and the Welsh hills beyond.

In 1566 the manor and lordship of Frodsham were leased by the Crown to Sir John Savage for a term of thirty-one years but in 1570 Sir John placed his interest in the hands of trustees through a deed of settlement in order to secure the preferment in marriage of his four daughters. He also acquired the office of seneschal of Halton, a position of great dignity and one which conferred much honour and influence upon its possessor. Sir John was the seneschal throughout the five years of Queen Mary's reign and again in 1560, 1570, 1571 in 1579 and 1592. He died in 1597 and was succeeded by another Sir John who became, like his father, constable and seneschal of Halton. Sir John Savage was the ninth so named to inherit the Clifton estates.

In 1611 James I was hard pressed to find the funds needed to maintain troops to quell a rebellion in Ulster. To raise the money the King created a new order of knighthood. The order was conferred upon those of the rank of gentleman who were prepared to find the cost of keeping thirty soldiers in Ireland for three years. Sir John paid a thousand pounds for which he was duly rewarded with the rank of baronet. He died in 1615 and was buried in the family chapel at Macclesfield. The succession then devolved on the eldest surviving son, Thomas, and so for the first time in over two hundred years there was not a John Savage as the owner of the Clifton estates. Sir Thomas was created a viscount to become the first member of his family to enter the peerage. He married the daughter and heiress of Lord d'Arcy and when their first son was born, the Prince of Wales, the future Charles I, stood as the child's sponsor at the baptismal ceremony. Sir Thomas was further honoured on 21st of August 1617 when on his return from a visit to Scotland, King James I was entertained at Rocksavage. With a vast train of courtiers the King dined at the house before hunting in Halton Park. After killing a deer the royal party returned to Rocksavage before riding on to Vale Royal the same evening.

Like many of the great men of his time Sir Thomas Savage was rapacious in his determination to increase his land holding. He also had few scruples about the morality of extracting the utmost rent possible from his tenants and he was always prepared to use the power of the law to support his claims to areas of heath and marsh which the townsfolk of Frodsham had always used as common land on which to graze their animals.

Sir Thomas Savage purchased the manor and lordship of Frodsham from the King and by 1616 he had also bought considerable additional land from other landowners. He was adept at taking land from those who could not produce a deed of ownership to their property even though the family might have lived on the smallholding for generations. Sir Thomas's ambition to own the whole of Frodsham soon provoked a lasting quarrel between him and the burgesses and freemen of the town. The townsfolk became alarmed at Sir Thomas' insatiable covetousness and they appealed to the King for help. The people accused Sir Thomas of enclosing common land so as to deny them their ancient rights to grass, turf, fern and stone. The burgesses also alleged that Sir Thomas had prevented them from fowling and fishing in the River Weaver and that he had so greatly increased rents as to *"most lamentably to oppress and endamage your said poore peticiioners in such cruell and unmercifull sort as unles some due and speedy releife be graunted by your Matie to your said poore subiets, it will be impossible that any of them should contynue to inhabite in those p'tes or to meinteyne their poore families and themselves under such greveous Tiranny"*. Unhappily for the townspeople, the King did not intercede on their behalf. Sir Thomas had considerable influence at court and when the Frodsham burgesses petitioned the Privy Council in December 1616 they met with no success and Sir Thomas had little difficulty in getting their pleas dismissed.

While Sir Thomas prospered, life became extremely difficult for the poor. The wet summers of the 1620s brought a succession of bad harvests which resulted in widespread famine. Many died "for the very want of food and maintenance to live". In Runcorn and Halton in the winter of 1623 the situation became desperate. Food prices soared and the parish poor relief was insufficient to cope with the distress. Some parishioners were obstinate in their refusal to increase their almsgiving. They were only prepared to contribute a pittance to help to alleviate the miseries of the chronic sick and the aged poor. It was an emergency situation which is vividly illustrated in a petition from Sir Thomas Savage addressed to the Justices sitting in Quarter Sessions at Chester. Sir Thomas complained bitterly of his neighbours' lack of charity towards the poor. He wrote, *'Forasmuch as at my late being at my house of Rocksavage great companies of poor people from the towns of Halton and Runcorn resorted to me complaining of want of relief. I shall hereby commend their miserable estate to your consideration desiring that you will in this time of scarcity direct some course for their relief as the statute requireth. The complaint is that many of the best wealth in that quarter want charity to yield help to the poor according to their abilities and that many charitable minds want means to yield such relief as they would. The remedy as I can conceive is by taxation as the law requireth, to lay the burden equally. I knowing I shall not need to use persuasion to so good a work of mercy and piety"*.

Sir Thomas Savage received further honours when he was appointed the Chancellor of the Queen's Court at Westminster by King Charles I.

Sir Thomas died in London in 1635 and his body was brought to Macclesfield to be buried in the family chapel.

With the death of Sir Thomas, his eldest son, Lord Viscount John Savage, became the owner of Rocksavage. In 1639 John Savage was created Earl Rivers but the family fell under suspicion for adhering to the Catholic faith. During an anti-Catholic drive in 1640 the Savage family was presented as being "recusant, malignant and delinquent". As their servants and tenants were inclined to follow the family's lead in matters of religion most of Cheshire's Catholic recusants were to be found either in the Runcorn-Halton area or around Beeston, the home of another branch of the Savage family.

At the start of the Civil War Earl Rivers declared his allegiance to the King and he put Halton Castle in a state of defence whilst his near neighbours, the Brookes of Norton declared for Parliament. The Roundhead success saw Halton Castle captured and its defences dismantled. Rocksavage was looted and rendered uninhabitable, the roof and some of the walls being thrown down. Earl Rivers was stripped of his titles and estates and he was fined for his loyalty to the Royalist cause. He retired to Frodsham Castle where he died on October 10th 1654. A few hours after the Earl's death with his body still in the castle, a fire completely destroyed the building. With some difficulty the servants rescued the Earl's body and carried it to Macclesfield where it was buried without the customary ceremony two days later.

Thomas, the new Earl was arrested on suspicion of plotting against the life of Oliver Cromwell. Eventually he was cleared of the charge and was released but for the next six years he lived in London because Rocksavage was still in a derelict state. When the monarchy was restored in 1660 Earl Rivers' estates were returned to him and Rocksavage was put into repair. The Earl remained in London until the house was ready and in the meantime he appointed a deputy-seneschal to look after the affairs of the manor of Halton.

Unlike his predecessors, Earl Rivers was a staunch Protestant and when the heir to the throne avowed his attachment to the Catholic faith the Earl was amongst the many who declared that he should be excluded from the succession. When the Duke of Monmouth made his semi-royal progress through Cheshire in September 1682 Earl Rivers and his son, Lord Colchester, entertained the Duke at Rocksavage. The march through the county was regarded by the authorities to be a seditious rising and for his part in providing hospitality for the Duke, Lord

The remains of the gatehouse at Rocksavage in the early years of the nineteenth century.

Colchester was tried at Chester Assizes. However, public sympathy was wholly behind a Protestant monarchy and Lord Colchester was dismissed with an order to keep the peace.

Three years after Monmouth's execution following his defeat at the battle of Sedgemoor in 1685, Lord Colchester rode to Exeter to meet the Prince of Orange. He was the first nobleman to offer his services to the prince. Lord Colchester died in 1693 and his father, Earl Rivers, died in the following year. The second son Richard, then became the owner of the estates. Richard had a distinguished career as a Privy Councillor and he became Master-General of Ordnance. Richard Viscount Savage died in December 1714 and his title and estates passed to a cousin, John Savage, who was a Catholic priest. However, the priest declined to accept the inheritance and with his death in 1728 the title of Earl Rivers became extinct. With the end of the direct male line of the Savages the Earl's only daughter, Elizabeth, claimed the estates. She was the wife of the Earl of Barrymore and when her claim was granted by a special Act of Parliament, the Earl and Countess set about restoring and enlarging the house of Rocksavage.

With the death of the Countess, the Clifton estates went to her only child, Lady Penelope Barry, who married the Honourable James Cholmondeley in 1730. Lady Penelope died without issue in 1742 and thus the blood of the Savages became extinct. The house of Rocksavage and the estates continued in the family of the Cholmondeleys. An account of the house in 1778 shows that it was still a stately home *"... the magnificent fabrick of Rocksavage overlooking the marshes and goodly waters round about the skirts of it and so contrived in the situation, that from the lower meadow there is a fine easy ascent up to the front of the house which, as you approach nearer still to it, fills your eye with more delight, as is the nature of true beauty and to see now the late additions of delectable gardens, orchards and walks would make one say it longs to be the abode of so honourable a master as it doth service to but his worth is like to have employment, where Honour herself cannot give too much attendance".*

The Cholmondeley family had their principal seat at Cholmondeley Old Hall near Bickerton in south Cheshire. The new owners of Clifton had no use for the great house of Rocksavage and gradually it fell into decay to become, by the closing years of the eighteenth century, a picturesque ruin. It is said that on one occasion a fox, hounds and horsemen charged in through the ruined front entrance and out by the back door. Too large to be converted to any other purpose, the old house became a quarry and over the years its stone was plundered to be used to build farm buildings and walls.

The Cholmondeleys retained their Clifton estates into the twentieth century with the eldest son being in his own right the Earl of Rocksavage.

Perhaps the most notable feature of the parish church of St. Michael in Macclesfield is the Savage chapel with its fine monumental effigies. Built as a chantry chapel in 1504 by Thomas Savage, the Archbishop of York, the chapel contains the ornate tombs and monuments of a number of John Savages and their ladies as well as the splendid altar tomb of Thomas, third Earl Rivers, who died in 1694. The flamboyant richness of the monuments gives some indication of the wealth and splendour of the owners of Rocksavage in the sixteenth and seventeenth centuries.

Sir John Chesshyre of Hallwood

Sir John Chesshyre, son of Thomas and Catherine Chesshyre, was born at Hallwood, Halton on November 11th, 1662. Thomas was the Bailiff of the Lordship of Halton and Whitley and because the Chesshyres were ardent Royalists the family had been inflicted with severe financial penalties during the rule of Parliament.

John Chesshyre entered Grays Inn and was called to the bar in 1689. He entered Inner Temple in 1696 and received the coif in 1705. In 1711 he became Queen's Serjeant to Queen Anne, was knighted in 1713 and was appointed His Majesty's Premier Serjeant-at-Law in 1727. Sir John earned a vast fortune from his profession. His fee books show that between 1719 and 1725 he received over £3000 in each year. At the age of 63 he confined himself to the Court of Common Pleas, *"contenting"* he said *"to amuse myself with lesser business and smaller gain"* and in 1732 he gave up regular attendance at court. Such was his wealth he was able to lend Lord Chesterfield the enormous sum of £20,000. Sir John had his portrait painted by the Court painter, Sir Godfrey Kneller. He was in great favour with royalty and was acquainted with the most influential men of his time.

One of the ways Sir John amused himself was to build and endow a small library near Halton church. In 1733 the library was completed and furnished with four hundred books. Most of the books were of eighteenth century printing and were mainly ecclesiastical histories and works of law. There were a few secular books including early "Tatlers" and "Spectators" but Sir John had designed the library for the incumbent of Halton and *"for any divine or divines of the Church of*

This fine south-facing feature of "Hallwood", Sir John Chesshyre's house, was demolished after becoming unsafe as a result of bombing during the war. "Hallwood" is now the "Tricorn" public house.

Sir John Chesshyre's Library, Halton.

England or other gentlemen or persons of letters". This provision enables Halton village to claim the distinction of having the first or one of the first free libraries in England. In the Rules and Orders relating to the library Sir John stated: *"It were to be wished that the curate for the time being would make use of the said room as his study, and in the winter seasons especially use the fire therein, whereby he may air the room and closer attend to his reading and meditations and he better freed from the interruptions of a family, or a temptation to esloigne or carry any book or books out of the said library for how little time so ever"*. Sir John intended that the curate (subsequently the vicar of Halton) would be the perpetual librarian.

Rather thoughtlessly, Sir John endowed the library with an income of only £12 a year for its upkeep. In 1849, a hundred and sixteen years after its opening, it was reported that the library *"contained 422 volumes chiefly in folio. Few additions have been made since the day of its foundation"*. By then the library had no function and no money.

In 1950 the fine oak panelling of the single room

had begun to show signs of rot, the roof had become so dangerous that *"the man who usually does the job says he dare not walk on it to patch it again and it is thought that with the next fall of snow the roof may come down altogether"*. The library furniture consisted of half a dozen good chairs and an excellent Queen Anne reading table for four persons with a folding flap to support a volume in front of each of them. In 1940 the condition of the books gave cause for anxiety. Many fine bindings were scarred or torn and some had become mildewed. During the war the books and the original catalogue which was printed on vellum, were sent to Stockport museum for safe keeping. Ten years later a "Manchester Guardian" report stated, *"It is hard to speak of the exact range of the books today ... because the original catalogue has never come back and neither the present incumbent of Halton, the Reverend S. Dawson, nor the present curator of Stockport museum knows what can have happened to the catalogue"*.

Though the little library was in a state of

advanced dilapidation in the early 1950s, the Ancient Monuments Association declined to contribute the necessary £500 for its restoration. Fortunately, the North-West Water Authority required the land occupied by the church hall, formerly known as the Hill School and when the new parish hall was built it incorporated a link passageway to the Chesshyre library which was completely renovated by the Parochial Church Council of St. Mary's with the financial compensation received from the Water Board. In June 1976 Mr. Hubert Chesshyre was present at the reopening of the library which his ancestor had founded nearly 250 years before. Sir John Chesshyre's library now serves as a parochial meeting room.

In 1739 Sir John built the present vicarage house of Halton. A handsome building of local stone,

the vicarage is dated and is adorned with his coat of arms. The chapelry was a poor living and in order to provide the curate with a reasonable income Sir John, in 1705, endowed the chapel with the sum of £200 which he increased in 1731 to £600.

Sir John Chesshyre died in 1738 *"suddenly as he was going into his coach"* and according to the *"Gentleman's Magazine"* he *"was worth above £100,000 all acquired by the Law"*. He spent most of his time in London either at his house in Isleworth, at his other home in Essex Street off the Strand, or at his Chambers in the Inner Temple. Sir John had expressed the desire to be buried in Runcorn church after a modest funeral. He wanted "no lying in state nor pompous train of coaches into Cheshire nor any unnecessary attendance". Nevertheless, the

Sir John Chesshyre's Library, Halton.

funeral appears to have been a grand affair, the expenses amounting to over £350. The funeral procession took five days to travel along the unmade roads from Isleworth to Runcorn. The undertaker's account still exists and it makes interesting reading:

For an elm coffin with an outside leaden
coffin and a plate of inscription .... £6 .. 0 .. 0
For a silk lining and a mattress quilted
with sweet powders to preserve
the corpse .... £3 .. 0 .. 0
For a superfine shroud, sheet, pillow
and gloves .... £2 .. 0 .. 0
For an elm case covered with black
velvet, set off with the best gilt nails,
4 pairs of the largest gilt handles and a
brass plate engraved, gilt with a
coat of arms and crest ....£17 .. 0 .. 0
For a velvet lid and feathers on
the corpse .... £1 .. 0 .. 0
For a hearse with six horses
for 12 days ....£12 .. 0 .. 0
For eight horsemen at 12 days each ......£48 .. 0 .. 0
For two mourning coaches with horses
for 12 days ....£42 .. 0 .. 0

Sir John's pyramidal monument of grey and white marble is hidden from sight behind the organ in All Saints parish church.

"In memory of Sir John Chesshyre who departed this life 15th May 1738
A wit's a feather, and a chief's a rod;
An honest man's the noblest work of God".

Lady Elizabeth, Sir John's first wife, died in London and was buried at Runcorn on September 8th 1705. The second Lady Chesshyre died in 1756. Robert Chesshyre, vicar of Runcorn, outlived his illustrious elder brother by a year.

Another well known worthy to frequent the Runcorn neighbourhood was Nicholas Blundell, the wealthy lord of the manor of Little Crosby who owned large estates in Lancashire including one at Ditton near Widnes. For social and business reasons he travelled extensively in Lancashire and Cheshire in the early part of the eighteenth century. Blundell was an enthusiastic diarist and he delighted in recording the details of his many journeys. The entries in his journal are informative and because of his inability to master the rules of spelling, quite amusing. Between 1705 and 1728 Squire Blundell made many references to Runcorn and its ferry. On his way to Chester in 1705 Nicholas crossed the river only to lose his sense of direction in featureless countryside near Weston village. He observed, "Went over at Runkhorn after which we lost our way and went to Windy Weston where we got a guide who brought us to Fradsom".

The ferry service was irregular and passengers could expect long delays. In 1714 Nicholas Blundell noted in his diary, "I came from Chester to Runkhorne where I stayed in the Boat Hous till we went over the water". A year later he again crossed by the ferry this time stopping at a local inn for a meal. He wrote, "I rid over in the Boat at Runkorn and did not lite till I came to the Ail Hous where we baited". Squire Blundell and his wife were welcome visitors at Rocksavage and on a number of occasions he records his pleasure on receiving presents of salmon and venison from the Rocksavage estate.

The Jacobites

The tranquility of the county was much disturbed during the Jacobite rebellion of 1715. A number of Cheshire gentry were Jacobite sympathisers and ten of them including Lord Barrymore of Rocksavage, met at Ashley Hall to consider their future course of action. They decided by a casting vote not to join the rebellion and later, to commemorate their fortunate decision, they had their portraits painted. At Rocksavage, Lord Barrymore, *"great in servants attending"* feasted the lucky conspirators. As J.H. Hodson records in his study of Cheshire, the guests were received *"with a fine ayr and full generosity"* ... *"the wine and ... old Beer perform a perpetual motion till six when a Health to our absent Friends and that they may return with Honour, prosperity and Glory concludes the Entertainment".*

After the rebels surrendered on 14th November, five hundred ragged and starving prisoners were escorted from Preston through Warrington, Runcorn parish and Frodsham en route for Chester Castle. Another hundred wretches were taken to Eastham for transportation to the colonies. Among these prisoners was a Matthew White who succeeded in escaping from the column at Horns Mill near Helsby. He made his way to Ince where he was befriended by sympathisers and allowed to settle in the village. Matthew married a local girl and over a century later some of his family moved to Runcorn where their descendants still reside.

A far more serious situation occurred with the second Jacobite uprising in 1745. To meet the threat of a Scots' invasion a militia called the "Liverpool Blues" was raised in the city. The men were dressed "in new Blew frocks, hatts and stockings" and they were to be maintained "for two months at least". When the Jacobite army was known to be bound towards the Mersey, the Liverpool Blues under the command of Colonel Graham, a professional soldier, with their carts and waggons "and a new tarpaulin for the powder cart", began to operate between

Runcorn ferry and the bridges at Warrington, Frodsham and Northwich. The countryside swarmed with armed men. The county militia was raised and Lord Cholmondeley and the Earl of Warrington marched the Cheshire regiment into Frodsham together with the Cheshire and Staffordshire militia.

As the "Young Pretender" and his Highlanders approached Cheshire the Liverpool Blues destroyed two arches of Warrington Bridge, dismantled part of Frodsham Bridge and other bridges in the neighbourhood of Manchester. The rebels crossed the Mersey at Stockport and Cheadle and marched south to Derby but they gathered little support in Cheshire and a few days later they were in full retreat to the north. There was no local fighting as the rebel army hastened out of the county to its defeat at Culloden.

Lord Barrymore of Rocksavage who, thirty years earlier, had been lucky to escape being branded a traitor, still adhered to the Jacobite cause. The old man sent his son to Derby with an offer to join Prince Charles in London but the son arrived two days after the rebel army had left on its retreat to the north. Once again fortune had favoured the family with the father and son escaping the certainty of imprisonment and possible execution and the forfeiture of their estate and possessions.

The alms houses on Halton Hill which were founded by Pusey Brooke were two hundred years old when they were demolished in the 1960s.

Bibliography

After abstracting information on the Civil War in north Cheshire from Leycester, Ormerod and Beamont, J.S. Morrill's *"Cheshire 1630-1660"* (1974) proved most useful. Fragments of information concerning the Civil War in this immediate neighbourhood have been gathered together from *"Discovering Cheshire's Civil War"*, a Cheshire County Council Publication of 1983; *"St. Mary's Church Halton, the Changing Scene"* (1976) by A.D. Jones; for the siege of Norton Priory see *"Warrington Guardian"* 2nd July 1853 and *Chetham Society* Vol. 65 (1909). Other details are to be found in *Cheshire Sheaf* June 1915 and in *Local Gleanings of Lancashire and Cheshire* Vol. II. Runcorn and Hale Ford are mentioned in an article in the *Transactions of the Lancashire and Cheshire Historic Society Session* IV (1851-52). J. Howard Hodson's *"Cheshire 1660 - 1780"* considers the county in the aftermath of the Civil War and there are references to the local scene in "Cheshire Quarter Sessions 1559-1760" of the *Record Society of Lancashire and Cheshire* Vol. 95 (1940). For the sections dealing with local society in the seventeenth century, material was collected from the wills and probate inventories deposited in the County Record Office at Chester. Sir Richard Brooke's will of 1632 is printed in "Cheshire Inquisitions Post Mortem 1603-1666" Vol. I of the *Record Society of Lancashire and Cheshire* (1934).

Education in Runcorn and Halton in the seventeenth century is mentioned in *Cheshire Sheaf* September 1896; J. Howard Hodson, *"Cheshire 1660-1780"*; and in "A View of Cheshire 1570-1620" by J. Phillip Dodd, *Cheshire History* No. 14, 1984.

The account of Rocksavage Hall at Clifton has been compiled from Ormerod, J. Howard Hodson and from *"Rocksavage and its History"* by William Handley. The following have also been consulted: "Sir Giles Overreach in Cheshire" by J. Phillip Dodd, *Cheshire History* 1983; *Cheshire Quarter Sessions 1559-1760* and *"The Great Diurnal of Nicholas Blundell"*, Vol. I 1702-1711; J.J. Bagley (ed.) *Record Society of Lancashire and Cheshire*. The story of the translation of Dutton Hall has been taken from *"Cheshire and its Welsh Border"* by Herbert Hughes (1966) and from the *"Warrington Guardian"* 24th February 1926.

Much of the account of Sir John Chesshyre of Hallwood bas been taken from *"Local Gleanings Relating to Lancashire and Cheshire"* Vol. II W.E. Axon (1879), from A.D. Jones, *"St. Mary's Church Halton"* (1976) and *"St. Mary's Church Halton, Historic Notices"* by E.K. Gregory.

Two articles by R.C. Jarvis relating to Jacobite activity in Cheshire touch on the local scene. "Turmoil in Cheshire" in the *Transactions of the Lancashire and Cheshire Antiquarian Society* (1943) and "The Town of Liverpool in the '45" in the *Transactions of the Lancashire and Cheshire Historic Society* Vol. 108 (1956). See also J.H. Hodson *Cheshire 1660-1780 "Restoration to Industrial Revolution"*, (1978).

A description of Sir John Chesshyre's house at Hallwood with an account of the building of Sir John's library and the vicarage house at Halton by A.H. Gomme is to be found in Vol. 135 of *The Transactions of the Historic Society of Lancashire and Cheshire* (1985).

The impact of plague in the sixteenth century has been ascertained from an examination of the parish registers of All Saints, Runcorn.

For an account of plague in northern England in the sixteenth and seventeenth centuries see "Plague, Poverty and Population in Parts of North-West England 1580-1720" by W.G. Howson in Vol. 112 (1961) of the *"Transactions of the Historic Society of Lancashire and Cheshire"*.

An early nineteenth century illustration of Runcorn as seen from the east.

Chapter 7
Parson Versus People

In 1816 the Reverend Frederick Master M.A., Fellow of Christ Church College, Oxford, began his long and turbulent ministry of the parish of Runcorn. The new vicar certainly possessed a most unfortunate manner which proved a serious handicap in his attempts to establish a working relationship with the parishioners and vestry officials and his troubles began soon after his induction.

A bitter dispute concerning the vicar's claim for an increase in his fees for performing the baptismal, marriage and burial services together with his rights and those of the parishioners regarding the placing of monuments in the church and churchyard, came to a head at a lively public vestry meeting held in the church on 30th November 1818. A letter from Mr. Master to the chairman, Captain Bradshaw, was read. It contained details of the additional charges proposed by the vicar as well as his claims to certain privileges in the administration of the chancel and the churchyard. The vestry took exception to what they considered to be serious encroachments on time-honoured traditions and in an atmosphere of resentment, a committee was appointed to seek legal opinion on these matters. The committee was also required to look into the practices and charges made by clergy in neighbouring churches.

On the 22nd April 1819 the opinion of counsel, Anthony Hart, of Lincoln's Inn Fields, was put before the vestry. The counsel considered four main areas of dispute. The first concerned the custom of burial within the church. Here the vicar contended that by virtue of his office as vicar he had an indisputable right, if he thought fit, to prevent burials in the church or its vaults and that the right of interment in church existed only with his consent. Furthermore, Mr. Master argued that he could charge any scale of fees he believed appropriate in the matter. However, counsel's opinion was that the vicar had no right to prevent families using vaults already made in the church, although the vicar, churchwardens, and Sir Richard Brooke could, acting together, forbid the breaking up of the church floors to make new graves or vaults but the vicar did not possess complete say on the subject. If he did refuse permission for burials in the church it ought to be only on the principle of preserving the church fabric from structural damage. As to the question of fees, the opinion stated that the vicar could demand only the fees for burial as specified in the terrier of 1696 and no other

rights were due to him.

The second area of controversy concerned the privileges of Sir Richard Brooke who claimed that he was entitled to erect seats and monuments in the chancel without paying fees as well as having the right to bury in his family vault. Sir Richard's ancestors had exercised these privileges since the sixteenth century in consequence of rights granted to them and him by Christ Church Oxford. The Brookes had always kept the chancel in repair and Sir Richard was duty bound to continue this obligation. As no mention of the chancel was made in the terrier of 1696 Mr. Master claimed it as the incumbent. But counsel's opinion did not favour him. It was pointed out that rights generally depend upon usage and as Sir Richard and his ancestors had always kept the chancel in repair, the vicar could not claim any rights to it. Sir Richard could fix monuments, hold his usual pew and bury in the vault but this did not mean that he had the right to grant others the right of burial or permission to erect monuments in the chancel.

The third subject of dispute affected "the poorer classes of inhabitants and their rights of burial in the churchyard and the fee payable thereon". Here the vicar claimed that the fees as fixed by the ancient terrier of 1696 were long out of date and too trifling to be still applicable a century and a quarter after they had been drawn up. In any case, Mr. Master argued these fees were charged only for the clerical office of burial and that he was entitled to claim extra fees for allowing the breaking of the ground. The fees as fixed in 1696 allowed five pence for the vicar and three pence for his clerk without any distinction whether the burial took place in new ground or old. The vestry committee noted that in 1777 attempts had been made to increase charges and considerable dissatisfaction had occurred at that time when the officiating minister had endeavoured to obtain an increase for his services. In an abbreviated terrier of 1778 the curate or minister of the time had attempted to get an agreement for increased charges. He had entered the following vague declaration in the terrier: "Item. Fees for baptisms, churching of women, marriages and burials we find changeable with the times". It appears that a vestry meeting was called to fix new charges but no minute of it was entered in the parish vestry book. However, one of Mr. Master's parishioners did possess an old memorandum book in which there was a table of dues as fixed and agreed upon at a vestry meeting held on 9th May 1779. This showed that the vicar's fee for performing the burial service had been advanced from five pence to a shilling. Counsel pointed out that the vicar was assiduous in basing his claims for tithes, glebe lands and Easter dues upon the 1696 terrier and that he recognised the ancient document when it favoured him but he did not recognise it when it specified the fees of his office. Counsel's opinion held that the vicar must *"rest his claim on the terrier of 1696 or he had no claim and that the churchwardens had no right to set up any table of new fees in the church. If they did so it would prove nothing"*.

Lastly, there was the question of the monuments and gravestones erected in the church and churchyard. Mr. Master declared that the parson had the whole of the freehold invested in him both in the church and in the churchyard and in consequence, he claimed the sole right of granting or refusing the liberty of erecting such monuments. He stated that he alone could decide what charges were due to him for giving permission. The proposed new charges were considerable and the vestry declared that they "amounted almost to a prohibition of enjoyment". On this issue the parishioners were utterly determined not to give way. They contended that "having always from the remotest period exercised this power and without the payment of such fees as those now claimed, that such a power cannot be taken from them either in the church or more importantly, in the churchyard where no person has any right to control the erection of a suitable monument".

The vicar's claim that he had the authority to choose the place of internment caused much indignation. It was pointed out that it was a natural and popular desire for parishioners to wish to be buried with or near to their relatives and they did not want any changes made. Here too, learned counsel found for the parishioners. They could erect monuments as their ancestors had done and the vicar could not prevent them from doing so. If he compelled them to pay for the privilege then he would be guilty of extortion.

After the reading of counsel's opinion at the April meeting of the vestry, prompt action was undertaken in order to defend the rights of the parishioners. A large committee of twenty-four members representing every village within the parish was formed and a deputation consisting of Sir Richard Brooke, Captain Bradshaw R.N., and the Reverend J. Cawley was delegated to remonstrate with the vicar against his claims and proposed increases in fees. The deputation was empowered to seek "an amicable adjustment of the claims and charges" but in the meantime a board on which was printed the church dues as stated in the terrier of 1696, was ordered to be fixed near the church and a thousand handbills giving the same information were printed to be circulated throughout the parish. The new committee was also empowered to settle the salaries of the clerk and the sexton beyond those fixed in the ancient terrier and after doing so, the new salary scales were printed on a board for public display and circulated by handbill. It was also resolved that if the parishioners were forced to pursue legal measures in order to maintain their rights and privileges, the costs should be met by the levying of church or other rates for the purpose and that Messrs. Tindall and Varey be appointed as solicitors to act for the committee.

Mr. Master was determined not to be deflected in his purpose and he sought legal advice which was presented to the vestry committee by his solicitor, Mr. Humberstone. In order to find a way through the impasse the vestry committee determined on compromise. The members realised that they could afford to give some ground without appearing to weaken their case and some adjustment could be made in order to satisfy the vicar's demands. After all, the clerical fees were absurdly low and they ought to be updated even though the committee declared that they found that the fees charged in neighbouring churches rarely exceeded those stated in the ancient Runcorn terrier. As for burials in church, members agreed that it was desirable to limit the practice as much as possible. In the matter of memorials the committee believed that it should be possible to reach an agreement with Mr. Master whereby he received a donation according to the size and form of the monument or gravestone.

The vestry therefore resolved *"that for the purpose of endeavouring to settle these unpleasant disputes amicably, the committee will not at present insist on the fees as stated in the ancient terrier but offers the following as future dues and fees of the vicar — the offer is made a compromise without prejudice to the strict legal rights of the parishioners"*.

Besides the proposals to increase the vicar's fees from five pence to one shilling and six pence for burials, from five shillings to six shillings for marriage by licence and from one shilling to three shillings for marriage by banns, the vestry committee offered a scale of "presents" to be made to the vicar when monuments and tombs were erected in the church or churchyard. For a large memorial erected in church the vicar was to receive a present of five pounds five shillings (he had demanded exactly twice this), for a grave with iron railings in the churchyard the vicar was to have two pounds ten shillings instead of the five pounds five shillings he wanted. A simple headstone merited the payment of five shillings which was a quarter of the charge proposed by Mr. Master. The vestry committee offered no concessions on the matter of family graves insisting that the custom whereby relatives had been buried together should continue.

The parishioners soon realised that they had underestimated the resolution of the vicar who adamantly refused to consider the compromise proposals. At a meeting held in the schoolroom on 27th October 1819 with Captain Bradshaw in the chair, a letter from Mr. Humberston was read. It stated that Mr. Master would not accept the fees and dues which had been offered by the committee. The vestry's response was immediate. It decreed that the vicar was to receive nothing other than the dues fixed in 1696 and there was no further mention of the "presents" which had been offered to him in order to secure his co-operation in the matter of the monuments and gravestones. The salaries of the parish clerk and the sexton, which had been increased a few months earlier by the committee, were now confirmed but no further salary increases or emoluments would be allowed. The committee then had the case for the parishioners and the vestry's resolutions printed and circulated throughout the parish.

The adversaries were now implacably settled for a long confrontation. In a letter to his solicitor the vicar complained bitterly of the lack of generosity in the parish. Mr. Master stated that he had *"endeavoured most earnestly to impress upon the means of the more liberal of his parishioners … without their support the clergy of the country must inevitably be driven from their charges … for want of a due feeling of liberality the established religion of the country will gradually be rooted up and a spurious fanatical religion be grafted in its stead"*. But the vicar had enlisted little support and his letter conveys something of his isolated position when he declared his firm intention of "remaining in my post surrounded by enemies".

Without doubt Mr. Master was remarkably unfortunate in the frequency with which he became involved in unpleasant confrontations and the dispute over his fees was just one of three major quarrels in which he had become embroiled within two years of his appointment at Runcorn. In 1819 the vicar was actually engaged in fighting three battles simultaneously — with the vestry for an increase in his clerical dues, with the tenants of Clifton over what they claimed were his excessive demands for vicarial tithes and — the most serious conflict of all, that with the parishioners and churchwardens over the condition and the responsibility for repairs to the ancient church.

The church was in a deplorable condition. The ancient fabric was so decayed through age and neglect that it was almost beyond repair. The result of years of makeshift patching-up and the damage caused by the insertion of poorly constructed additions and alterations was plain to see. The false economy of cheap rebuilding had resulted in a situation where there was doubt over the very stability of the old building. Much of the church was nearly six hundred years old and it was obvious that without major repairs it could not be expected to last much longer. Even then such repairs would be a temporary expedient — a holding operation to make the building safe for a few years whilst funds were collected to provide for its replacement. In any case, the church was too small to cope with the increase in the congregation which grew considerably after 1810 and the introduction of galleries in 1802 had done little to ease the overcrowding at Sunday services. It was time for drastic action and from the start of his ministry Mr. Master treated the problem as an urgent first priority. On taking up his appointment the vicar immediately expressed his concern about the state of the tower which appeared to be developing a dangerous overhang. The members of the vestry agreed that the tower should be surveyed quarterly and within a few months their worst fears were confirmed. They approached Mr. Harrison, a prominent Chester architect, for his opinion and advice and in the meantime they gave orders that the bells were not to be rung.

In June 1817 Mr. Daniel Stewart's report was read to the vestry. In order to remove the immediate danger, Mr. Stewart recommended that the top of the tower should be taken down as far as the string course. The report did not mince matters: *"The old part of the church is going fast to decay. The south front of the chancel inclines considerably outwards and is only retained in its present position by the roof"*. The south aisle was barely fifteen years old but the surveyor declared it to be "built in a very slight manner". It was sinking and this was causing gaps to appear round the windows.

Mr. Stewart listed a number of essential repairs which would be necessary to keep the building secure for two or three more years but he was firm in his view that the right course of action would be the complete demolition of the church with a replacement as soon as possible. The vestry had asked for two surveys and the second, carried out by Mr. W. Turner, architect of Whitchurch, confirmed Mr. Stewart's findings. Of the south aisle Mr. Turner observed, *"The purlins and ceilings have evidently given way and a*

*Watercolour of the medieval parish church as seen from Church Lane
showing the 1802 rebuilding of the south aisle.*

piece cut from one of the principal binders evidently shows that the timber to be in a perishing state. The most dangerous part is the tendency of the walls on the north side to give way and being eight to nine inches out of perpendicular and receding outwards. The roof is covered on the south side with Cumberland slate but on the north side with flag slates of a porous quality of about four times the weight of the slates on the south side. The outer wall and roof of the side aisle has the same inclination outwards and upon the whole state this part of the church, together with that which was new roofed in 1802 cannot be repaired with safety and convenience but should be wholly taken down".

Mr. Turner reported that for the time being the tower could be secured by using bands of iron but he urged the vestry to *"Think forty-five feet wide and thirty feet high with a gallery at the west end, doors to the middle and side aisles and each side of the chancel made about four feet wider to accommodate the communicants so that a convenient and respectable church might be obtained for this parish".*

In the light of the architect's surveys the vestry immediately put essential repairs in hand. Charles Nickson in his "History of Runcorn" gives an account of the improvements carried out. A vestry minute of 21st September 1817 records a resolution "that the present hearse house be laid open to the body of the church". It would appear that the hearse house adjoined the church but an examination of early nineteenth century etchings and paintings has failed to indicate its position. Possibly it was situated at the east end of the north aisle. A new hearse house was then needed and this was built at the south-east corner of the churchyard in Church Street where it remains today as an electricity sub-station.

The cost of the repairs and improvements totalled £132 of which the churchwardens had raised £64 by levies which meant that they had a debt amounting to £68. According to Nickson six more levies were made in order to clear the arrears. In Runcorn, the levy or church rate on land and property averaged about £13, thus £79 was collected by this means. Of course the meagre sums expended by the vestry would not have met even half the cost of the repairs deemed necessary by the architects and it is obvious that much of the remedial work decreed as being absolutely vital was not carried out. It appears that some of the less serious areas of dilapidation were botched up but nothing was done about the tower, the walls of which were bulging out alarmingly to the north and west.

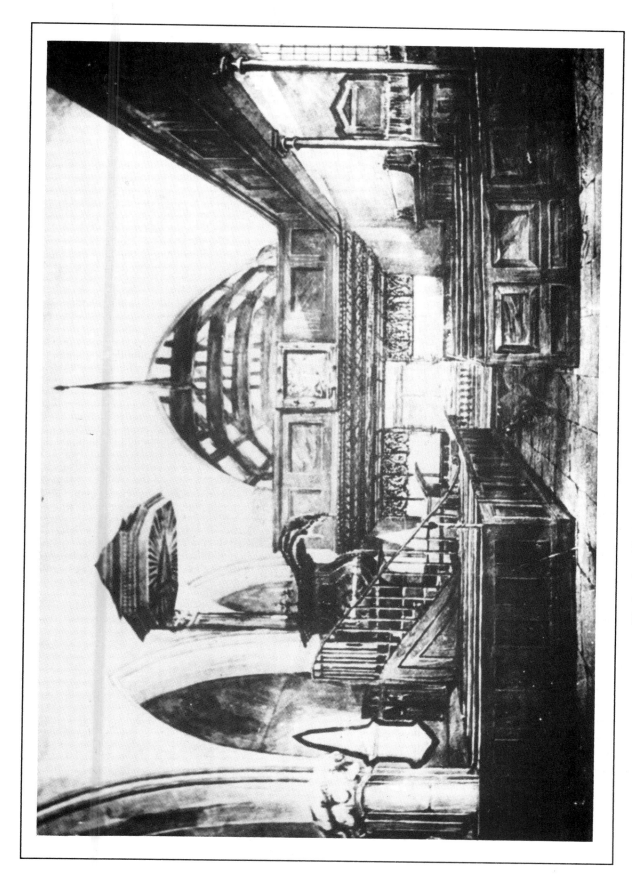

The interior of Runcorn Parish Church which was demolished in 1846.

The mortar of the belfry was perished and much of the masonry was loose.

The vicar received yet another architect's survey this time from a Mr. Slater who, in a few brief sentences utterly condemned the old building. Of the tower Mr. Slater said simply: "It is dangerous to suffer it to stand". He believed that such was the advanced state of ruin, repairs would be impossible to carry out. *"The old part of the building indicates speedy ruin. If the chancel roof is taken off, its south wall will fall"*.

Mr. Master placed the reports before the vestry and demanded immediate action on the matter. It was decided that the tower should "be taken down to the foundations and rebuilt under the direction of the churchwardens". Tenders were invited and plans prepared to put the church in better repair but the work was postponed until a dispute between the churchwardens of Runcorn and those at Daresbury chapel over the contributions the latter were obliged to pay toward the repairs, had been settled. The Trustees of the Duke of Bridgewater were also at odds with the churchwardens over the proportion of expenses to be borne by them.

By the middle of May 1820 the vicar's impatience at the delay could not be contained. He was so exasperated by the apparent incompetence of the vestry and by the indifference of the parishioners in general that he wrote an irate letter to the archdeacon in which he forcibly expressed his outrage. Mr. Master demanded not only instant action but vengeance as well. He was prepared to go to any length to have his church restored and to support his case he enclosed the surveyors' reports. The vicar wrote:

"At a general meeting of the parishioners the tower was ordered to be pulled down and rebuilt but in consequence of the danger that would be attendant upon such a step being taken as to the remainder of the church, the churchwardens did not think it right to comply with the order.

In consequence of the great inattention on the part of the parishioners as to the support of the House of God in not ordering a more general repair and also in consequence of the inattention on the part of the churchwardens to the particular order as far as it refers to the tower of the church, the said Reverend Frederick Master thought it proper to cite the churchwardens before the ecclesiastic court of Chester — to which no attention has been made.

In thus submitting to the archdeacon of the diocese of Chester the several reports of the surveyors as to the dilapidation of the church the said Reverend Frederick Master does so with the fullest confidence that the archdeacon has the power to compel the parishioners of Runcorn to repair their parish church in the fullest

manner and to punish the churchwardens for their neglect of duty and that his interference will be the means of preventing the Reverend Frederick Master from laying the case of the parish of Runcorn before the House of Lords. Assured that this step will not be rendered necessary, the said Reverend Frederick Master is convinced that the archdeacon of the diocese of Chester will give the subject his earliest consideration".

30th May 1820.

The vehemence of the vicar's impassioned letter had the desired effect for Sir Richard Brooke, Captain Bradshaw and Mr. Janion of Rocksavage together with the churchwardens, were called to Chester to give their account of the delays in carrying out the repairs. Shortly afterwards the bishop ruled that immediate action had to be taken to ensure the safety of the church and the renovations which enabled the old building to survive for another quarter of a century were put in hand. The tower was allowed to remain standing because the surveyors believed that its removal would cause the rest of the church to collapse!

The unpleasantness engendered by this contest did not deter Mr. Master from entering vigorously into further conflict with his parishioners — this time over the matter of church tithes. This ancient tribute whereby a tenth part of the produce of the land and its stock were assigned for church purposes, had been reallocated at the Dissolution of Norton Abbey when the tithes of the parish of Runcorn were divided into the great or Rectorial tithes and the small or Vicarial tithes. The rector of Runcorn was a lay-man, Sir Richard Brooke, who, like his ancestors held the rectory on lease from Christ Church College, Oxford. Sir Richard was entitled to the great tithes of geese, hay and pigs whilst the vicar had the right to the small tithes of minor produce and labour which were difficult to collect. Even the amount of tithe to which Mr. Master could lay claim was not clear. During the long incumbency of the eccentric absentee, Mr. Alcock, the late vicar had been popular because of his reluctance or forgetfulness in collecting the tithes which were due to him. Mr. Alcock was a wealthy man and, far away in his Devon living, he gave little attention to Runcorn parish.

Odious quarrels involving litigation over the question of the rights to the great tithes were endemic in Runcorn parish and the place gained a notorious reputation because of the frequency of the bitter disputes over the matter. In April 1819 Mr. Master claimed tithes amounting to the tenth lamb and tithes of milk, turnips, hay and horse grass from the Rocksavage tenants of Lord Cholmondeley. The tenants took exception to the vicar's demands which they considered to be excessive and Lord Cholmondeley's agent gave them his support declaring the Mr. Master was only entitled to thirteen shillings and four pence a year in Easter dues and six shillings and eight pence for hay and grass. Six years later the vicar was still involved in a dispute over his tithe entitlement and in October 1825 he took legal action against Acton Fletcher and other defendants. Eventually the question was settled when the vicar was found to be entitled to the small tithes to which potatoes were decided to belong. He also had the right to the whole of the tithes of Weston village.

The frequent law suits which arose in the parish of Runcorn were finally ended by the Tithe Commutation Act of 1836 whereby the tithes were converted into a rent charge based on the prevailing price of corn. The rectorial tithes were commuted for £81..18s..4d and the small tithes for eighteen shillings.

Mr. Master was involved in further discord at a parochial meeting which was convened to consider the most appropriate method of expressing the sorrow of the parishioners at the death of King William IV. In the seventeen years which has elapsed since the death of George III the country had three times mourned the demise of the ruling Monarch and Queen Victoria's coronation would be the third coronation to be celebrated within this period. These occasions demanded a traditional outward show of loyalty and patriotism from both the officials of the town and its inhabitants and often small townships experienced difficulty in meeting the costs of this obligatory mourning or rejoicing for royalty. At a meeting held in the Parish Church on 29th June 1837 consideration was given to ways of showing the grief felt at the death of the King. A resolution was carried to the effect that certain features of the interior of the church should be draped with black cloth as a mark of parish mourning. *" The sum of £20 be allowed from the parish funds for the purpose of putting the parish church of Runcorn in mourning and that when the cloth be taken down again, it be left in the care of the churchwardens for the purpose of being put up again on any similar occasion or to be distributed to the deserving poor by the vicar and churchwardens."* This recommendation was put to Mr. Master for his approval but the vicar and churchwardens adamantly refused to sanction the idea and consequently the church was not put in mourning.

In spite of the paucity of parochial funds Mr. Master had succeeded in having the church repaired but soon he was subjected to more financial pressure. The National School,

although only nine years old, was proving so popular that by 1820 it was obvious that it would soon need to be expanded or replaced by a larger building. Then there was the ever present problem of the decrepit vicarage. A few years previously Mr. Keyt had carried out renewals and restoration to both the church and the vicarage but unfortunately the work was not well done. In May 1825 Mr. Master complained that *"The vicarage house built by the late W.E. Keyt with his own money........was not well built and will, hereafter, be a source of considerable expense. The barn also built by W.E. Keyt is slight and the roof is in danger of falling in"*. However, there was little chance of the vicar being able to find money to improve his manse for the universal demand for elementary education quickly made the question of school enlargement his most pressing task. The work was put in hand and in 1833 Mr. Master had the satisfaction of seeing the opening of the new parish school in Church Lane. The original school situated at the south-east corner of the churchyard was then removed.

There were other urgent needs. The rapid growth of population made necessary the enlargement of the parish burial ground and in 1832 the churchyard was extended at the cost of £1,100, the improvements being carried out after the levying of a church rate of 9d in the pound. New boundary walls, iron fencing and gates were erected. The churchwardens of the time were determined that their work should be remembered for the lock on the entrance gates in Church Street stills bears their names, "J. Donald. W. Banks. Churchwardens 1833". Predictably, when Mr. Master greatly increased the fees for interment in the new ground there was renewed anger in the town.

In 1817 Ormerod described the church as being "embosomed amongst venerable trees" but by 1846 most of the ancient yews had gone. The churchyard improvements of 1832 had resulted in the removal of the trees which overhung the footpath which skirted the river on the north side of the church and their destruction had caused something of an outcry in the town. The old church was an eyesore. Viewed from the south it was a patched and crumbling edifice set amidst "an immense accumulation of upright gravestones". It was a most unimpressive building and by the beginning of Queen Victoria's reign during a period of religious revival when new churches were being built all over Britain, public pride in Runcorn demanded that the old church should be replaced by a more imposing building.

By 1835 all notions of further renovation of the medieval church had been abandoned in favour of building a new one. In less than twenty years since his induction, the vicar had seen the population of Runcorn treble to more than 6,000 inhabitants. He summed up the situation in a letter to Lord Graves to whom he wrote soliciting a donation for the new church. On February 17th, 1835 Mr. Master wrote , *"At a meeting held in the schoolroom and presided over by Sir Richard Brooke to take into consideration the best mode of supplying the religious wants of a very enlarged and increasing population, it was resolved to erect by voluntary contributions a new parish church. The present church is in a very dilapidated state and is incapable of holding more than 300 poor persons. The situation in Runcorn is very peculiar. It contains a population of 6,000 inhabitants who are principally supported by inland navigation but there are few in such circumstances as would enable them to contribute to the erection of a new church."* Lord Graves was invited to send his donation to the bank of Parr, Lyon and Greenall in Warrington.

Mr. Master now directed his considerable energies to the task of raising the money needed to build the fine new parish church that he did not live to see.

But, always involved in controversy, the vicar continued to express forthright views on local issues. In August 1828 he publically upbraided the select vestry over its inability to reduce drunkenness and crime in the township and a few years later he conducted a campaign against the inland waterways companies when the practice of Sunday working became widespread. He believed *"That the sailing of packets on the Lord's Day is especially offensive to Almighty God and injurious to the morals of the community, causing disorder, confusion and gross irregularities on the day set apart for the divine worship."*

Over the years Mr. Master's abrasive and uncompromising attitude had made him many enemies and in December 1836 there occurred an unsavoury incident in which the vicar was the innocent victim of a nauseous conspiracy engineered by two of his parishioners. Just after Christmas, Runcorn was stunned by the news that a servant girl in the vicarage had given birth to a child which she claimed had been fathered by Mr. Master. The child had been born in the vicarage and had lived for a few hours. After its death the girl had been arrested and remanded in the bridewell under suspicion of murdering the child. In spite of the fact that it soon became obvious that the girl was bordering on the insane and that she was guilty of improper conduct with a number of dissolute men, the two parishioners went ahead to promote a suit against the vicar "in the interests of religion to have the charge properly investigated." The case took two years before it was heard in the Consistory Court of the Diocese of Chester in September 1838. The

vicar was represented by Charles Wilkins, barrister-at-law and his solicitors were Messrs Tindall and Varey.

The absurd and contradictory accusations levelled at Mr. Master were shown to be utterly false and the vicar was found innocent of any improper conduct whatsoever.

Frederick Master was Vicar of Runcorn for another seven years. His wife having died in 1824, he married again and it seems that the last years of his incumbency were infinitely more placid than the earlier ones had been.

He died on 2nd May 1845 but whereas thirty years before the parishioners had been pleased to subscribe to erect a monument in memory of popular vicar Keyt, it was left to Mrs. Master to provide a marble in remembrance of her husband.

> *The Reverend Frederick Master A.M.*
> *Fellow of Christ Church Oxford*
> *and for 29 years the respected Vicar*
> *of this parish*
> *died 2nd May 1845 aged 62 years*
> *And as a memorial of his private virtues*
> *and a token of her affectionate esteem*
> *this tablet*
> *was erected by his widow*
> *Elizabeth Master*
> *The above Elizabeth Master*
> *died June 21st 1864 aged 66 years.*

Perhaps Mr. Master was a demagogue, an obstinate and unswerving martinet who knew nothing of the art of compromise. He certainly showed tenacity of purpose and some allowance can be made for his demeanour. He was a scholarly man in a poor village parish in which there were very few with whom he could share common interest. From the day of his appointment he was confronted by immense financial burdens. The church was rapidly going to ruin, the vicarage seedy and threadbare whilst it was obvious that as the population of the town increased, the school premises would become inadequate and would soon need to be replaced. There was little money to finance the essential repairs and renewals and the vicar could not rely on the small merchant and propertied class to provide all the necessary funds.

Tactless and insensitive on occasion Mr. Master may have been , but there is no doubt that he was an indomitable labourer utterly dedicated in his mission to provide the town with an elegant new church. His battles are long forgotten and for many years now even his memorial has been hidden from sight behind the organ in the new parish church which was completed three and a half years after his death.

Two views of Mr. Master's Parish School which replaced the original National School in 1833.

Bibliography

The problems encountered by the Reverend Frederick Master can be found in a document deposited in the local collection at the Shopping City Library - *"The case and Opinion of Counsel obtained on Behalf of the Parish upon the Subject of the Dues and Fees Payable at the Church at Runcorn with the Ancient Terrier of 1696 and the Resolutions Adopted by the Meetings of the Vestry and Committee"* (1819). The Consistory Court proceedings are detailed in a pamphlet in the records at the Warrington Library (P1384) *"An Authenticated Report of the Speech of Charles Wilkins, Esquire, Barrister at Law, in Defence of the Reverend Frederick Master, Vicar of Runcorn in the Consistory Court of Chester, 13th September 1838".*

The disputes over the repairs to the Parish Church and the vicarage house are taken from Charles Nickson's history and from Architects' Reports on the Parish Church of Runcorn 1819, Chester County Record Office (EDP 234/6); Letter from the Reverend Frederick Master to the Archdeacon 20th May 1820, Cheshire C.R.O. (234/6); Glebe Terrier of the Parish Church of Runcorn Cheshire in County Record Office (EDV8/75/3). The letter from Mr. Master to Lord Graves is quoted from the *Runcorn Guardian* of 4th May 1973.

Other information was taken from the Runcorn Vestry Minute Book of the Meeting for 22nd August 1828.

The disputes over tithe payment can be seen in the litigation of Mr. Master v Acton Fletcher and other defendants in October 1825, County Record Office, Chester (EDV8 75/3).

The Tithe Awards for the various townships within the Parish of Runcorn for 1844 have been printed by Halton Borough Council as *"Halton Historical Publication No. 12".* This document is a good guide to local land use and property ownership in early Victorian Runcorn.

Chapter 8
New Churches and Chapels

The Reverend John Barclay M.A. who was appointed vicar of Runcorn in 1845, was born in York on Christmas Day 1816. At Christ Church College, Oxford he had a distinguished career being awarded first class honours in 1838. He was ordained priest in 1841 and was appointed tutor to his college where he proved to be an able teacher held in high esteem by students and colleagues. After a few years of academic work, this scholar of ancient Greek and Roman literature left Oxford to devote the rest of his life to the parishioners of Runcorn.

During the last few years of Mr. Master's incumbency strenuous efforts had been made to raise the funds needed to provide the new parish church and a few months after Mr. Barclay's installation the vestry minutes record that the parishioners unanimously decided, "That as the present church is not equal to the requirements of the parish, a new church should be erected on the site of the old one". Events now moved quickly and in September 1846 the vicar preached the last sermon in the old building. From the stately three-decker pulpit he

addressed the congregation with the appropriate text, "Arise and let us go hence." The parishioners crowded into the ancient box pews many of which were carved with dates, names and initials of people long dead. The banner of the Loyal Runcorn and Weston Volunteer Infantry hung from the chancel arch and below it on the Georgian parapet above the rood beam, was fastened a board upon which were painted the King's Arms of George III. The work of dismantling had already begun and there were large gaps in the walls from which monuments and commemorative tablets had been removed in order to be cleaned and stored away before being installed in the new church on its completion. The vicar preached an excellent sermon and the congregation, aware of a sense of occasion, was saddened at the passing of the church which had been the centre of parish life for centuries.

The work of demolition proceeded in order that the site should be fully prepared and ready for the laying of the foundation stone by Sir Richard Brooke at Easter 1847. During the removal of the

The new parish church of All Saints which was consecrated in 1849.

old foundation two tombstones of the Aston family were discovered. The following in old English characters was let into them in lead :-

"Hic jacet Richardus Aston Miles qui obit anno domini MCCCC nonaginta III. Jhu Mercye" (Shield of Aston)

"Hic jacet domina Matilda Aston. Lade Helpe" (Maltese cross)

Just as Mr. Master's surveyors had foretold thirty years before, very little of the material of the old church could be re-used. However, the bell metal was valuable. The tower of the old church held a ring of five bells, one of which, the tenor bell, was removed to be installed in Holy Trinity church, Runcorn where it still remains. It weighs twelve hundredweights and the inscription reads :-

SOLI DEO IMMORTALIA SIT GLORIA 1628

The bell has the foundry mark of William Clibury of Holt. The other four bells of the old church which weighed 32½ hundredweights, were taken to the Whitechapel foundry in London and the metal allowed for in the cost of a new ring of eight bells for the new church cast in 1851.

As previously mentioned, some fragments of the magnificent rood screen were salvaged to be incorporated in the new choir stalls and the altar rails were saved to enhance the new building. The old pulpit was bought by Thomas Hazelhurst for the Methodist Chapel in Farnworth, Widnes where, without its pedestal and sounding-board it remains in use to this day. The Royal coat-of-arms and the bequest board or table of benefactors, were kept to ornate the new church. The old box pews and the remnants of ancient glass did not survive but the organ and some furniture were preserved. Nothing else was saved but it seems that for some years one or two carved stones from the old church remained as curiosities in the churchyard. The author has a Victorian photograph which shows a medieval capital together with a keystone which bears the date 1755. Perhaps the oldest object to be saved was the fragment of a medieval grave slab of the 12th century which can still be seen in the present church. The parish registers of baptisms, marriages and burials are extant from 1558.

For more than two years while the new church was under construction, divine service was held in the National School as parish school was then called and on January 11th 1849, in the presence of a large congregation of clergy and parishioners, the new parish church of All Saints was opened and dedicated by Dr. John Graham, the Bishop of Chester.

The church building costs which amounted to £8052, were met by public subscriptions and by parish rate. The new church had sittings for 1060 parishioners. Six seats were reserved in aid of the choir, a few appropriated under a faculty to certain farms and holdings, whilst Sir Richard Brooke and the vicar each had a pew. The remaining seats were *"free and unappropriated following out the view of the first founders of parish churches that they should really be poor men's churches where the Gospel should be preached without money and without price"*.

The last church rate to be levied in the parish of Runcorn was one of eleven pence in the pound which was raised on 15th March 1855 for the purpose of liquidating a debt of £3000 due to Miss Harriet Worthington who had advanced the money on the security of the church rate. The levying of the church rate was decidedly unpopular and there was much opposition to this method of raising finance. Dissenters hated having to pay but the collection of the money was pursued with vigour by the All Saints churchwardens. The following item in the "Warrington Guardian" of 6th September 1856 serves to illustrate the churchwardens' devotion to duty. *" Sharp Practice. On Thursday the Reverend William Meldrum, formerly minister of the Reformed Methodists in Runcorn, was in town on a visit to friends when he was accosted by Mr. Josiah Rigby, churchwarden, with the compliments of the day and adding that he was delighted to see him so well and he heartily shook him by the hand while with the other tendered him a church rate paper informing him that it was his duty personally to demand six shillings and eight pence. Mr. Meldrum expressed astonishment that on a visit to the town after an absence of fifteen months he should be thus dunned for a rate the very existence of which he had never known nor ever been asked for while a ratepayer in the town but, not wishing for any unpleasantness, he at once paid the money"*.

A poll was conducted among the ratepayers of Runcorn and it showed that the majority wished to discontinue the collecting of the church rate. There was also considerable opposition from the people of Daresbury as to the sum that they could afford to give towards the new parish church of Runcorn. Many believed that the demands were beyond the slender resources of the township but eventually it was agreed that Daresbury should pay £1300 towards the costs of the new church.

The new All Saints was built to the designs of Anthony Salvin in the Early English style of the thirteenth century and Runcorn stone was used in the construction. The casings of the doors, the window frames and the tracery are of fine freestone whilst the interstices are filled with rough faced walling stone. The windows of the aisles and those of the clerestory are circular with quatrefoil lights. Above the square tower there is an elegant octagonal spire which was originally surmounted by a finial and gilded weather vane fifty metres above the ground. The gables are adorned with pinnacles which are nineteen metres in height. The original roof was Westmorland slate whilst the timbers of the roof are of Memel fir. The clock was installed in 1851 by John Handley of Runcorn.

The interior of the church is impressive, the long sweep of the five bays of pointed arches of the nave arcades create a pleasing effect with the general impression being one of space and height. Sculptured corbels in the form of heads adorned in thirteenth century head-dress support the boarded roof. Sir Richard Brooke gave the stained glass window of the chancel the three sections of which represent the Last Supper, the Crucifixion and the Ascension. The window which lights the south aisle was presented by the vicar. The seats are of American oak whilst the chancel was paved with Minton's encaustic tiles.

The organ was presented to the old church in 1827. It bears a brass plate with the inscription *"This organ was presented to the Old Parish Church of Runcorn by Jane, Relict of the late John Orred, Esq. of Higher Runcorn"*. Some years ago the organ was modernised and enlarged and most of the original pipes were retained in the rebuilt instrument.

Among the items of furniture brought from the old church is a curiously designed table said to have been used as a communion table. It is constructed with a central pillar from which spring curved braces reaching the corners in large spirals with smaller ones below. The gift of a Sir Richard Brooke, the table is undated but has the inscription, *"Ex Dono Richard Brooke, Baronette"*. There are two sanctuary chairs one of which is a fine Jacobean example, and also a plain domestic chest having one lock and with three drawers at the bottom.

The Communion plate includes a handsome silver chalice and paten inscribed, *"The Lady Mary Brooke, of Norton, her legacy to the Parish Church of Runcorn in Cheshire, the honour of Jesus Christ, and the use of those who have faith in His Blood. September 1670"*. An undated cup by William Mutton of Chester is very similar to the one in the church at Thornton-le-Moors which was made in 1567 and a silver flagon bears the inscription, *"For Runckorn Church, the gift of the Honourable The Lady Elizabeth Savage, daughter of Thomas, late Earle Rivers, for the use of the Parish Church of Runckorn, Com. Chester 1704"*.

Since the opening of the church the interior has been improved by numerous memorial gifts. The altar rails which had been taken from the old church were replaced in 1900 by new ones of alabaster which were presented by Miss Edith Barclay in memory of her father. According to F.H. Crossley writing in the Transactions of the Lancashire and Cheshire Antiquarian Society in 1938 "the (old) rails were rescued from the lumber of a joiner's shop and are now in a church in Wales". Unfortunately Crossley give no information as to their whereabouts. Although Salvin's new parish church is a most pleasing design it was soon realised that the chancel was too dark and gas lighting had to be used during morning services. To remedy this three new lancet windows were opened in the wall arcading in March 1900. The alterations greatly enhanced the chancel and the parish magazine records that the parishioners were unanimous in their satisfaction at the improvement.

The fine marble reredos was also the gift of Edith Barclay given in 1888, whilst the lancet windows in the west wall are a memorial to Philip Whiteway and his wife. Of the mural tablets preserved from the old church, those in the chancel commemorate various members of the Brooke family of Norton and former vicars of Runcorn. Stained glass windows on the south side were given in memory of James and Mary Wilding and in remembrance of William Wilson M.D. of Norton Hill and of John Rigby Hughes. The font covering is inscribed to the memory of Dennis Brundrit whilst the carved panels of the pulpit recall the devotion of James Littler, a former chorister and choirmaster. An oak clergy stall perpetuates the memory of Sir William Dudley who was an active worker for the church for many years. Lady Dudley was also a staunch friend of All Saints and her work is commemorated by the console of the organ which was given when the organ was modernised.

In the churchyard there is an ancient sundial with an octaganol shaft and stepped base. The dial has long worn away but the sundial was once an essential means of setting the early primitive clocks which were notoriously unreliable. Nearby is the oldest gravestone on which the date 1626 is still legible. One or two graves have interesting epitaphs but none so striking as that which pays tribute to the industrious town crier of the early decades of the nineteenth century. The undated inscription reads:

> To the Memory of
> SOLOMON SHEPHERD
> Heroes have died in defence of their country
> The world has at various times
> lamented the loss of eminent
> Statesmen, Divines, Physicians and other Wise men
> But the Parish of Runcorn
> has to lament the loss of one who
> in the several characters of
> Sexton, Bell ringer, Grave digger

and Crier executed his
offices faithfully.

A few years after the completion of All Saints the last of the ancient yew trees in the churchyard was removed. It was estimated that the tree was nine hundred years old.

Although by 1850 the Anglican community could admire their impressive new Parish Church, the old inconvenient vicarage house remained and it was not until 1912 that the Reverend Howard Perrin (later Canon Perrin) built the present house to provide himself and later incumbents with a home which afforded some degree of comfort.

The Reverend John Barclay's association with Runcorn was to last for forty-one years. Energetic, kindly and unstinting in his labour not only for the welfare of the parishioners, but for the people of Runcorn in general, John Barclay was well liked and respected throughout Cheshire. An ardent supporter of every worthy cause, he readily accepted public office serving as chairman of the Runcorn Board of Guardians for fifteen years and as chairman of the Runcorn Free Library Committee. He was particularly keen to see the advancement of education and for nine years he was chairman of the Runcorn School Board.

In 1865 Mr Barclay was appointed Honorary Canon of Chester cathedral and shortly afterwards, Rural Dean of West Frodsham. Among his honours Canon Barclay received the appointment of Select Preacher for the University of Oxford in 1856 and for several years he held the position of Proctor for the Archdeaconry of Chester in the Convocation of York.

During the first years of his vicariate Mr. Barclay had to guide the parish through the difficult period between the demolition of the old church and the opening of the new. Later, when Runcorn was growing apace he promoted the building of the Newtown Mission and the Shaw Street school in 1868. He also provided St. Peter's Mission, the proposed nucleus of St. Peter's parish for the town's maritime community at the Bridgewater Docks. His work for the parish church is remembered in that he reorganised the choir and it became one of the first surpliced choirs in the diocese outside the cathedral. Canon Barclay was an accomplished preacher and it is recorded that he made the services at All Saints both attractive and popular. Towards the end of his life Canon Barclay saw work begin on the church of St. Michael and All Angels in Greenway Road which replaced the Newtown Mission in 1887. He died nine months before the building was completed.

The occasion of Canon Barclay's funeral on 30th August 1886 saw a public demonstration of affection that was more spontaneous than any ever before paid to the memory of a man in public life in Runcorn. A vast crowd assembled at the graveside and a hundred men of the 2nd Cheshire Volunteer Rifles paid a last tribute to their former honorary chaplain with three volleys. A family man, Canon Barclay was survived by his wife Matilda and by his daughters, Edith and Alice. He may still maintain a presence at today's services at All Saints for the present vicar, Canon Thomas, believes that it is possible that the stone heads which are carved in the mouldings on each side of the choir vestry door represent Canon Barclay and his wife. The stone clergyman is wearing a Canterbury Cap, the traditional headware of an Anglican priest, but beneath it can be seen a flowing hair style very similar to that worn by Canon Barclay.

The first year of Queen Victoria's reign saw the completion of a new Anglican church in Runcorn when Holy Trinity was consecrated in 1838. Holy Trinity was designed by Joseph Hartley, a Runcorn architect and built by William Rigby, a local builder. Neo-gothic in style and built of local stone the church has lancet windows with an embattled western tower with pinnacles. The Church Building Society made a grant towards the building costs and the remainder was provided by public subscription. John and Thomas Johnson, soap manufacturers, were the largest subscribers. They supplied the endowment and were patrons of the living. The first incumbent at Holy Trinity was the Reverend John Davies M.A. The ecclesiastical parish of Holy Trinity was formed from All Saints in 1840 with 40 acres of glebe and residence in the gift of trustees. The church already had the benefit of the Anglican Mariners' Mission Church in Irwell Lane. This had been built for the town's watermen by the Earl of Ellesmere in 1831, the incumbent of Holy Trinity being the minister.

In 1841 the Trustees of the River Weaver Navigation Company built a church at Weston Point for their employees and their families. The Trustees were generous for they also provided the minister's house, paid his stipend and made allowances to the church cleaners and choristers. A school was built for the boatmen's children and the schoolmaster's salary was paid by the Trustees. This chapel of ease was called Christ Church and its architectural style is geometrical gothic. Built of Runcorn or Weston sandstone Christ Church, Weston Point, has a fine octagonal spire and the plan of the church is in the form of a cross. When the church was newly-built it stood on a small headland which jutted into the Mersey. By 1894 the Manchester Ship

Christ Church, Weston Point, showing Salt Union works and the lighthouse during the construction of the Manchester Ship Canal.

Canal had replaced the river on one side of the church whilst the Weaver Navigation Canal formed another boundary. Two inlets between these canals left Christ Church on an island so there is justification in the claim that the church is the only one still in use on an uninhabited island in Britain.

The long association of the ancient chapelries with the mother church was severed in mid-Victorian times. Halton became an independent parish in June 1860 and Aston in the April of the following year. Thelwall became a separate parish in 1870 and Daresbury in February 1880. From the time a chapelry became independent its curate-in-charge became the vicar of the new parish. Changes also occurred in the parish of All Saints when it became necessary to divide the town into a number of more easily managed districts. Originally it was thought that the pattern of settlement would be best served by new churches at Weston, at Newtown in Greenway Road with another in Dukesfield. In time new churches were built in Weston and in Newtown but St. Peter's mission in Dukesfield closed in 1872 due to lack of support from the newly-formed Bridgewater Navigation Company. The company refused to provide a permanent site for a church and consequently, St. Peter's parish never came into being.

When the Bridgewater Trustees had managed the waterway they encouraged missionary activity at their docks. In 1840 they provided an old barge to be used as a floating church and when in 1866 the timbers of the barge-church were found to be rotten, the Trustees made a building available to serve as St. Peter's Mission Church. With the closure of St. Peter's there would be no parish specifically dedicated to the temporal and spiritual welfare of Runcorn's maritime community. However, in 1875 the Mersey Mission to Seamen founded a Seamen's Mission in the town and through the tireless efforts of William Shaw, the first lay missioner, sufficient funds were available by 1890 to build a Seamen's Institute in Station Road. The building comprised a church with leisure facilities for boatmen and seamen and their families and it was opened in 1891. The new Institute was well attended and the missioner's first annual report noted that there were 898 narrow boats registered at Runcorn and 1857 sea-going vessels and river craft visited the port.

In 1890 Mr Shaw and his dedicated volunteer helpers made 3,106 visits to ships, river flats and canal boats and another 1,849 visits to the homes of seamen and boat people. The Mersey Mission to Seamen, in addition to providing a tranquil haven for ship's crews, also achieved much in its efforts to relieve distress during periods of unemployment and hardship.

The church of St. John the Evangelist at Weston was built of local stone between 1895 and 1898 and in order to raise funds to meet the building costs, a novel method of soliciting donations was initiated. St. John's choirboys appealed to the choristers and choirboys of cathedrals and churches all over the kingdom and the response was immediate and gratifying with over 5,000 gifts of money being received. The enterprise attracted the attention of people of affluence and many donations were received from titled personages and those of rank as well as from the clergy and church sodalities throughout the land. St. John's, Weston and St. Michael's, Greenway Road, were formed into parishes independent of All Saints in 1931.

Protestant Nonconformity

The influence of Protestant nonconformity which changed the character of English society spread rapidly across Cheshire in the last decade of the eighteenth century. John Wesley had preached in the neighbourhood of Aston and Preston Brook in 1781 and 1782 and Methodist preaching had commenced in Runcorn as early as 1781. According to J. Janion in his "Introduction of Methodism into the City and some parts of Cheshire" which was written in 1833, preaching in Runcorn was conducted "sometimes out of doors and sometimes in the house of a friend". When Methodist workmen from Dutton and Aston found work in the Weston quarries, Methodism became established in Weston village and Janion records: *"A few months after we became householders (in 1790) we invited the travelling Methodist preachers to our house in Weston ... and they gave us a sermon once a fortnight. Here we had preaching under our own roof for thirty or forty years"*.

When they attempted to conduct their services in the open, the peripatetic Methodist preachers found that they were not welcome in Runcorn. The Reverend W. Myles visited the township with a pioneer party of preachers in 1789. The group was ejected by force and did not succeed in accomplishing its aims. In spite of the setback however, a small group of worshippers later that year, secured a house in High Street which they fitted out as a place of worship. But the early Methodists persisted in their determination to conduct out-door services and the preachers attracted attention by ringing a hand bell. In Halton too, the first services were held in the open, the preacher taking his position at the junction of the village street and Holt Lane. One wet day a sympathetic villager invited the Methodists into her cottage and for several years services were held there until a small chapel was built in 1818.

At first, adherents to Methodism were few. The Reverend William Jones when recalling his early life in Runcorn, noted that in 1801 there were only sixteen members "with a very small and inconvenient preaching room". But by 1808 when Mr. Jones left the town to enter the Methodist ministry, a new chapel had been built in Well Lane and there were forty members of the society.

The growth of Methodism advanced with the growth of the town. The first Sunday School was opened in a room in Holloway in 1800 and classes were held there for twenty years until increasing numbers forced the school to move to a building in Martins Gardens (Nelson Street) which was used as a pin factory in the week.

The "Old Soapery" chapel in Well Lane was situated to the south of the Bridgewater Canal and to attend Sunday services there the Sunday School children crossed over by means of a light footbridge which spanned the canal at the top of Martins Gardens. By 1825 however, there were 155 children attending Sunday School in the pin factory and conditions were becoming impossible. The situation was eased only when Brunswick Chapel in Brunswick Street was opened in 1827. The new building was large with deep galleries on three sides and, below ground level, a long room was provided to accommodate the Sunday School. A house for Runcorn's first resident Methodist minister was built adjoining the new chapel.

Methodism continued to flourish in Runcorn and within twelve years of Brunswick's opening both the chapel and the Sunday School premises were considerably enlarged. Without doubt the Methodist cause was advanced by the dedication and energy of the Sunday School teachers. It was not unusual for men and women to serve in this capacity for forty years and two of the Brunswick teachers were actually associated with the work of Christian instruction for sixty years! In 1850 an average of 290 scholars and 38 teachers attended Sunday School at Brunswick chapel but a year later there occurred a great division in Methodism caused by the Reform Movement. In the secession of 1851 over 160 Sunday School children and teachers left Brunswick to attend the United Methodist Church in Ellesmere Street. Although this was a severe loss, the Brunswick congregation and the Sunday School recovered and within a few years it became obvious that the chapel would soon prove inadequate for the demands made on it.

On July 12th 1864 the foundation stone of St. Paul's Wesleyan Methodist church in High Street was laid and two years later on November 13th 1866 the building was opened for divine service. The new church was the largest Methodist chapel in the Liverpool district and the entire building costs of over £8,000 were met by Thomas

Hazlehurst, the soap manufacturer. Mr. Hazlehurst was a very wealthy man and when his wife died on her twenty-eighth birthday he resolved to use the £60,000 that he had received from her estate together with much of his own money in the building of Wesleyan Methodist chapels and schools.

With its broad Italianate colonnaded stone facade, balconies and towers surmounted by domes, St. Paul's was one of the few buildings of distinction in Runcorn. The handsome interior offered perfect acoustics for the powerful organ and the church was brilliantly illuminated by gas chandeliers which were suspended from an elegant panelled ceiling.

Thomas Hazlehurst began his chapel building in Runcorn with Camden Methodist Chapel in Lowlands Road in 1862 and in 1871 he built Halton Road chapel at a cost of £8,000 to replace the small Zion Chapel in Frederick Street which had served the Mill Brow area since 1848. In 1872 Mr. Hazlehurst built Weston Point chapel; Trinity Church, Frodsham in 1873 at a cost of £9,000 and Trinity, Halton in 1875, the year before he died. Thomas Hazlehurst contributed generously to many Methodist foundations in Lancashire and Cheshire. He laid the foundation and memorial stones of over a hundred chapels and schools and pride of place in his house, "Beaconfield", was a display case containing ninety-nine presentation silver trowels and mallets.

Originally, Runcorn was part of the Northwich Methodist circuit. In 1812 it formed part of Warrington circuit and in 1848 it became, with Widnes, a separate circuit. Runcorn divided from Widnes in 1869 and from Frodsham in 1872. The Methodist movement in the county continued to grow despite the various schisms which occurred within the denomination after the death of John Wesley. The Primitive Methodists were at first conspicuous by their custom of conducting open-air services. Later they held their meetings in a cottage in Nelson Street before building a chapel in Regent Street in 1838. Within a few years the congregation had outgrown the Regent Street chapel and a move was made to a new chapel and schoolroom in Greenway Road in 1871. After the detachment of a large section of the Brunswick congregation in 1851 the defectors of the Reform Branch of the Free Wesley Methodist Society held their services at the Forester's Hall in Devonshire Square. By 1853 they had begun to build a chapel and schoolroom in Ellesmere Street, much of the building work being done through voluntary effort by members of the congregation.

The thriving Victorian Sunday School movement was nowhere more successful than at Brunswick. The School register for the Centenary year 1900 lists 64 officers and teachers and in 1888 during the construction of the Manchester Ship Canal when the population of the town and district showed a large temporary increase, the

St. Paul's Wesleyan Methodist church. Its destruction in 1969 prompted Nickolaus Pevsner to declare: "The town centre has thus lost its one distinctive building".

afternoon attendance at Brunswick Sunday School was 492 children and teachers.

The two Methodist day schools did not last for long and the voluntary provision of education ended when the managers of Granville Street School and Brunswick School handed them over to the control of the Runcorn School Board in 1895.

The Congregational Church became established in Runcorn mainly through the efforts of the Reverend William Alexander of the Congregational church in Prescot who, in 1807 held services in the "White Hart" and in private houses in the town. At first the small group of worshippers depended upon preachers from the "Lancashire brethren who have arranged to supply the place on week-day evenings until more regular and permanent preaching can be obtained".

The Congregationalists were always closely allied to a religious denomination called the Countess of Huntington's Connexion and it was from friends in the Connexion at Warrington that funds were forthcoming to build the first Congregational chapel of St. John in the centre of Runcorn township in 1818. Both Congregationalists and Connectionists worshipped together for about ten years until a dispute resulted in a number of brethren leaving to form a new congregation. The new group received the support of Mr. William Pennington, a local property owner, who in 1830, built for it St. Luke's Chapel and schoolroom in Mason Street. A few years later St. Luke's was fortunate to receive the patronage of John Tomkinson, quarrymaster of the Mill Brow and Runcorn Hill quarries. Mr. Tomkinson realized that Runcorn was expanding westwards and he bought what was soon to become a central site and provided the means to build Bethesda Chapel and schoolroom at a cost of £6,000. When Bethesda was opened on 29th September 1835, St. Luke's was superseded but the little Mason Street chapel continued to be used for another 130 years.

Built of local red sandstone, Bethesda was unpretentious. It had two tiers of windows in castellated walls and a short chancel. In 1861 a school was built on land adjacent to the chapel. Bethesda also had a small burial ground. A serious fire in 1891 destroyed much of the church and the interior had virtually to be rebuilt. In common with all denominations at the beginning of this century, Bethesda had a successful Sunday School. A report of 1907 stated that there were 200 scholars and "new classrooms have become absolutely necessary".

The Welsh Presbyterians had first held services in the town during the Regency period and a gravestone in the Parish churchyard commemorates the Reverend J.E. Jones who died aged 73 in 1860 after "Having been a faithful minister with the Welsh Presbyterians for upwards of 50 years". In 1849 the Welsh Presbyterian Church bought and renovated the original Congregational chapel which had been built by the Huntington Connexion in St. John's Street and for the next forty-four years the building accommodated an ever-growing congregation and a Sunday School. By 1893 however, increasing pressure of numbers had forced the elders to seek new premises and in that year the present schoolroom in Victoria Road was opened. The foundation stone of St. John's Presbyterian church was laid in 1904 and the building was opened in 1905. After the church had moved to the Victoria Road site, the old Huntingtonian church in St. John's Street was bought by Sir John Brunner who presented it to the town for the use of the public.

The Welsh community in the town grew quickly during the first three decades of the nineteenth century as seamen, dock workers and quarrymen from Wales settled in Runcorn. One of the earliest Welsh religious centres on Merseyside was the Welsh chapel in Back King Street which was built in 1829. Before that date Welsh seamen had held prayer meetings aboard a barge in "chapel basin". The Duke of Bridgewater's Trustees contributed £10 per annum towards the cost of the venture but nothing more is known of its history. A Welsh chapel was built in Rutland Street in 1856. According to customs officials, half of the 4,418 ships to visit Runcorn in 1865 were Welsh vessels and the essay prize at the Welsh Eisteddford held in Caerleon in 1866 was the gift of Welshmen living in Runcorn.

The Roman Catholic population of Runcorn in 1840 was less than two hundred and during the eighteenth and early part of the nineteenth centuries, Sunday observance meant a ferry crossing to the mass centre in Widnes. Before 1748 mass was celebrated at Lowerhouse in Widnes and after that date, at a house in Appleton village. The first resident Catholic priest in Runcorn was the Reverend Edmund Carter who, from 1842, held mass in a house in Irwell Lane, then in Stenhill House and later in a hay-loft in Heath Road. Father Carter stayed for one year before he was raised to the dignity of a canon and transferred to Bolton. His successor, the Reverend Gerald Ward, built the first St. Edward's church in Windmill Street in 1846.

The industrialisation of Runcorn and a resulting increase in the number of Irish immigrant workers made necessary the provision of a Catholic day school for their children and on 8th July 1866 a school was established in the upper room of the Windmill Street church. As the number of pupils increased, more of the chapel-school was taken over for educational purposes and by 1880 it was obvious that the congregation would have to abandon the church to classrooms. On 2nd September 1888 a corrugated iron church, which cost a total of £724, was opened in Irwell Lane. Although this building was intended to be a temporary expedient, it was to remain in use for another sixty-eight years until it was replaced by the present St. Edward's in Ivy Street in 1956.

The Baptists had a small chapel in the centre of Runcorn. In 1845 they built their place of worship in Bridge Street opposite the present public swimming baths. Hope Hall was used for services until the beginning of this century when the Baptists sold the premises.

HALTON ROAD CHAPEL, RUNCORN.

Two of Thomas Hazlehurst's Wesleyan Methodist chapels, Halton Road and Trinity, Halton.

Bibliography

In addition to Charles Nickson's history the following were used for the account of the present Parish Church. *"Runcorn Parish Church"*, Centenary Publication (1949); *"A Visitor's Guide to the Parish Church of All Saints, Runcorn"* by D.G. Thomas (1978); Pigot and Company, *Cheshire Directory* (1838); *Kelly's Post Office Directory* (1906) and the Parish Magazine of the Parish Church 1896 to 1901. Information was also obtained from Canon Barclay's Annual Letters to the Parishioners of Runcorn, from *A History of the Church of St. Michael and All Angels, Runcorn* by E.R. Woodcock (1967) and from "History of Runcorn Parish Church and Jubilee Proceedings" *Runcorn Guardian* 14th January 1899.

References to the church furniture of the Parish Church can be found in "Concerning Certain Designs in Screens and Stall work Found in the Borderland of England and Wales" by Fred. H. Crossley in the *Transactions of the Lancashire and Cheshire Historic Society* Vol. 97 (1945); "Cheshire Church Furniture" by Fred Crossley in Vol. LIII of the *Transactions of the Lancashire and Cheshire Antiquarian Society* (1938); the Centenary Magazine of Farnworth Methodist Church, Widnes 1849-1949; *"Chester Silver"* by Maurice Ridgeway (1972) and in *Cheshire Sheaf,* January 1879.

For the other churches see "The Church of St. Peter, Aston by Sutton" by Raymond Richards, *Transactions of the Lancashire and Cheshire Historic Society,* Vol. 101 (1949) and Vol. 102 (1950); *St. Mary's Church, Halton* by A.D. Jones (1976), *"Cheshire"* by Nikolaus Pevsner and Edward Hubbard (1971); *Holy Trinity Church, Runcorn,* Centenary Publication (1938).

The account of Non-conformity in Victorian Runcorn was obtained from: *The Methodist Recorder* 29th March (1906); St. Paul's Wesleyan Church Souvenir of Jubilee Services (1917); *A History of the Cheshire County Union of Congregational Churches* (1907); by F.J. Powick and from the Roman Catholic *Diocese of Shrewsbury Centenary Record 1851-1951.*

For the history of church missionary work at the docks see *Mersey Mission to Seamen (Runcorn Branch) 1875–1921* in the local collection at Runcorn Shopping City library. An account of Christ Church, Weston Point — "The Spire Among the Ships" by Gordon Roxby appears in *Port of Manchester Review,* (1972).

Chapter 9
The Parish Constable and the Overseers

From Tudor times the parish was the unit of ecclesiastical and local government. The centre of its administration was the parish vestry and the first entries in the Runcorn vestry minute book date from 1751. They record the appointment of parish officers. When his turn came, no able bodied man could escape the obligation to serve as Parish Constable, Overseer of the Poor or Overseer of the Highways. The unwilling and inexperienced officials received their unpaid appointments with ill-grace but all had to act for a year in one capacity or another. In small townships it was likely that a man would be required to serve on a number of occasions during his lifetime.

Perhaps the most onerous task was that of Parish Constable. He was responsible for law and order, administration concerning the militia, collecting taxes and the relief of destitute vagrants. Sometimes it was deemed necessary to appoint two constables but they could expect little support in carrying out their unenviable work.

The Overseers of the Highways or to use the contemporary misnomer, "the surveyors", were elected annually to amend all the public roads within the parish boundaries. They had statutory powers to call on every householder, cottager and labourer to work on the roads for eight hours on six specified days in the year. The reluctant labourers had to bring their own tools and the local landowners had to provide horses and carts. The unwilling and often rebellious workforce was to carry out road repairs without pay and with little guidance from surveyors who knew next to nothing of the essential techniques required. Although the hamlets of Halton and Runcorn were quiet places with little through traffic to cause serious problems to the soft surfaces of the tracks which served as roads, nevertheless constant levelling and draining were required. The one main highway to cross the parish boundary was the road from Chester to Warrington and the responsibility for its maintenance lay with the villages through which it passed.

The Overseers of the Poor were responsible for the welfare of paupers, the aged poor and those who were too sick to earn a livelihood. Every penny of the overseer's limited funds had to be accounted for and he was usually hard pressed in his attempts to alleviate poverty among the poor whose numbers never decreased but grew inexorably as the population increased.

The first entry in the minute book for Runcorn township is a record of the vestry meeting on 10th June 1751 when the accounts of the constables and overseers were audited. Usually it was the practice to appoint officials at Easter but in Runcorn by 1762, it had become customary to have three meetings in the year when the officers were given their appointments. For instance on January 14th 1762 John Archer and John Muskett were elected as supervisors of the highways. On 22nd April William Wright and John Billings became Overseers of the Poor whilst on 29th October the constables were Richard Banner and William Wright. The vestry minutes allow us tempting glimpses of every-day life in Georgian Runcorn. An entry in the vestry minutes of 1776 refers to disputes which had occurred involving the use of the parish hearse. (The hearse was required for journeys of some distance. Before the consecration of Aston churchyard in 1635 Runcorn was the usual burial place for the inhabitants of Aston and Sutton). At the meeting on 29th September 1776 the vestry laid down rules and conditions to be observed before the hearse could be used:

"That whereas there hath been some disputes concerning hiring of the hearse belonging to this parish this is to notify to whom it may concern that the charge shall be for the future as follows:

First every person that makes use of the said hearse shall pay for it to the clerk sixpence for his trouble in cleaning it again.

Secondly every parishioner shall have a right to take the said hearse to any part of the parish that is within the liberty where the parishioners pay towards the repairs of the said hearse paying sixpence as aforesaid, but if any parishioner have occasion to take the said hearse out of the said parish, that is out of the liberties that pays towards the repairing of the said hearse, they shall pay a further shilling for every mile it goeth from the outside of the said liberty …

Thirdly every person that make use of the said hearse not being a parishioner and taking it out of the said parish shall pay the clerk as aforesaid one shilling for every mile they take it — to be accounted from this church. As witness our hand".

James Starkey
Peter Cooper
Peter Johnson
Peter Okell.

The constables' accounts for the parish of Runcorn throw light on the various responsibilities of their office. Typical entries include the following expenses incurred by Thomas Dutton and Thomas Parr who were the parish constables in 1781.

1781	£	s	d
Paid John Grice for a gudgeon for Sour Milk Lane Gate (Pool Lane)	0	0	6
Paid for a lock for the pinfold door	0	0	10
Paid for a town chest	0	10	6
Paid for gunpowder for November 5th	0	0	6
Paid John Dutton for 2 dozen of sparrows	0	1	0

Every year the constables paid out sums of money for dead sparrows. In a township of thatched cottages they were regarded as a serious pest and were caught in many ingenious ways. Their heads were presented to the churchwardens as proof of the constables' expenses. Bullfinches were unwelcome because they fed on the buds of fruit trees and shrubs. In 1781 the constables paid for 520 dead sparrows at a halfpenny each and 30 bullfinches at two pence per head.

Another item of expense which appeared every year shows the constables' responsibilities concerning the militia. A militia act was passed in 1757 and every village had to supply its quota of militia men. After 1762 a total of 28 days drill became standard practice. Militia duty was unpopular and many did not care to spend time in what they considered to be pointless drilling and marching. The constable had to draw up lists of those liable to serve in the ranks and men were frequently selected by ballot.

		£	s	d
1784	To a journey to Knutsford with the militia	0	1	6
1798.	With Bate, the lawyer 3 days and three nights to identify and serve the supplementary militia substitutes according to the Act of Parliament	1	0	0
1802	Journey to Hoo Green returning a list of militia men	0	2	0
	Journey to Knutsford balloting for the army reserve	0	3	0

On 13th December 1788 the vestry appointed the town's first salaried officer.

The nineteen men who made up the vestry signed the following declaration:

"Wee, the inhabitants of Runcorn have jointly agreed that Kerfoot Jennion takes upon him to serve all the Town's Offices for the sum of £5 to be paid to the said Kerfoot Jennion yearly out of the town lays".

Although the vestry appears to have had every confidence in their newly appointed town manager they were parsimonious in spending public funds and the meagre payment offered for carrying out a variety of time-consuming and burdensome duties could not have attracted many candidates for the post.

On the day of Kerfoot Janion's appointment the vestry made a bye-law about trespass. Anyone found trespassing in the township or of "making cross rodes should forfit three shillings and sixpence each to the Bennifit of the Poor and Kierfoot Jennion Overseer of the Poor to Recover the same".

Wandering pigs which rooted up roads and destroyed vegetable gardens were a constant nuisance and at the same meeting the vestry issued orders with the warning that: "... any *person or persons having any pigs Trespassing upon any Persons land from the 2nd of February to the 5th November any Pig or Pigs under three months old to have a single Ring in his snought and from that age a duble Ring or to forfit three shillings and sixpence to Kerfoot Jennion Overseer of the Poor for the said township".*

One of the constables' most difficult tasks was the collection of money for the maintenance of unmarried mothers and their children. Illegitimate pauper children could represent a severe drain on the Poor Law fund and if possible the fathers had to be identified and made to pay a regular fixed sum. The constables' accounts and those of the Overseer of the Poor record their activities in this respect:

		£	s	d
1809	Paid for an order of bastardy upon Cobbet Lovett and taking him and Sarah Lamb to Warrington	0	9	6
1812	Received from William Oakes in part to acquit him of a bastard child of Betty Silvester	10	0	0
1827	Journey to Liverpool in search of John Crouchley having a warrant against him for arrears of bastardy	0	8	0

The sum of £97 .. 5 .. 11 was collected from the fathers of illegitimate children in 1826 and payment to the mothers seems to have averaged about five pounds each.

Even the tiny hamlet of Runcorn had its share of petty crime and on 2nd September 1806 at a town's meeting at Job Wilson's, the Bowling Green Inn, it was decided that the township needed a roundhouse or bridewell. The vestry approved plans for a bridewell with "Stone walls not less than two feet thick, seven feet high and to the square of nine feet each way", but the committee baulked at the cost of building and the thickness of the walls was reduced to one and a half feet. The work was to be completed for "Forty guineas without any extra expenses whatsoever". The bridewell occupied a site in Bridge Street opposite the present public swimming baths. It was a typical village lock-up with no windows, the light entering through the domed roof. Over the years the roundhouse suffered much wilful damage and it was often in need of repair. The constable's accounts show that frequently he had to provide a new door and locks.

The village stocks were much used and they were renewed during a period of increased petty crime in 1824. The vestry decided to spend two pounds on refurbishing the stocks but there was one dissenting vote, that of Dennis Brundrit who considered the ancient form of punishment to be degrading and cruel.

Some examples of entries relating to breaches of the law are given below:

		£	s	d
1803	To taking a boatman to Chester Castle	0	10	0
	To taking and detaining Kirkham and Jackson for stealing apples.	0	2	0
1826	Expenses on Charles Pownall (son of Phoebe Astbury) having being in custody 2 days charged with having been the cause of his mother's death by beating and abusing her.	0	4	0
	A man to go to Chester for coroner's warrant for inquest on Phoebe Astbury. Three shillings expense on man and three shillings on horse.	0	6	0
	Paid Mr. Case for Morbid Dissection of the body and attention	2	2	0
	For women cleaning the room	0	2	6
1827	Expenses of apprehending Richard Orme and John Morgan for disorderly conduct in assaulting the constable in the execution of his duty and taking them before Mr. Lyon where they were bound over to appear at the sessions.	0	3	0
	Paid Randle for 2 lanthorns for watch	0	7	0
	Paid for a pair of snap handcuffs	0	9	6
	Paid Mr. Wilson for straw for the Roundhouse at various times	0	3	0

One of the duties which devolved on the constable was that relating to coroner's inquests and throughout the records there are numerous items concerning this aspect of his work. The following will suffice by way of example:

		£	s	d
1792	Paid for a coffin, church dues, washing for a drowned person	1	10	0
	Paid jury for Margaret Smith	0	4	0
	To coffin, funeral expenses paid for a Welsh boy drowned	1	10	0
	Paid jury for Jos. Hindle's man	0	4	0
1801	Jurors for a man drowned at Halton	0	4	0
1820	Pd. jurors and fetching coroner for strange man and coffin and funeral expenses and carriers.	1	12	0

Part of the constable's duty was to ensure that vagrants from places outside the township did not attempt to settle in the village where they might become involved in criminal activity or worse, die and have to be buried at parish expense. Some of the vagrants were passing through the district to settle in their own parishes and they had passes stating their destinations. The constable was obliged to hurry them on their way by giving them small sums of money if it was necessary.

		£	s	d
1782	Pd. to 3 men with each a pass	0	3	0
1792	Paid to poor persons with passes	0	2	2
1801	Paid for a vagrant warrant	0	7	6
	Paid to different poor families and sailors travelling by way of a pass	0	8	0
	Poor man in distress	0	1	0

At the end of the Napoleonic War there was a huge increase in the number of vagrants and former soldiers and their families passing through the town by way of the ferry. In the period 1815 to 1818 the small sums paid to travellers mounted up to become a considerable drain on parish funds.

On 1st and 2nd June 1817 ninety-five soldiers' wives were paid for with passes for the Liverpool sailing packet at a cost of £18 .. 10 .. 5½ .

		£	s	d
1815	Pd. a quantity of soldiers when detained by frost at Runcorn	0	16	0
	Paid Mr. Turner for meat and Peter Brown for ferry for the above	1	6	0
1817	Woman and two children with a pass	0	1	0
	Soldier's wife and three children	0	1	6

Poor man taken ill at
Runcorn .... 0 ..2 ..6

These are typical of the scores of payments made to destitute people by the constables during the three year period.

From among the more interesting items in the constable's account book the following miscellany has been compiled:

		£	s	d
1781	Paid for a book to gaither by	0	..0	..6
	Journey to High Leigh to return (list of) ale sellers	0	..1	..0
	Paid for burds	0	..4	..8
1782	To John Kirkham for a witness	0	..3	..6
	To warning a town's meeting	0	..0	..4
	To writing a ley book	0	..0	..6
1784	To Mrs. Orford for liquor	0	..9	..4
	To assessing the land and window tax	0	..8	..0
	To signing a list of freeholders	0	..0	..6
1792	To John Fryer for a stone trough and carting	0	..5	..0
1802	To 4 days taking stock of population	0	..12	..0
	To one day taking account of firearms	0	..3	..0

Often the constable's funds proved insufficient and at the end of his term of office he was out of pocket. Thomas Cornes, the parish constable for 1782 noted: "the town's indebted to Thos. Cornes, Constable for £ 0..9..7½" and his successor George Radley noted "out of Pockett £0..4..9¾". The vestry carefully scrutinised the accounts and in 1803 they begrudgingly accepted constables Robert and Kerfoot Janion's accounts but demanded restitution from some individuals who had been a charge on the parish. *"We whose names are herunto subscribed agree to sign the above charges that the constable apply to John Houghton, James Ryder, Joseph Howard, The Trustees and Agents of the Duke of Bridgewater, H. Henshall and Mary Hughes for the respective sums of money charged to the Township of Runcorn on their accounts and receive the same from them if possible and credit the town with what they receive in the next year's accounts and for the time to come such charges will be allowed".*

The accounts of the Overseers of the Poor for Runcorn parish survive only from 1808.

		£	s	d
1808	Pd. to Mr. Oliver for mending Betty Cowley's child's shoes	0	..1	..6
1810	Making shifts, petticoats and bedgowns for Okel's child	0	..2	..6
	Pd. Ruth Ackerley when her children were bad	0	..5	..0
	Pd. Mary Gorton for taking care of Ackerley's children	0	..15	..0
	Pd. Mary Gorton for washing for Ruth Ackerley	0	..3	..0
	Pd. Ruth Ackerley's rent	2	..10	..0
	To warrant going to Wilderspool and fetching James Ackerley home	2	..13	..0
1826	Pd. coals for Samuel Shaw when sick	0	..2	..11
	Casual relief for Samuel Shaw, candles, paper, etc.	0	..5	..0

In 1813 the following record of money received by the Overseer of the Poor was entered in the account book:

	£	s	d
Received from Mr. Meacock in lieu of Poor rate for the locks of the Trustees of the late Duke of Bridgewater	40	..0	..0
Received from Old Quay in lieu of Poor rate	2	..10	..0
Assessed from a poor rate April 22nd 1812	120	..19	..0
Assessed from a poor rate October 14th 1812	105	..17	..6
Assessed from a poor rate January 12th 1813	124	..14	..0

The total of outdoor relief distributed in 1826 to "weekly paupers" came to £294..9..6 whilst "payments for bastard children" totalled £97..5..11. The overseer forced vagrants out of the parish and left them to become a nuisance in another village.

		£	s	d
1808	Paid Bayman's wife to take her to her settlement	0	..5	..0
	James Osborne to go to his settlement	0	..4	..0
1811	Order of removal for Thomas Booth and children	0	..3	..6
	Paid Thomas Booth	0	..2	..6
1812	Journey and expenses to Hoo Green with Margaret Dutton Gig hire	1	..0	..0
	Journey and expenses in removing her to Liverpool and stopping all night	0	..18	..0

In the closing years of the eighteenth century there was widespread unemployment in agriculture which resulted in tremendous pressure on the Poor Law system. The poor rate demand rose to unprecedented levels. The parish paupers had become a threat and the attitude of officials towards them became less sympathetic. The Runcorn vestry no longer wished to maintain the poor in their own homes by paying outdoor relief. The following sad entry in the minute book reflects this hardening of attitude:

1800 "Town's Meeting. April, 8th. Resolved that the Overseer should enter into arrangement with the Halewood Poorhouse on the best terms he could to take the poor of the Township".

The third parish official was the Supervisor or Overseer of the Highways whose office dates back to Tudor times. However, the earliest reference to local communications by road appears to be that recorded by Ormerod who mentions Frodsham Bridge in the thirteenth century. The name Philip de Pont occurs in 1271. Apparently in 1341 there was a chapel on the bridge for the benefit of travellers. In 1419 John Done, the Forester, of Delamere, was ordered to select an oak for repairs to the bridge. At the beginning of Queen Elizabeth's reign the bridge was in need of repair and James Benet in 1559 gave six shillings and eight pence "to ye mending of Fradsome Bridge" and in 1593 William Robinson had a penance commuted to a payment of ten shillings which was paid to repair the bridge. Ormerod tells us that Frodsham bridge was rebuilt of brick in Elizabeth's reign "builded most part of brick, the longest bridge in all Cheshire". Later this was taken down to be replaced by "four fair arches all of stone".

In 1618 the Overseer of the Highways for Runcorn received orders that he was to join with the overseers of neighbouring hamlets to keep the approaches to Frodsham bridge in good repair. *"The causey (causeway for carts) at the end of Frodsham bridge is to be maintained by the inhabitants of Sutton, Weston, Runkorne, Clifton and Halton"* and the Justices of the Peace were ordered at the Quarter Sessions to see that regular maintenance was carried out.

It was the duty of the supervisor of the highways to make sure that landowners attended to blocked ditches and overhanging hedges and trees. If they neglected to do so the overseer was empowered to have the job done and charge the landowner for the work. After 1700 it became usual for a parish to dispense with the hopelessly inefficient statute labourers and instead levy a rate to hire labour for road maintenance but paupers were often employed in road repair. The upkeep of roads in Halton and Runcorn simply meant keeping a fairly level surface of gravel or quarry waste and it was not until well into the nineteenth century that the district saw its first scientifically constructed roads.

The records of Runcorn's surveyors of the highways for a few years after 1815 (by which time he was a paid official) are still in existence. They show increasing expenditure year by year as the township began to grow.

		£	s	d
1815	Mr. Kirkham on acc. for paving stones	44	16	0
	Stanley Leathwood for paving and labouring work	59	18	5
	Wm. Coy for mason work	4	12	7
	James Shallcross for carting	10	12	3
	William Rigby, surveyor, for salery	10	0	0
1816	Stan Leathwood for picking and loading stone on the shore side and labouring	1	12	0
	William Wright as acc. for Roundhouse	6	8	1
	Mr. Grindrod for side stones and sough stones	2	8	6
	Pd. John Hignet for finding quicks in Holloway	0	4	6

By 1816 the first factories had been established in the town and industrial slag and clinker was being used for road surfacing.

		£	s	d
1816	Pd. to Messrs. Johnson and Hazlehursts men for sinders	0	10	0

The discharging of a barge laden with cinders was a streuous task and it took a considerable time. An allowance for beer for the labourers is included in the cost.

		£	s	d
1816	Paid. A flatt load of sinders discharged and allowance	4	10	0

The overseer needed every penny he could obtain and his accounts show sums of money borrowed from the town's Friendly Societies.

		£	s	d
1818	Pd. interest on £180 borrowed from the New Inn Sick Club	9	0	0
1820	Paid the sick club at the New Inn	62	0	0
1821	Paid interest on money borrowed from the women's club	3	10	0
1823	To interest of money paid to the Female sick club	3	10	0

The highway rate of 1817 amounted to £227 raised from a rate of a shilling in the pound in April followed by a second levy of sixpence in the pound in July.

Halton was a township independent of Runcorn but its rudimentary parish administration was precisely the same as that in Runcorn, indeed as it was in countless other small communities throughout England. The job of constable was universally hated. Each cottage in turn had to supply an able-bodied man to serve as town constable for twelve months. As the appointment was unwelcome it became a general practice to pay someone else to do the job and it was not unknown for some to attempt to avoid the onerous task by resorting to dishonest claims. The surviving town book of Halton commences in 1698 with a careful record of all who had not served as constable during the previous sixteen years. The entry lists "An account of the houses that have not served constable since the year 1682".

The Halton Overseer of the Highways had much the same problem as overseers everywhere. In 1703 there is an item concerning damage to the roads in the village. Offenders with carts were liable to a fine of three shillings and fourpence of which one third was to be awarded to the complainant and the remainder was to be used to pay for road maintenance. A similar fine was liable to be paid by offenders who allowed cattle to stray on to the highways. In 1746 an entry in the town book reads: *"No person shall pasture any cattell in the lane leading from Runcorne to Halton called Runcorne Lane without attending in pane three shillings and four pence".*

The Halmot Court at Halton dealt with petty offences such as common nuisance, highway or ditch disrepair and the like. An entry of 11th August 1753 has a resolution to *"... Prosecute anny person or persons that pulleth down or carrieth away anny hedges belonging to anny person in the township of Halton and that the charge of prosecution shall goo out of the township's charge namely out of the poor leay — one shilling to the complaneor".*

Another interesting order of 1746 prohibits the sale of gorse within the township because it was required to fuel "the oven and furnace". The ashes of plants were needed in quantity for the making of a crude, home-made soap and it seems that Halton Common was becoming denuded of its gorse bushes. *"We order that no person or persons shall mowe gorse uppon Halton Commons to make ashes of to sell but be for the use of the Township inhabitors ... and if any person do burn it to sell they shall be prosecuted by the town and that no certifficate persons shall get any".* A "certificate person" was a 'foreigner' from another village who had been granted a certificate of settlement. Often they were regarded as being of less status than the indigenous folk and no stranger would be allowed to settle in the community if there was any possibility of him becoming a liability. Only craftsmen and the comfortably-off would be accepted. Evidence of this practice can be seen in the following order which was proclaimed at the halmot court in Halton in 1715:

"We order that no inhabitant what soever in the township of Halton therunto belonging shall sell or lett any person or persons belonging to another town or township any house or houses under the value of tenn pounds. The person not bringing a certificate before he or she enters upon any part or parcel of the said (property) the aforesaid Burgase, Burgesor or Inhabitants so doing shall forfeit the sum of £5 for doing such fault so committed". This enormous fine to be paid by offenders against the halmot bye-law illustrates the anxiety and suspicion when strangers moved into the community. Only when it was certain that the newcomers were unlikely to become a drain on parish charity would they be grudgingly accepted.

The constable's account book for the township of Weston still exists. The first entries were made in 1702 by John Hales and they were, in the main, concerned with defining the ownership of property boundaries within the village. A resolution of 1703 records the liability for keeping in good repair the fencing and hedges of fields which abutted the common land. *"Agreed that all the Ringyards at Lambsickle, Lydiate Pale and all other fences adjoining the common except Milfield shall be made up before Candlemas (2nd February) and the gates to be hung up at the same time".* The jurors of the township also decided that they would *"From time to time repaire the breaches betwixt Lambsickle, Robert Gregge's railes and John Wright's mickley hedge upon the forfeiture of one shilling per year".* At the end of his term of office the constable's expenses were audited: *"September ye 30th 1703. John Hale's accounts were examined and it appeared he was out of purse £0..1..4½".* John Hale was followed as constable by Robert Gregg and on April 27th 1704 the latter was fined because a couple of pages in the account book were found to be damaged. *"Robert Gregg for defacing or att least suffering ye Town Booke whilst trusted in his custody to be torne and defaced £0..0..4".*

The Overseer of the Poor for Weston township also kept his accounts in the town book and they show something of the severe demands made on the slender resources of the village by the aged and the destitute.

		£	s	d
1751	To cloes for Daniel Green	0	6	6
	To shirts and making		4	6
	To paire of shoes		4	3
	To a new paire of breeches and making		3	10
	To a new hatt		1	2
	To a new paire of stockings			10
1752	Paid to Saml. Siddeley for Daniel Green's two quarters board		17	6
1753	Paid for Daniel Green's waistcoat and breeches		6	2
	To Daniel Green's cloathes	0	11	9
	To linen cloth for Daniel Green			3
1754	Thomas Simms paid two quarters for Daniel Green's table	1	15	0
1755	Paid to Daniel Green's funeral and expenses	0	13	2

To James Cartwright for a paire of shoes		4	.. 6
Paid to a paire of clogs			7
1757 Paid Widow Bentley's quarter rent		7	.. 6
Widow Bentley paid Doctor Dunbabin a pound of sugar physic and attendance		8	.. 5
Sent to Samuel Prescott towards burying his daughter		10	.. 0
1760 Paid to a lode of coles for Thomas Kirkham 19 baskets at 6d per basket		9	.. 6
1773 Pd. to Mary Ellison for mate and lodgings for Charles Griffiths		1	.. 6

	£	s	d
1779 Charles Griffiths expenses in the militia	0	.. 0	.. 3
1783 Bread, butter and cheese for Charles Griffiths	0	.. 0	.. 3
To half a ton of coles from Frodsham Bridge for Charles Griffiths	0	.. 4	.. 3
To drawing the coles	0	.. 1	.. 0

Weston township included Weston Point and the marshes at the mouth of the River Weaver. Drowning was a frequent occurrence and in 1772 alone there were four separate instances of fatalities in the river. One or two of the many entries concerning death by drowning have been selected from the Weston constables' accounts:

	£	s	d
1763 To four persons going on jury for two children drowned	0	.. 2	.. 0
1767 To funeral expenses on two men that were drowned	1	.. 7	.. 10
1770 Paid for going for the coroner and carrying a drowned child to church	0	.. 3	.. 6
Paid to Thomas Accarly for a coffin	0	.. 4	.. 0
Drawing the child into the town from the river	0	.. 0	.. 6
To jury and burying same	0	.. 6	.. 0

The duties of the township officials often took them on journeys to Quarter Sessions in Chester or Knutsford and their travelling expenses are detailed. Richard Janion, the constable of Weston in 1770, gives his expenses:

	£	s	d
1770 To my journey to Daresbury to be sworn Constable	0	.. 0	.. 6
To Knutsford to return list of overseers of the highways		2	.. 0
To High Leigh to return freeholders list			10
Paid at the turnpikes			4½

The following miscellaneous items from the Weston constables' accounts are of interest:

	£	s	d
1782 Paid for postage for 3 letters from Macclesfield			11
1803 To going to Northwich concerning militia men			8
1808 Expense of getting Fanny Wright married at Warrington		8	.. 0
1810 Repairing marsh gate		1	.. 0
Repairing heath gate		8	.. 0

The Weston records show that certain families were long established in the village. For instance there were Greggs, Heaths and Hales in the sixteenth century and their descendents were still living in the township in the eighteenth century. In 1747 William Bankes, John Wright and George Orred were the principal farmers and members of their families were to become the prominent landowners of Victorian times. The tithes of Weston township, both great and small, belonged to the vicar of Runcorn. The Church Ley for Weston in 1750 amounted to £1..6..0 and eight years later a rate was laid by the Runcorn vestry on all inhabitants of the parish towards the repairs of the church. The amount paid by Weston township amounted to £1..0..6½ and that for Clifton £1..4..4.

Early Local Government

The arrangement made in 1788 whereby Kerfoot Janion had taken on the task of holding all the offices in the township does not appear to have been of long standing for in 1792 Samuel Wylde and John Thomason submitted their accounts as parish constables. However, at a special town's meeting on April 9th 1799 Joseph Fox was appointed as overseer of the poor and parish constable. The vestry minute records the following: *"We do agree to appoint Joseph Fox as the standing officer for the said township, to perform the office of overseer of the poor, assessor and collector of the land tax and other taxes, and also the office of constable of the said township and we do likewise agree to allow the said Joseph Fox the yearly salary of twenty-one pounds per annum for the performance of the offices of the said township and the salary to be instead of all expenses, journeys etc. incident to the said offices".*

The increase in the new officer's salary is an indication of the growth of Runcorn township with a consequent increase in the official's duties. Joseph Fox did not remain long in office for in 1801 William Johnson held the post of constable. It was during Mr. Johnson's term in office that the first national census of population was taken and the returns show that in Runcorn township in 1801 there were a mere 1379 inhabitants.

For decades the vestry had met in the Parish Church when its duties were similar to those carried out by the Parochial Church Council of today. During the eighteenth century however, its scope widened and the vestry became progressively more concerned with issues of a municipal nature. Furthermore, as the century progressed, there was an increase in the number of vestry members who were not members of the Church of England. By 1798 it had become the practice to hold vestry meetings immediately after divine service on the first Sunday of the month but they were held in the Boathouse Inn, the White Hart (Royal Hotel) or in the Bowling Green Inn (Wilsons Hotel). The vestry had by now jurisdiction to regulate almost every aspect of life in the township.

At a town's meeting in July 1807 the vestry considered the assessment of the rates to be paid on the properties administered by the Duke of Bridgewater's Trustees. The warehouses, locks, basins, tonnage, dues and wharfage were rated at £1,200 per annum and the Trustees immediately appealed against the rating. They proposed instead to make an annual contribution of £40, to be applied for the same purpose as the poor rate and after some deliberation the vestry accepted. The arrangement was a remarkably generous concession on the part of the vestry for the Trustees escaped by paying £40 a year which was equal to three shillings in the pound on an annual value of about £267.

In 1804 the Runcorn to Latchford Canal of the Mersey and Irwell Navigation Company was opened for traffic. The Old Quay Canal, as it became known, had its terminus in the centre of Runcorn township at the Boat House Pool. The vestry rated the new undertaking at £50 per annum and the Mersey and Irwell Company promptly appealed. Instead they proposed to pay a contribution of thirty shillings a year in order to be excluded from the rate and the vestry accepted the terms. These arrangements appear to have been continued without amendment for some years.

At a town's meeting in 1811 it was decided to establish a weekly market in the town. It was stated that this would *"be very convenient and advantageous to the inhabitants of Runcorn and the vicinity"* and notices advertising the market were placed in the Liverpool, Manchester and Chester newspapers. It was also decided that there should be fairs for the sale of horses, cattle, sheep and goods on two days in the year, the last Friday in April and the last Friday in October. The parish constable was ordered to circulate handbills advertising the events. From the start the weekly market and the fairs were not wholly successful but they continued to be held for many years. Even after twenty-three years (by which time the

town's population had almost trebled) the events were still struggling to survive and a directory of 1834 noted that *"neither the fairs nor the market are well attended".*

The town's water supply was the Sprinch Brook which flowed in an open stream from the Sprinch field across the road near the Royal Hotel and into the creek known as the Old Gut. On 15th April 1813 the overseer of the highways was ordered to make a *"convenient watering place for the use of the public".* It appears that Mr. Rigby, the overseer, was slow in carrying out his instructions, for, six months later, the following minute was entered in the town's books: *"It is further agreed that if Mr. Rigby neglects to make the watering place he shall forfeit £3 of his salary".* There is no further reference to Mr. Rigby's failings in this respect but four years later he was reprimanded by order of a new town's committee because of *"the concern and dissatisfaction to the protracted delays to their orders and directions and the observed nuisances they have pointed out to him in different parts of the town (which are) allowed to continue".*

The old vestry system of local government underwent a change in 1814 when at a town's meeting in the "White Hart" the following resolution was passed, *"It is unanimously agreed that a committee be appointed to inspect and manage the town's business to consist of nine persons to meet quarterly and to serve office for twelve months, five of which shall be competent to act ... It is further agreed that in the case of any of the committee men neglecting or refusing to attend shall pay the sum of two shillings and sixpence as a fine for non-attendance unless a sufficient cause can be produced to the satisfaction of the above Committee".* All the members of the committee were men of influence and standing in the township. They were Thomas Hazlehurst, turpentine and resin manufacturer; Francis Salkeld, a grocer; Samuel Meacock, the local agent of the Bridgewater Trustees; Job Wilson of the "Bowling Green Inn"; William Johnson of the "Bridgewater Arms"; William Wright, tanner and quarry master; Thomas Sothern, shipbuilder; William Greenwood, grocer; and Ralph Green, solicitor.

One of the new committee's first actions was for the better regulation of the public houses. They resolved that the bellman and town crier, Solomon Shepherd, should receive an additional guinea a year for *"tolling the bell every Sunday evening from Michaelmas to Lady Day at eight o'clock and from Lady Day to Michaelmas at nine o'clock. It is also agreed that the innkeepers will use their best endeavours to close their houses (to stop the tap) to all dissolute company on Sunday evenings at the above hours and on other days of the week they will close their houses at ten o'clock in the evening".* It is said that members of the committee actually visited certain inns and beer houses to see if the ruling was being obeyed.

Like the previous vestry, the new committee found difficulty in obtaining satisfaction from the work of the overseer of the highways, William Rigby, and they decided to appoint someone to have control over all the town's officers. The man they appointed was a retired naval officer, Captain James Bradshaw R.N. Bradshaw, soon to become the Deputy Superintendent of the Bridgewater Trust, became the most influential personage in the township. Recently arrived in the town, he took up residence in Bridgewater House. Captain Bradshaw was a very determined and capable administrator. He was a man of authority and he quickly stamped his imprint on the management of Runcorn township. He had volunteered his services to the committee and the record of the town's meeting held on November 1st 1817 notes: *"Captain Bradshaw having handsomely offered to take upon himself this duty and to execute the same to the best of his ability, it is resolved that the Town's Officers are directed to obey such orders and directions Captain Bradshaw shall think fit to give for the better regulation of the town in the execution of their several duties"*. James Bradshaw quickly assumed the leadership of the committee and he proved to be a dynamic and perceptive chairman who was to serve the township for many years.

The state of the town's roads left much to be desired and for a couple of years the committee seemed to have been concerned with little else. There were insufficient funds for road repair and in January 1818 it was decided to borrow £250 *"with a view to relieving the heavy expenses necessary to put the roads in proper state for the accommodation of the public, a deputation consisting of the chairman, Mr. Wright and Mr. Allen be requested to wait on Sir Richard Brooke to request his assistance herein"*.

Besides being in a poor state of repair the roads were foul with manure — a saleable commodity which the committee considered to be the property of the town. In an attempt to improve matters they decided to ask for tenders for road scraping, Mr. Rigby being ordered to have handbills printed and posted informing the public that individuals were not to remove manure after the 25th December. Mr. William Wright's offer for road cleansing was accepted and he undertook to clean and scrape the highways from Delph Bridge to the Boathouse Inn and from the Royal Hotel to the foot of the Town Bridge to where the road led to Higher Runcorn. Mr. Wright was *"guaranteed the property of the scraping together with a payment of £13 per annum. Penalty for any neglect therein £5"*.

Church Lane was put in repair using industrial cinders and an application was made to the Old Quay Company requiring them *"to fill up to a proper slope the Old Road (Irwell Lane) leading into Runcorn"*. A new road called Fryer Street was opened in 1818 *"with a view to obviating the present nuisance"*. Here no explanation is available as to the nature of the nuisance. The Overseer of the Highways was directed to *"cause a quantity of boulder stones to be got from the beach and fixed so as to defend the new wall by Delph Bridge and to take proper measure for preventing carters from watering their horses at the canal or drawing their carts in the footway"*. (At the bottom of Delph Bridge). The road from *"Soapery Bridge to the Pickow and from thence to the Holloway is to be done with Delph rubbish and cinders and a hard raised footpath of moderate width is to be marked out with side boulders"*. The church path leading to the Duke's stables was also put in good order.

The next subject to occupy the minds of the committee was the problem of illegal settlement on the common or heath. Some years before, the common land was in danger of being enclosed when the Duke of Bridgewater and Lord Cholmondeley each coveted areas of land around Runcorn Hill. Fortunately for the town the two noblemen could not agree on how to divide the waste land and it remained common land. But for a number of years squatters had gradually encroached on the common. Poor people mostly, there were probably some amongst them who believed in an ancient folk tale which stated that they had a right to permanent settlement if they managed to erect a dwelling in one night! The new vestry, no doubt spurred on by the chairman, Captain Bradshaw, decided to clear the common and on 26th September 1818 they resolved to *"lay waste"* the encroachments. The flimsy dwellings and enclosures of sixteen people were pulled down and another five individuals were ordered to remove the cow sheds and pig sties which they had erected.

Once again the supervisor of the highways came under attack. The committee charged Mr. Rigby with making encroachments. He was a builder by profession and he often abused his powers as overseer by storing his building materials on the highway. The committee noted that he had *"frequently been remonstrated with on the impropriety of making the highway into a timber and flag yard. Such conduct in a hired officer is insufferable. He cannot find fault with others whilst he is the greatest aggressor himself"*. Mr. Rigby was warned that his salary would be under review if he persisted in obstructing the road near his premises.

The committee was very active in its efforts to improve the town's thoroughfares. It now ordered the summons before a magistrate of Mr. Gilbert, the agent of Mr. Cooper of Grove House, who was the town's principal landowner. The foot road along the river bank to the east of the Parish Church ran through Mr. Cooper's land and his agent was summoned to show cause why he should not repair it. On 27th November 1820 the committee expressed deep dissatisfaction at the poor condition of the public roads: *"Owing to the very filthy state of the roads generally in this town it was ordered that the overseer employ the paupers of the town to scrape and cleanse the same forthwith"*.

It was the tradition to separate the road from its footpath by means of a line of white painted posts. A number of posts which marked Churchfield Path (which ran from the Town Bridge to the church, probably along the line of the present Bridgewater Street) were removed. They were re-erected as guards to protect the footway along Bridge Street from the Sprinch to the roundhouse. The committee was not prepared to spend its slender resources needlessly and refused to upgrade two thoroughfares. *"The road from the church to Castle Rock is not a bridle road belonging to the town and has never been repaired by them and the road from the church to Higher Runcorn (so far as the Duke's Canal) is only a footpath and is in excellent repair"*.

The official census returns for 1821 give the population of Runcorn to be 3,103 inhabitants with 542 houses. The town was growing steadily with newcomers arriving every week. The committee viewed with alarm the increase in robberies and other misdemeanours and it was pointed out that *"it is expedient for the respectable inhabitants to co-operate together in endeavouring to discover the offenders"*. It was resolved to form an association to *"keep watch and ward"* during the night. A committee was appointed to organise it and orders were given to put the round house in proper repair. The limits of the watch from east to west extended from Windmill Street on Delph Bridge to Welsh Row Bridge (Waterloo Bridge) and north to south, from the river to the Old Soapery on the south side of the Bridgewater Canal.

A select committee of both Houses of Parliament in 1818 and 1819 recommended alterations in parish vestry constitution for *"the Relief of the Poor"*. From this time onward the entire management of the poor was entrusted to a special committee which came up for election every year. At a town's meeting in the autumn of 1822 a *"select vestry was appointed in accordance with the act recently passed"* and seven prominent merchants and farmers were elected. They were Joseph Moulsdale, principal officer of customs; John Prescott, farmer; Philip Whiteway, stone merchant; Thomas Hazlehurst, soap boiler;

Charles Simpson, slate and flint merchant; John Hignett, farmer and William Jardine. At their first meeting the select vestry passed a resolution to do all they could to stop begging and vagrancy in the township.

The town had grown considerably since 1781 when the constable had purchased a chest in which to keep the town's documents and now the tradition of conducting the town's business in the "Boat House Inn" or in the "Bowling Green Inn" was out of favour. A more dignified venue was needed and as the building of a town hall was beyond the resources of the township the vestry rented a cottage in which to conduct its meetings. During 1822 and for the next twelve months road maintenance was again the priority. Weston village in 1803 had been described as *"being out of the way of roads"* and twenty years later it was still a detached community. The magistrate's order to *"put in repair the road over Runcorn Hill"* (presumably Weston Road) was an expensive project and the vestry asked Quarter Sessions for more time to be allowed before the work should be carried out.

On August 20th 1823 the right of way to the ferry was challenged when a gate and fencing were erected across the lane leading to the river. A town's meeting was called and a strong resolution was passed: *"That the Surveyor of the Highways be authorised and directed to take down the gate and fencing which is placed across the highway leading to the Ferry at the south end of what is commonly called Pig Lane — and further — in case of the Surveyor aforesaid refusing or neglecting to put this order in force by noon tomorrow, that the town will indemnify any person or persons who will or may remove the same, as well as any person or persons against whom any proceedings arising out of the business may be instituted"*. The trouble had arisen because of the resiting of the ferry crossing. The ancient landing place had been the "Old Gut" or the Boat House Pool, a natural inlet or creek which was situated in the centre of the township. This pool had been enclosed by the Trustees of the Duke of Bridgewater and by the "Old Quay" or Mersey and Irwell Company. The ferry crossing was then removed to a new location near to the Parish Church. Deprived of the right to use the Boat House Pool, the vestry took immediate action when the road to the new ferry landing was claimed to be private property. The prompt action taken by the vestry seems to have been totally effective for there is no further reference to the dispute in the town records.

The town's major outlet was the turnpike road from Runcorn to Northwich which was completed in 1820 and, reading between the lines, it appears that the turnpike trustees were guilty of attempting to claim the ferry road as part of their highway, for the minute relating to the matter records the following resolution: *"Resolved that Mr. William Wright and Mr. Thomas Hazlehurst be requested by this meeting to attend the earliest meeting of the Commissioners or Trustees of the road leading from Runcorn to Northwich with a view of ascertaining whether a certain road leading from the north-west end of Church Lane to the river at or near Castle Rock is part of the said road and consequently a Highway or not".*

Other matters dealt with in 1823 include the repair of the pinfold for stray farm animals on Mill Brow, the fencing of the quarry at Delph Bridge and the repair of *"that part of the highway which leads past the stables of the Bridgewater Canal to Pig Lane".*

Drastic action was taken to curb the nuisance of stray dogs roaming the town and the vestry ordered the levying of a special rate on dog owners. The overseer of the highways was *"empowered to appoint a person (after notice is given through the town by the bell-man) to kill every dog that might be found loose in the streets until the next vestry meeting and that the person so appointed be paid two shillings per diem and two shillings for every dog he might kill and that he may be indemnified by the town".* At the next meeting of the vestry it was decided to continue the draconian measure.

At a Court Leet on the 8th October 1824 the old parish constables were removed from office and new ones were appointed. It seems that the old officers were reluctant to give up their positions and they refused to surrender their insignia of office. The records contain the following resolution: *"Resolved that a deputation of three or four persons be appointed to call upon the late constables to request them to deliver up keys, staffs, handcuffs and all other materials belonging to the town in their possession. In case of the constables refusing to comply with the above request then the present constable be authorised to procure keys, staffs, handcuffs and other materials for the town's use at the town's expense".* As there is no further reference to the dispute it must be assumed that the matter was settled without acrimony.

Twelve months later the vestry appointed Mr. William Harding to be assistant overseer of the poor, vestry clerk, constable and collector of rates and taxes at a salary of £60 per year with travelling expenses for all journeys undertaken over five miles from the town's offices. Mr. Harding was a very able public servant and he held his various offices for nearly a quarter of a century.

The prevalence of petty crime had become a vexatious problem and Mr. Frederick Master, the vicar, made an appeal to the vestry which prompted quick action. *"That in consequence of the representation of the Vicar requesting the Churchwardens and select vestry to take into consideration the disorderly state of the town in respect to drunkenness it is resolved that the churchwardens and constables be requested to use their utmost endeavours to put the laws in force against all and every person or persons offending against the laws in being for the suppression of vice and immorality and that this vestry will support and uphold them in their endeavours to suppress the present disorderly state of the township and that the constables do give public notice to that effect, first individually to each publican and secondly, by posting bills in different parts of the town".*
As usual the roundhouse was in need or repair. It was inadequate for the needs of the township and the vestry decided not to renovate it but to construct a new one. It was now that the possibility of building a municipal headquarters was considered. A sub-committee was appointed to explore the *"building of a suitable lock-up house or bridewell … in support of the laws and peace of the inhabitants and to extend such a building for the further purpose of the town's use in offices and dwelling for the paid constable as well as the possibility of affecting the establishment of a Justice's Petty Session at Runcorn".* The committee was required to find a suitable site and submit costs. The chairman of the committee was James Bradshaw and on 22nd April 1830 he presented its report.

The site chosen for the town hall was in the centre of the township at the junction of Bridge Street, High Street and Mersey Street. The land was given by the Bridgewater Trustees for the payment of a nominal annual rent of five shillings. The committee was also able to report that it had received the support of the local J.P. as well as that of the Chairman of the County Quarter Sessions for holding Petty Sessions in Runcorn. It was pointed out that *"the heavy expenses now incurred by the want of the projected establishment would be reduced if the plans be carried into effect and the result will prove a considerable annual saving to the ratepayer and which may be rated at not less than £80 per year".*

The report was unanimously adopted, the committee was thanked for its efforts and plans were prepared and approved. The new town hall, constructed mainly of local stone, was built by William Rigby for £450, the money being borrowed at 5% to be paid off in three years. The facilities included a large court room for petty sessions and public business as well as living accommodation for the constable. In the basement there were seven cells for prisoners on remand. The town hall was completed in 1831.

At the completion of the town hall Mr. William Harding was re-appointed assistant overseer of the poor, assistant surveyor of the highways and constable of the township at an improved salary

The first town hall of 1831 and the fountain which was erected in 1857.

of £75 per annum. The first vestry meeting was held in the new building on July 22nd 1831 when it was resolved to repair the road from Big Pool Brook to "Moffland Lane". The principal business of the meeting was to appoint a town doctor following the death of Dr. Case. The vestry decided to appoint Dr. Case's son, Dr. Thomas Case, to the position because he now had to support his mother. The vestry meeting in October decided *"That an oil lamp be purchased for the outside door of the Sessions House and one for the inside of the lobby of the new Town Hall"*. It was to be another seven years before Runcorn had its gas works and for some years after that there was no public lighting of the streets. The vestry at this meeting ordered Mr. Harding to purchase four pairs of blankets and four rugs for use in the new bridewell.

The Cholera

Although it was a small place away from large centres of population Runcorn did not escape the visitation of cholera which first appeared in Britain's cities in 1831. The vestry anticipated the possibility of a local epidemic and on 9th December 1831 laid plans to reduce the risk of infection. A Board of Health was formed to promote cleanliness in the township and to organise the removal of unhygienic nuisances. The following members constituted the Board:

Captain James Bradshaw, Chairman; the Reverend Frederick Master; the Reverend John Walsh, the Methodist minister; Reverend George Fowler of St. John's; the surgeons, Samuel Myles, Edward Myles, Thomas Case, John Dunn and R. Grindrod, in addition to twelve other vestry members and men of consequence in the township.

The Board was soon called into action the following summer when cholera was identified in the areas of poor housing off Mersey Street. The town was divided into five districts with a number of members of the Board charged with the responsibility of keeping an eye on developments in each area. Public subscription was raised in order to equip a temporary hospital near the Bridgewater Canal which was granted rent free by the Bridgewater Trustees and the Board provided blankets and other necessities for cholera cases who were promptly isolated in the hospital. The efforts of the Board to contain the infection seems to have been successful but between 18th June and 25th October 1832 there were 36 cases of cholera, eighteen of whom died of the disease. About £130 was expended on the hospital during the emergency.

By May 1833 it was obvious that the danger had passed and the Board concluded its efforts by passing a vote of thanks to the indomitable Captain Bradshaw *"for his unwearied and zealous attention to the duties of chairman of the Board of Health at a time which required great sacrifice both of time and comfort to himself".* The Bridgewater Trustees were also thanked for the use of the hospital. Four months after receiving recognition for his services during the epidemic Captain Bradshaw died by his own hand. It was expected that after serving for 15 years as Deputy Superintendent to the Bridgewater Trustees he would succeed his father, Robert Haldane Bradshaw, as Superintendent. The father had the right under the Duke of Bridgewater's will, to appoint his own successor and he appointed not his own talented son but James Sothern, one of his staff. The disappointment proved too much for James Bradshaw and he cut his own throat.

Two of the victims of the cholera have gravestones which record the visitation. Beside the north door of the Parish Church is the grave of Jane, the wife of the Reverend John Walsh who was a member of the Board of Health. The inscription on the stone reads:

"Beneath this stone was deposited the remains of
Jane, the beloved and affectionate wife of the Reverend J. Walsh, who died of cholera, September 2nd 1832, aged 36 years and 10 months. To her sudden death was sudden glory. For more than twenty years she had walked in the light of God's countenance and adorned her Christian profession by an unblameable conversation.
She was a woman of meek and quiet spirit, eminently patient in affliction, and greatly loved by all who knew her. Here also lie the ashes of Joseph, her infant son, who died two days after of the same disease, aged 14 months.

Cholera claimed John Dunn, the surgeon. His grave is also to be found in the Parish Churchyard. The stone has the inscription:

"Sacred to the memory of John Dunn, Surgeon, who departed this life August 26th 1832 aged 28 years. His amiable and obliging manners endeared him to all who knew him; his laborious exertions were kind and indefatigable to the sufferings of others during the rage of cholera when he fell a victim to that disease.

Although the epidemic had occupied the attention of the vestry for some months other matters were not neglected. The members were aware of allegations that some of the town's pawnbrokers were carrying on business of a dubious nature and by so doing they were encouraging theft and drunkenness in the township. The vestry claimed that *"after careful investigation of every circumstance relative to the manner in which the pawnbroking business is carried on in this place it does appear that considerable blame is attached to the parties engaged therein for the culpable manner in which they have lately acted, thereby tending to encourage theft and dishonesty".* The constable

received instructions to supply the pawnbrokers with copies of the vestry's resolution to act against any pawnbrokers who broke the law. Mr. Harding was also ordered to have printed and posted up a hundred handbills warning the poor not to frequent public houses.

In 1833 the first effective Act of Parliament fixing legal limits for the working hours of children and young persons in factories was passed. Children under nine years of age were not to be employed and those under 13 years were not to be employed for more than eight hours a day. Young people between the age of thirteen and eighteen were not to be employed for more than twelve hours a day or for sixty–nine hours a week. The vestry was quick to implement the ruling and the constable was instructed to visit Messrs Wood and Stubbs' pin manufactury in Martin's Gardens (Nelson Street). Mr. Harding was to interview the manager to express the vestry's view that *"The time the children are kept at work in the evening viz. eight o'clock is too long (from 7a.m. to 8p.m.) and they (the vestry) think that 10 hours of the day viz. from 7 to 12 noon and from 1 to 6p.m. is long enough for the children to be kept at work".*

By the Poor Law Amendment Act of 1834 the relief of the poor was no longer made by the select vestry but by a relieving officer appointed by a Board of Guardians of the Poor, the new body responsible for Poor Law administration. The Act decreed that outdoor relief was to be abolished and people unable to support themselves were to be accepted into poorhouses which were made as unpleasant as possible so that likely inmates would be encouraged to seek work. Parishes were encouraged to combine into "Unions" in order to finance the cost of building a local workhouse. Fortunately, Runcorn was spared a workhouse for more than twenty years and the poor continued to receive outdoor relief until Dutton workhouse was opened in 1857.

Under the provisions of another Act, the Lighting and Watching Act of 1833, the town decided at a meeting held on June 14th 1836 to adopt the Act as far as street lighting went and to light some streets with gas lamps. A Board of Lighting Inspectors was elected and Mr. John Crippin was appointed treasurer with Mr. John Tindall as the secretary. Street lamps were ordered and it was resolved that the lamp posts should be made of *"good solid English oak ten feet six inches long, eight inches square at the base tapering to four inches at the top and to be of octagonal shape and well dressed".* This resolution was later rescinded but no order for iron lamp posts appears in the minutes. In 1839 it was decided that two pounds three shillings and sixpence was to be paid to the Gas Company for each lamp. Later in the year the vestry allowed the gas inspectors the sum of £220 for the year.

In the first week of 1839 the region was struck by a hurricane. A storm of unprecedented ferocity devastated shipping at Liverpool and caused widespread damage and casualties across the country. An eye-witness recorded in his diary something of the situation in Runcorn the day after the storm. *"I find that in consequence of the tremendous gale of last night, the most awful calamities have taken place in this town and particularly on the river. It is dangerous to walk in the streets this morning on account of the chimneys and slates which are falling. I was quite prepared to go home but I find that both Runcorn packets are sunk. The sight of the river is truly terrific, on every hand you see nothing but wrecks. Several people have been killed during the night from the falling in of the roofs of houses. In the town and neighbourhood nine persons have been killed. In this river and on the banks the loss of life has been frightful".*

Urban Growth

In the first forty years of the last century Runcorn's population increased more than five-fold to reach nearly 7,000 inhabitants by 1841 and as the century progressed the town spread westwards from its original nucleus at the Boat House Pool towards the Parish Church. More development took place with quarrymen's cottages at Mill Brow, Frederick Street and Windmill Street.

There were no planning regulations or bye-laws to prevent the crowding together of hastily thrown up small dwellings. No provision was made for main drainage or for a system of sanitation. There were no arrangements for the disposal of house refuse and the filthy ashpits became a constant source of infection during the summer months. In the courts and tiny houses of the slum area or "Rookery" off Mersey Road, typhus and smallpox were not unknown and child mortality was heavy. Since there was no piped water supply and very few wells, every gallon of water had to be fetched from the Sprinch Brook. Ruth Roberts, Francis Cox and others made their livings as water carriers. The streets were cinder thoroughfares, unlit and ill-kept.

The town's rapid expansion caused major problems. The little Parish Churchyard was now too small to cope with demand and an order was made at the general parish meeting for the diverting of Pig Lane leading to the ferry and the opening up of a new road on the west side of the church to enable an extension to be made to the burial ground. But this was seen to be a short term solution to the problem for it was obvious that within a few years a large cemetery would be needed.

The growth of industry also brought difficulties. The unsightly dumping of alkali waste on the fields south of the Bridgewater Canal caused an outcry and when this resulted in the serious pollution of the Sprinch Brook there was universal uproar. The first sign of trouble appeared towards the end of 1840 when at a town's meeting the Bridgewater Trustees were informed of *"a very offensive nuisance that the public are at present suffering rendered by the filling up of the Sprinch with refuse from the Soaperies which contaminates the water used by the public".* The Trustees took prompt action and pipes were laid in order to prevent further contamination. However the water supply improved for only a few months and by September in the following year the pollution was worse than it had been previously. The Bridgewater Trustees owned the land adjacent to the Sprinch and they had allowed the tipping of waste from the soap works in order to raise the level of the site so that it could be utilised for building. The town committee which had been formed to deal with the problem demanded immediate action by the Trustees to alleviate the nuisance and in a strongly worded communication they expressed the anger felt throughout the township. *"The culvert laid down has not had the effect of removing the nuisance or even abating it and the water which the inhabitants have ever enjoyed remains so impure and so impregnated as not to be by any means fit for use and they hope that no time may be lost in adopting such measures as may be calculated to remove the great nuisance so justly and loudly complained of".*

A reply to this letter of protestation came from Mr. Smith of the Trust. He was desperate to find a quick solution to the problem which had generated so much anger and condemnation towards the Bridgewater management. The Trustees were guilty and Smith was designated to be their peace maker. He wrote to the Committee: *"May I beg you will inform me specifically of the nature of the claims you have on the Trustees and what is required that they should do further with any suggestions that the Trustees can reasonably be expected to accede to".*

Within a month the condition of the brook deteriorated so much that the Trustees were forced into urgent action and instructions were given to lengthen the culvert beyond the point of contamination. As a gesture of good will and to pacify the Committee it seems that the Trustees were prepared to pipe the water to a more convenient spot near the town hall if arrangements could be made with the owners of adjoining property. But the proposed arrangements did not satisfy the Committee and a town's meeting was called so that the matter could be laid before the ratepayers. Messrs.

An early nineteenth century painting of Runcorn windmill.

Tindall and Varey, solicitors, were requested to give the Trustees notice *"that the Committee will not sanction the stopping up in any way or the interfering with the present Sprinch well"*. At the meeting it was resolved that *"the Sprinch well be kept open at both ends as it always has been"*.

There is no doubt that from now on the Trustees made strenuous efforts to solve the problem. The tipping of factory refuse was discontinued and the land was levelled with quarry waste and canal dredgings. It had taken over two years to resolve the matter to the satisfaction of both parties. The town's water supply was wholesome once again and the Trustees were able to develop their land for building.

Urbanisation brought additional demands when the Vestry was faced with the fact that serious fires in the township were a probability and so the members gave some thought to providing a fire engine. They were pleased to record their thanks to God for sparing the town from catastrophic fires. The resolution of 23rd October 1840 concerning the provision of a fire engine is a prayer of thanksgiving: *"It was unanimously agreed upon that this meeting, whilst they would express their gratitude to that Allwise Providence who had hitherto mercifully protected them from the calamities of fire, nevertheless deem it their imperative duty, in humble dependence upon the same Providence for the protection of their lives and property against the perils of fires Providence dictates and as experience in other large and populous places has proved to be necessary.. To that end they recommend that a fire engine or engines be provided"*. As usual a sub-committee was established to seek information and costs but no report was presented because the Bridgewater Trustees had bought a fire engine for their own use and they consented to its use for the extinction of fires in the town. Perhaps the Trustees now wished to ingratiate themselves with the town fathers after the quarrel over the Sprinch.

For a few years into the reign of Queen Victoria Runcorn township still retained something of its rural origins. In 1840 the occupiers of houses with gardens in High Street received notice to prune trees and hedges which were overhanging the footpath and a minute in the town's books records that Mr. Whiteway had agreed that his orchard wall in High Street should be set back in order to widen the street and provide a footpath. In spite of earlier resolutions to discontinue paying for sparrows' heads, the trappers were still being paid a penny-halfpenny a dozen out of the highway rate in 1842. The Board of Surveyors in 1840 gave much of their attention to the improvement of footpaths in the principal streets in the town. The church field path from Doctor's Bridge to the Parish Church was found to be

"almost impassable" and notice was given to the owners of the land to put it in good repair. By 1840 both High Street and Bridge Street were beginning to present continuous building frontages and shops were starting to spread to occupy sites on both sides of Church Street, formerly Church Lane. Increasing traffic meant that the ancient lanes had to be widened. Before 1843 High Street was a narrow lane fronted by cottages with small gardens. In that year the enclosing walls and hedges were taken down and the railings of Bethesda chapel were set back in order to widen the street. It seems that in most cases land required for road widening was given willingly by public-spirited owners. By 1844 definite improvements in street maintenance were obvious and the town bought its first street watering cart. In that same year the town resolved to adopt the whole of the Lighting and Watching Act. The part previously adopted was for lighting only. From now on paid watchmen were employed to patrol the town by night. A number of the vestrymen were appointed inspectors and from this time onwards they formed a governing body as far as lighting and watching were concerned. John Wright was appointed chairman with John Tindall as secretary. The members of the committee were Robert Hedley, William Forster, James Rigby, John Hignett, John Ockleston, Thomas Trefall Rigby, W.B. Gibson and William Whittaker. Mr. R. Richardson was appointed Watchman and Constable for the township at £70 a year and residence in the town hall. An assistant constable was engaged for Saturday and Sunday nights at five shillings a week. In 1846 a permanent assistant constable was appointed at £1 a week and "clothing in part". Two "Burleymen" (bye lawmen) Josiah Savage and William Rigby, were employed to see that the bye-laws were enforced whilst John Shepherd became "Pig pounder, bailiff and common crier". Some of the newly-appointed officials were uncertain as to the limits of their jurisdiction. The Sprinch brook formed the boundary between the ancient parish of All Saints and the new ecclesiastical parish of Holy Trinity which came into being in 1840. It was reported that some officials who resided *"to the east of Sprinch brook could not serve because the steward refused to swear them as he considered the brook to be the boundary of the Manor of Runcorn"*. (In 1840 the boundary between the townships of Halton and Runcorn lay to the west of Delph Bridge. Mill Brow, Pool Side (Heath Road), Foundry Lane, part of Bridge Street as far as Cholmondeley Place and part of Irwell Lane were then within jurisdiction of Halton township).

By 1843 the population had increased so much that it had become impossible for one official to discharge efficiently the combined duties of

Assistant Overseer and Collector of the Poor Rate as well as carrying out the duties of Constable. At a meeting on September 10th 1844, it was decided that the office of Assistant Overseer and Collector of Rates and Taxes should be held by someone who was not connected with public office whilst the post of Deputy Constable and Overseer of the Highways would be held by another appointee.

The poor communications to Runcorn caused much concern. The town was isolated with only the tenuous link by ferry to the north and further disadvantaged by the barrier created by the Bridgewater Canal, which, because of its narrow bridges, slowed commerce by road. Delph Bridge was a particular source of complaint, its sharp turn being a serious hindrance to the passage of waggons and carts. From about 1842 the town had been pressing the Bridgewater Trustees to improve the narrow bridge and its approaches. Four years later major works were carried out when, to the satisfaction of the public, Delph Bridge was widened and the approaches on both sides made more convenient. Town Bridge sometimes called the Doctors Bridge, was also very awkward being steep and very narrow sufficing only for one cart to pass over at a time. This bridge linked the town to the cart ways of Lowlands Road and the Holloway leading to Higher Runcorn and Weston village. As there was yet little traffic to these outlying districts there was no pressure on the Trustees to improve the bridge.

As the work was in progress on Delph Bridge attention was also given to Mill Brow which was lowered by several feet and at the same time crossings of paving stones were set into the road surface at the ends of certain streets in the town. In July 1848 Wellington Street, Bridgewater Street, Regent Street, Egerton Street, Peel Street and Brook Street were adopted by the town as public thoroughfares. Two years later it was resolved to *"make a good road across the Common leading to Weston"*. During the construction of this road the Board of Inspectors were again faced with the problem of squatters on the Heath. They took prompt action and cleared the encroachments of fifty-two enclosures and shacks by breaking down fences and walls. Squatters were always present on the fringes of society and their illegal settlements were alleged to be the source of much criminal activity.

The committee certainly regulated the lives of the town's officers. On 4th June 1850 it was ordered that in keeping with the dignity of their office, Constable Blake should attend the churchwardens at Holy Trinity Church every Sunday morning and Mr. Richardson, the Head Constable, should attend the service at the Parish Church.

The census returns for 1851 indicate that the population of Runcorn was six and a half times what it had been fifty years earlier. In 1851 there were 1,818 houses with a total of 8,688 inhabitants. Industry was booming and unemployment in the town was slight with only 58 men declaring that they were out of work. Seventeen men and fifty-four women were listed as paupers. The rural character of Runcorn shows in the fact that ninety-two men and five women were employed in agriculture, most of them living in Higher Runcorn or between Delph Bridge and Halton. Two hundred and sixty-three women and forty seven girls were employed in domestic service. On the day the census was taken there were 220 persons living on canal boats and barges within the boundaries of Runcorn with a further 234 recorded on craft at Weston Point. The rateable value of Runcorn township in 1851 amounted to £26,465.

The 1843 tithe map of the township shows that Higher Runcorn and the land to the east of Holy Trinity church was still, in the main, meadow and pasture with one or two arable fields. Some of the ancient field names had endured the centuries to give evidence of their former uses: Brick Kiln Field, Tan Yard Field, Marl Field and Smithy Field. There was a Millfield in Weston and in the sixteenth century, the windmill stood somewhere near the present water tower. Clifton also had a Millfield. The names of families who had lived in the township centuries before were perpetuated in field names with Muskett's Acres, Cooper's meadow, Alcock's Big Acres, Parr's Croft, Woodward's Hill and Greg's Acres. Some of the field names bear testimony of agricultural land won from waste or woodland with such names as Long Ridding, Little Poop Ridding and Big Poop Ridding. By 1843 the main streets of today's Runcorn were in being as roads or footpaths. Present-day High Street, Bridge Street, Moughland Lane, Holloway, Greenway Road and Irwell Lane follow the identical line of the lanes and pathways of the ancient township and the same is true of the roads in Halton village. Some of the old street names give clues to their history: Windmill Street; Mill Street, which was situated near to the steam mill at Old Quay; Ferry Lane; Pool Lane, which led to the creek or Pool of Runcorn. Pool Lane had been known in the eighteenth century as Sour Milk Lane or Buttermilk Lane. Until well into modern times Westfield Road was Cock and Hen Lane whilst present-day Balfour Street was Waterfall Lane. Lodge Lane in Halton was the road to the ancient hunting lodge. Spark Lane indicates the presence of the smithy whilst Pump Lane was the source of the village water supply.

For some years the administration of Runcorn

township had been managed from a cottage in Vicar Street. By 1848 these premises were totally inadequate and new offices were built on land next to the town hall. This new building was to serve as the town's public office until the administration moved to Waterloo House in Waterloo Road which became the new town hall in 1884.

Runcorn's principal landowners in early Victorian times included the Orred family of Higher Runcorn. When Vicar Alcock died in 1798 his great nephew, John Orred and his great nieces, Ann, Elizabeth, Jane and Mary Orred inherited land under his will. By 1850 Ann Orred owned property in Weston and in Higher and Lower Runcorn. In Weston township the main landowners besides Ann Orred were Thomas and John Johnson, the soap and alkali manufacturers; the quarry owners, James Collier, John Tomkinson and John Wright; Philip Whiteway who was a shipbuilder and quarry master and William Bankes, farmer. The Bridgewater Trustees and the Mersey and Irwell Navigation Company also owned agricultural land in Runcorn township whilst the Marquis of Cholmondeley, the Lord of the Manor of Runcorn, owned much of Clifton with other land and properties throughout Halton and Runcorn.

Sir Richard Brooke dominated Norton and Stockham with considerable holdings in Halton, Acton Grange and Moore. From Tudor times the Brooke family had played a role in county matters, Colonel Henry Brooke in 1644 had served as High Sheriff of Cheshire and from then until the early nineteenth century every generation of the family provided a Sir Richard Brooke who held the office. However, during the Victorian period the Brookes began to play a lessening part in county affairs although they continued their active interest in local matters, serving as Justices of the Peace, Volunteer officers and as chairmen of various local committees. Whilst it is true that the ancient impost of the tithe demand, due to Sir Richard Brooke, was a source of some local resentment, the Brooke family was universally held in high esteem. They were paternalistic squires, fair employers and enlightened landlords. On November 17th 1865 in a spontaneous display of respect for the late Sir Richard Brooke, the sixth baronet, Runcorn's Commissioners and leading citizens together with a large assemblage of townsfolk, met the funeral cortege in Halton road. All the shops in Bridge Street, High Street and Church Street were closed as the great procession passed on its way to the Parish Church.

Pre-industrial Runcorn. "The shore all the way to Weston Point is protected by a low ridge of rock rising almost perpendicular from the beach. The lovers of botany may find a pleasing variety of plants both maritime and inland varieties in the vicinity of this place". John Aikin 1795.

Bibliography

Much of the information in this chapter has been gathered together from documentary evidence. Among the primary sources used were: the Account Book of the Overseers of the Poor for the township of Weston (1704-1812) and the Constables' Accounts for Weston (1702-1812) which are deposited at the County Record Office, Chester. The Town Book of Halton township which dates from 1698 is deposited in the local history library of the Municipal Library in Warrington. John Simpson's printed *Abstract of the Minute Book of Runcorn 1751-1851* is to be found at the Runcorn Library, Shopping City, Runcorn. A most useful, comprehensive survey of early town management in Runcorn is William Handley's "After Many Years" and his "Local Memoranda" which were written for the *Runcorn Weekly News* in 1902.

Other documentary sources included: The Constables' Accounts of Runcorn township (1781-1834); the Accounts of the Overseers of the Poor (1810-1834) and the Surveyor of the Highways records of Runcorn township all of which are in the local history collection at the library, Shopping City, Runcorn.

Useful detail appertaining to land ownership in Runcorn in the early nineteenth century has been obtained from the Runcorn Tithe Map of 1844 and from "A Littoral Survey of the Port of Liverpool" by J. Boult in the *Transactions of the Lancashire and Cheshire Historic Society* Vol. 22, 1869.

The references to Frodsham Bridge have been taken from Ormerod, from *Cheshire Sheaf*, October 1925 and from "Ancient Fords, Ferries and Bridges in Cheshire" by William Harrison in *Transactions of the Lancashire and Cheshire Antiquarian Society* Vol. XIV, 1896.

Further detail has been gleaned from *"A Visitor's Guide to Runcorn and its Vicinity"* by G. Fowler (1834) and also from *"Weston. Historical Notes and Walk"*, St. John's Church, Weston (1977).

Top Locks in the early 1930s.
Photograph "Liverpool Daily Post and Echo".

Chapter 10
The Bridgewater Canal

Situated far from any main road or centre of population both Runcorn and Halton in the mid eighteenth century were little known outside the immediate locality. The ferry crossing at Runcorn had some local importance but the township itself was a cul-de-sac, a lonely rural settlement of no consequence with a scattered population of a few hundred people. The nucleus of the hamlet was a group of small dwellings by the 'Old Gut' where the Sprinch brook entered the river. Here there was a small wooden bridge called Pool Bridge which linked the houses on one side of the creek with those opposite.

By using the remembrances of elderly people, John Simpson, who was born in Runcorn about 1818, wrote an account of the village as it was about 1760 before the coming of the Bridgewater Canal. He tells us that there were few substantial houses. Indeed, he doubted if there were more than thirty dwellings all told. Below Delph Bridge in "Towngate", now Canal Street, there was then a large house which was the home of the Wright family but, by the time Simpson was writing in 1860, the house had been sub-divided into labourers' cottages. At the top of Bridge Street in 1760 there were a few thatched cottages on the left hand side going down and below them on the same side, a large house known as the "Old Hall'. This house seems to have been the home of a well-to-do family. Simpson tells us it was "large, lofty and well finished" and much more impressive than another 'Old Hall' in High Street. Where the "Wilsons Hotel" now stands there was a small pot house called "The Ship" and on the site of the market hall (today's public swimming baths) one or two more cottages. Opposite them there was another old house which was the home of a family of some standing in the township. The "Royal Hotel" was then a tiny thatched public house called the "White Hart".

By the Sprinch stream was the site of Runcorn's ancient water mill and Simpson tells us that in 1831 when the foundations of the new town hall were being excavated heavy timbers which had formed the dam or the framework of the medieval mill were discovered. According to tradition the Sprinch brook was at one time the boundary between Runcorn township and Halton. The former "Boat House Inn" in Mersey Road is believed to date from Elizabethan times when it was two cottages.

Where High Street met Church Lane there were

a few more thatched cottages but there were no other buildings between them and the Parish Church. Further up High Street on the site of the present St. Paul's Health Centre was Camden Croft, an old farm with a barn and outbuildings and a little further on, a thatched tavern called "The Raven". Beyond this was a stone-built Jacobean house which, by Victorian times, had become known as the "Old Hall". This house lasted into the days of photography and from photographs and earlier paintings it is shown to have been a sizeable farm house with a cobbled yard and stone-built stables and shippons.

A black and white timber-framed house occupied a site somewhere near the present South Bank Hotel and Simpson tells us that there was a "Jessamine Cottage" nearby. In Higher Runcorn in 1760 there were four or five cottages near to the vicarage, two or three more on the road leading to the river and, apart from a couple of houses and the farm in what is now Heath Road, very few others. Such was Runcorn hamlet in the first year of George III's reign.

Weston village had one or two imposing sandstone houses dating from the previous century, notably the Old Hall and the Manor Farmhouse, but there were barely a hundred and fifty inhabitants in the hamlet and Weston Point did not exist.

But the situation was about to change and from being an unknown place of little consequence, Runcorn was soon to become a vital link in Britain's inland waterways system during the Industrial Revolution. In December 1761 James Brindley visited Runcorn with the intention of surveying a route for the extension of the Duke of Bridgewater's Worsley to Manchester Canal to the Mersey. Brindley considered the possibility of making the terminus of the new canal at Hempstones, just east of Runcorn village and he spent a couple of days studying the tides and gauging the depth of water at this point.

His travelling expenses were presented in his unorthodox spelling: *"Expenses for his Grace Duk of Bridgwater to pay for traveling Chareges by James Brindley. December 21st to inspect to flux and reflux at Ham Stone ... 2 dayes charges ... £0..6..6".*

The story of the promotion and construction of the Bridgewater Canal has been told by many historians and various accounts are available in our public libraries. The present work does not seek to retell the story but one or two contemporary accounts of the great undertaking might serve to illustrate local events.

The proposed route for the canal passed through the estate of Sir Richard Brooke at Norton and Sir Richard was not pleased with the way the plans were developing. He had carried out an expensive remodelling of his mansion, laid out landscaped grounds and gardens with a lake and he was appalled at the prospect of boatmen poaching his game and wildfowl. Sir Richard valued the tranquillity of Norton and he did not want to see unsightly canal works anywhere near his house. When the Bridgewater Canal Extension Act was passed in 1762 it stipulated that the cut should not be made within 325 metres of the house; the towing path had to be on the southern bank; no quays, buildings, hedges or fences were to obstruct the views from the mansion, and except for the period during the construction of the canal, no vessels were to be moored within a thousand metres of the Priory. The Act also laid down that the streams which supplied Sir Richard's mill pool could not be diverted and that all excavated spoil from the excavations near the estate should be removed from the site within a year.

Sir Richard did not see the necessity for a canal. He believed that the Mersey and Irwell Navigation Company could carry far more than the existing Liverpool-Manchester trade by the old river route. He thought that the proposed canal would cause inconvenience to his tenants and other landowners by dividing farms. Much valuable land would be lost and the undertaking would drain away waters which supplied the rivers so that the Mersey and Irwell Navigation would be adversely effected during dry seasons. Sir Richard also doubted the practicality of a terminus at the Hempstones and he wrote to the Duke pointing out that the most experienced Mersey watermen believed *"that at nip tides you will not have sufficient water to carry on your boats from Hempstone to Runcorne"*. The plan for the canal to exit at Hempstones was abandoned when the Duke agreed to link his canal with that of the Trent and Mersey at Preston Brook but the detour added greatly to his soaring expenses.

For years Sir Richard Brooke determined that the canal should not pass through his demesne and his resolute opposition only weakened in the face of public opinion which was whole-heartedly in favour of the canal. Sir Richard then demanded an exorbitant charge for the right to cross his land, costs which the Duke could not afford. Nevertheless, work on the canal commenced shortly after the passing of the Act to allow the extension of the waterway from Stretford to the Hempstones in 1762. Sir Richard showed no sign of relenting even when the works were largely complete and the Runcorn locks

had been opened on January 1st 1773. At Norton a mile of canal remained to be dug and in the meantime the Duke's barges had to be unloaded and their contents carted around the Priory estate. At Astmoor a range of buildings was erected for packhorses and carts. This wearisome operation added to the Duke's overburdened expenses but Sir Richard's opposition was crumbling as merchants and shippers became exasperated at the delays to growing trade caused by his obstinacy. Throughout the region there was a desire to see the great waterway complete: *"It is the universal wish of the country that the only remaining obstacle to the completion of the canal may be speedily removed and that the dispute between his Grace and Sir Richard Brooke be amicably adjusted and the public eased of an expense of one shilling and eight pence per ton which must be paid for the land carriage of goods over the intermediate space of ground"*. In December 1775 Sir Richard Brooke bowed to the inevitable and a compromise was reached — thirteen years after the passing of the Act for the extension of the Bridgewater Canal to Runcorn.

By March 1776 the canal was complete throughout its length to Manchester. The fact that the canal towing path is diverted from one side of the waterway to the other for a considerable distance beyond Astmoor Bridge remains as evidence of the long dispute and Sir Richard Brooke's determination to keep boatmen away from his gardens and wild life.

The construction of the Bridgewater Canal was carried out with careful forward planning and attention to detail. The scheduling of building material and the removal of the spoil was carried out efficiently and there was little disruption in the daily life of the small communities through which it passed. At the opening of Runcorn locks a local account noted: *"It must be added to the honour of his Grace and the reputation of his agents, that there never was a work, either public or private, better conducted or carried on with greater order and regularity in the execution, or punctuality in respect of payment, nor with less cause of complaint than this has been"*.

The Bridgewater Canal was designed for the sole purpose of carrying freight but it also helped to lessen the isolation of Runcorn for shortly after the canal was complete, the Duke built passenger boats to satisfy the curiosity of tourists who came to see his canal. He then established a regular passenger service between Warrington and Manchester by which travellers were conveyed for a penny a mile. The boat journeys were cheap and convenient and the Duke offered to let the boats for £60 a year but as there were no takers he had to run them himself. Within a couple of years the boats had become so popular that the

Duke found that they were making him clear profits of £1,600 a year and so the service was extended to Runcorn.

The passenger service from Runcorn Top Locks, to Manchester took eight hours and the boats could each accommodate about a hundred people. The coming of the canal made possible comfortable travel and many people used the passenger boats in order to visit markets in Warrington, Lymm, Altrincham and Manchester. The sedate journey through the Cheshire countryside was appreciated by passengers who could avail themselves of light meals served by the stewardess. A German visitor has recorded his experience of travel by the canal boats: *"For the comfort of passengers a covered passenger boat which resembles the Dutch canal boats, goes twice a week from Manchester to Runcorn and return. One cannot travel more pleasantly, in more comfort or more cheaply than in these boats. Their length is fifty-six feet, width eight feet and the height inside at the centre is seven feet. At the top of the deck stands a post on which is hooked the towing rope by which it is drawn by a horse, at the foot of this post lies a pulley, block and tackle whereby a sail can be hoisted by the boatman at the helm and can be held in the desired direction. The barge goes five English miles every hour and calls at two stations where the horses, which stand ready in specially built stables, are changed and where the passengers often halt for longer than an hour, the journey from Runcorn to Manchester being completed in eight hours. The charge per person for the whole trip in the general quarters is two shillings and three pence and three shillings and sixpence for the special accommodation"*. The packets started from Top Locks with more passengers boarding at Delph Bridge. The Duke of Bridgewater took particular pleasure in travelling by his own boats.

The Duke had encountered many difficulties during the building of his great work but in one respect he was fortunate. At Runcorn there were quarries which produced excellent stone which was the ideal material for the construction of locks and basins. Josiah Wedgewood visited Runcorn in June 1773. Like many other sightseers he was awed by the size of the undertaking and by the ingenious methods which were used in the building of the locks. He thought that the locks were *"truly wonderfull ... I was quite astonished at the vastness of the plan and the greatness of stile in the execution. The walls of the locks are truly admirable, both for strength and beauty of workmanship. The front lock next to the sea (for such it seems when the tide is in) in particular, whose walls are composed of vast stones from one to twelve tons weight, and yet by the excellent machinery made use of, some of which is left standing, they had as perfect command of these huge masses of rock, as a common bricklayer has of the brick in his hand ... the whole seems to be the work of Titans, rather than a production of our pigmy race of beings."*

James Brindley was often absent on canal projects in other parts of the country and it became the duty of John Gilbert to oversee the engineering of the lock staircase. The work was completed three months after Brindley's death. Amid feasting and rejoicing the "Heart of Oak", a vessel of 50 tons from Liverpool, passed twenty-seven metres up the ten locks into the canal on New Year's Day 1773. Six hundred of the Duke's workmen were entertained on the side of the locks with roast beef and good liquor and there were many toasts including "Prosperity to trade and navigation" and "Prosperity to the town of Runcorn". The Duke's health and those of John Gilbert and General Cholmondeley, the Lord of the Manor of Runcorn, were toasted as well as the

Sir Richard Brooke, the fourth baronet, resisted the Duke of Bridgewater's plans to cut his canal through the Norton Priory estate.

health of "All honest fellows who have exerted themselves in the execution of these works". However, the ceremony at the opening of the locks was little more than a publicity exercise for the completion of the undertaking was to be delayed for three more years by the intransigence of Sir Richard Brooke.

The locks were the wonder of their time. Built to accommodate barge traffic, nine locks each had a fall of two metres with the river lock having a fall in excess of six metres at low water to permit vessels to enter and leave the canal on any tide.

The locks soon became a popular tourist attraction. In June 1780 Samuel Curwen, a

Bridgewater House, the Duke of Bridgewater's Runcorn Residence.

refugee from America during the War of Independence, sailed along the canal in a passenger boat which he said held a hundred sightseers. The journey from Warrington to Runcorn took two hours after which Mr. Curwen inspected the locks. He observes, *"The ascent from river to canal is 74 feet in a distance of short ¼ mile ... the time taking up and letting a boat into the canal from the lowest lock is 2½ hours and Mr. S.S. and myself often did the whole process, which we're told was the usual time"*. Samuel Curwen also gives us a glimpse of the local social life. He dined at the "White Hart" and he writes *"The inn was crowded with great numbers of jolly lads and lasses, met to congratulate our landlady's daughter lately married and just returned home after a week's absence. The concluding scene of Sunday, being considered in England a relief from*

labour is generally spent in the alehouses by the middling and lower sorts in merry-making".

Four years after Curwen's visit two Frenchmen came to see the Duke's locks. M. de Givry and M. Dulubre were impressed by the scale of the undertaking and by the magnitude of the shipping and commercial activity at Liverpool, but, unlike Mr. Curwen, it seems that they did not find English taverns to their liking for M. de Givry noted in his diary: *"At Runcorn we made one of the worst possible breakfast-dinners"*.

In order to oversee the construction of the Runcorn end of his canal, the Duke built a large house as an occasional residence near to the line of locks. To the south of Bridgewater House were the warehouses, docks and basins. The Duke soon found that the Mersey deposited mud and sand in the sailing channel beyond the canal entrance and in order to obviate this nuisance, he cut a narrow channel across Runcorn promontory from Castle Rock to the lock gates. This cut, known as the "Duke's Gut", did not always function satisfactorily but, when it did, the strong ebb tides rushed through the channel to clear away the mud at the canal entrance. A permanent arched bridge was built across the Gut at its eastern end. It was similar in design to the familiar hump-backed bridges to be seen along the canal and because it was sited at Ethelfleda's rock it was known as Castle Bridge.

Many of the navvies or 'navigators' who had built the canal were accommodated in old ships moored at the river's edge. They left the town when their work was finished but there was some increase in Runcorn's population as labourers, craftsmen, overseers and company agents from outside the area found employment in the undertaking. Employment opportunities increased and boatmen, dock porters, warehousemen, lockmen and stablemen were recruited locally. Housing expanded in the area close to the docks. Among the first houses to be built were those in Welsh Row, English Row, Crescent Row, Gilbert Street, Sothern Street and St. James Street and, at the eastern edge of the township there was some housing development at Delph Bridge. This new housing illustrated the impact the docks and canal had on Runcorn hamlet for, with the coming of improved transport facilities, traditional building material ceased to be used and the houses were built of brick, Welsh slate and imported timber carried on the waterways.

The Trent and Mersey Canal was authorised by Act of Parliament in 1766 and it joined the Duke's canal at Preston Brook. When it was finished in 1777 it opened up communications between Liverpool and the Midlands. Unlike the Duke of Bridgewater's wide canal, the Trent and Mersey is a narrow-gauge waterway, the locks permitting only the passage of craft of narrow beam. This meant that the manufactured goods from the Midlands had to be discharged from the narrow-boats at Runcorn or at Preston Brook and then transhipped into larger river craft to be carried to Liverpool there to be discharged once again for loading into sea-going vessels. Eight years before the completion of the Bridgewater undertaking it had become obvious to certain Liverpool merchants and shippers that time and money would be saved if it became possible for canal boats to pass from the Midlands and Manchester straight into Liverpool by way of an aqueduct over the Mersey at Runcorn Gap and then, by means of a new cut, to the Liverpool quays. The newspaper "Williamson's Liverpool Advertiser" reported on 19th July 1768 that James Brindley met several leading men of Liverpool "to ascertain the expense that may attend the building of a bridge across the Mersey". The ambitious project was not proceeded with because of the enormous costs involved. The idea of carrying the Duke's canal from Runcorn by means of high embankments and arches across the river and valley of the Mersey is quite staggering. However, if Brindley's aqueduct had been built it would have been the greatest civil engineering undertaking of the century and certainly a most fitting monument to his genius.

From the middle years of the 1770s an ever increasing trade passed through Runcorn. The Duke's canal carried boats laden with iron goods and crated pottery from Staffordshire and with coal and bales of cloth from Manchester, down the locks into the tideway for the port of Liverpool and the world market. The canal even won some of the river Weaver salt traffic with substantial cargoes of rock salt being transported to the refineries at Liverpool. The reverse trade to Manchester included cargoes of raw cotton, wool, roofing slates, sugar, grain and timber whilst flints, ball clay and china clay were taken to the Staffordshire potteries.

A tidal basin was constructed at the entrance to the canal in 1775 and this allowed craft to be assembled before ascending the locks, but few coasting vessels arrived at Runcorn in the first years of the canal's existence because the Mersey's difficult sailing channels were not marked by navigation buoys and only river craft of shallow draught could cross the awkward approaches to the canal. However, determined efforts were made to improve matters. The tidal basin was enlarged and in 1791 a new dock was finished. When the dock was opened in November there was a feast provided for the workmen and the Duke gave a roasted ox with additional meat, potatoes and beer for the navvies each of whom received a free spoon or pepper pot as a souvenir of the event.

The Duke of Bridgewater was often seen in Runcorn. Dressed in outmoded clothes and frequently grimy after watching the unloading of coal barges, the Duke took a keen interest in the everyday activities of his waterway and sometimes he could be heard giving his instructions in an affected broad Lancashire accent. Over the years he made frequent visits to reside in the house which he had built near to the locks. Bridgewater House or, as it was generally styled, "The Big House", was connected to the public roads by a private coach road which was laid out between the line of locks and the reservoirs.

The Bridgewater Canal was the vital route by which the products of the mills of Manchester and its hinterland and the manufactured goods from the Midlands reached the Port of Liverpool. The coming of the canal brought about a considerable reduction in transport costs. In 1792 it cost £2.50 to send a ton of pottery by road from Josiah Wedgewood's works at Etruria to Liverpool but when he transported his wares by the canal it cost him only thirteen shillings and four pence (70p). In 1767 the land carriage from Liverpool to Manchester was £2 per ton and by the Mersey and Irwell Navigation it was sixty pence a ton but by the Duke's canal only thirty pence a ton. Carriage by the Duke's waterway was also quicker and safer than by the other routes.

The initial impact of the Bridgewater Canal on Runcorn township was not as great as might be expected. It is true that there was some slight increase in population but even a quarter of a century after the completion of the Duke's work the census returns for 1801 show that there were only 228 houses and 1,397 inhabitants in the town. The Manchester and Salford directory of 1802 noted the beginnings of Runcorn's commercial growth; *"Runcorn is becoming an astonishing place of business ... it is a place of summer resort for sea bathing being very much recommended by physicians for its saline as well as its salubrious properties"*. As yet Runcorn was a place of some consequence only because of its strategic siting as the terminus of the Bridgewater Canal. The canal traffic passed through the town and although the Runcorn quarries were known beyond the immediate district and a ship building and repair industry had been established, it was not until the second decade of the nineteenth century with the coming of the first factories that there was significant urban expansion.

In July 1804 the 7¾ mile Runcorn to Latchford Canal of the Mersey and Irwell Navigation Company was opened. It was cut under powers embodied in the Mersey and Irwell Navigation Act of 1720 which gave powers to make new cuts without the necessity of further recourse to Parliament. This "Old Quay Canal" enabled vessels to proceed to the canalised River Mersey beyond Warrington without them being neaped by the ebb tide at the shallows at Fiddlers Ferry. The new canal had its terminus near the centre of Runcorn township and the Old Quay Company hoped that it would enable them to compete more effectively with the Bridgewater undertaking. The company claimed that their new cut would reduce the time taken from Liverpool to Manchester to twelve hours but it was rarely accomplished in less than eighteen hours.

For most of its length the Runcorn to Latchford Canal was crossed by light turn-bridges and the absence of locks and fixed bridges enabled river flats to use a small sail to assist the horses if the wind allowed. The rivalry between the two canal companies was keenest in the passenger-carrying service. For nearly a quarter of a century the Duke of Bridgewater's canal packet boats had enjoyed lucrative business. In August 1806 the Mersey and Irwell company introduced passenger boats on to their waterway. The down boats from Manchester completed the journey to Runcorn in eight hours — that was one hour less than the Duke's boats but the up boats took the same time to reach Manchester as did the Bridgewater boats.

The Old Quay passenger boats were of heavier construction than those of the Bridgewater Trustees. They were towed by three horses instead of two, the middle horse moving unridden whilst the others were ridden without stirrups by boys whose feet rested on the traces. The fare from Liverpool to Manchester was three shillings and sixpence — about the same as the Duke's but the Old Quay route was not so picturesque. A contemporary account states: *"Although the course of this navigation chiefly leads through the Mersey and Irwell rivers, the prospect is shut out by winding, muddy banks so lofty that at least seventy yards of towrope are used, and the extremity of which is fastened high on the mast above the cross-trees"*.

The connection between Runcorn and Liverpool was by passenger sailing packet. The Liverpool directory for 1803 advertised the service, *"The Runcorn packet sails every day for Runcorn about four hours before high water. First cabin two shillings, second cabin one shilling and sixpence. William Woods, master of the packet"*.

In 1800 the absence of good roads made land travel difficult. Satisfactory road surfaces became common after 1820 but before then the passage of heavy wheeled traffic in winter could quickly reduce the best-made road to ruin. The nearest main highway to Runcorn was the Chester Turnpike which ran through Preston Brook and Daresbury to Warrington. At a meeting of the turnpike's trustees on February 2nd 1787 the following resolution was passed: *"Ordered ... That the gate keepers at the respective Toll Gates be directed to acquaint the persons using narrow wheel waggons with four horses that after Michaelmas Day next, information will be lodged against such persons and that Notices in writing be affixed on the Toll Gates.*

Also ... any vehicle having nails projecting more than a quarter of an inch above the surface of the tyre would be charged ten shillings at every gate they passed through". Carriers were thus forced to use waggons with smooth broad wheels on the grounds that they did less damage to the soft surface of the road.

The coming of the turnpikes was a benefit to trade and commerce because they cut travelling times but they did not resolve all the problems for the new roads often proved difficult to maintain. For instance, the loose gravelled surface of the Runcorn to Northwich turnpike needed constant and expensive renewal after periods of severe weather.

The Old Quay Canal looking east to Wigg works.

The locks of the Old Quay Canal.

Bibliography

The most influential works concerning the impact of the Bridgewater Canal on the economy of Merseyside are *"Canals of North-West England"* (1970) by Charles Hadfield and Gordon Biddle; *"Canal Ports. The Urban Achievement of the Canal Age"* (1977) by J.D. Porteous; *"The Canal Duke"* (1961) by Hugh Mallet and F.C. Mather's *"After the Canal Duke"* (1970). The Bridgewater undertaking has also been dealt with by G. Wheat in *"On the Duke's Cut"* (1977); *"Canals to Manchester"* (1977) by D. Owen and the Bridgewater Department of the Manchester Ship Canal, Handbook (1973). the references to the canal builders were taken from *"Lives of the Engineers"* (1862) by Samuel Smiles: *"James Brindley"* (1956) by Laurence Maynell and *"The Canal Builders"* (1981) by Anthony Burton.

Also used were *"A Collection of the Several Acts Relating to the Canals of the Late Most Noble Francis, Duke of Bridgewater"* (1820); *The Palatine Note Book* (1884) Vol. LV and *"Cheshire 1660 - 1780 Restoration to Industrial Revolution"* (1978) by J. Howard Hodson. Although primarily concerned with the Liverpool end of the Bridgewater operations, Linda Little's "The Duke's Dock in Liverpool" in *The Transactions of the Lancashire and Cheshire Historic Society,* Vol. 133 (1984) provides interesting detail of the importance of Runcorn during two centuries of commercial traffic on the canal.

For the history of the Mersey and Irwell Navigation Company the *"Mersey and Irwell Navigation to Manchester Ship Canal 1720 - 1887"* by Alfred Hayman (1981), Federation of Bridgewater Cruising Clubs, is a most useful publication and J. Corbridge's *"A Pictorial History of the Mersey and Irwell Navigation" (1978)* contains some interesting illustrations of the waterway in the Runcorn area.

Information on the Chester Turnpike is from "The Chester Road, Helsby, Turnpike and Tolls" by W.R. Hawkin, *Cheshire History,* Vol. 6 1980.

Chapter 11
Runcorn, A Health Resort

A few years into the nineteenth century the nation faced a crisis when, during the Napoleonic War, the country was threatened with invasion from France. In the official returns for 1804 Cheshire is credited with raising 5,600 men in readiness to repel an enemy landing. In Runcorn two companies of infantry numbering 146 men were equipped to form the Loyal Runcorn and Weston Volunteer Infantry. The officers came from the local landowning and merchant class. Captain James Adam was the first commanding officer and his officers were Captain Thomas Bate, Lieutenants Thomas Sothern and Samuel Wylde and Ensigns Charles Hickson and William Bankes. In Norton a cavalry troop of sixty men was raised. The Norton Volunteers were commanded by Captain Peter Heron with Lieutenant Richard Brooke, baronet,

and Samuel Dod, Cornet. The Runcorn and Norton Volunteers co-operated with those from Frodsham in field manoeuvres. The Frodsham Volunteers comprised a corps of three hundred infantry formed into four companies.

There can be no doubt that at first the activities of the Volunteers provided some diversion for the quiet township but, when the threat of invasion receded, Runcorn resumed its sleepy ways. The Runcorn and Weston Volunteers remained in being for ten years before being stood down at the end of the war. On July 4th 1818, three years after the battle of Waterloo, the colours of the Volunteer Corps were deposited in the Parish Church. Led by their former commanding officer, Captain Bankes of Weston, the men were addressed by the new vicar of Runcorn, Mr. Frederick Master, who prayed that

Belvedere boarding houses which were "built for the accommodation of summer visitants".

there would be *"no future occasion to withdraw the ensign but should that ever be the case I feel fully confident that you will exhibit the same firmness of mind and intrepedity of spirit which you have hitherto done"*. After the ceremony the ensign was hung from the chancel arch where it remained for twenty-eight years. When the new church was completed there was no place for the old banner and it was used as a floor cloth.

For many centuries the Runcorn area remained little changed and even today when the urban scene is one of sprawling industry and housing, it requires little imagination on the part of the observer to appreciate that the prospect of a hundred and fifty years ago was an unspoiled vista of rare beauty. In 1800 the view across into Lancashire was entirely rural, a landscape of marsh, pasture and woodland. Widnes did not exist and the tiny hamlets of Ditton, Appleton and Farnworth would be hidden in the distance. A few landmarks could be seen : the tower of Farnworth church, Bold windmill, the spire of Prescot parish church and the mill on Ditton Brook but, apart from a few scattered farmsteads, little else. At high water however, the river presented a busy scene with dozens of single-mast sailing barges making their way to and from the Sankey Canal or Warrington — a scene more reminiscent of a pleasure regatta than the commercial activity of the Industrial Revolution.

Across the Weaver to the west, the view to Frodsham, Helsby and the Welsh Hills was magnificent. Of the Mersey estuary an observer wrote, *"At that time, from Weston Point the whole country was wooded with trees of noble proportions … and all the way along the beautifully wooded shore were banks of glittering sand stretching away at low tide as far as the eye could see"*. The river Weaver was then a vital industrial thoroughfare and scores of small sailing craft carrying salt to the refineries at Liverpool could be seen every day passing under Frodsham bridge.

By 1790 the county directories were lauding the attractions of Runcorn as a summer watering place. It was reported that the area had become *"visited by genteel, fashionable and gay parties for the sake of gratifying their imaginations with views of fine landscapes which would beggar art to describe"*. From another source in 1800, we learn that the district *"is of late much visited by parties of pleasure and invalids. The air is impregnated with health, the salt bathing is very good"*.

Angling and bathing in the river were popular pastimes but both could be dangerous and in his "Account of Runcorn and its Environs" written in 1803, the Reverend John Greswell gives a warning about the rapid tides at the narrows *"It may not be improper to caution the angler and bather*

to be on his guard against the rapid rise of the tide which has sometimes been productive of distressing and dangerous accidents. From the shelving nature of the shore a retreat in some parts upon an emergency may be very difficult"*. During the summer months both shores of the river were popular with pleasure seekers and the ferry was busy conveying people across to Widnes or 'Runcorn Gap' as it was then known. The "Boat House Inn" at the ferry landing in Widnes was known over a wide area as the "Snig Pie House" on account of the excellent pies served by the landlord and made from eels fresh caught in the river.

Pre-industrial Runcorn had a reputation as a spa or pleasure resort and by the end of the Georgian period the district was renowned as a place which *"is well suited to invalids of strumous habit and convalescents from various types of fever"*. Visitors from Liverpool and Manchester came to benefit from *"the pure air which generally proves very friendly and favourable"*. Certainly the neighbourhood was very picturesque and a traveller in 1795 noted : *"Lovers of botany may find a pleasing variety of plants both maritime and inland varieties in the vicinity"*.

The township had its two distinct areas. "Lower Runcorn" was the village situated at the river around the inlet of the Boat House Pool whilst a second, smaller area of scattered dwellings was to be found where present day Highlands Road and Moughland Lane meet. This latter was "Higher Runcorn". The divisions are ancient in origin for the Higher Runcorn of 1800 was "alterior Roncover" in twelfth century documents. It was "Runcoure Superior" in 1295 and "Over Runcorne" in a manuscript of 1428. In a document of 1635 Lower Runcorn is "Runkhorne Abatis". One or two ancient field and place names also survived the centuries. Runcorn Heath in 1370 was 'Runcoreheth', the Stenhills in 1315 was "Stenehul", whilst Moughland Lane appears as "Mothland" in a manuscript of 1687.

An eighteenth century plan showing the route of the Bridgewater Canal where it passes through Runcorn township is deposited at the Boat Museum at Ellesmere Port. The plan shows that much of the land bordering the canal was in the ownership of Vicar Alcock and his brother Matthew. Matthew had considerable holdings to the west of the Big Pool in the area now occupied by Langdale Road, Norman Road and by Runcorn cemetery. The vicar had lands on both sides of the canal stretching from present day Victoria Road at its junction with Heath Road to Runcorn Bridge (Savages Bridge). Mr. John Cooper owned much of the land between Top Locks and the river whilst John Orred was in possession of practically all the land stretching from Higher Runcorn to the line of locks. Daniel

Orred had the fields bordering the river to the west of the Duke's canal as well as property in Heath Road. Kerfoot Jannion and John Fryer were men of substance with fields along Bridge Street, whilst a large area between today's High Street and Church Street was the property of a Mrs. Banner.

The land to the east of Heath Road from Delph Bridge to where Boston Avenue is now situated was common land or waste, as was an area to the north of the canal opposite today's "Wilsons Hotel".

A suggested date for the plan is 1780. It shows the township's watermill on the Sprinch stream opposite Mrs. Orford's "White Hart" in Mersey Road and also the town quarry or "delf" below Delph Bridge. Opposite the "Boathouse" there was a brewery adjacent to a small group of houses owned by the vicar and Mr. Cooper.

Although the plan is a useful source of information, it is limited in scope for it details only those properties which abutted the canal. The Duke's warehouse, limekiln, coalyard and canalside buildings are indicated but only in the area between the canal and the river is there sufficient detail to enable an estimate of the number of houses to be made. In 1780 there were about forty dwellings between Delph Bridge and Savages Bridge and the river, with three or four others along Heath Road. One or two of the commercial premises in today's High Street still retain architectural features which indicate Runcorn's late Georgian development.

From about 1800 the town began to show the first signs of increased commercial activity. The Reverend John Skinner, Rector of Camerton in Somerset, remarked on the growth of the township when he visited Runcorn in 1804. He noted that *"the town is small but growing almost daily with many comfortable houses erected in the village. In summer the place is resorted to by company from Liverpool who retire here to enjoy the pure air. A plan is in agitation to make salt water baths ... In respect to rides and walks in the summertime there cannot be a finer spot".*

Whilst it may be true that there was a noticeable increase in shipbuilding and shipping, Runcorn still remained a cul-de-sac unknown outside its environs. Communications were as primitive as they had been a couple of centuries previously. The only way to the north was by way of the unreliable ferry which provided a service if there was a demand. By 1803 however, there was the regular passenger service by sailing packet to Liverpool in 1806 the Mersey and Irwell Navigation Company entered the canal passenger carrying business and their packets from the Old Quay docks soon began to provide

serious competition to those of the Bridgewater Trustees. The old ford crossing between Hale Head and Weston was rarely used but there is a record of the vicar of Hale, on removing to Wrexham in 1808, carting all his household goods by way of the ford. But it was a dangerous route and few ventured across although the Lord of the Manor of Hale, John Ireland Blackburne MP, stated in 1828 that he had often driven his horse and gig across.

As for made roads in the first years of the nineteenth century — there were none. Runcorn was by-passed by the main road from Chester to Warrington and by much of the traffic on the river. Although the town had, for a quarter of a century, been the terminus of the Bridgewater Canal, it did not profit greatly from the undertaking as trade had passed through the town en route to important centres of population. But this position of isolation became less acute in 1820 with the construction of a macadamised turnpike road between Runcorn and Northwich.

Between 1820 and 1830 Runcorn's fame as a watering place was at its height. In 1822 salt water baths were built on the river's edge below the Parish Church. The baths proved to be very popular during the summer months and a contemporary account describes the facilities. *"These baths have been erected at the expense of nearly £700 and comprise every requisite for salt water bathing with the greatest comfort, cleanliness and privacy. Here are two large separate closed baths which are filled with water from the river at each tide. A warm bath and shower may likewise be obtained at the shortest notice as a person will constantly reside on the premises. There are also many separate dressing rooms for a single person or party. It should be mentioned however, that the building has sustained considerable damage from the violence of the storms with which this shore has been visited".* In order to accommodate the increased number of visitors, Belvedere Terrace boarding houses were built in 1831.

The attractive situation of Regency Runcorn made it an ideal place for the establishment of boarding schools for the sons and daughters of Liverpool business people and by 1825 a number of schools had been opened. From about 1815 Mr. Blake, the proprietor of Hallwood Academy in Halton, was advertising his school for young gentlemen in the Liverpool newspapers and by 1835 there were half a dozen boarding schools and as many private day schools in the town. One of the boarding schools was owned by two clergymen, the Reverend J. Allen and the Reverend W. Whitworth who had their school for boys in High Street, whilst Mesdames Margaret, Mary and Eliza Harrison had a boarding school for young ladies in Church Street. Sophia Lees had her "respectable seminary" for young ladies in High Street and Mesdames Goodine and Potter had a boarding and day school for girls in Pennington Place. For the local children, one or two private, single teacher day schools were situated in rather less salubrious neighbourhoods. For a few pence a week these schools offered basic education to the children of the less well-off and to the sons and daughters of non conformists who did not wish their children to be educated in the Parish School. Mr. Robert Naylor was the proprietor of a day school in Brunswick Street, Mr. Bernard O'Connor had his school in Fryer Street whilst that of Mr. Josiah Metyard was to be found on Mill Brow.

Runcorn's select boarding schools were not destined to become institutions of long standing for they became early casualties of industrialisation. Before mid-century the town was no longer an attractive resort and the business people of Liverpool and Manchester were looking for boarding schools which were situated in parts of the country which were more picturesque and healthier than sooty mid-Merseyside. A local newspaper of June 1858 carried the following notice, *"First class ladies seminary of Higher Runcorn to be let. The establishment has borne a high reputation for more than half a century. The house and garden situated on Runcorn Hill command extensive views across the River Mersey and the Welsh Hills. The air is salubrious, the scenery unrivalled and the taxes moderate. Commodious pews in the Parish Church belong to the house".* This establishment seems to have been one of the last boarding schools in the town. The census returns for 1851 indicate that it was run by two spinster sisters, Eliza and Emma Marston, with the help of an assistant teacher. Of the fourteen boarders attending the school in 1851, nine were from towns outside the local area. Their places of birth include London, Liverpool, Manchester, Yorkshire and Shropshire. As late as 1874 a local directory lists Mr. James Craig B.A. as the proprietor of the Collegiate School, Irwell House in Irwell Lane.

Bathing parties and parkland at Runcorn about 1830. The paddle steamers and the factory chimneys indicate the beginning of industrialisation. The Duke's Gut and Castle Bridge are to the right. (Painting, Cheshire County Libraries, Runcorn)

Bibliography

Contemporary accounts of early nineteenth century Runcorn are to be found in *"A Description of the Country from Thirty to Forty Miles Around Manchester"* (1795) by J Aikin; *"An Account of Runcorn and its Environs"* (1811) by J Gresswell; *"A Visitor's Guide to Runcorn and its Vicinity"* (1834) by G Fowler and in *"Diary of Richard Lea. What was Runcorn like in 1838?"* in the Holy Trinity Church Centenary Publication (1938).

A number of county directories give interesting detail notably, Pigot and Company, *"Cheshire Directory"* (1828); *"Handbook and Directory of Runcorn"* (1846) by W Walker; S Bagshaw, *"History, Gazetteer and Directory of the County Palatine of Chester"* (1850) and *"Universal British Directory"* (1792).

Information about the Runcorn and Weston Volunteer Infantry and the Norton Volunteers has been taken from "Local Gleanings of Lancashire and Cheshire" Vol.II, March 1878, *"Cheshire Sheaf"*, January 1879 and *"Returning the Colours Belonging to the Late Corps of Runcorn and Weston Volunteers"* (1818), a pamphlet deposited in the local collection, Shopping City Library, Runcorn.

Runcorn Town Bridge (now known as Doctor's Bridge or Savage's Bridge) in 1891.
The notices include a cattle auction, excursions by railway and free passages to Australia.

Narrow-boat women shopping at a grocer's stall in Bridge Street.

Chapter 12
Victorian Runcorn

Runcorn's celebrations to mark the Coronation of Queen Victoria on June 28th 1838 were described by William Handley in a local newspaper article written in 1902. Mr. Handley's sources of information were "a written record of an eye-witness" and the recollections of elderly people who were present at the coronation festivities sixty-three years before. His article presents a most illuminating picture of the occasion which began with the distribution of "upwards of two hundred pounds of as good beef as was ever eaten, with plum pudding and four hundred pounds of bread" to five hundred and twenty poor families in Runcorn and its neighbourhood.

At six a.m. on the morning of the coronation the town was awakened by a nineteen gun salute — one volley for each year of the Queen's life and by ten o'clock the procession began forming in front of the town hall. Led by some 1,400 children from the Sunday schools dressed in their best attire and each wearing a medal suspended on a white ribbon, the procession moved off towards Runcorn Hill in glorious sunshine. After the children came the Friendly Societies; the Oddfellows, the Foresters, Shepherds and Rechabites, the members dressed in the distinctive livery of the societies, carrying banners and accompanied by marching bands. Then came Mr. William Harding and his four constables, a trumpeter on horseback followed by "The Champion of England" mounted on a grey charger attended by his squire also mounted and carrying a banner. The pageant was followed by the gentry and townsfolk marching three abreast.

The procession moved up High Street to Doctor's Bridge where it was joined by the gunners with the cannon. By way of Lowlands Road and Holloway the procession proceeded through Higher Runcorn to Beetle Hill where the various groups assembled in pre-arranged order. An eye-witness declared that there were seven thousand people present. The National Anthem was sung (According to Mr. Handley it was "the old version composed by Henry Carey in 1740"), and the cannon fired volleys in salute followed by three hearty cheers. The procession then reformed to make its way across Runcorn Heath via Cawleys Lane to Heath Road. It was a mile and a quarter in length as with bands playing, it crossed Delph Bridge to reform into ranks in front of the town hall. The Champion and his squire then took up position at the front

of the assembly and a proclamation was made "for all persons who could deny Her Majesty's right to the Throne to come forward, or for ever hold their peace". No traitor came forward to challenge the Champion and after more cheering the children dispersed to the schools for cakes and buns, whilst the employees of the soaperies were given free meals at the works by the owners. Mr. Handley tells us that "The civic fathers dined, at their own expense, in the good old style, at the Royal Hotel, under the presidency of Philip Whiteway with feast, song and toasting". In the afternoon there were sculling and rowing matches on the river. The evening's activities included children's races held on a large stretch of open ground bounded by Bridge Street, Penketh Lane and the Bridgewater Canal known as the "Green Turn". "By the lofty poplars where the limpid waters of the Sprinch Brook meandered on its way to the river" there was a greasy pole surmounted by a leg of mutton, the prize for the successful climber.

After dark there was a firework display and "a brilliant illumination provided by the Gas Company". At midnight the crowds made their way to Castle Rock to witness the climax to the day's festivities. Moored in mid-river was an old barge which had been given by the Bridgewater Trustees. It was laden with tar, resin and quantities of gunpowder and after being set alight it provided a tremendous spectacle of explosion and flame until it burned to the waterline. The eye-witness who recorded the day's events recalls : *"The greatest good humour prevailed among all classes, all party and political feuds forgotten and the only feeling there seemed to be was that too much honour could not be done on such an auspicious event. Everybody appeared to be gratified by the day's proceedings which terminated without anything taking place to mar the day's pleasure".*

Poverty, Charity and Self-Help

In a previous chapter mention has been made of the parochial attempts to provide for the basic needs of the poor and aged by means of the parish poor fund or poor rate. However, individual charity also played an important part in poor relief. Indeed, from the first year of Edward VI's reign the parish clergy were obliged by law to preach regularly on the subject of charity and they constantly urged and shamed the well-off into giving. The obstinate and uncharitable who refused to contribute were reported to the bishop who put pressure on them in order to obtain an appropriate donation. If necessary, and in the last resort, the Justices of the Peace were empowered to assess a man's worth and then demand from him an amount of money to be paid to the Overseers of the Poor.

One of the few items to survive the demolition of the ancient Parish Church is the benefaction table or bequest board. The faded gilded lettering can still be read and it recalls charitable donations made in the seventeenth and eighteenth centuries: *"A memorial of ye Benefactions of sundry pious and well-disposed Christians, who have justly deserved to be publicly distinguished as lovely for the imitation of their posterity. To the Parish Church of Runcorn. Halton Chappel Mr. Robert Chesshire towards ye repair of Runcorn Church ye yearly interest of £20; John King, clerk, for ye use of a preaching Minister at Halton, ye yearly sum of £5; Mrs. Mann for ye like, ye yearly interest of £12..10s; Mr. John Chesshyre, for ye like, ye yearly interest of £12..10s; William Weston for ye like, yearly summe of 15s; Mrs. Squires for ye like ye yearly interest of £25; Mr. Mason for ye like, ye yearly interest of £25; Mr. Roger Wilbraham of Nantwich ye yearly interest of £25; Thomas Middlehurst of Norton, for ye like, ye yearly interest of £5; by unknown benefactions, for ye like, ye yearly interest of £6; Sir John Chesshyre, Sergeant-at-Law, for ye use of ye Minister of Halton, £200. For ye use of ye poor of Runcorn Mr. Robert Dobbs ye yearly interest of £5..10s; William Runcorn, ye yearly sum of 6s..8d; Thomas Grice ye yearly sum of £2; Thomas Breck, ye yearly interest of £15; Mr. Squires, ye yearly interest of £12..10s; Mr. William Liptrott, ye yearly interest of £10; Mr. Fynmore of Buckley etc., ye yearly interest of £10; John Hale, ye yearly interest of £3; by unknown benefactions ye yearly interest of £5. For ye use of ye poor at Halton. Mr. Robert Dobbs, vicar, ye yearly interest of £8; Mr. Robert Chesshyre ye yearly sum of ten shillings; John King, clerk, ye yearly interest of £50; more to poor widows born and living in Halton, ye yearly interest of £20; more to poor scholars, ye yearly interest of £10; Mrs. King, ye yearly interest of £20; Robert Jennings ye yearly interest of £4..3s; William Runcorn, ye yearly sume of 6s..8d; Mr. Robert Acton, ye yearly interest of £5, Mr. Maloney, ye yearly interest of £12..10s; Mrs. Squires, ye yearly interest of £12..10s; John Chesshyre, sergeant-at-law, ye yearly interest of £10; William Weston ye sum of 15s. To Halton Schoole By unknown benefactors ye yearly interest of £180; Thomas Grice, ye yearly sume of £2; William Weston, ye yearly sum of £1. Thomas Breck ye yearly interest of £5; William Bushell ye yearly interest of £5".*

Besides leaving money to the poor and to the church another popular work of piety was to leave it for the "mending of the ways" — the repair of roads. John King, cleric, in 1635 left the yearly interest on £5 for the maintenance of the highways in Halton.

In 1692 the sum of £22..10s, being the amount of benefactions given to the poor of Runcorn by Mr. Liptrott, Mr. Finmore, Elizabeth Heath and John Buckley, was used to buy a piece of land in Runcorn called the Oldershaw. The rent from the land was then applied to poor relief. In 1756 other benefactions and money from the poor stock were used to buy one and a half acres in Churchfield. The income derived from these investments was used by the trustees to *"apply twenty shillings yearly for buying bread to be given out on twenty Sundays in the year to the poor attending Divine Service at the Parish Church and the remainder to be divided among the poor on St. Thomas's Day"*. By 1850 one of the fields was being let for £10 a year and the other for £8 and this money was distributed to the poor by Miss. Orred who was the sole surviving trustee. Miss Orred also had the administration of the Alcock Charity. Thomas Alcock, the vicar of Runcorn, left certain lands with a yearly payment of £2..10..0 to the poor to be distributed on St. Thomas's Day together with an annual payment of £2 for the master of Halton School and £3 for the promotion of psalmody in Runcorn church.

Every St. Thomas's Day (December 21st) the revenue from three charitable investments was distributed to the poor of Halton at the Castle Hotel by the vicar of Halton and his churchwardens. In 1872 the interest on £401..12..6d deposited in Parr's Bank in Warrington was given to the poor. This money had originally been invested in Turnpike Trusts. Under the will of Thomas Eaton which was proved at Chester in 1810, the chief rent of properties in Warrington benefitted the poor of Halton to the amount of £6..14..0 annually. The Bolton charity, which consisted of the rent of a field in Halton, yielded £9 a year, one third of which went to the vicar at Halton, a third to Halton Grammar School and a third to the poor of the village. It is interesting to note the decline of charitable payments in the twentieth century with the arrival of the old age pension. In 1874 fifty-four poor persons, mostly widows, received sums of either ten shillings, seven shillings and sixpence, five shillings or two shillings and sixpence each from the St. Thomas's Day Charity at Halton. In 1885 fifty-seven people received the charity, in 1903, fifty two; 1912, twenty-seven; in 1921 eleven. In 1932 there were only four people receiving help from the charity and the last payments were made in 1933. In 1932 Mrs Hannah Craven died. A poor widow, she had been in receipt of the charity for forty-one years.

A member of the Brooke family founded a private charity in Halton for the benefit "of six poor persons who have lived as house-servants of the Brooke family". Pusey Brooke who became Surveyor-general of Hampshire and Dorset, by his will dated 1767, founded the almshouses on Halton Hill. Each former servant was to receive four shillings a week and the houses were endowed with the yearly sum of £54. Such altruism was uncommon in the eighteenth century and Pusey Brooke showed a spirit of humanity which was far in advance of his time.

The Orred charity was an annual almsgiving for the destitute of Weston village. There were 144 recipients of this charity when it was distributed to the poor of the village at St. John's church on December 27th 1899. The total sum distributed was twenty-seven pounds, seventeen shillings and six pence, which averages at three shillings and ten pence. Times were difficult for there was much unemployment in the district and an article in St. John's parish magazine illustrates the poverty prevalent in the area; *"Several of the old beneficiaries have been in receipt of the charity for more than twenty years ... We believe that some were disappointed this year because their amounts were not increased but when it is stated that more money was given away than was received and that fourteen new applicants were refused through sheer necessity it is evident that there can be no increase unless several are knocked off the list — an act which the Trustees have no intention of doing".*

Throughout the last century the various religious denominations made strenuous efforts to relieve the misery of the poor in times of underemployment due to trade recession or when farm labourers, quarrymen and boat people were laid off because of frosty weather. The "Warrington Guardian" of 17th December 1879 reported on the work of the Mersey Mission to Seamen. During four days of bitter weather when the canals were frozen 468 free meals were served to the families of boatmen and after the divine service on the Sunday morning, 128 children were treated to tea and buns.

Besides the Dorcas Society and the Runcorn Ladies' Charity which had been distributing clothing to widows and orphans in the 1830s, there was All Saints Fresh Air Fund for Sick Children. This benevolent fund was established at the Parish Church in order to provide "a change of air for convalescent little ones". In 1897 the parish magazine reported that nine children had been given three or four weeks holiday at West Kirby Convalescent Home. The vicar, the Reverend Alfred Maitland Wood, urged the parishioners to support the bazaarette in aid of the Fresh Air Fund so that adult convalescents, "who were sometimes even more helpless than the children", could also be sent away for a rest cure.

Another laudable enterprise was organised by the Parish Church to aid the sick poor of the town. This was the provision of a district nurse. In 1888 an approach was made to the Institute for Nurses at Worcester requesting the superintendent to recommend a district nurse for Runcorn. The costs of about £85 per annum were to be provided from All Saints' funds. The services of the nurse were available to those who could not afford to pay for medical attention and she would attend the poor irrespective of religious belief or want of belief. The parish magazine notes, *"Generally speaking, Nurse Evans will not sit up at night, nor will she attend cases of infectious disease. It is plain enough she cannot work both day and night and plain too that if she goes to a case of infectious disease she cannot go to other cases for fear of carrying the disease. The nurse will, for the present, be found at No.1 Wellington Street. Applications for her services must be written on a slate which will hang by the door. Applicant must state name, address and complaint of the patient".* The nursing service soon became of great value to the sick and elderly. In the first seven weeks of her appointment it was reported that Nurse Evans made 842 visits to 59 patients. Her work was quickly recognised as being essential for the welfare of many in the poverty-stricken Rookery and Mrs. Maitland Wood made strenuous efforts to collect funds and linen to be used to support the nurse in her labours.

Until 1857 the Runcorn Poor Law Union provided outdoor relief to those in desperate need. The Union included thirty-six townships and the thirty-nine elected Guardians met at the Board Room in Preston Brook on every alternate Friday. Before 1857 the destitute were at least spared the final ignominy of incarceration in a workhouse but in the October of that year the local newspapers advertised the posts of master and matron for the workhouse which was nearing completion at Dutton. Applicants had to be man and wife and they had to be competent to keep books and accounts. The salary was to commence at "£80 per annum with rations". Designed to accommodate 232 inmates and costing £7,500, Dutton workhouse was described in the late Victorian directories as "a commodious and handsome brick structure with stone facings".

In order to draw attention to the poverty in Runcorn and in particular to the plight of the children of the town, the Y.M.C.A. *"decided to give a free breakfast to a thousand poor children in the Public Hall on January 7th 1881 ... More than double that number made their appearance in the hall ... With much difficulty they were provided with a wholesome breakfast".* Such a show of want was not anticipated and although the Association managed to give every child a meal, the expenses incurred were beyond the treasurer's resources and an appeal had to be made to the membership so that the bill could be paid.

In eighteenth century Britain the humiliation and degradation of the parish paupers could be observed every week as the destitute went to the house of the Overseer of the Poor to receive a pittance in outdoor relief. Regarded as society's failures, they were branded as either indolent or reduced to poverty through improvidence, crime or drink. Widows, orphans and the aged poor lived on the edge of starvation. When a labourer and his wife grew old and infirm they were in a desperate situation unless they were fortunate enough to receive assistance from their children. In the diary of an unknown lay-preacher which is deposited in the Norton Priory Museum is the following entry for January 1841, *"William White near the Boat House was found dead in bed this morning. He was (advanced) in years and it appears that he died from want".*

The desperate poor pawned and repawned their few belongings, ensnared sparrows for a few coppers, occasionally found menial work for a day or two and frequently turned to petty crime simply to exist. However, as there was no local workhouse, Runcorn's paupers were spared the ultimate degradation of being committed to the poor house although most considered that dependence on out-door relief was disgrace enough.

Workers in regular employment could make some provision for accident, illness or old age through the Friendly Societies and probably through the influence of the Duke of Bridgewater who encouraged thrift amongst his new employees, Runcorn saw the early establishment of "Sick Clubs".

"The Duke's Club" was instituted in August 1790 for the purposes of "relieving the sick and maimed members and for burying their dead". The irrationality of the expensive burials reflects the labourer's horror of a pauper's funeral. If, after paying thirteen shillings a member of the Duke's Club died, his dependents would receive £8 "for a decent burial". After two years' subscriptions, his family would receive £10 and after five years' membership a man's burial grant would amount to £15. After paying thirty shillings a member was entitled to sixpence from every member of the club if his wife died. A member who fell sick or lame after paying thirteen shillings *"shall on the same being duly certified, receive eight shillings a week during his infirmity except that such infirmity or disability proceed from debauched or intemperate method of living".*

At a meeting of the Duke's Club at the "Packet Inn" in December 1818, the Club's rules were amended, "for the better government of the Society" and a steward was appointed by no less a personage than the Superintendent of the Bridgewater Trust, Robert Bradshaw. It was agreed that the members' subscription should be a shilling a month. The declared aims of the Society were "To promote good morals and brotherhood. Love and Serve each other" and in order to foster friendship, there should be an annual dinner. The rule concerning the annual dinner is worthy of quotation in full : *"There shall be an annual dinner for every member for which each member shall pay one shilling and sixpence for meat and a further sixpence for liquor. On Whit Monday every member shall attend the house of Mr. William Johnson, the "Packet Inn" at nine o'clock in the forenoon when a statement of accounts of the Society for the preceeding year will be given by the steward after which the members are to proceed to attend divine service at the church. Each member not attending to forfeit a shilling to the master of the house and sixpence to the Club unless he can show just cause for non-attendance. No liquor to be drunk in the clubroom that day until the return from church".*

The Runcorn Friendly Society was established in January 1806 and its rules and aims were similar to those of the Duke's Club. Here too, it was the tradition to have an annual dinner. One benefit of membership is worthy of note. *"Every member incapable of following his business by reason of old age shall, every Saturday during his life, by applying to the treasurer receive three shillings a week".*

The Runcorn "Friendly Society of Women", instituted in 1811, was one of the first in the country and in the year of its inception 127 members were enrolled. Halton village also had a Women's Friendly Society. The Halton Female Friendly Society was formed in 1815 as a mutual self-help club. By paying regular subscriptions the members were able to establish a fund from which they could claim maternity benefit, death grants and assistance in times of hardship. From the beginning the "Halton Ladies' Club" as the Female Society became known, held an annual anniversary procession which developed to become the main social event in the village in Victorian times. After attending a service in St Mary's church the ladies, dressed in their best attire, wearing blue and white sashes and all carrying white staffs, walked in procession to the parish boundary in Halton Road.

Halton "Ladies' Day" became a gala occasion and on returning to Halton Castle the members would enjoy a tea party and there was dancing in the evening. Led by Lady Brooke and the Runcorn Harmonic Band, the procession attracted large crowds of sight-seers with the men reduced to the role of mere spectators. The tradition lasted over a hundred years with the final procession taking place in 1920.

The Friendly Societies succeeded in providing some measure of insurance for hard times and as previously noted, they prospered so that often they were able to lend money to the town for the maintenance of the roads.

By 1830 Runcorn had branches of a number of Friendly Societies that were national institutions including the Independent Order of Oddfellows, the Ancient Order of Foresters, the Ancient Order of Shepherds and the Rechabites. Each society had its distinctive dress for public ceremonies as well as emblems and banners and usually they provided a drum and pipe band on walking days.

In the last decade of the eighteenth century the Friendly Societies received official encouragement and this helped to make them popular but during periods of economic recession the dread of "being buried on the parish" was the most effective recruiting agent for the societies. Between 1813 and 1815 the number of poor people in Halton township who were permanently dependent on poor relief increased from 28 to 40 and in addition to these there were other villagers who required occasional help from the poor rate. The money expended on the poor increased from £278 to £309. Even though times were hard and permanent employment difficult to find, many took advantage of the membership of a Friendly Society. An official return shows that in Halton the Societies increased their membership from 46 to 76 in the three years.

Even the Parish Church had a Friendly Society for the benefit of those parishioners who had been connected with the school either as pupils or teachers. It was a modest venture paying out two shillings a week during times of sickness plus the services of a doctor and a grant of £2 was paid towards the cost of defraying funeral expenses. Members of the "Runcorn School Friendly Society and Sick Club" were required to pay "a halfpenny to the general fund and a monthly payment of a penny for the advice and services of the surgeon". The Parish Sick Club was well patronised with receipts amounting to £87 in 1859. St. Michael's church parishioners in Greenway Road established their "Dividing Club" in 1891 and its aim and objectives were very similar to those of the Parish Church Friendly Society.

Self-help was further encouraged with the establishment of the Runcorn Savings Bank in 1846. Its object was "to give the humbler classes a safe and beneficial investment" and to promote "a beneficial effect upon the industrious habits of the working class". Of the bank's 579 depositors in 1859 eleven Friendly Societies and forty-seven charities contributed most of the £13,000 on deposit.

The Runcorn Penny Bank was opened in the parish schoolroom on February 26th 1859.

Halton Ladies' Club. The annual walk in 1909.

Under the management of the clergy assisted by the Sunday School teachers, the bank accepted deposits from a penny upwards and it was open for one hour on Saturday evenings. In its first year £364 was deposited and some measure of the popularity of the bank can be seen by the fact that ten years later deposits had increased to over £830. Without doubt this parish enterprise was a boon to many in times of unemployment and hardship. Encouraged by the success of the Runcorn Penny Bank the people of Weston village began a Penny Bank in the schoolroom in May 1864.

Of course there were many who through extreme poverty could not avail themselves of the services of a Friendly Society or the Penny Bank. For some of the desperate poor, help could be obtained from the "Runcorn Dorcas Society", a voluntary body established in 1832. The aims of this society, which depended entirely on public generosity for its funds, were *"to visit and provide articles of clothing for those persons whose circumstances will not admit of their purchasing such garments as are necessary to protect them from the weather. The attention of the Committee is particularly directed to widows and orphans"*.

"The Ladies' Charity" was commenced in 1831. Its object was *"to afford relief to poor married women in child-bed at their own houses by the use of bed linen and by furnishing such other necessities as their situation might require"*. Funds were raised entirely from public subscriptions and donations.

In an attempt to encourage thrift and the prudent management of the family purse, a clothing club was instituted at All Saints church. This "Runcorn Church Clothing Club" came into existence in the late 1850s and for many years it proved to be a valuable investment for hard–pressed working people. Every week throughout the year the members paid subscriptions and in October before the onset of winter, their savings were returned to them with an added dividend. The bonus money came from a fund which had been contributed by the business and professional community. The Brookes of Norton, the Orred family of Weston and the clergy were generous contributors to the fund. The scheme was popular and the idea was adopted by St. Peter's Mission and later in the century, by St. Michael's parishioners in Greenway Road and by those at St. John's in Weston.

The self-improvement ethic and the cult of worldly success and respectability were virtues which were held in high esteem in the Victorian era. Freemasonry in Runcorn dates from the formation of the Ellesmere Lodge in 1859 and about this time a number of agencies whereby a working man and his children could progress in life came into being. Long before the establishment of a national system of education was introduced in 1870 the various religious denominations had taken on the responsibility of educating the young. First in the field was the Church of England with the Parish School of 1811 and Holy Trinity Infants' School of 1839 with a boys' and girls' department built in 1848. Granville Street Methodist School also dates from 1848 and twenty years later a Methodist day school was started at the Brunswick chapel with another in Weston village in 1873.

Until the setting up of the School Boards following the Education Act of 1870, the churches continued to be the providers of elementary education. In 1863 a Church of England school was built in Weston village. The school and the headteacher's house were built on land given by Major Orred who also gave a donation of £500 towards the school building fund. The new school also served as St. John the Evangelist's Mission for the Anglican community at Weston. In his letters to the parishioners, Vicar Barclay wrote of the astonishing demand for schooling in Weston. The number of children on the roll of the new school rose from 46 on the opening day to 153 a year later. Mr. Lloyd, the schoolmaster and his sister who was the assistant teacher, were appointed at a combined salary of £60 per year.

St Michael's School in Shaw Street was opened in 1868 for the children of Newtown. The school was under severe pressure from the start and before 1900 three enlargements to the premises had been made in order to cope with the ever increasing roll.

Canon Barclay and his curate, Mr. Garven of the Floating Church Mission in Duke's Fields, were keen advocates of free education for all and a day school for the benefit of the migratory canal boat children was opened in 1865. The school building which was provided by the Bridgewater Trustees, was situated half-way down the line of locks. Within a couple of years there were 108 pupils on the roll under the supervision of a trained certificated teacher and an assistant. The school relied heavily on the financial support of the Trustees but when the waterway passed into the ownership of the Bridgewater Navigation Company in 1872 the new company's directors refused to make any contribution to the school or to the Sunday School and they were forced to close.

For those Runcorn children who were held to be too dirty or verminous for the ordinary day schools, a Ragged School was built by John and Thomas Johnson on Mill Brow in 1853. The

Ragged School was supported by subscriptions from the public.

In spite of hard times many parents made determined efforts to keep their offspring at school but in 1860 it was reported that some parents of children attending the Parish School were finding it difficult to afford the few coppers needed to pay the "school pence" to educate two or more sons and daughters. Even the families who lived on the narrow-boats who seldom mixed with the townsfolk and who had avoided formal education, now began to send their children to school. When the boats were tied up at Runcorn the children attended the local schools for a few days. They carried their own registers which recorded their attendance at dozens of schools along the country's inland waterways.

Education was also available for adults. In 1850 most working folk "made their mark" because they could not even write a signature. At Holy Trinity National School classes were provided "for the education of adults who have hitherto not had that privilege".

About 1835 the Runcorn Literary Institute was established. Its principal objective was *"to promote a general knowledge in subordination to religion and to provide facilities for moral and intellectual improvement by the provision of a reading room, classes and delivering lectures on literary and scientific subjects"*. By 1853 there was a Mechanics' Institution which was associated with the Literary Institute and which catered for the mechanics and artisans who were employed in the new factories on both sides of the river.

"A Visitors' Guide to Runcorn" which was published in 1834, informs us that the town had a "circulating library" which was kept by Mr. Walker, printer and publisher and that there was a newsroom in the town hall which was open every day. From another source we learn that a public library with 650 volumes was opened in premises in High Street in 1858. The Runcorn Free Library (the present municipal library) dates from 1882.

The Co-operative movement helped to further working-class progress in education and well-being. From its humble beginnings in a small shop in Devonshire Square with few customers in 1862, the Runcorn Industrial Co-operative Society soon developed into a thriving concern with shops throughout the town and in 1869 the committee opened a branch in Widnes. In both towns the Society expanded enormously. But the Co-operative Society was more than a business venture, for it taught working folk the benefits of mutual self-help and sound business practice as well as exerting a moral and intellectual influence which created a desire for education and social advancement.

Runcorn was the birthplace of a famous Victorian man of letters. Sir Thomas Henry Hall Caine was born in Runcorn in 1853. A noted dramatist and novelist, Caine was a friend of the painter, Dante Gabriel Rossetti, who encouraged him to write romantic novels. These were very popular with "The Deemster" written in 1887, "The Manxman" of 1884, "The Christians" (1897), "The Eternal City" (1901) and "The Prodigal Son" (1904) being the best known. He also wrote "Recollections of Rossetti". In 1891 Caine went to eastern Europe to report the plight of the Jews who were fleeing the pogroms in Russia and during the First World War he devoted himself to disseminating British propaganda in the United States. Of Manx blood on his father's side, Caine lived in the Isle of Man where he was a member of the House of Keys from 1901 to 1908. He was knighted in 1918 and was made a Companion of Honour in 1922. Sir Thomas Hall Caine died in 1931.

A pavement pot seller in Bridge Street at the turn of the century.

Bibliography

The charities of Runcorn, Weston and Halton are recorded in *"The Report of the Commissioners on Charities in England and Wales Relating to the County of Cheshire 1818 — 1837".* Additional information has been taken from Canon Barclay's Letters to his Parishioners of Runcorn; G. Fowler's *"A Visitor's Guide to Runcorn and its Vicinity"* (1834), Smith's *"Runcorn Almanac"* (1885); *"Kelly's Post Office Directory"* for 1896 and the Parish Magazine of All Saints 1888, 1889, 1899.

The rules of the Duke's Club (revised 1819) are to be found at the local history library in Warrington Municipal Library (ref.P12441) as are the rules and regulations of the Runcorn Friendly Society, 1806 (ref.12691) and the Runcorn Friendly Society of Women 1811, (ref.MS276). Halton Ladies' Club annual walk is reported in the *Warrington Guardian* for 17th July 1858. Adult education is mentioned in the Runcorn Literary Society and Mechanics' Institute in the *Warrington Guardian* for 20th October 1853 and 12th December 1857. The Ragged School at Mill Brow is also mentioned in an item in the *Warrington Guardian* for 1st October 1853. For Dutton workhouse see the *Warrington Guardian* for 23.10.1856; 27.12.1856; 1.8.1857; 24.10.1857; 28.11.1857; 28.8.1858 and 20.6.1864. Details of the attempts by the churches to promote thrift and to alleviate suffering from poverty have been taken from the monthly Parish Magazine of the All Saints 1896 – 1901 which includes information from St. Johns, Weston and St. Michaels, Greenway Road.

An insight into the establishment of the local Co-operative movement can be found in Walter Millington's *"Jubilee History of the Society 1862-1912"* published by the Runcorn and Widnes Industrial Co-operative Society Ltd. (1912).

Chapter 13
The Coming of Industry

For centuries Cheshire's fame has rested on its dairy produce. Since Elizabethan times Cheshire cheese has been renowned and during the Civil War in the seventeenth century, it was the staple diet for both the Royalist and the Roundhead armies. In the eighteenth century the cheese was carried to a warehouse at Frodsham Bridge for transhipment to Liverpool for the London market. In the days before refrigeration cattle were slaughtered at Martinmas and beef from the local farms was shipped via the Mersey and Weaver rivers. From early in the Georgian period, locally produced bacon, butter, oatmeal, malt, oats and barley were transported by both rivers to the port of Liverpool.

The rapid growth of population in Liverpool and Manchester created large markets for Cheshire dairy produce and the area around Runcorn and Halton supplied substantial quantities to both cities. The need for increased food supplies brought about a transformation of the landscape and within a hundred years of the end of the Civil War the trees of Halton deer park had disappeared to make way for pasture land for dairy and beef cattle. The large open fields and common pasture had also gone to be superseded by small fields enclosed by hawthorn hedges.

Before the days of railways there was intense competition between the Mersey and Irwell Navigation Company and the Bridgewater undertaking to secure the potato trade of Aston, Preston Brook and Sutton. It paid farmers to improve their land and marling and the application of bone dust paid dividends in creating rich fertile pasture and plough land. The Runcorn Bone Mills Company was established in 1843 and the company encouraged local farmers to buy its bone meal by offering the annual prize of a silver cup for the best farm produce which had been grown using their fertilizer. The canals also carried night soil from the towns as well as the manure of the city streets which together with Derbyshire lime was used to enhance the fertility of the soil. Fleshings from Runcorn's tanneries and canal dredgings were also used to enrich the fields. Farmyard manure was a valuable commodity and by the terms of his lease, a tenant farmer was usually forbidden to sell it or remove it from his farm.

As the demand for food in the expanding cities increased so the local farms responded with greater production. Sir Richard Brooke added to his profitable acres by reclaiming an area of marsh which bordered his estate on the river at Norton and by 1820 his embankments were causing sandbanks to form in the river's navigable channel, much to the chagrin of the shippers and merchants who had vessels trading to Warrington and Manchester.

The canal companies had a lucrative business in the carrying of agricultural produce but much of the trade was eventually taken by the railways. An early victim of railway competition was the daily "Moore Milk Boat" which carried churns of milk from the local farms to Manchester. The railways also transported young Irish cattle from Birkenhead docks to be fattened on farms in the district.

By 1830 farming was attracting handsome profits and a number of prominent business people began to engage in agriculture as a secondary occupation. The Johnson brothers, soap manufacturers of Runcorn, farmed extensively and in the 1850s and 1860s they exhibited cattle and sheep at the Birmingham Agricultural Show. John and William Brundrit, shipbuilders and quarry owners, also took a serious interest in farming and they exhibited sheep and poultry at various county shows. It can be seen that as late as 1851 agriculture was still very much an industry of significance in Runcorn. In that year the census returns show that a hundred people from Higher and Lower Runcorn were employed as farmers or as farm labourers.

In 1850 the vista of the countryside as seen from Halton Hill presented, in every direction, a patchwork of small hedged fields of potatoes, barley and pasture which stretched to Runcorn township to the west, Frodsham to the south and across the plain of Cheshire to the horizon in the south-east. This prospect was to remain little changed for another century and a quarter until the arrival of Runcorn new town.

The Quarries

The outcrops of pink and red sandstone which are to be found at Runcorn and Weston were laid down over 200 million years ago. Quarrying was the first industry of the district and from the early medieval period quarries were being operated in Halton, at Windmill Hill and at Clifton as evidenced in the building of Halton Castle, Norton Priory and the ancient parish church of Runcorn. Both Halton and Weston villages still retain stone houses dating from Elizabethan and Stuart times and the great house of Rocksavage

One of the Weston quarry tramroads used to convey stone to the stone loading wharf at Weston Point.

was built of local stone in 1568. By the early years of the eighteenth century Runcorn's durable sandstone was in demand in the neighbouring towns. In 1749 it was carried up river to Wilderspool from where it was carted to Grappenhall to be used for paving. At the beginning of the nineteenth century large-scale quarrying was taking place at Weston, Runcorn Hill, at the Stenhills and at Mill Brow.

The grey and red stone of the district is free from clay which makes other sandstones perishable. Being easily worked, it is ideal for building purposes and whilst it is soft when first quarried, it quickly hardens into a material which withstands the rigours of the weather indefinitely. Stonemasons preferred Runcorn stone because of the complete absence of pebbles which caused problems when working with other building stone. The best of the local stone could be worked to produce intricate detail and the colour of the material varied from dark red to grey, with a streaked grey and red stone which produced an attractive veined and marbled effect and which was always in demand. One strata of a whitish-grey colour produced a stone *"that both in appearance and durability is equal and indeed can only with some difficulty be distinguished from the best Derbyshire building stone"*. Another strata yielded a stone which made ideal grindstones which were used in many of the world's tool manufacturing centres. This solid stone had a uniform grain and a gritty nature. It was entirely free from deposits which could make grinding a dangerous process and the stone did not glaze with constant use.

From about 1820 there developed an enormous demand for Runcorn stone due to the vast dock construction then taking place at Liverpool. Much of the stone used in the city's docks came from William Wright's quarry on Runcorn Hill. John Tomkinson, a Liverpool man and the builder and patron of Bethesda Chapel, Runcorn, also engaged in large-scale quarrying. He bought the Mill Brow quarry which had been in the possession of Mr. Grindrod and which later belonged to Messrs. Woodward and Co. John Tomkinson also acquired a quarry in Weston. By 1840 stone was being extracted from many sites in the town. William Wareing Perrey had a quarry at Mill Brow, Dennis Brundrit worked two at the Stenhills and John Janion and William Shaw also had workings there. William Bankes had a quarry at Weston and Sir Richard Brooke owned another in Halton. The employment opportunities available in Runcorn and Weston soon attracted quarrymen from Cumbria and North Wales to the town and for about sixty years from 1820, the reputation of the local stone was at its height. According to a Cheshire directory of 1850, no less than 700 workmen were employed in John Tomkinson's Weston quarry.

At first horses were used to haul the stone but later the quarries were equipped with locomotives and steam cranes. Dram roads were constructed to convey the stone down the steep hillside to the stone loading wharfs and railway sidings at Weston Point. At Mill Brow the stone was transported by means of a tramway to a wharf on the Bridgewater Canal at the Big Pool.

After 1880 the best of the stone was worked out and Mill Brow ceased production in 1894, Runcorn Hill in 1900 and much of the Weston quarries soon after. When the quality of Runcorn and Weston stone was at its best, it was in demand for public buildings over a wide area of the north of England. Hore Cross Hall in Staffordshire and the neighbouring church of Holy Angels near Burton-on-Trent, Peel church in the Isle of Man, Finsthwaite church near Lake Windermere, Holy Trinity in Southport, St. Cyprian's at Edge Hill, Liverpool and Tabley House and Tatton Hall near Knutsford are a few examples of buildings where Runcorn or Weston sandstone was used. The enormous masonry of the Perch Rock Battery, the estuary fort at New Brighton, was quarried at Runcorn between 1826 and 1829 and in 1838 John Tomkinson's quarry supplied the stone for the foundations of the great railway viaduct at Stockport. Between 1868 and 1874 Chester cathedral was extensively recased with stone from Wright's quarry. The famous architect, Sir Gilbert Scott, preferred Runcorn stone when he restored ancient sandstone churches. At Chester, Scott did more than restore the friable fabric of the cathedral. He added to the building with an extension to the tower and he erected pinnacles of Runcorn stone to the choir. At St. Mary's, Nantwich, one of the architectural treasures of Cheshire, much of the original soft red sandstone had weathered badly and between 1854 and 1861 Sir Gilbert Scott replaced large areas of rotten masonry with Runcorn stone. In another restoration at St. Mary's over a thousand metres of Runcorn stone was required. Many of the older buildings in Runcorn are of the local stone. Holy Trinity church (1838); All Saints (1849); St. Michael's, Greenway Road (1887); St. John's, Weston (1898); St. John's, Victoria Road (1904) and in Halton, St. Mary's, which was consecrated in 1852. The Runcorn Railway Bridge (1868); the first town hall in Bridge Street (1831); the Mariners' Mission, Irwell Lane (1831) and the old market hall which is now the town's public swimming baths, are all built of local sandstone.

Because it was ideal for carving, the best of the fine-grained stone was used where precise detail was required as in the fireplaces at the home of the Cavendish family at Holker Hall near

Quarrying was the first of the town's industries.

This photograph of a local quarry shows very large blocks of stone being transported by tramway.

Cartmel and in some of the delicate sculpture in Liverpool's Anglican cathedral. Almost three hundred tons of close-grained stone from Weston quarry was used in the interior of the cathedral and the foundation stone was cut in Orme's quarry at Weston.

When steam driven craft were introduced onto the inland waterways the canal banks had to be strengthened with retaining walls and much of the work of reinforcement was carried out using locally produced stone. Some stone was crushed to make hardcore for roads and quarry waste made ideal ballast material for sailing ships. Runcorn ballast has been jettisoned from Liverpool ships at ports all over the world.

William Wright's 85-acre quarry was worked by his son, John Linacre Wright, until 1883 when the family relinquished the quarrying rights to William Guest and Son of Greenway Road. Guests later acquired the more profitable Weston quarry and the Runcorn Hill quarry passed to its last owners, Messrs. Orme and Muntz. After the closure of Runcorn Hill the Weston quarry continued to supply stone until it was abandoned in 1942.

Dennis Brundrit, druggist, shipbuilder and quarry master of Runcorn and Philip Whiteway who had recently arrived in the town, entered into partnership in 1823 as stone merchants and shipbuilders. Brundrit realised the potential market for the sale of Welsh granite. The hard wearing stone was perfect for road making as it could withstand the constant passage of heavily laden waggons with their iron tyres better than any other roadstone. The partners purchased the Penmaenmawr and Gimblet quarries and soon Brundrit and Whiteway's setts, curb and crossing stones were being used by the authorities in many of the industrial towns of the region. When street tramways became popular in the second half of the century, Welsh setts were required as ballast between and on both sides of the lines. Brundrit and Whiteway also supplied granite chippings to be used for macadamised road surfaces and for many years their small coastal vessels were engaged in carrying Welsh stone to Runcorn docks and also to other ports in the North-west and to Ireland. The partners built their own craft at their Mersey Street shipyard and they also built vessels to satisfy the needs of other merchants who were engaged in carrying slate, salt, coal and pottery materials.

Shipbuilding

The rise of the town's shipbuilding and repair industry which began about 1790 can be attributed to the development of the inland waterways of the region and the growth of Runcorn as a canal port from the early decades of the last century. The upper reaches of the Mersey do not provide the best sites for shipyards. The river is shallow and the course of the winding navigable channel is uncertain from one month to the next. However, river conditions on the Weaver at Frodsham Bridge afforded a better prospect for a shipyard site and during the eighteenth century the rapid expansion of the Cheshire salt trade brought about the establishment of a small shipbuilding and repair yard at Frodsham. Here river craft and small coasting vessels were built. The oak which was needed for ships' frames was still available from Delamere Forest and American and Baltic timber imported into Liverpool was easily obtained. As Liverpool's maritime commerce increased her merchants needed more vessels of every type and because the supply of barges, sailing flats and coastal schooners could not be met by the major builders, the Liverpool ship owners placed their orders for new craft at the small shipyards on the upper Mersey.

The Duke of Bridgewater had boat repair facilities at the terminus of his canal but the first sizeable vessels to be constructed for him in Runcorn's primitive yards were half a dozen schooners and barquentines which were launched between 1791 and 1800. The pace of ship construction expanded and the frequency of launches increased three-fold in the first forty years of the century with vessels being built at the Castle Rock, Belvedere and Mersey Street yards. The Runcorn shipyards prospered at the expense of the Frodsham yard and craftsmen from the latter were induced to seek work in Runcorn where the opportunity for long-term employment was better.

By 1850 Runcorn had won a considerable reputation for building ships of quality. A number of vessels were built to trade on the longest ocean routes and among the craft launched from Brundrit and Whiteway's Mersey Street yard there were two full-rigged ships. Some of the first paddle-steamers to operate on the Mersey were built locally and later in the century, Runcorn-built schooners were designed to trade to Newfoundland and South America.

The half mile of Mersey Street was the scene of considerable industrial activity with vessels being built or under repair. Sawyers, ships' carpenters, caulkers, painters and blacksmiths could be seen working on the hulls of ships which were enclosed in wooden scaffolding. The sounds and smells were those familiar wherever wooden craft were built. A blend of odours — sawn timber, pitch, linseed oil and paint and, all day long, the sound of the caulkers' mallets and the ring of the

The launch of the "Despatch", the last Runcorn-built schooner, at Brundrit and Hayes' yard, May 1886.

blacksmith's anvil could be heard. Ancillary maritime trades proliferated and for a hundred years from the Regency period, the town had many small independent establishments of specialist craftsmen who supplied the shipyards and the local shipping with their requirements. There were anchor smiths and chain makers, block and pump makers, riggers, mast and spa makers, fog horn manufacturers and makers of ships' stoves. One small business supplied ships' lamps, another navigation buoys. Others specialised in boat repair whilst a couple of small enterprises advertised their hull cleaning and ship painting services. There were a number of sail-making lofts and three rope walks.

Small wooden sailing craft were built at a number of places on mid-Merseyside; at Sankey Bridges, Fiddlers Ferry, Widnes and at Warrington. The last of the Runcorn builders operated until 1888 when the construction of the Manchester Ship Canal brought about the end of the industry although wooden vessels were still being repaired on local slips into the 1930s. Canal barges and narrow boats continued to be constructed at the Castle Rock and at boat building yards on the Big Pool until well into the twentieth century.

The Tanneries

Tanning is an ancient industry which has long been practised in this area. Because Cheshire was always a dairy county with large herds of cattle it is not surprising that there were many small village tanyards which were set up to process the local skins and hides. These farmyard tanneries were able to obtain oak bark from which to make tanning extract from the woods and forests and it is likely that by the eighteenth century every hamlet had a farmer who engaged in tanning as a secondary occupation. It is certain that at this time there were small tanyards in Runcorn, Astmoor and in Preston Brook. Early in the last century a Mr. Graham had a tanyard at Old Quay, whilst another in Halton Road was being operated by a Mr. Walker. The latter establishment changed hands in the 1830s when it was acquired by John Ockleston. Tanning was long established in Astmoor with one yard in existence in the middle of the eighteenth century. Frank, William and Henry Reynolds were operating a tannery at Astmoor in 1830 and a trades directory of 1834 lists Henry George Davies as having a tanyard there. In addition to his thriving quarry on Runcorn Hill, William Wright had tannery premises in Bridge Street

By the first decade of this century Runcorn had become the country's leading centre of leather production. These photographs show Highfield tannery in the 1960s.

and between 1841 and 1851 yet another tannery was started on the northern bank of the Bridgewater Canal opposite Ocklestons. This concern was later taken over by Mr. J.N. Lello before being bought by Thomas Walker of Bolton to become Highfield Tannery in 1888. In the late 1860s Robert Pierpoint opened his tanyard in Halton Road.

By 1865 tanning in Runcorn had become big business and as often is the case, war conditions were responsible for the upsurge in trade. The armies of Victorian times depended on leather (there were no substitutes for it) and army boots, belts, harnesses and many other items of leather were in increased demand during the Crimean War, the Indian Mutiny and the American Civil War. Throughout the nineteenth century the mechanisation of Britain's factories and mills brought about a need for leather belting for machines and engines. At the same time the huge growth in population meant that there were additional millions requiring to be shod.

A number of reasons may be advanced to show why Runcorn developed into one of the largest centres of leather production in Britain. In addition to the early advantage of there always being a ready supply of hides and oak bark from the Cheshire countryside, the Mersey estuary provided an easy way of disposing of the unpleasant waste liquors of the tanning processes and it was also via the river that the tanneries were able to export their finished hides. All the larger tanneries were sited on the Bridgewater Canal and it was by way of the canal that they received their coal supplies, raw hides and imported tanning materials from Liverpool docks. From the last years of the nineteenth century the tanneries were fortunate in being able to obtain Lake Vyrnwy water from Liverpool's pipeline. This water is unusually pure and it was a great benefit to the industry. Of course the proximity of the port of Liverpool was a major factor in the rise of Runcorn's tanneries. Hides imported from North and South America, India, West Africa, western Europe and New Zealand came through the port of Liverpool as did the various tanning materials. These included mimosa from South Africa, sweet chestnut from France and Italy, sumac from Cyprus, myrabolans from India and querbracho from South America.

According to the local folklore, an early tannery at Astmoor supplied leather to make the boots which were used by the Duke of Wellington's army during the Napoleonic War. There is no doubt about the important contribution made by the Runcorn tanneries to the war effort in two World Wars. During the First World War the demand for leather was such that in 1915

Hazlehursts' disused soapworks was adapted to become Camden Tannery.

Soap and Chemicals

Alkali manufacture in Runcorn had its origins in the Regency period and it pre-dates the establishment of the chemical industry in Widnes by more than thirty years. As early as 1816 two factories in Runcorn were producing soap and turpentine and within a few years both the works had developed into major manufacturing concerns which were producing chemicals as well as soap.

Under the will of the Reverend Thomas Alcock who died in 1798, his great niece, Elizabeth Burton inherited land together with an orchard and garden abutting the southern bank of the Bridgewater Canal above Runcorn township. In 1799 Elizabeth married John Johnson, a local farmer. Johnson possessed acute business acumen and within a few years he had increased the value of his wife's inheritance by mortgaging the land and by building houses on it. Johnson speculated further by taking out additional mortgages in 1803 in order to establish a soap works, a rope walk and a slate factory but he did not live long enough to see the full blossoming of his enterprises, for he died in 1816 at the age of thirty-seven by which time the manufacture of soap had become his primary business interest. By 1822 Messrs. Hayes, Ollier and Company had leased the Johnson works and in addition to soapmaking they were producing resin and turpentine. It seems that an arrangement was made whereby the lease was to last only for the duration of the minority of John Johnson's sons and when the young men became of age, the factory reverted to the control of the Johnson family.

Ideally sited to receive and despatch materials by the Bridgewater Canal, the soapworks of Thomas and John Johnson prospered so that by 1832 it was producing 1,500 tons of soap annually. In that year the brothers paid £38,000 in soap duty. The tax on soap was then three pence per pound weight. Within a year of the reduction of the duty to three-halfpence per pound in 1833, Johnsons' output had soared above 2,000 tons and by 1841 the works had expanded to such an extent that its rateable value had tripled in a decade.

Soon other entrepreneurs were attracted to the locality. Two Liverpool men, Dennis Kennedy and Thomas Maguire purchased land in 1833 on the Weaver Canal at Weston. They took out a mortgage of £1,000 from the Bankes family of Weston to enable them to build a works to manufacture soap and chemicals. But the

Halton Grange, built by Thomas Johnson, the soap manufacturer between 1854 and 1856. In 1932 the house became Runcorn's town hall.

venture proved unsuccessful and when the partners defaulted on their mortgage, their factory and some adjacent land was bought by the Johnson brothers. The Johnsons had made a shrewd bargain for their own business was increasing rapidly and the new site would afford them the opportunity of building new plant on land which was favourably sited to receive supplies by water.

The other successful soapery was that founded by Thomas Hazlehurst in 1816 and its rise to prominence parallels that of the Johnsons. Thomas Hazlehurst was born in 1779 and his name first appears in local records in connection with the management of Runcorn township in 1806. He laid the foundation of his fortune in salt and coal-carrying on the river Weaver and he was engaged in some kind of manufacturing process before he founded his soap works for in 1815, both he and Thomas Johnson were selling large quantities of industrial cinders to the local Overseer of the Highways. Hazlehurst's works were built at Camden Croft in High Street on the opposite side of the Bridgewater Canal to that of his rivals and within twenty years business was booming to such an extent that production had grown to 1,260 tons in 1832 and the firm paid soap duty amounting to £23,000 for the year.

The trades directories of 1840 list Johnsons and Hazlehurst as "turpentine distillers, soap, vitriol and soda manufacturers and chemists". Both companies were making their own soda for soap manufacture by the offensive Leblanc process. This method of alkali manufacture necessitated the building of tall chimneys in order to disperse hydrochloric acid fumes into the atmosphere and by 1836 both works had chimneys which were landmarks in the area. In December 1836 "Hazlehurst", a chimney of 93 metres was completed and a local newspaper reported that *"the immense pile contains more than half a million bricks and is computed to be about 2,800 tons in weight. The coping stone on the top weighs ten tons. There is a twin chimney in the town (Johnsons) which is not quite so high".* Thus it can be seen that the two Runcorn soapworks were making alkali at least ten years before John Hutchinson built the first Widnes chemical works at Woodend in 1847.

The geographical position of Runcorn made it the prime location for the alkali industry. The works were conveniently sited equidistant from the coal mines at St. Helens and the salt of the Cheshire saltfield. They were also well placed to receive limestone from North Wales and pyrites from Ireland and Spain by way of the river and the canals.

Between 1840 and 1860 the Johnson brothers created an industrial empire. They determined to own the sources of their raw materials and by 1860 they possessed a saltworks at Winsford, limestone quarries in Wales, a coalmine in St. Helens and a factory in Widnes which produced resin. To transport their raw materials and finished products the Johnsons owned four schooners, ten sailing flats and a number of smaller vessels.

The expansion of the two Johnson factories was spectacular. In 1850 they developed their Weston works and they built a very large chimney of 110 metres to carry away the acid fumes from the plant. However, the great chimney was not completely successful in dispersing the fumes and for some years after its completion the brothers were involved in disputes over blighted crops, trees and gardens. It seems likely that the aggrieved complainants did not seek legal redress because the Johnsons were *"almost the largest employers of labour in the district and the most liberal of paymasters".* It was also reported that the brothers *"have not merely a local standing but possess almost a world-wide reputation ... They were earnest contributors to the erection of Holy Trinity church ... Promoters of the daily Infant and Sunday schools ... Supporters of the Ragged School"* — and they were also members of the Runcorn Improvement Commission.

Throughout the 1850s the soaperies boomed. Messrs. T. & J. Johnson's works were the largest in the area and in 1860 they opened an office in Liverpool in order to facilitate their business to the United States. Their agent in Liverpool was Charles Wigg who was to start a successful chemical works of his own in Runcorn a few years later. Hazlehursts were also involved in trade with the United States and they had a considerable business in the export of carbonate of soda.

Other, smaller chemical works were built in Runcorn but they did not prosper to the same extent as the two original firms. Messrs. Rooke & Hunter had their plant in Halton Lane (Halton Road) where they made acid. This works was in being in 1834 but it seems to have gone out of business about 1850. Another short-lived enterprise was the chemical works of William Collier which was established near to the Weston factory of T. & J. Johnson in 1859. Collier, a former works manager of Johnsons, was unable to compete with his formidable rivals and within three years he was forced to sell his works to the brothers. In 1854 Messrs. Haddock and Parnell were unsuccessful in their endeavours to obtain land on which to build a works. They applied to the Trustees of the Duke of Bridgewater to sell or lease them a site in the Runcorn area on which to build a factory but the Trustees wanted to avoid coming into conflict with Sir Richard Brooke whose Cuerdley tenants were complaining that their crops had been damaged by industrial fall-out from the Widnes works and they therefore refused the application.

After the Bridgewater Trustees' refusal to sell land for the building of chemical plant, the industrial development of Runcorn slowed until 1860 when the partners Charles Wigg, Neil Mathieson and Duncan McKecknie set up a works at Old Quay to make soap and extract copper. The two Scotsmen, Mathieson and McKecknie, had been managers in the Johnson works and Charles Wigg had been Johnsons' export manager in Liverpool. Early in the partnership the manufacture of soap was abandoned and the Old Quay plant concentrated on the production of copper. Within a short time McKecknie had a disagreement with his partners and he left to start a copper refinery in St. Helens. Not long afterwards Mathieson also departed to establish a new works in Widnes.

Charles Wigg's works at Old Quay soon became a thriving concern and within fifteen years of its foundation the factory was shipping a larger volume of freight through the Bridgewater, Old Quay and Weaver docks than any other works in the area. In 1875 seventy thousand tons of material was despatched and received at the works and the company carried iron ore and sulphur and chemicals between Widnes and the port of Liverpool in the firm's own flats and steam barges.

From 1850 onwards there developed a close liaison between the Runcorn chemical manufacturers and those in Widnes and managers and workers travelled to employment from one town to the other. Besides this exchange of expertise there was also the movement of capital investment across the Gap. The Johnsons had their Iron Bridge Works on the St. Helens Canal in Widnes, J.H. Dennis, the copper smelter, had financial interests in Wigg's works, Robert Shaw of Runcorn was a partner in Hall Brothers and Shaw of West Bank, Widnes, a company which produced salt cake, bleaching powder and caustic soda.

In Victorian times the pollution of the atmosphere by primitive chemical processes was appalling and the Alkali Act of 1863, which prohibited the release of corrosive fumes directly into the air, was slow in being implemented. Three years after the passing of the Act the situation in Runcorn was still unsatisfactory. After a particularly bad emission of acid gas in the summer of 1866, Mr. Blake, the Inspector of Nuisances for the Runcorn Highways and Sanitary Committee, reported to the Committee on the effect the pollution had made on

vegetation in the town. The fumes had come from Johnsons' works and Mr. Blake attempted to get the brothers to take action in order to alleviate the problem. He was unsuccessful in his efforts and Thomas Johnson responded by threatening to have the Inspector dismissed from his job if he complained in the future. It was reported that "Mr. Johnson made use of a great deal of harsh language ... he said that he would leave no means unturned to upset Blake from his position". The Johnson family had made the town and the brothers were relentless businessmen who defended their interests and who would not tolerate interference in their operations from anyone, and that included the officials of the Improvement Commissioners.

Noxious gases caused problems to the east of the town. When Charles Wigg and his partners began to operate their plant at Old Quay they encountered furious opposition from Sir Richard Brooke whose house was little more than a mile away from the new works and the Norton Priory mansion lay directly in the path of the prevailing wind from Wiggs. Soon the baronet was complaining that his crops had wilted and his trees had been damaged by industrial pollution. Sir Richard also alleged that his pasture was spoiled so that he could not fatten his cattle. His injunction against the partners named Neil Mathieson as being responsible for the nuisance and this was probably the reason for Mathieson leaving Old Quay works to start a new enterprise in Widnes whilst Charles Wigg, in association with his sons and his son-in-law, Dr. Edward Steele, carried on the Runcorn works under the name of Wigg Brothers and Steele. Sir Richard's complaint was the first of many and twelve years later his son, the seventh baronet, was demanding reparation for damage to crops allegedly caused by fumes from Wiggs.

Despite the passing of the Alkali Acts of 1863 and 1874 and the Noxious Gases Act of 1880, there was no obvious lessening of atmospheric pollution on mid-Merseyside. The Widnes works were by far the worst offenders with a million tons of coal a year being burned in the furnaces so that the place came to be described as "the dirtiest, ugliest and most depressing town in England". But Runcorn also made a substantial contribution to industrial smog. Writing of the town in 1881 Thomas Helsby, the editor of George Ormerod's "History of the County Palatine and City of Chester" said *"Noxious vapours from the chimneys of the chemical works are carried at times as far as High Legh ... and trees and vegetation generally for miles round are blasted and it is certain that there has been a great decrease in the value of all the farms in and around Norton, the most of which, at present, are too inconveniently situated to be turned into building land"*. Helsby may have been guilty of exaggeration but by 1875 the pink sandstone of Runcorn's churches was a uniform black and the Mersey had become a drain for the effluent of dozens of industries and towns from Manchester to the sea.

By 1860 the Johnson brothers were at the zenith of their success. In addition to their thriving factories in Runcorn, the colliery in St. Helens had proved a valuable asset and the brothers won a profitable contract to supply steam coal to naval and merchant ships using the port of Liverpool. The Winsford saltworks and the limestone quarries in North Wales produced more than was needed in the Runcorn works and the brothers found a ready sale for the surplus to other manufacturers. But the Johnsons were about to over-reach themselves to become involved in adventures which would lead to financial difficulties and to their eventual bankruptcy.

The Johnson's industrial empire was destroyed by their avarice. During the American Civil War business to the United States fell away but Thomas and John Johnson saw a way of enormously increasing their profits by running the Union blockade to supply the Confederate states with the materials they required for their war effort. They succeeded in passing one steamer through the blockade to realise a profit of £70,000. The success of the adventure tempted the brothers to invest heavily in a number of blockade runners but this time with disastrous consequences for the steamers were lost in a naval battle at Charleston. The Johnsons could not withstand the huge losses incurred and the affair led first to the flotation of the company as a public concern and eventually to their ruin.

In 1865 the Johnson Company became the Runcorn Soap and Alkali Company and the new concern purchased all the brothers' properties in Runcorn, Weston, Widnes and Winsford. The promoters of the new firm were Thomas Campbell and Francis Shand described as Liverpool merchants, Peter Boult and John Higson, brokers of Liverpool and William Keates, copper smelter of Liverpool. The other promoters were Neil Mathieson and Charles Wigg. Among those investing in the Runcorn Soap and Alkali Company were the soap manufacturers William Gossage of Widnes and Thomas Hazlehurst of Runcorn. Duncan McKecknie also had a financial interest in the new company.

The Johnson brothers kept their St. Helens colliery but not for long. They had borrowed large sums to finance the American venture and in 1869 they were forced to sell the coal leases in order to pay their debts. Two years later they were declared bankrupt. Pressed for money, John Johnson attempted to sell his house, Bank House, to the Improvement Commissioners but the house could not easily be adapted for public use so the offer was declined. Thomas Johnson was obliged to sell his mansion, Halton Grange, which he had built in the style of Queen Victoria's residence, Osborne House in the Isle of Wight. The house was bought by his rival in business, Thomas Hazlehurst, for £10,428 in 1874. (Halton Grange was purchased in 1932 by the Runcorn Urban District Council to become the Town Hall.) After the fall into bankruptcy John Johnson lived another twelve years. He died in 1883 and his brother survived him by a year.

The Runcorn Soap and Alkali Company came into existence at a most fortunate time for in the decade after the end of the American Civil War, there was intense activity at both the Runcorn works to satisfy the demands of the market in the United States. The manufacture of Johnsons' pale yellow soap ceased when the new company was formed and the works concentrated on the production of basic heavy chemicals such as sulphuric acid, salt cake and hydrochloric acid. The recovery of the Lancashire cotton industry after the calamitous recession caused by the American Civil War resulted in a large increase in the production of bleaching powder and the Runcorn works were busy in meeting the demand for the product.

Although fierce competition had brought about the end of soap making at the Runcorn Soap and Alkali works, Hazlehursts were able to expand this side of their business. In spite of a temporary recession when supplies of tallow had been hard to find during and immediately after the Crimean War, Hazlehursts had grown steadily and many of their brands of pale, brown and mottled soap were known nationwide. The company also manufactured wax candles, night lights and Eau de Cologne. The range of their products was remarkable. By 1895 they were advertising "Honest" soap, "Marvel Washer", "Crown" and "Anchor" blue mottled soap. The toilet soap included "Bouquet", "Pearl" and "Sun" soap and by the early years of the twentieth century the variety had increased to include "Marigold", "Skylark", "Balloon", "Engine", "Tower", "Antelope" and others. Hazlehursts realised the importance of attractive presentation and their products were packaged in colourful wrappers which helped them to win a world market. Their Gold Medal Soaps won awards for quality at exhibitions in London, Paris, Calcutta, Australia and in New Zealand.

The manufacture of soap was Runcorn's premier industry in the nineteenth century and before the duty of three-halfpence per pound weight was removed in 1853, the town's soaperies were contributing £80,000 a year to the national exchequer.

Following the establishment of the soapworks new industry was not long in making its appearance. The Bridgewater Foundry and Engineering Works of E. Timmins & Sons was started on the canalside at Delph Bridge in 1827 to produce castings for the soap and alkali works. Timmins also made the town's first lamp posts. The foundry quickly gained a reputation for precise engineering and they even made steam engines for a number of paddle-steamers which were built in the local yards in the 1830s. The works went on to specialise in artesian well-boring and later, in the manufacture of pumping engines and air compressors. Timmins progressed to become one of the town's major employers. On the occasion of the centenary of the foundry in 1927 about ninety fitters, moulders, pattern makers, carpenters and wheelwrights posed for the commemorative photograph. In addition to this workforce the firm had a well-sinking department of nearly a hundred craftsmen. Over many years Timmins' enjoyed international recognition for their expertise in well drilling.

Among the town's smaller industries was the steam mill of Hardy and Wylde at Old Quay. The six storey building was a landmark in the district and on the occasion of a fire at the mill in 1857 it was reported that there were "six stones which are at work day and night producing between 500 and 600 tons of oatmeal". The steam mill had made the windmill on Delph Bridge redundant and in the 1850s the sails were removed leaving the tower a reminder of the days when the mill was the town's only mechanised activity. At Old Quay there was an industrial pottery which produced drain pipes and chimney pots. Other industries included Robert Hedley's school writing slate manufactury, a brickyard, a chain works and a small factory producing elastic stockings.

By 1850 Runcorn was a bustling little industrial town of some 8,700 inhabitants. It was rapidly losing its image as a resort and the description of the place by Nathaniel Hawthorne, who was the United States Consul in Liverpool from 1853 to 1857, is probably well defined. Hawthorne was not impressed and he wrote that Runcorn had *"Two or three tall manufacturing chimneys with a pennant of black smoke from each, a church or two. A meagre, uninteresting, shabby brick-built town with irregular streets, not village-like but paved and looking like a dwarfed, stunted city. We cannot conceive in America, anything so unpicturesque as this English town"*.

As for rural Widnes or Woodend, the landscape was about to suffer a profound change. Throughout the 1850s factories had sprung up around the St. Helens Canal and a decade later, they were being built around West Bank Dock. John Hutchinson had built the first alkali works in Widnes in 1847 and within twenty years the view into Lancashire was one of factory chimneys, waste tips and the ugly towers of the chemical plant.

While the devastation of the local countryside was calamitous, there was produced in the new factories a material which would bring infinite benefit to mankind. Chloride of lime or bleaching power, was a powerful disinfectant. It was used in purifying water supplies and its use ended the menace of cholera in Britain after 1860. The demand for the product became immense and thousands of tons were despatched in casks from Runcorn and Widnes to towns all over the world.

Industrial Recession and Progression

For most of the two decades from 1850 Runcorn's trade and industry thrived but by 1874 two events occurred which were to have far reaching adverse effects on the prosperity of the town. One calamity had been advancing steadily and remorselessly for a number of years. This was the almost catastrophic silting of the navigable channel and the approaches to the town's docks. The other event to occur in 1874 and which was not recognised as a menace by local industry, was the establishment of a factory by Brunner and Mond in Northwich in which alkali was produced by a new and cheaper method. Both the natural calamity of silting and the Solvay process of chemical manufacture were to bring recession and unemployment to Runcorn.

By 1874 conditions at the approaches to the Bridgewater and Old Quay docks were becoming impossible for safe navigation. The sandbanks blocked the dock entrances and as a result the coastal trade and the shipbuilding and repair yards experienced severe depression. At the same time there was unrest in the Bridgewater labour force. Three years before the Bridgewater Navigation Company was formed in 1874 there had been trouble when the dock workers went on strike for increased pay. The Bridgewater Company came into being when the Mersey was at its most perverse and the Company experienced labour difficulties from its inception. When the new company rationalised its trading activities in 1874 the dockers viewed the changes with the deepest suspicion. They went on strike demanding more money and in doing so they dislocated traffic when the quick turn about of vessels was essential because of the problems caused by the sanding of the channels.

After 1877 the capricious Mersey channels began to improve but labour relations at the docks remained unsatisfactory. When in 1879, the Bridgewater Company proposed to reduce the dock workers' wages by seven and a half per cent in order to bring them in line with the wages of unskilled workers in the local factories, there was an instant walk out.

In February and March 1884, there was serious disruption of trade when the Bridgewater flatmen received notice that the Company was to cut their wages by a shilling a week. The strikers were informed that if there was not an immediate return to work their earnings would be reduced by a further shilling a week when they did resume work. There were big processions of striking flatmen in Runcorn which were impressive in their orderliness. The men marched through the town "preserving admirable order and singing hymns … their appearance evoking much astonishment among the townspeople". Led by the Salvation Army band, the hundred and twenty watermen marched from Delph Bridge via Shaw Street and Lowlands Road to Devonshire Square and public feeling was aroused sufficiently to cause subscriptions to be raised for a strike fund. In the end the flatmen returned to work on the Company's terms. The strikers' wages were reduced by two shillings a week and, as some jobs had been taken by other men during the stoppage, a number of flatmen were thrown out of work.

As the 1880s approached, the local alkali works began to experience severe competition from Brunner-Monds. The Runcorn factories found that Brunner-Mond's Solvay process of soda manufacture had all but made their Leblanc method of production obsolete. Brunners could make soda at a much lower cost and within a couple of years of the establishment of the Northwich works, the firm had made substantial inroads into the Leblanc firms' alkali business on both sides of the Mersey. Brunner-Monds' success meant employment opportunities in Northwich but recession and contraction in Runcorn with local manufacturers reducing wages and laying off men. The "Warrington Guardian" of 8th February 1879 reported on the situation in Wigg Brothers and Steel's works when the salt cake makers were told that their earnings were to be reduced to bring them in line with the workers at the Runcorn Soap and Alkali works in Runcorn and Weston. The newspaper account states, *"The Runcorn Soap and Alkali Company's men voluntarily offered to work at these prices rather than have the works close but even at the reductions they are compelled now to close the Runcorn works as they cannot carry on without a loss. Messrs. Wigg Brothers and Steele have done all in their power to keep the works going rather than turn off men but since the reductions early in December the men have neglected their work and have not made the quantity they ought to have done, thus causing a great waste of fuel".*

When the crisis in the chemical industry worsened the Runcorn Soap and Alkali Company decided to build a new plant using the Solvay process but, with adverse conditions developing in foreign markets, the situation in the Leblanc factories did not improve. There was a world depression in chemicals with fierce foreign competition and dumping. Furthermore, the American market was in severe decline due to the imposition of protective tariffs by the United States against the principal Leblanc manufacturers. If the future looked decidedly bleak for the mid-Merseyside works a new development at Weston Point did not augur well for the industrial prospects of Northwich.

At the very time that the success of the Brunner-Mond factory in Northwich was beginning to pose a threat to employment in the Leblanc alkali works of Widnes and Runcorn an event occurred which was far more menacing to the industry in Northwich and to the Cheshire salt producers. In 1882 a small company called the Mersey Salt and Brine Company laid a pipeline to carry brine from the vast salt deposits under the estate of Mr. A.H. Smith-Barry at Marbury near Northwich, to salt works built at Weston Point. This was the first time that a brine pipe had been extended beyond the boundary of the salt field and the implications of the development were not fully appreciated by the Cheshire salt refiners, or by the Trustees of the River Weaver Navigation on whose waterway almost the whole of the salt trade of Cheshire was carried. The salt manufacturers and the Weaver Trustees ignored the new project and private landowners across whose land the pipeline was laid, readily agreed to its construction. In Northwich the pipeline was seen as an insignificant enterprise and it was not realised that if the brine was simply pumped out of the salt field to be manufactured elsewhere, the rateable value of Northwich would decline and trade would depart elsewhere to bring eventual ruin not only to the local saltworks but to many other commercial and business interests as well. Before long it was seen that the Mersey Salt and Brine Company's works at Weston Point could produce salt at costs considerably less than those of the works in the salt region. For one thing, the St. Helens coal and slack needed by the refiners in large quantity was much cheaper in Runcorn than in Northwich and for another, the heavy Weaver

An ocean-going vessel loading salt at the vacuum plant, Salt Union, Weston Point.

Bagging salt at the vacuum plant, Salt Union, Weston Point.

freight charges did not apply to salt produced at Weston Point. The new company believed that it was in a position to command the bulk of Runcorn's coasting and foreign salt trade which was averaging about 200,000 tons per annum and the directors hoped that they could supply the Runcorn chemical works with brine and subsequently extend the pipeline across the river to the works in Widnes and St. Helens.

When Salt Union was formed in 1888, the new firm became the owners of the Mersey Salt and Brine Company and plans were considered by which the pipeline could be enlarged. By now, however, the industrialists of Northwich and Winsford were aware of the formidable competition they were facing and they mounted opposition which succeeded in slowing Salt Union's expansion plans for some years.

Among the smaller companies established in Runcorn by 1880 were Lyons & Sons, manufacturers of soda ash and caustic soda at the Old Quay Alkali works; William Earp, lead smelters; J.J. Rooke and Company, alkali manufacturers of Bates Bridge and John Cliff of Lambeth who had the Old Quay pottery which manufactured drain pipes. There was a significant development a few miles out of Runcorn in 1886 with the transfer of the Britannia Telegraph Works to Helsby from Neston on Wirral. The factory grew rapidly and soon work people were travelling by railway from Runcorn to their employment in Helsby. Eventually the Helsby cable works was to become a major source of employment for hundreds of Runcorn men and women.

In order to survive the competition from the Solvay ammonia soda factories and from the foreign manufacturers, forty-eight of Britain's Leblanc firms combined to form the huge United Alkali Company on 1st November 1890. The merger included fourteen firms from Widnes as well as Wiggs, the Runcorn Soap and Alkali works at Runcorn and Weston and the chemical side of Hazlehursts. The founding of the United Alkali Company coincided with a great slump in chemical manufacture with a resulting decrease in employment in the locality. When the United Alkali Company drastically reduced its manufacturing capacity at the Runcorn works in 1895 it was rumoured that as many as 1700 men were to be laid off and the Runcorn Council appealed to the Company not to close the works as they were "the backbone of the trade of the town". When the United Alkali Company established its new ammonia-soda plant at Fleetwood in 1893 the effect was soon felt in Runcorn in lay-offs and hardship.

Hard times persisted for some years with chemicals, shipping and quarries all in decline. On the occasion of Queen Victoria's Diamond Jubilee, the "Runcorn Guardian" of June 6th 1897 reported gloomily, "Although labouring under somewhat adverse conditions the townspeople have decided to enter with enthusiasm into the Jubilee celebrations". Earlier in the year the Medical Officer of Health for Runcorn had attributed the population fall to 18,000 to the emigration of unemployed workers from the town. In the midst of the depression there was one heartening occurrence — the arrival of the Castner-Kellner Alkali Company at Weston Point.

Castners was created by the Aluminium Company of Oldbury which decided to locate its new chemical works at Weston Point where the land was cheap and where there was an easily accessible source of brine. The new company held the right to exploit the patents of Hamilton Young Castner of New York and Carl Kellner of Vienna both of whom were on the board of directors. Another director was Sir William Mather, a well-known manufacturer of the electrical power equipment, which was essential for the new process of electrolysis of brine. In their prospectus the Castner-Kellner Company declared that they would be able to manufacture caustic soda and bleaching powder at half the current market prices.

Castner-Kellner's method of decomposing salt by electricity entailed the use of large quantities of mercury and there was some anxiety expressed over the possibility of atmospheric poisoning caused by the release of mercury. These fears proved to be groundless and in 1897 Castners began to take brine for the processes. The new factory was an immediate success and over the years the works has expanded to become the mainstay of employment in the locality. It has outlived the four Runcorn factories of the United Alkali Company as well as most of the Widnes works which were in production in 1891.

The vital expansion of local industry in the twentieth century would not have been possible without an improved water supply and in 1892 the great water tower at Norton was built as a balancing reservoir on Liverpool Corporation's pipeline from Lake Vyrnwy. Within a few years the soft Vyrnwy water would be available to the domestic users of Runcorn and it would prove invaluable in some of the town's industrial processes. Built of Runcorn sandstone, Norton water tower is 34 metres high and its tank holds 3,000 tons of water (672,000 gallons). The supply to Liverpool is carried by means of a ten foot-wide tunnel under the Mersey. Carved in the frieze at the top of the tower is a Latin inscription, "*This water, derived from the sources of the Severn, is brought to the City of Liverpool, a distance of eighty miles, through the mountains and over the plains of Wales and the intervening country, at the cost of the municipality, in the year of Our Lord 1892*".

Women and girls dredge for coal in the drained Bridgewater Canal at the Runcorn Soap and Alkali works.

Bibliography

For a description of the local scene before the arrival of industry William Handley's "After Many Years" and "Local Memoranda" which were published by the *"Runcorn Weekly News"* in 1902 were helpful. (Warrington Library, ref.P50761) The effect of local land reclamation on river navigation receives the attention of the British Association for the Advancement of Science, *"Report from the Mersey Inquiry Committee"* (1856).]

The notes on the quarries were taken from F H Crossley's article in the *"Chester Archeological Society"*, Vol.34 Part II (1940) from *"Notes on the Restoration of Chester Cathedral"* by the Dean of Chester (1974); and *"Old Cheshire Churches"* by Raymond Richards (1947). Other facts were obtained from *"Quarrying at Runcorn"* by the Mersey Valley Partnership' *"Daily Life as a Quarryman"* by Jack Kinsey, at the Norton Priory Museum and from the Tithe map of Runcorn township (1843). A most useful source of information is an article on Messrs Orme and Muntz quarry which is deposited in the local history collection at the Shopping City Library, Runcorn.

For background reading on the building of wooden coastal craft, the most comprehensive survey is Basil Greenhill's *"The Merchant Schooners"* (1968). For local shipbuilding see the present author's *"Schooner Port"* (1981). There is a useful historic account of local boat building in "Sprinch Dockyard, Runcorn 1883-1977" by K M Holt in the *"Port of Manchester Review"* for 1978.

Much of the material used in the account of the tanning industry has been taken from material deposited by Mr. C.C. Posnett at Catalyst, The Museum of the Chemical Industry, from the *"Runcorn Official Handbook"* for 1920, 1926, 1952 and 1960 and from Pigot & Co., *"Cheshire Directory"* (1828) and J. Slater *"Directory of Cheshire"* 1855 and 1890 and White & Co. *Runcorn Directory 1887*.

For soap and chemical manufacture see *"The House of Hazlehurst 1816-1916"*, Lever Brothers publication (1916) and *"Alkali Firms in Widnes and Runcorn"*, Catalyst, The Museum of the Chemical Industry publication. The background reading to alkali manufacture included Charles Nickson's *"A History of Runcorn"* (1887) and D.W.F. Hardie's *"A History of the Chemical Industry of Widnes"* (1950).

Gordon Rintoul's *"Chemical Manufacture in Runcorn and Weston 1800-1930"* is a scholarly survey and it is to be found in the Museum of the Chemical Industry. A good guide to the sequence of events is the chronology compiled by the Runcorn library — *"A Chronology of Runcorn and Its Environs"*.

Further information of local chemical firms is to be found in *Warrington Guardian* 14th February 1857 and the account of industrial pollution in the district has been taken from the papers of the Brooke of Norton documents — Damage to Crops by Industrial Processes (1863, D24B1 and D24B7/15; 1873 D25A1) County Record Office, Chester. See also the papers of Dr. R. Dickenson at the Cheshire County Record Office (ref.D3075).

For the story of Salt Union and the development of the Mersey Salt and Brine Company see *"Salt in Cheshire"* (1915) by A. F. Calvert.

Chapter 14
The Coming of the Railway

The railway was late in coming to Runcorn but as early as 1829 there had been a proposal to link Liverpool to Birmingham by railway with the line crossing the Mersey at Runcorn Gap. The financiers who proposed the undertaking were anxious not to offend the canal interests and their spokesman, John Moss, assured William Huskisson, the MP for Liverpool, that a bridge crossing the Gap was ideal because "a railroad to Runcorn interferes with no canal". Notwithstanding, the Liverpool to Birmingham railway scheme was denounced by Robert Bradshaw of the Bridgewater Trustees and by shippers and merchants who believed that a bridge would hamper traffic on the river. The idea came to nought but fifteen years later, interest in railways to Runcorn revived with the promotion by the Grand Junction Railway of a Preston Brook to Runcorn line with a branch to the Bridgewater docks and ultimately with an extension to Liverpool. The plans received wholehearted support at a public meeting held in January 1846, but the scheme was withdrawn after the Board of Trade objected to the proposal. This set-back was soon seen to be a more serious reversal than the local merchants had realised. A number of rival ports which were also engaged in the coastal trade such as Fleetwood, Garston and Birkenhead succeeded in acquiring railway links and they began to attract some of Runcorn's traditional trade away from the Bridgewater Trustees. It was now realised that if Runcorn was to prosper it was a matter of urgent priority that efforts should be made to secure the vital rail link to the town and its docks. At a meeting of the ratepayers in May 1858 it was resolved unanimously that *"a committee be appointed to lay a synopsis before the London North-Western Railway Company with a view to inducing them to make a branch line of the railway from either Moore, Warrington, Aston or from some other station on their line and to take into consideration the possibility of building a bridge over the river at Runcorn"*. However, it was to be another ten years before local aspirations were realised and Runcorn was situated on the main Liverpool to London railway line. And yet, oddly enough, there was a Runcorn railway station in existence seventeen years before the town's main line station was completed in 1868. The "Runcorn" station of 1851 was some miles out of town on the Chester to Warrington line at Sutton Weaver. At that distance beyond the town's boundary the name was hardly appropriate and shortly afterwards it was changed to "Runcorn Road" and when the town station was opened, Runcorn

Road station was changed to Halton station.

Shortly after the Warrington to Chester railway was opened an accident in the Sutton tunnel cost the lives of seven passengers. On Chester Cup race day in April 1851, a train packed with returning racegoers experienced difficulties when its under-powered locomotive laboured to cross the Frodsham viaduct. A following train which was hauled by a more powerful engine tried to help by pushing the first and both entered the tunnel at Sutton Weaver only to stall inside. Before a warning could be given a third train entered the tunnel and the collision occurred. At the subsequent enquiry to discover the causes of the accident it was stated that in addition to the locomotive's failure to cope with its load, the carriages were so over-loaded that in one carriage at least the springs were bearing down on the wheels. Over a century after the disaster a number of gold coins were found when the permanent way was being renewed inside the tunnel. They were probably the winnings of an unlucky racegoer who was involved in the accident.

Even though by the middle of the century the railways had come tantalisingly close to Runcorn, the town had benefitted little from them. Whilst it is true that from 1833 there was a gradual increase in the number of passengers crossing by ferry to the St. Helens to Runcorn Gap Railway station at Woodend in Widnes, the rail journey from there to Liverpool or to Manchester was a slow, complicated one by roundabout routes and of course, there was no carriage of freight by rail to and from Runcorn.

The Bridgewater Trustees were anxious to establish a rail link to their waterway and in 1853 a short branch line was constructed from the Chester to Warrington railway to the canal-side warehouses at Preston Brook where the Duke's Canal joined the Trent and Mersey Canal. The Trustees hoped that this enterprise would promote new business with barges from Liverpool discharging cargoes into railway waggons but the venture never amounted to much because of the high freight charges imposed by the railway company.

Thus rapidly developing Runcorn was forced to endure its long period of isolation into the mid-Victorian era. Until the London and North Western Railway and its Ethelfleda Bridge were complete in 1868 passengers for Liverpool had to rely on the Bridgewater Trustees' steam ferry-boat service.

Runcorn Ferry and the River Bridge Schemes

The narrowing of the Mersey at Runcorn creates a situation which has been described as being "the site designed by nature for a bridge" and yet the Gap was not crossed by a permanent road bridge until 1961. Before the beginning of the twentieth century heavy goods being carted between Lancashire and Cheshire had to be hauled over Warrington Bridge, a roundabout route which was both time-consuming and expensive.

By the last decade of the eighteenth century the merchants of Liverpool who were frustrated by the delays and costs in communicating with London via Warrington, began to exert pressure for the building of a road bridge at Runcorn. The first scheme had been Brindley's aqueduct proposal of 1768 by which the Duke of Bridgewater's Canal would have been carried over the river but the finance was not available and the canal had to end in Runcorn.

The growing commercial prosperity of Liverpool had brought about improved communications between the city and other centres of population but the vital road to London remained unsatisfactory and the cause of much exasperation. A bridge at Runcorn was necessary to lessen the time taken by goods and mail destined for London and in 1800 Ralph Dodd, a civil engineer from London, put forward his plan for a bridge at the Gap. He proposed a cast iron structure of three or five arches which would be wide enough to carry an aqueduct along the centre with a roadway on each side for vehicles and pedestrians. Dodd's ideas were not taken up and thirteen years later James Dumbell of Mersey Mills in Warrington put a proposal to the Mayor of Liverpool for a high level bridge which would not impede traffic on the river. Mr. Dumbell did not submit detailed plans because he feared that others would steal his idea but it seems likely that he favoured the construction of a suspension bridge. Following Dumbell's scheme, a William Nicholson deposited bridge plans in 1813 but his proposals did not succeed in attracting the attention of men of influence and it was not until 1816 that serious consideration was given to bridging the Mersey at Runcorn Gap.

On 22nd October 1816 a public meeting was held at the "White Hart Inn" with the object of forming a committee "for carrying the (bridge) undertaking into effect". There was an impressive gathering of "noblemen and gentlemen" and the Marquis of Stafford, the Marquis of Cholmondeley, the Earl of Derby and the mayors of Chester and Liverpool were invited to serve on the committee. At a meeting held at the "White Hart" in November the Committee examined the various plans and estimates which had been submitted for their consideration. It seems that six schemes were laid before the Committee : a stone bridge of seven arches, an iron bridge with five, a timber bridge with two arches and another with five, a chain bridge with a span of 487 metres carrying a roadway 33 metres above high water and an iron bridge of similar dimensions. The Committee also considered letters from three other engineers, Jesse Hartley of Pontefract, Ralph Dodd of London and Thomas Telford.

The Committee resolved to meet again early in 1817 to receive further plans and estimates and a resolution was passed asking Liverpool Council to "give their countenance and support to the Undertaking". However, the Bridge Committee did not succeed in achieving the essential support of the Council and the movement to provide a Mersey crossing at Runcorn lost its impetus, but two years later Liverpool Council revived the interest when in December 1818 they presented a Parliamentary Bill relative to a bridge at Runcorn Gap.

The plan was for a suspension bridge and the chosen design was that by Telford who claimed that as a result of his experiments he could provide "a roadway independent of timber,

Telford's designs for a bridge at Runcorn Gap.

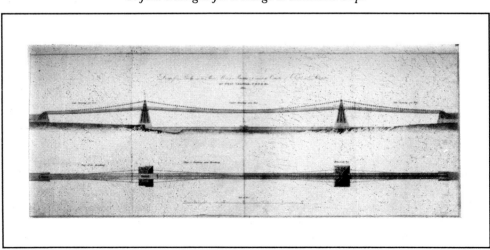

which is impervious to water, has perfect elasticity and appears indestructable". Telford's bridge was of heroic proportions. The centre span was 305 metres across and each of the side spans was to be 152 metres in width. The bridge was to be constructed using the latest techniques. Instead of being carried by chains the road platform was to be suspended by means of laminated iron cables. In his biography of Telford, Samuel Smiles described the Runcorn Bridge as being "very magnificent ... and perhaps superior even to the Menai suspension bridge". At a cost of £84,890 the bridge would reduce the time taken for the carriage of mail between Liverpool and London by eight hours. The first estimates of Telford's Runcorn Bridge were considered to be much too high as was the revised costing at £62,500. The proposals were not adopted and the bridge scheme was abandoned.

Undoubtedly, Thomas Telford was a bridge builder par excellence but modern engineers have voiced doubts over the suitability of his plans for Runcorn Gap. Writing in 1958, L.T.C. Rolt declared, *"Looking at the drawings today with an unprejudiced eye, one is forced to the conclusion that it was as well the bridge was never built. The design would have offered far too little resistance to the lateral wind pressure acting upon so great a span".* So neither Brindley's huge aqueduct nor Telford's great suspension bridge were to be built and perhaps both were conceptions which were too grandiose to be feasible. However, if they had been built Runcorn would have become by Regency times, the best known river crossing in the world. It was to be a hundred and forty-three years after the abandonment of Telford's plans that the present Runcorn-Widnes road bridge became a reality.

Telford's vast suspension bridge was never to be, but he did carry out important canal works in the Runcorn area. From 1810 onwards he was engaged in completing the Weston Canal for the Weaver Navigation Trustees. The canal was designed to by-pass the difficult lower tidal channel of the river. Telford also carried out considerable harbour works at Weston Point.

The failure to build Telford's suspension bridge extended the life of Runcorn ferry by another ninety years and until the completion of the railway bridge in 1868, communications to the north were to remain wretched. At the beginning of the century the Marquis of Cholmondeley leased the ferry for £10 a year. There was little traffic across to Runcorn Gap (Widnes) but by 1802 there was a daily passenger sailing packet to Liverpool. The ferry service to Widnes was primitive and desultory. At low water travellers were often required to transfer to another boat at a sandbank in mid-river and when they arrived

at the other side they had to struggle across a muddy beach carrying their luggage. Sir George Head described an uncomfortable crossing in 1836 when he complained of delay and the lack of landing jetties : *"In the first place the public are ferried across by a couple of men who are not always to be found at a moment's notice. Next the landing place at Runcorn is at all times extremely incommodious and thirdly, that on the other side is still worse".* Another source of resentment was the fact that Mr. William Hurst of West Bank House, the owner of much of Woodend, received payment for all goods landed in Widnes by ferry passengers and traders, whilst he and his tenants had right of free passage across the ferry.

Before the industrialisation of Widnes, people from Runcorn regarded Woodend to be an attractive spot for outings on Sundays and holidays. In his "Old Widnes and Its Neighbourhood", Charles Poole extols the beauty of rural West Bank : *"Leafy groves of trees that covered the slopes above Runcorn Gap ... spreading beech and lime, towering oak and sycamore flourished amid ferns and wild flowers in abundance".* During the summer months the ferry did profitable business carrying pleasure seekers across to the Boathouse Inn at Woodend in Widnes.

With the completion of the St. Helens to Runcorn Gap Railway and the extension to the Sankey Canal to Widnes in 1833, the ferry crossing began to assume a greater importance as more passengers from Runcorn and the surrounding districts crossed the river in order to reach Liverpool, Manchester or St. Helens by the railway. But the great upsurge in ferry passengers started with factory building in Widnes. From its beginnings with the establishment of John Hutchinson's No.1 works at Spike Island in 1847, the evolution of the Widnes chemical industry was spectacular and by 1855 there were seven alkali works clustered round the termini of the railway and the canal.

When John Hutchinson arrived in Widnes he found a population of just over two thousand people living in the area and although he recruited much of his labour force from among Irish immigrants in Liverpool, he was also able to engage experienced chemical workers from the soap and alkali factories in Runcorn. As the new chemical works in Widnes began to attract more labour and expertise from across the river, so the ancient ferry service developed into a vital crossing and by the middle of the century it was being let by the Marquis of Cholmondeley for £400 per year which was forty times the lease of forty years previously. However, the service offered to the public remained inefficient and irregular and by 1853 conditions were so bad that a public meeting was held in the Runcorn town hall to discuss the situation in the hope of finding a remedy. It was a lively meeting. The ferrymen were accused of idleness, drunkenness and indifference to the needs of the public and the Marquis was severely criticised for not providing suitable landing places. A committee was formed to convey the feelings of Runcornians to Lord Cholmondeley and to ask him to reduce the exorbitant toll of two pence for crossing by the ferry.

On 31st January 1854 the Marquis of Cholmondeley granted the lease to Mr. (later Sir) Gilbert Greenall MP, representing the directors of the St. Helens Railway Company. The new lease reflected the astonishing growth in importance of the ferry in half a century. From a meagre £10 a year, the rental had increased over a hundred-fold. The twenty-one year lease was granted at a rental of £920 per annum for the first term of seven years, at £1,000 for each year of the second term of seven years and at £1,100 per annum for the third term. The conditions of the lease required the lessee to repair and maintain the landing places and also to supply three boats and enough ferrymen to provide a regular service.

In order to improve the ferry service the railway company considered the use of amphibious craft which would be equipped with wheels so that they could be hauled across the sandbanks but the curious innovation does not appear to have been tried. The ferry boats were fitted with sails but these were soon reported to be *"in a torn and dilapidated condition and the sailing of the boats is very much impeded in rough weather and the passage is a matter of considerable hazard"*. The Runcorn Improvement Commissioners tried throughout the 1850s to get the Marquis to provide suitable jetties and a waiting room but to no avail until an accident, in which a number of farm animals were drowned, forced Lord Cholmondeley's agent to try to improve matters.

The long awaited amenities at Runcorn included a waiting room and booking office with a notice board which gave the ferry charges and also the departure times of the trains from Runcorn Gap station in Widnes. The ferry charges in 1854 were as follows :

	s	d
Passenger for every passage		2
Passenger for a passage to and fro on the same day		3
Pig		1
Man and horse		6
Gig and horse including two passengers	1	..0
Bull or cow		4
Score of sheep		10
Barrels of ale, beer etc.		6
Sack of wheat		6
Package per cwt.		6
Coffin containing a corpse and including six bearers	3	..0

From Waterloo Road a long narrow causeway was built across the mud and rocks to terminate at a flight of steps which led to mooring posts at the low water mark.

Passenger traffic by the ferry soared in the next few years and in 1861 Lord Cholmondeley claimed that two hundred thousand foot passengers had crossed the river during the previous year. Four years later pressures were such that boats were crossing every five minutes in order to cope with demand. The ferry was a valuable asset and the Marquis opposed the London and North Western Railway Company's plan for a bridge at Runcorn. In his petition against the Railway Company, he declared that the buttresses of a bridge would endanger the ferry boats by causing new sandbanks to form in mid-river. Lord Cholmondeley's arguments were feeble and when he realised that his opposition to the railway company could not succeed, he proposed instead that the company should purchase then abolish the ferry and undertake to make the railway bridge available for pedestrians and that Lord Cholmondeley himself or his lessee should have the benefit of the bridge tolls. This scheme did not find favour with the railway company and so the ferry remained in use for a further thirty-six years after the completion of the bridge. In the meantime the lease for the ferry was assigned to the London and North Western Company which began work on the Runcorn to Widnes railway bridge in 1863.

The story of the building of the Runcorn Railway Bridge has been described in some detail by Charles Nickson in his history of Runcorn. However, over twenty years before the completion of the bridge an Act of Parliament had been obtained by the Grand Junction Railway (later the L.N.W.R. Company) to bridge the Mersey at Runcorn Gap. The railway company wanted a quick route north from the Midlands to the Atlantic-facing and rapidly growing Port of Liverpool. By the terms of the Act of 1846, the Grand Junction Company proposed to construct a bridge with a clearance of 30 metres. above high water and the spaces between the piers was to be at least 85 metres. The powers of the Act were not used within the time limit of seven years and as a result the project lapsed.

In 1861 another Act of Parliament gave the

The railway bridge under construction in 1864.
The view across to West Bank, Widnes.

London and North Western Railway powers to construct a line from Aston, south-east of Runcorn, to Ditton on the Warrington and Garston line. The first stone of the bridge over the river was laid on Tuesday April 12th 1864 by Philip Whiteway J.P., the shipbuilder and quarry owner of Runcorn. By November 1866 the great piers of the bridge were largely complete and the first two girders were settled into position on the stone abutments on the Cheshire side of the river. This was an occasion for rejoicing with the firing of cannon and the ringing of church bells. A dinner was provided for the workmen in the evening and, in holiday atmosphere, "Champagne was handed out ... and the health of the workmen and other toasts were heartily drunk".

The bridge works caused serious problems for those river craft which were making their way to Old Quay docks, to the Widnes dock of the St. Helens Canal or further up river to Warrington. Unpowered craft could not proceed up the river because of the great lattice of staging and scaffolding which grew until it barred much of the passage to shipping. The railway company provided small steamers to tow sailing vessels through the obstructions and Admiralty lights were erected on the staging of the bridge together with steel bells each weighing three hundredweights. These were tolled two hours thirty minutes before high water and for one hour thirty minutes after high water during foggy weather. In spite of these precautions there were casualties with small craft receiving damage from colliding with the works.

The sixth and final girder was placed in position on February 14th 1868 and on May 21st the locomotive "Cheshire" with twenty waggons containing five hundred people, passed over the bridge to Widnes. The "Cheshire" then returned to Runcorn before crossing to the middle of the bridge where Mr. L.B. Wells, the railway company's engineer, made a speech.

The bridge has three spans each of 93 metres and the foundations of the piers are built upon sandstone 13.7 metres below the river bed. The girders are 23 metres above high water mark. On the Cheshire side, the line is carried by way of a viaduct of thirty arches each of 12.5 metres, with another three each of 18 metres, then by means of a deep cutting through Higher Runcorn and out to level country towards Sutton Weaver. The year of completion for the bridge is given as 1868 but its opening for goods and passenger traffic is usually recognised as being 1869 which was when the whole route between Weaver Junction and Ditton came into operation. The bridge has two names, locally it is known as Ethelfelda Bridge because its foundations on the Cheshire bank are on the site of Ethelfleda's tenth century Saxon fortress but further afield the bridge is known as the Britannia Railway Bridge.

With the completion of the railway bridge Runcorn at last lost its position of isolation for it was now situated on the main line from Liverpool to London and the Midlands. The coming of the railway was a boon to the Bridgewater Trustees because they acquired a vital branch line to their docks and this placed them in a better position to compete with other ports in the North West. The bridge had a footway and from the day of its opening hundreds of work people crossed the river twice a day to their employment in Runcorn or Widnes. The railway made the Runcorn to Liverpool steam ferry service redundant and within a few months of the opening of the line the Bridgewater Trustees withdrew their passenger-carrying boats.

The ancient ferry to Widnes continued a spasmodic service but very few passengers used it after 1869. The crossing became intermittent although the boats still remained useful for carrying light freight and farm animals.

Runcorn Railway Bridge shortly after its completion in 1868.

Bibliography

The efforts of the Improvement Commissioners to promote a railway to Runcorn are reported in the *"Warrington Standard"* of 26th June 1858 and in the *"Warrington Guardian"* of 31st May 1858. *"The Sutton Tunnel Railway Accident of 30th April 1851"* by W. Hawkin is deposited at the Cheshire County Record Office. This paper gives a full account of the accident with the report to the Commissioner of Railways into the causes of the accident.

A description of the difficulties encountered by passengers crossing the ferry is to be found in Sir George Head's *"A Home Tour Through the Manufacturing Districts of England in the Summer of 1835"*. The long running attempts made by the Improvement Commissioners to improve the conditions at the ferry crossing is recalled in *"Schooner Port"* by H.F. Starkey as are the early schemes for bridging the river. *"Runcorn River Crossings"*, an archive teaching booklet issued by the Cheshire Education Committee is a good summary of the various nineteenth century plans to build a bridge at Runcorn.

A comprehensive account of the building of the Runcorn to Widnes Railway Bridge is to be found in *"Old Widnes and Its Neighbourhood"* by Charles Poole (1906).

Bridgewater docks and the Duke's house in the early years of the nineteenth century.

Chapter 15
The Port of Runcorn

When in 1481 the burgesses of Chester succeeded in persuading King Edward IV as Earl of Chester, to grant them the complete monopoly of the county's trade with Ireland, the possibility of port development on the Mersey came to an end. We have little evidence of shipping at Runcorn in the medieval period but it is possible that the township was becoming a landing place of some consequence before the King ended its prospects with his order to the sheriff to arrest all vessels attempting to discharge cargoes from Ireland at Runcorn. Sixty years after Edward IV had issued this order John Leland described Runcorn as "now a poore hamlet". Perhaps Leland's use of the word "now" is significant and this decline in the prosperity of the township dated only from 1481. Was Runcorn showing signs of developing into a prosperous maritime community only to be reduced to "a poore hamlet" by the action of the Chester merchants? We do not have the answer and another three hundred and twenty years were to pass before Runcorn had developed into a thriving sub port of the port of Liverpool.

With the completion of the Sankey Canal in 1757 there was an increase of traffic on the upper Mersey and when the Duke of Bridgewater's Canal was opened throughout its length to Manchester in 1776 prospects for maritime trade at Runcorn brightened considerably. By 1785 the Duke's line of locks ended in a tidal basin. Here there was a warehouse and two locks up from the tideway, a small dry dock. To the south of Bridgewater House there was another warehouse and in 1791 a dock was built specifically for the sailing flats which carried cargoes from the Duke's dock in Liverpool. The Runcorn dock was available for independent carriers who paid tolls on tonnage carried on the canal. At first no provision was made at Runcorn for the berthing of the larger sea-going craft because the Mersey's shallow, twisting navigable channel was not marked with buoys and cargoes of flints and china clay destined for Runcorn from the south coast had to be discharged at Liverpool and then transhipped in flat bottomed craft to Runcorn.

It is evident that, by the end of the eighteenth century, some marking of the shipping channel had taken place for regular cargoes were being unloaded at Runcorn. Roofing slates from North Wales were being discharged for distribution by way of the inland waterways and considerable quantities of potters' materials were being transhipped into narrow-boats for Stoke-on-

Trent. From about 1800 Liverpool displaced London as the leading port for the importing of raw cotton and through traffic forwarded to Manchester via the Duke's Canal or by the Old Quay Canal included shipments of cotton, wool, flax, hemp, dyewood, timber, roofing slates, sugar, rice, tea and grain. Cargoes from Manchester to Liverpool consisted mainly of textiles, manufactured goods and coal. The opening of the Trent and Mersey Canal enabled salt to be transported via Runcorn and in the four years to 1782 nearly twenty-two thousand large crates of pottery were carried by the Duke's boats at 7½d per crate. In 1790 it was reported that forty-two boats each fifty tons burthen were employed on the Bridgewater Canal and that they made on average three trips to Liverpool every fourteen days.

Runcorn's beginnings as a minor port within the customs port of Liverpool date from about 1800. By then several local men had financial investments in a number of small craft which were trading out of Runcorn. Most of the first men to own shares in shipping were the Duke of Bridgewater's agents and managers from Manchester and Runcorn who formed business associations to become co-owners of coasting vessels. For example in 1786 John Gilbert, the Duke's principal agent and Benjamin Sothern, an important official at Runcorn, formed a business association with two Worsley men. The partners owned seven small vessels trading in coastal waters. Four of the ships were two masted-'galliots' each of about 73 tons and built in Northwich whilst the others were sailing flats. Of course in a small township of less than 1,500 inhabitants, there were few local merchants and shippers of consequence but from the early years of the nineteenth century more businessmen began to invest in shipping as a secondary interest. The Duke of Bridgewater and later his Trustees encouraged independent carriers to use the canal and docks and many did avail themselves of the opportunity to do so. They included Thomas Pickford, Worthington & Gilbert and Hugh Henshall & Company.

The rise of the port of Runcorn can be attributed to a number of factors. By 1805 there were two canals with outlets into the Mersey at Runcorn and traffic to the Sankey Canal had increased. At Weston Point the Trustees of the River Weaver navigation completed their Weston Canal which they built in 1810 in order that craft could avoid the difficult entrance at the mouth of the Weaver.

The expansion of maritime commerce in the locality resulted in the establishment of ship building and repair yards at Frodsham and Runcorn. By the Regency period the upper Mersey had become a very important highway by which the bulk of the raw materials of the textile, pottery, glass, soap and salt refining industries were carried. The canal port of Runcorn was to play a vital part in promoting the economic development of large cities. Before the days of good roads and railways, the mills of Manchester depended on the improved Mersey and the canals for their supplies of raw cotton and for the transport of their cloth to world markets. Similarly the prosperity of Stoke-on-Trent was built upon supplies of pottery material from Cornwall, Devon and France carried on the upper Mersey and transhipped at Runcorn to the Five Towns, the canal craft returning with cargoes of crated pottery. Equally, Liverpool's rise to prominence in the early eighteenth century was largely due to the Cheshire salt trade which supplied the town's early industries whilst salt was exported to Europe and North America from the port.

Navigation on the upper reaches of the Mersey was never plain sailing. The navigable channels are constantly migrating and the movement of craft before the river was well marked with buoys and perches was often a hazardous operation. Shippers and merchants were anxious that landowners whose estates bordered the river should do nothing which interfered with the tidal scour. The embanking of marshes to reclaim land and the building of chevrons into the river so as to slow the velocity of the tide in order to protect the shore line were unwelcome nuisances to the maritime community. The unpredictable channel, the rocks and shallows and rushing tides of the river presented a formidable challenge to the masters of small craft navigating to Runcorn and Warrington.

By 1817 Runcorn had become a port of some prominence and in that year there was a relaxation in the regulation concerning the export of dutiable goods from its docks. A local report noted, *"The great connection which Runcorn forms between the coasting and inland trade gives to it all the bustle of a considerable port and a supervisor is now established here for whom a suitable office or customs house has recently been built on the wharf. The privilege of clearing out certain commodities from here without touching the great port of Liverpool has recently been granted by the Commissioners of Customs".* However, Runcorn was to remain a creek port within the port of Liverpool for another thirty years before it finally gained its complete independence of Liverpool.

The principal agent in the development of the port of Runcorn was the steam tug-boat. The Mersey's capricious channels in the upper reaches were a barrier to maritime trade while cargoes were carried in sailing vessels but the highly manoeuvrable paddle-tugs could make the best use of the tides to convey trains of barges quickly up river. The first merchants in the region to perceive the advantages of steam towage were Runcorn businessmen who financed and built the first steamers to operate successfully on the Mersey. Outside interests supplied the first steam ferry-boat to provide a passenger service on the river when in 1815, the paddle-boat "Elizabeth" began to ply between Liverpool and Runcorn. "Elizabeth" could make progress against the wind and tide and it did not go unnoticed that the little steamer had proved herself to be very useful as a tug-boat when she came across the Runcorn sailing packet which was becalmed. "Elizabeth" proceeded to tow the packet for ten miles to Runcorn. Unfortunately, "Elizabeth's" engine was unreliable and after a year she was sold to be converted into a horse packet, the paddles being worked by heavy carthorses which revolved a treadmill. The horse packet was unsatisfactory because the horses became ill with the constant rolling of the boat so the paddle-wheels were removed and the vessel was converted into a sailing barge.

In 1816 two wooden paddle-steamers, "Prince Regent" and "Duke of Wellington" were completed in Runcorn yards. They were used as passenger packets operating between Liverpool, Runcorn and Warrington. The little craft were very successful and they shortened the time taken from Liverpool to Runcorn considerably. The passenger service was profitable and by 1819 a regular coach service was established to convey ferry-boat passengers from the bottom locks at Runcorn to Northwich and the road between the two towns was turnpiked in that year. Ellen Weeton visited Runcorn in the summer of 1817 and her "Journal of a Governess" describes her trip by steamer, *"they make a rather laughable appearance. They go puffing and blowing and beating their sides and labouring along".*

Unaccountably, the canal companies were slow to see the advantages in using steamers and there was no immediate development of towing facilities. As far as can be ascertained the first steamer to be employed as a tug on the upper river was the paddle-boat "Eagle". In 1824 she was used to tow barges from Queen's Dock in Liverpool to Runcorn from where the barges were horse-drawn via the Duke's canal to Manchester.

It was nearly ten years after the first paddle-boat had made its appearance that the Bridgewater Trustees and the Mersey and Irwell Company

A view of 1840 with steamers leaving Old Quay Docks.
The medieval church, the windmill and the salt water swimming baths can be seen as well as shipping in Bridgewater Docks beyond Castle Bridge.

had their own steamers. When they hired tug-boats the companies had been forced to pay exorbitant fees. They now ordered tugs and there was a building boom in the Runcorn shipyards in the 1820s with half a dozen steamers under construction. After 1830 the navigation companies realised the fact that the Liverpool to Manchester railway was a serious competitor and more tugs were ordered. From this time onwards many of the sailing flats were dismasted to become "dumb" towing barges and the more powerful steamers of the day were each capable of towing up to twelve loaded barges. The decade saw the start of what was soon to become an immense barge traffic on the upper estuary and in order to facilitate navigation by night, two lighthouses were built, one at Hale Head and the other at Ince on the Cheshire shore. The Bridgewater Trustees were responsible for the bulk of shipping above Garston and they took on the obligation of marking the sailing channel with buoys and perches and later with light-vessels.

During the 1840s the maritime trade to Runcorn grew substantially and the Mersey and Irwell Company toyed briefly with the idea of cutting a canal from Garston to Runcorn Gap to enable vessels of 150 tons to proceed to their Old Quay docks but the idea was abandoned in 1841 as being impracticable. Trade at Runcorn docks soared and in the years 1840-1842 there was an average of 55,000 tons of raw cotton passing through the Bridgewater locks. Immense quantities of potters' materials were shipped from Cornwall and Devon in coasting schooners and the material was piled up on the Bridgewater quays awaiting shipment to the Potteries. Sir George Head writing in 1836 included a description of the docks in his "Tour of the Manufacturing Districts of England". Sir George was impressed by the volume of trade and by the neat appearance of the wharfs. *"The enormous heaps of material piled up ready for embarkation would be sufficient, one would think, to freight all the barges on the line for months to come, consisting of substances used in the manufacture of British china such as flints from Kent and Sussex, pipe clay from Devonshire and Dorsetshire, besides a soft stone containing an abundance of mica from Cornwall and Wales ... The whole extent of ground is laid out with the care and order of a pleasure garden".* The pottery crate warehouse was a landmark and Sir George writes, *"The warehouse is very remarkable ... a striking object on the bank of the river, exceeding in size most other buildings in this country of like description".*

In order to meet the intense competition from the Liverpool to Manchester Railway a new type of canal passenger packet — the swift boat was introduced. Constructed of light material, the swift packets were pulled by galloping horses to complete the 28 mile journey via the Bridgewater Canal from Runcorn to Manchester in four hours. The Mersey and Irwell Company also introduced swift boats. The fast packets kept to a strict schedule and they had priority passage when passing other traffic. The Mersey and Irwell's river steamer "Tower" delivered its passengers from Liverpool for Manchester conveniently alongside the canal packet boat at Old Quay and the company made much of this arrangement. Their advertisement in the "Liverpool Mercury" for 1st May 1840 promised passengers *"a delightful and healthy excursion ... avoiding the inconvenience of passengers removing their luggage and having to walk half a mile in all states of the weather at Runcorn as these packets always come alongside each other".* This was a reference to those passengers who sailed from Liverpool by the "Duke of Bridgewater" and who were required to toil up the slope to Top Locks carrying their baggage before their canal journey to Manchester. The Duke's Trustees promptly made arrangements for baggage handling advertising that, *"Steady porters will attend the packets and packet houses. Luggage is removed from one packet to the other free of charge".* The swift canal packets provided a twice daily service with "Swallow", "Dolphin", "Eagle" and "Waterwitch" operating to Manchester every day except Sunday. In 1844 the Mersey and Irwell Company was purchased by the Bridgewater Trustees thus ending seventy years of fierce competition.

The steam ferry service to Liverpool was very popular but the journey could be made uncomfortable by "the low society on board who are allowed to drink, smoke, swear, etc. and the journey took two hours instead of one". In the 1840s the paddle-steamers "Blanche", "Bridgewater","Eclipse" and "Tower" were employed in carrying passengers between Liverpool and Runcorn and the boats also had "liberty to tow" if the opportunity occurred. A contemporary timetable gives the names of Runcorn's packet houses. These were Mr. Wilson's Hotel in Bridge Street, Mr. Rigby's "Boat House Inn" in Mersey Street, Mr. Percival's "Lord Nelson" tavern and Mr. Bolton's "Castle Hotel" in Halton. The steamers picked up passengers at Weston Point and the packet house there was Mr. Baines' "Weaver Hotel". Weston Point was well served by the steam packets for a paddle-boat from Northwich called there for passengers for Liverpool. Passengers landing at Runcorn for Northwich found the "Tally-Ho" coach awaiting their arrival. There were two coaches for Northwich, one from the Bottom Locks for Bridgewater passengers whilst the other set off from the "Royal Hotel" with those who had arrived at Old Quay. The fare for the voyage to

Liverpool in "Eclipse" in 1838 was one shilling and sixpence (7½ pence) "in the best appartment" and one shilling (5 pence) "in the second appartment". During the summer months the river paddle-steamers took excursion parties for trips to the North Wales coast.

With the volume of Liverpool to Manchester trade expanding dramatically on the Bridgewater Canal and on that of the Mersey and Irwell Company in the first two decades of the nineteenth century, improvements to both waterways became necessary. In June 1825 the

A three-masted barque at the Duke's pottery crate warehouse, Bridgewater Docks,
with china clay sheds in the background.

Two masted Mersey "jigger" flats off Runcorn in the early years of the present century.

Fishing smacks on the upper Mersey.

Mersey and Irwell Company began new works which would facilitate trade at Old Quay. A large dock was constructed with two sets of locks into the river, one to be used by incoming craft and the other to be used by vessels leaving the canal. Further improvements carried out at Old Quay in 1829 allowed vessels drawing 16 feet of water to enter the docks at Spring tides. Not to be outdone, the Bridgewater Trustees also put major improvements in hand on their waterway. The Trustees realised that the slowness of passage through the Bridgewater locks had been a main factor in promoting the case for the Liverpool to Manchester Railway and in order to quicken traffic, a new line of locks was opened at a cost of £35,000 in 1828.

During the ten years from 1835 to 1845 trade boomed at the port of Runcorn. In 1835 five hundred vessels left the town's docks. Ten years later three times that number of ships carried cargo from the port. To cope with increasing business the Trustees built a new dock called Francis Dock which was opened in 1843. In view of this success local merchants began to agitate for independence from the port of Liverpool and on 5th April 1847 Runcorn's growing importance was recognised when the town was designated an independent customs port and certain wharfs were declared to be "legal quays" where dutiable goods could be landed. The new customs port of Runcorn extended from Warrington Bridge to Eastham to include both shores of the Mersey. In keeping with its enhanced status a new customs house was built in Old Coach Road in 1847.

From the beginning it was obvious that the customs port of Runcorn would not be a success. A few foreign vessels did arrive bringing oats from Denmark and oak bark from Belgium but the high hopes of a developing foreign trade did not materialise and on 12th April 1850 Runcorn's short-lived independence came to an end and the boundaries of the port of Liverpool were amended to include all the waters of the Mersey and Weaver rivers. However, at the very time that the bonded port of Runcorn failed, the Navigation Laws were repealed and this action allowed foreign ships to compete with British vessels. Immediately the prospects for foreign trade brightened and in the next decade small foreign vessels began to arrive at Runcorn in numbers to load salt for the fishing industries of France, Holland, Germany, Belgium and Denmark.

In spite of its loss in status in losing its independence as a customs port, Runcorn's maritime trade prospered. This was partly due to the rapid growth of industrial Widnes. The factories at Woodend began to receive pyrites, chemical ores, coal and firebricks and from 1862, Ditton Brook Ironworks was busy taking iron ore, limestone and coke. Into the Bridgewater and Weaver docks came potters' clay, china clay, flints and whitening. From Caernarvon, Bangor and Dinorwic over forty thousand tons of roofing slates were despatched to centres of population by the Bridgewater Canal. In 1852 about forty-two thousand tons of Scottish pig iron was sent to Midland foundries via the canal. Substantial quantities of timber to be used as propwood in the Lancashire and Staffordshire coal mines arrived from Ireland. Copper ore destined for the refineries in St. Helens was landed at the Runcorn quays and quantities of bones, oak bark, sand and felspar were imported for the local factories. In addition to this trade, there was also the larger canal trade which passed through Runcorn to and from Manchester without the necessity of being discharged onto the quayside.

Outgoing cargoes from the local docks mainly consisted of two staple commodities, namely coal and salt but the products of the soapworks, the tanneries and the alkali factories were transported to Liverpool by barge to be sent all over the world.

Runcorn was always a shallow-draught port with the largest of the schooners using the docks rarely exceeding 150 tons. Because the railway was late in coming to the town (the vital rail link to the Bridgewater Docks was only laid down in 1868) the Bridgewater Trustees and their successors had to exploit every means to survive the competition from the railway ports. This rivalry induced the Trustees to provide free towage to and from the Sloyne anchorage off Tranmere, for the sailing vessels using their docks.

The shipping merchants of Runcorn had long suffered the affliction of the levy of the Liverpool Town Dues. This was a tax imposed by the Corporation of Liverpool on all goods imported into or exported from the port of Liverpool. As Runcorn was a creek of the port of Liverpool, the town was obliged to pay according to the volume of Liverpool's trade. The money raised was used by the Corporation for the benefit of Liverpool docks but no expenditure was allocated from the Town Dues for lighting and buoying, or improving the river above Liverpool. The Runcorn merchants declared that the monies raised in Runcorn should have been used in the vicinity of Runcorn. As the town's trade increased so did the levy. In 1836 Runcorn's share of the Liverpool Town Dues amounted to £1,172 and by 1855 this had risen to £3,182 for the year. Controversy between the local interests and the Liverpool Corporation had been intense for some years and when the docks at Liverpool and

The river tug "Earl of Ellesmere" had a very long life. She was nearly seventy years old when she went to the breakers in 1926.

Birkenhead were transferred to the Mersey Docks and Harbour Board in 1857 the industrialists of Runcorn, Warrington, Widnes and St. Helens introduced a Bill into Parliament which required the Mersey Docks and Harbour Board to sell them the Town Dues on the up-river traffic. The act was passed in 1860 and the merchants paid £105,000 as their share of the Town Dues. The dues continued to be levied on upper Mersey shipping by the Upper Mersey Dues Trust until 1877 by which date the debt and the interest on the money borrowed had been repaid.

In 1876 the Upper Mersey Navigation Commission was constituted. The Commission was empowered to take over the lighting and buoying duties formerly carried out by the Bridgewater Trustees and, from 1872, by their successors, the Bridgewater Navigation Company. The new Commission levied charges on owners operating vessels within the stretch of river from Bank Quay to Eastham. The Commissioners were also permitted restricted powers to submit requests for river improvement work to the River Mersey Conservancy Commissioners who could sanction improvements to a limit of £500 per year.

From about 1859 Runcorn's maritime trade showed a startling increase and on January 1st 1862 the town was once again appointed an independent customs port. The Alfred dock

which was completed in 1860 was equipped with hydraulic cranes and two years later a telegraph line was introduced to connect the Bridgewater Trustees' offices in Manchester with their dock in Liverpool. The line was suspended across the river at Runcorn Gap.

Throughout the 1860s business at Runcorn's docks continued to grow steadily. The foreign trade was well developed by 1870, with schooners loading salt for Russia, Denmark, Iceland, Norway and the Low Countries. Salt was also carried across the Atlantic to the saltfish industry of Newfoundland in hundred-ton coastal schooners. A new traffic began about 1870 with cargoes of animal bones, horn piths and bone ash from Rio Grande do Sul in Brazil. The evil smelling cargoes were destined for Runcorn's bone mills newly re-established at Sutton Weaver or for the potters of Stoke-on-Trent.

The Bridgewater, Old Quay and Weaver docks accommodated scores of sailing flats and coastal schooners and at high tide the Mersey resembled a festival with small craft moving to berths on both sides of the river. This satisfactory state of affairs continued until about 1871 when the menace of shifting sands began to appear and silting started to occur in the sailing channels and at the dock entrances. By 1875 the silting had all but ruined the port of Runcorn and it was reported that "A dangerous sandbank, nearly destroying the entrance to Runcorn docks has

Bridgewater Docks, Runcorn 1886.

driven a large amount of trade to Liverpool in 1875". Sandbanks also formed in front of the shipyards and few vessels of any size were launched in the eight years after 1870. Desperate measures were taken to ensure the approaches to the docks were kept open. Tug boats towed rakes along the river bed so that the ebb tides would scour away the loosened sand and mud. This strategy was successful in keeping traffic moving until the ever-changing Mersey altered its tactics and the Duke's Gut began to function satisfactorily to clear away the silt from in front of the lock gates.

After five years of nearly catastrophic silting, the port of Runcorn made a quick recovery as the navigable channels improved. Coastal schooners crowded the Runcorn and Weston Point docks. They came from ports great and small all round the coasts of Britain. Practically all were engaged in the slate, coal, salt or pottery material trades. The schooners were registered at Bristol, Barrow, Liverpool, Glasgow, Bideford, Lynmouth, Padstow, Caernarvon and Amlwch. Foreign schooners loaded salt for the fishing industries in Scandinavia, the Low Countries, France and Germany. By 1880 the customs port of Runcorn was an undoubted success. Schooners carried salt to Newfoundland and returned with cargoes of saltfish for the Mediterranean countries and Runcorn vessels were to be found discharging saltfish at ports in Italy, Spain, Greece and Turkey. They then loaded fruit for the return voyage to British ports.

The list of wrecks and casualties among local vessels in the last century is a long one. Runcorn sailing vessels were small wooden craft rarely exceeding 100 tons. They carried heavy bulk cargoes of coal, salt, china clay and pig iron. Before the legislation of 1876 schooners were often undermanned and overloaded. Very often Mersey sailing flats were converted into coastal schooners, a role for which they were not suited for the extra canvas made such craft unstable in heavy weather. In 1861 Canon John Barclay was so moved by the distress among dependants of seamen lost at sea that he asked the clergy of all the denominations in Runcorn to make a simultaneous appeal on behalf of the Shipwrecked Mariners' Association. Canon Barclay writes that his suggestion was "cheerfully adopted" and the appeal raised thirty pounds for the charity. Runcorn registered craft were lost off Newfoundland, South America and all round the coasts of Britain. The local newspapers often carried items headed "Loss of Runcorn Schooner". The menace of winter gales must always have occupied the thoughts of the men of the little schooners and their families.

The schooners and flats were owned by many local people of quite modest means. Innkeepers, shopkeepers, tradesmen, farmers, widows, clergymen and clerks were prepared to invest in shipping and the names of hundreds of Runcorn folk are to be found listed as shareholders in the registers of Runcorn vessels. The peak year for

A typical Runcorn owned schooner, "Gleaner" was built at Carrickfergus in 1883. She was lost with her crew in November 1918.

Narrow Boats "Java" and "Pekin" at the Bridgewater Docks in 1905.

locally registered shipping was 1881. Of the 9,275 tons of shipping registered at the port in that year, one hundred and ten vessels displaced more than fifty tons and forty-three were less than 50 tons. Runcorn was always a sailing ship port and in that year only four small steamers were registered at the port.

The Bridgewater Navigation Company bought the Duke's canal and the old Mersey and Irwell Navigation with their docks and warehouses in 1872 and three years later a new dock, the Fenton, was opened at a cost of £50,000. It was equipped with the latest in hydraulic cranes and tips. Railway sidings were added and three large sheds were built for the storage of china clay. The dock was also equipped with the latest high level tramway.

Victorian Runcorn had the vital nautical atmosphere of a busy port. The docks were crowded with ships and seamen from Norway, Germany, Ireland, Cornwall and North Wales were to be seen mixing with the local flatmen and narrow-boat folk in the public houses. The shopkeepers relied on the patronage of ships' crews and they advertised their willingness to deliver orders to the docks at a moment's notice. There were "family and shipping grocers", "family and shipping butchers", "ship and house painters" as well as sailors' outfitters and seamen's eating houses. The local optician sold mariners' compasses and navigation instruments and a river pilot had a ship's hull cleaning business. The contemporary newspapers and directories carried advertisements for half a dozen ship brokers and a couple of ship chandlers. There was even an inshore fishing industry of some consequence. In 1872 there were fifty-three sailing smacks registered at the port of Runcorn. The little boats were used for shrimping and catching fish off the mouth of the Dee and off the Lancashire coast.

A sizeable proportion of the town's workforce was employed at the docks or on the canals. The narrow-boat people in their traditional dress seemed to be separate from the rest of the community. They were a hardy group, many of them spending all their working lives on the boats. Some had houses ashore whilst others paid a few pence for rooms for a couple of nights while their craft were tied up at Runcorn. In 1886 there were 823 canal boats registered at the port and by the turn of the century this number had risen to over a thousand.

After 1875 the Mersey's navigable channel began to improve, the problems of silting at the dock entrances began to ease and there was a recovery in maritime trade. However, all new dock construction and the further development of the port of Runcorn ended with the completion of

the Tollemache Dock in Weston Point in 1885 — the year in which the Manchester Ship Canal Bill received the Royal Assent.

From about 1890 difficulties occasioned by the Ship Canal works caused a decline in Runcorn traffic and trade suffered from then until 1894 when the Customs Port of Runcorn was abolished and it became part of the new Port of Manchester.

The Manchester Ship Canal

At various times from the reign of George IV onwards groups of Manchester merchants had shown enthusiastic support for the concept of a canal for ocean-going vessels from the Mersey estuary to Manchester. By 1882 steps had been taken to make the plan for a ship canal a reality with the first Manchester Ship Canal Bill being deposited for the Parliamentary Session of 1883. However, the intention to bring a seaway through Merseyside was not received with universal satisfaction. For a start, as early as 1882 the Upper Mersey Navigation Commissioners had declared their opposition to the proposals and the Widnes Local Board opposed the Bill on the grounds that the canal works would have an adverse effect upon the Mersey's sailing channel. This would make navigation to Widnes Dock and West Bank Dock difficult for the scores of small craft operating each day between Liverpool and Widnes. The shipowners of Runcorn were anxious that their interests should not be unfavourably affected by the canal and of course, there were many whose land and property lay in the path of the canal and who wanted adequate compensation if their businesses or houses were taken.

The passage of the Ship Canal Bill through Parliament was a tedious affair but after the first two attempts had failed the third Bill received the Royal Assent on 6th of August 1885. Five months before this the Runcorn Improvement Commissioners had conducted a poll among the ratepayers upon a resolution to empower them to oppose the Manchester Ship Canal Bill. Later in the month, a meeting of the town's shipowners agreed to leave their interests in the hands of the local authority but they insisted that the Ship Canal Company should concede to their demands for the continuance of free towage on the river for locally owned vessels of up to 500 tons. The shipowners were trying to exploit the situation and were looking a long way into the future for there were no craft of more than 150 tons displacement registered at the port of Runcorn in 1885.

The contract for the construction of the Ship Canal was signed on 8th June 1887 and the first

*The Runcorn to Latchford Canal of the Mersey and Irwell Navigation Company (Old Quay Company).
Canalside properties have been demolished to make way for the Manchester Ship Canal. Photograph about 1888.*

"Noah's Ark Café". Catering and accommodation for the workers engaged on the
construction of the Manchester Ship Canal.

sod was cut at Eastham by Lord Egerton of Tatton on the 11th November. The Bridgewater Navigation Company was purchased by the Ship Canal Company for the sum of £1,710,000 and the new company thus acquired the Bridgewater Canal and its docks and properties as well as the Mersey and Irwell's Old Quay Canal and its docks.

The first large ocean-going ships to be seen in Runcorn arrived when the Manchester Ship Canal Company commenced to use the completed section of the waterway from Eastham to Weston Mersey Lock in 1892. The company established a temporary port at the mouth of the River Weaver at Weston Point. It would be another eighteen months before the canal was complete to Manchester and in the meantime the mushroom port of "Saltport" flourished. As the name suggests, salt cargoes shipped down the Weaver formed the chief export commodity. Soon Saltport became a busy place with steam cranes unloading salt from barges or discharging timber on to the wharfs. The ships using the new port were very large when compared to the small craft using Runcorn's docks. Sailing vessels up to 2,500 tons displacement towered over the fields as they unloaded cargoes of American pitch pine. In less than six months in 1892 over 90,000 tons of new business came to Saltport and on 11th August 1893 it was reported that eleven ships with a total cargo carrying capacity of 20,000 tons were discharging at the port.

On 2nd June 1892 the Manchester Ship Canal Company gave notice to the shippers of Runcorn of their intention of closing temporarily all the entrances between the river and the navigation systems at Runcorn and Weston Point with the exception of the Delamere Dock at Weston Point. These arrangements came into operation on July 1st and the Ship Canal Company made provision for the clearance of cargoes at Runcorn at no extra costs to the importers and shippers. The Company still towed incoming vessels via the Mersey into Weston Point docks, or through Eastham locks, then via the completed section of the canal to Saltport. At both places barges were available to convey cargoes at the Company's expense to Runcorn by way of the Runcorn and Weston Canal.

The task of keeping trade moving during the excavations in front of the docks was a formidable one for hundreds of schooners continued to arrive from the south of England with pottery material or with slates from the Welsh ports. The Ship Canal Company's efforts to provide an efficient service were successful and after a year-long closure the Bridgewater Dock river entrance was opened for traffic on 12th July 1893. When the water was admitted into the Ship Canal to Runcorn it ended the uncertainty of entry into the town docks for large vessels. Before the coming of the canal it was not unusual for a large ship to have to wait eight or ten days in the estuary before proceeding to

Excavating the Manchester Ship Canal at Old Quay in 1891.

Runcorn. The canal enabled ships to reach the town's docks regardless of the state of the tide. When the laybye was built, tall ships which could not be towed to Manchester because they could not pass under Runcorn Railway Bridge began to unload cargoes of grain, timber and whale oil which were lightered up the canal to their destinations in Warrington and Manchester. The laybye could accommodate the largest merchant vessels of the day being 500 metres in length with a depth of water of nearly eight metres alongside. When the canal was completed there was no further need for Saltport and the jetties were dismantled to leave no trace of the temporary port.

The water was admitted into the Ship Canal by stages. On 28th September 1891 it was opened as far as Weston Marsh Lock for the accommodation of River Weaver traffic and on 8th July 1893 it was opened to Old Quay. On the 17th November 1893 the water was admitted between Runcorn and Latchford and the waterway was completely filled from Eastham to Manchester a week later. The great seaway was opened for traffic on New Year's Day 1894 with Queen Victoria performing the ceremonial

opening on May 21st.

To enable shipping to enter the canal from the river the Ship Canal Company built four locks in the vicinity of Runcorn. Weston Marsh lock at the mouth of the Weaver became the entrance to the Weaver Navigation whilst Weston Mersey lock enabled shipping to enter the Weaver docks. The Bridgewater Docks were served by the Bridgewater lock and Runcorn Old Quay lock entrance was built near to the site of the old Mersey and Irwell Company's Runcorn to Latchford (Old Quay) Canal dock. All the locks were busy from the time the canal opened for, although the new waterway provided an easy route to the estuary, it was not usual for small sailing vessels to be towed via the canal from Eastham to Runcorn and Weston Point docks. However, when there was insufficient water in the Mersey at low tides, the Manchester Ship Canal Company was prepared to allow vessels bringing the traditional cargoes of pottery material, bone ash and slates to be towed up the canal free of charge but the normal entry for schooners to Runcorn and Weston Point was via the river to Weston Mersey, Bridgewater and Old Quay locks. The Ship Canal Company continued the practice

A narrow beam Bridgewater Canal tug assembling a train of barges at the Bridgewater Docks.

of its predecessors in supplying paddle-boats to tow barges, flats and schooners to and from the estuary.

The arrival of the Manchester Ship Canal had a lasting impact on the Runcorn waterfront. The Duke of Bridgewater's Gut and Castle Bridge across to No Man's Land were removed. The old salt water baths below the Parish Church also disappeared as did the ferry slip and the docks, locks and tidal basin of the Old Quay Company's Runcorn to Latchford Canal. The steam flour mill which was situated on the river's edge at Mill Street was demolished. Further up river, Old Quay Mill with its offices and wharf were pulled down together with the Old Quay mortar works and the adjacent pottery with its offices. Among the many smaller properties removed were a number of cottages, a couple of brick yards, timber yards and the outbuildings of a number of agricultural smallholdings.

The Ship Canal was built through the townships of Weston, Runcorn, Halton, Moore and Acton Grange. Much of its rural route was through Sir Richard Brooke's estate. Rough pasture and marsh, woodland, good grazing land and footpaths were effected by the work but Sir Richard did not present opposition to the canal works as did his obstinate ancestor a century and quarter previously.

Runcorn's shipbuilding industry was already dying when work on the Ship Canal started. The days of the wooden sailing vessel were coming to an end and the local shipyards had not moved with the times. They had remained primitive. Their managements were content to satisfy the regional demand for small coasters and river craft and they did not install the equipment needed to build the iron and steel vessels which were required by the end of the century. Soon after the completion of the Ship Canal the "Runcorn Guardian" noted *"Shipbuilding has become an industry of the past and this has proved prejudicial to the interests of the district"*. The newspaper article stated that the directors of the Ship Canal had been asked *"to grant concessions to Runcorn but with comparatively little success and since the completion of the undertaking considerable depression in trade has been experienced"*. When the great wall between the canal and the Mersey was being constructed it was not possible to launch large vessels from the shipyards and the 145-ton schooner "Despatch" which was launched in 1886, was the last coasting vessel to leave the local slipways although ship repair and barge building continued for many years after the completion of the Ship Canal. The Manchester Ship Canal directors did make some concessions to Runcorn. They sited their tug boat depot at Old Quay and in addition, a new boat repair yard was established at Runcorn Big Pool on the Bridgewater Canal. The Sprinch yard was claimed to be the finest of its type in Britain with facilities to enable six barges to undergo repair at any one time. The yard was responsible for the maintenance of over two hundred canal craft.

The Runcorn to Latchford or Old Quay Canal had been in steady decline for many years before it was swept away by the Ship Canal. It had however, a vital role to play during the building of the Ship Canal for much of the building material needed for the construction of Salford Docks was transported via Old Quay. Not every trace of the Old Quay Canal disappeared, for stretches of the old waterway between Runcorn and Moore were left and in time what remained of the canal became an attractive feature of the rural landscape. Unfortunately, a few years ago the canal was drained and today its route is an overgrown ditch barely discernible among the weeds and rushes.

For a couple of years Runcorn and district experienced a large increase in population when the workforce employed in the building of the Ship Canal found accommodation in the town. The census returns for 1891 show that there were five thousand more people than there had been ten years previously and local construction on the canal works was only at its beginning. It was a boom time for Runcorn's shopkeepers, licensees and lodging house keepers and there were increased employment opportunities for local people but the arrival of the navvies and their families put pressure on the limited housing available and also upon the schools. Because of the acute shortage of school places the Catholic school managers decided to build a second school in the locality and a small school was built in Weston Village. When the Ship Canal was finished, the navvies and their families left the district and the numbers on the roll of the Weston school fell until it was no longer viable. It was closed in 1902 and the building was bought by Sir John Brunner who presented it to the local community to serve as the village hall.

The migration of the Manchester Ship Canal construction workers after 1893 resulted in a fall of nearly six thousand in the population and two years later there were five hundred houses to let or for sale in the town. The days of employment opportunity also departed with the completion of the Ship Canal which coincided with a depression in local industry. The canal works had an adverse effect on Runcorn docks and there was also a general decline in trade on the old inland waterways. The promoters of the Ship Canal had predicted that their undertaking would attract many new industries to line its banks but this did not happen in the Runcorn area and there was no increase in job prospects. The canal did place Wigg works on deep water and a few years after its completion, Salt Union at Weston Point developed a new plant which enabled large ocean-going vessels to load alongside the works.

Surprisingly, the ancient ferry crossing survived the coming of the Ship Canal. In 1895 both the Borough of Widnes and the Runcorn Urban District Council threatened legal action to ensure that the directors of the London and North Western Railway Company honoured their statutory obligations by preserving the ferry service. At the same time, the Runcorn Council requested the railway company to reduce its toll on the railway bridge footway "because of the great depression in trade both here and in Widnes". After being closed for four years during the construction of the canal, the ferry was reopened on March 11th 1895. The Ship Canal Company provided a boat capable of holding thirty passengers for traversing their waterway from the ferry steps to a pier in the canal wall and the railway company provided the other boat which crossed the river to Widnes. Intending ferry passengers now had the added inconvenience of ascending the canal wall in order to transfer from one boat to the other.

It has been said that the Manchester Ship Canal is "in sheer magnitude the greatest civil engineering project of the Victorian Age". Within six months of the opening, 630 sea going vessels passed through Runcorn to Manchester Docks. The new canal could handle the largest cargo vessels then afloat and from 1894, the sight and sounds of ocean-going ships and their paddle-tugs added unique character to Runcorn and Weston Point. Soon veritable processions of big ships became commonplace. Tall windjammers with their top masts lowered to clear the railway bridge were towed along the canal. Often at night, two or three large steamers were to be seen tied up at the wall to the east of the bridge. With all lights ablaze, the ships presented a striking spectacle on the town's waterfront.

In 1911 in order to allow the passage of larger vessels, the curve of Runcorn bend immediately to the west of the railway bridge was increased in radius. This permitted the navigation of ships of greater tonnage and soon a number of vessels with an overall length of up to 170 metres and with a beam of 19 metres were towed to Manchester.

An ocean-going vessel passing Old Quay swing bridge shortly after the opening of the Ship Canal.

The ferry crossing with the old baths.
The Ship Canal is being built with the piles of the sea wall in position.
The furnaces of the disused Ditton Brook Ironworks can be seen under the span of the bridge.

Bibliography

For the general background reading for the development of the port of Runcorn see J.D. Porteous *"Canal Ports. The Urban Achievement of the Canal Age"* (1977); *"After the Canal Duke"* (1970) by F.C. Mather and *"Schooner Port"* (1981) by H.F. Starkey. The Handbook of the Bridgewater Department of the Manchester Ship Canal Company (1973) and an article in the *"Port of Manchester Review"* (1976) by W.E. Leathwood "Workshop of the World" also deal with the origins of the port in Runcorn.

The story of the promotion and construction of the Manchester Ship Canal has been exhaustively explored by Bosdin Leech in *"History of the Manchester Ship Canal"* (1907) and more recently by D.A. Farnie *"The Manchester Ship Canal and the Rise of the Port of Manchester"* (1980). Another useful source of information is *"Port of Manchester"* (1901) published by Hind, Hoyle and Light Ltd. Maps and plans of the Manchester Ship Canal's route through Runcorn, Weston and Halton townships which were presented for the M.S.C. Parliamentary Bill of 1885 were also used.

Chapter 16
The Improvement Commissioners

From the early decades of the nineteenth century Britain's expanding urban areas began to demand a more effective form of local government and new authorities were set up by individual Improvement Acts which brought into being Boards of Commissioners who were to undertake specific duties. At a public meeting held in Runcorn on 25th September 1851 steps were taken to start proceedings leading to the application to Parliament for an Improvement Act. A committee was formed to expedite the resolution with Mr. William Pritchard, the secretary and manager of the gas works, being appointed secretary and Robert Chesshyre Whiteway as chairman. The Runcorn Improvement Act was passed in June 1852 and in October the election of the Commissioners took place.

The first Board of Commissioners had sixteen elected members. They were Messrs. John Hignett, William Hazlehurst, J.L. Wright, James Cawley, Thomas Johnson, John Rigby, William Brundrit, John Johnson, Charles Hazlehurst, H. Beswick, James Rigby, John Simpson, R C Whiteway, T.C. Stelfox, Philip Whiteway and W.B. Gibson. The Improvement Act stipulated that the Trustees of the Duke of Bridgewater and the Mersey and Irwell Navigation Company could each provide a commissioner. The Trustees duly appointed Mr. William Howarth and for their Mersey and Irwell Company they nominated Mr. George Forrester. Thus eighteen members met for the first time on November 1st with Mr. John L. Wright in the chair.

Under the Runcorn Improvement Act the Commissioners were empowered to pave, drain, light, police and clean the town and also to improve conditions by providing such facilities as a library, a cemetery and a market hall. The Commissioners had powers to borrow up to £50,000 on the security of the rates and they were to create a sinking fund for the redemption of each loan at the end of a period of thirty years. There is no doubt that the new Board faced an uphill task for Runcorn in 1852 was unpaved, ill-lit and without building bye-laws. The town was "almost entirely wanting in those amenities of civic and social environment ...considered absolutely necessary for public health and well-being". William Handley writing in 1902 referred to the problems which confronted the first Commissioners. In his "Sketch of Early Local Government in Runcorn" Mr. Handley states, *"It was often remarked that Runcorn was the end of the*

world having but one way in and the same way out. The number of streets or lanes in 1852 was sixty-five, none of them constructed according to modern ideas, being little more than earthen or cinder roads some flagged with footways. The sewers were open-jointed stone drains with their sub-soil polluting facilities and untrapped connections directly communicating with the dwellings of the inhabitants ... There was no cemetery, no waterworks, and the banking facilities were limited to a few hours on one day a week".

The passing of the Runcorn Improvement Act brought progressive civic administration to the town. Towards the end of 1853 the Improvement Commissioners appointed Mr. Michael Barker to succeed Mr. John Buckley, the Clerk of the Highways, who was killed whilst crossing the railway line at Widnes station. Mr. Barker received the designation "surveyor" and in his account of early town management we are told by William Handley that, *"There being no special provision in the Improvement Act prescribing the appointment of a surveyor, Mr. Barker's appointment was made subject to the approval of one of Her Majesty's principal Secretary of State and his appointment bears the approval by signature of the Home Secretary of the time, Lord Palmerston".* We are told that the new surveyor was required to make a declaration "in solemn and statutory manner" that he would perform his duties *"diligently, faithfully ...to the utmost of his power, skill and ability ...without favour or affection, prejudice or malice to any person whomsoever".* There is no doubt Mr. Barker proved to be an excellent public servant for, fifty years later, he was still serving the new local authority, the Runcorn Urban District Council.

By 1850 it had become obvious that the continued development of urban Runcorn depended upon the availability of an improved water supply for both domestic and industrial users. The existing supply from the Sprinch, supplemented by water from a few wells was totally inadequate for the needs of the growing town. The situation was discussed in a "Warrington Guardian" editorial of 6th August 1853 which referred to a plan to form a waterworks company. *"A prospectus has been issued by the Runcorn Waterworks Company stating their intention to apply during the next session of Parliament for an Act of Incorporation with powers to raise £14,000 with further powers to borrow £3,000".* In the next edition of the newspaper a week later, there was another brief reference to the waterworks but no information about the precise plan and design of the project was given. The article simply stated, *"The neighbourhood of Runcorn is eminently suited for villas but building has been retarded because of the inadequate water supply ... The engineers state that they can supply wholesome water at moderate cost. A small outlay will construct the works and the Company will supply the Improvement Commissioners with a cheap water supply for sanitary purposes and for extinguishing fires without the necessity for fire engines"*. However, the scheme never materialised and four years later the same newspaper gave a description of a "handsome stone water fountain which ornaments the front of the Commissioners' Offices given by the Earl of Ellesmere". The fountain was erected in June 1857 and for many years it was a feature of the town centre. Water was conveyed from the Sprinch well to the fountain opposite the town hall and *"The top of the fountain is surmounted by a large globular lamp (Naylor's Patent) for the labouring classes of the community. The fountain is ten feet high and is set on a circular base of nine feet diameter"*. But the new fountain did not represent a significant advance in public amenities for it did not increase the water supply and the town did need a fire engine. In October 1857 the Commissioners purchased a fire engine with all the requisite implements for £230. It was described as being "a double action engine with an eight inch stroke. It can lift one ton of water per minute and is of the most powerful description made".

Within a couple of years the water supply problem was demanding the Improvement Commissioners' urgent attention and they looked at three schemes by which the flow could be increased. The Commissioners considered first a plan to form a lake by building a dam across the Sprinch above the Big Pool. This plan was soon discarded when it was calculated that in dry years the proposed reservoir would be unable to supply more than 14,000 people and the Commissioners were planning a water supply to cater for the needs of a future population in excess of 20,000. The costs of building the reservoir and the filtration system as well as a pumping station at a total cost of £35,000 were also deemed to be excessive. A second plan was for the using of the subterranean water of the new red sandstone formation under the town by means of a shaft sunk near to the head of the Big Pool from where the water would be pumped to a reservoir on Runcorn Hill. This idea was ruled out as it was believed that the underground supply of fresh water at this site was limited and a few years of extraction would result in salt water gradually taking its place. It was thought more desirable to sink a shaft on high ground and Runcorn Hill was chosen as the place for the new waterworks. Mr. Hawksley, a consultant engineer, agreed with Mr. Cunningham, the

Commissioners' engineer, in his view that *"The water works should be placed in an eminently clean and beautiful situation, never likely to be crowded by buildings and manufactories ... I have much experience of the beneficial effects produced by placing the water works of a town in an agreeable situation, and from laying out the grounds within the enclosure in an ornamental manner. Whenever regard is had to these conditions the Water Works speedily become the accustomed resort of the inhabitants when in search of amusement or recreation"*. Mr. Cunningham saw only one drawback in his scheme — the cost of transporting coal for the pumping engine up to Runcorn Hill. In his report to the Commissioners he suggested that this could be overcome *"if there might be an arrangement made with the owner of the tramway up to the quarries by which the empty waggons occasionally be made available for bringing up the coal from the wharf at a very moderate cost"*. The bore hole was to be drilled to a depth of 128 metres. The estimated costs came to seventeen thousand pounds of which the engine, boilers and pumps cost three thousand pounds; the engine house, boiler house, chimney shaft, two cottages, workshop and boundary walls cost £3,600 with the well-boring costing two thousand pounds. The reservoir charges were assessed at £3,500 with the trenches, mains and engineering work at £4,500.

Mr. Cunningham's plans were submitted to the Improvement Commissioners in July 1861 but they were slow to take action and it was not until August 1864 when Mr. Hawksley's report confirmed the soundness of the Runcorn Hill scheme that the contractors received the instruction to commence work. The contract for the waterworks was awarded to a Mr. James Whalley of Wigan who, after a year's work on the project was declared bankrupt. According to an article in the Runcorn "Free Press", "the company directors were then forced to rely upon their own resources and they employed workmen to complete the task that Whalley could not finish". The waterworks began operations in March 1868 when water was pumped into a covered reservoir on Beacon Hill at the rate of 40,000 gallons an hour. The difficulties encountered during the construction of the waterworks involved an expenditure of nearly three times the original estimate.

From 1868 Runcorn had an excellent water supply. The "Free Press" noted *"The water is sufficiently safe for domestic washing purposes (for which it is admirably adapted) as it as soft as rain water with none of the impurities from roof or atmosphere and for brewing, distilling or other manufactories it will doubtless be the quality required ... The clear, pure, crystal water will be distributed by pipes which are now being laid to parties in the three townships (even as*

The waterworks. The pumping station on Runcorn Heath.

elevated as the *"Castle Hotel" in Halton) on application for it"*. The waterworks company retained the system for twenty-five years before selling to the town in 1893.

One of the first projects undertaken by the Improvement Commissioners was the provision of a market hall. In February 1853 a sub-committee was formed consisting of John and Thomas Johnson, the soap manufacturers; John Linacre Wright, tanner and quarrymaster; Philip Whiteway, shipbuilder and James Cawley. The committee considered a number of sites in various parts of the town including one which was owned by the Johnson brothers. It was agreed that this Bridge Street site was the most suitable and it was bought from the Johnsons for £1,800. However, by selling the land to the Commissioners the Johnsons created an unforeseeen problem when it was discovered that they had inadvertently breached the provisions of the Improvement Act and by doing so had disqualified themselves from serving as Commissioners for that year at least. An election had to be called to appoint two new Commissioners to replace them.

Also on the site of the proposed market hall was a fair sized house with a garden belonging to Mrs. Wylde and adjacent to this property were a number of old cottages. Just below the market site was "Barber's Whint" and the public bakehouse. All these were purchased by the town and pulled down to make way for the new market.

Mr. Barker, the surveyor, was responsible for the Italianate design of the new market. The hall was built of brick with stone dressings and rusticated quoins. It contained fourteen shops with an open central area which was provided with stalls for greengrocers. The new building was opened on 27th September 1856 when it was reported that the displays of meat, fish and poultry were excellent but it was not the food which attracted the large throng on the opening day. Crowds of sightseers came to see the brilliant gas lighting and by ten o'clock on Saturday night the market was so densely crowded that business nearly came to a standstill. The market hall was the first major project for which Mr. Barker was responsible.

The urgent need for a town cemetery was another priority and by 1858 the newly-elected Runcorn Burial Board had acquired land in Greenway Meadows for the purpose of making a cemetery. In June that year the "Warrington Guardian" carried an advertisement inviting architects to tender for the work, *"The Runcorn Burial Board are desirous of receiving plans and estimates for the creation of two plain neat chapels detached (one for the use of the Established Church and*

the other for Dissenters) with an entrance lodge, gates and receiving house and for laying out the burial ground". When the cemetery was opened in March 1860 it became necessary to make the old field path from Savages Bridge to Higher Runcorn into a road. With the creation of Greenway Road an area of streets of small houses came into being between the cemetery and the Bridgewater Canal. The new streets eventually included Shaw Street, New Street, Surrey Street, Cavendish Street and Albert Street and because they formed a distinct new community away from the old township the district became known as Newtown.

The Board of Commissioners did not neglect the old cemetery at the Parish Church and they renewed the boundary wall from Clarence Terrace to the Ferry landing. The contractor for this work faced unforeseen difficulties due to the nature of the ground. The minute of 8th June 1866 shows his predicament over the work and also his anxiety about payment for extra labour. *"The Chairman read a letter from Mr. George Hunt asking for an allowance for the erection of the churchyard wall over and above the amount contracted for, owing to the foundation having to be sunk deeper than the old one, which was built on river mud and which gave way. Resolved that Mr. Ramsdale write to Mr. Hunt informing him that when the erection of the wall is completed the Board will entertain his application".*

Of the total rateable value of Runcorn in 1852, the Bridgewater Trust with their Old Quay Navigation or Mersey and Irwell constituted a fifth. William Handley states that the Trustees paid twice as much in rates as any other industry in the town. At the inauguration of the Board of Improvement Commissioners there were twenty-five industrial enterprises and they comprised three soap works and chemical works, two quarries, three tanneries, two steam mills, the windmill, two slate works, two iron foundries, one chain works, one ropery, one maltkiln, one brickyard, one pottery and the gas works as well as a number of smaller concerns.

From the very first the Improvement Commissioners were under pressure to improve communications to other towns. Letters began to appear in the local newspapers urging the Commissioners to petition the railway companies to provide a branch line to the town with a rail and footbridge across the river.

Typical of the correspondence is the following from the "Warrington Guardian" of 5th June 1858 in which the writer speaks of a growing rivalry between Runcorn and the rapidly growing new town of Widnes, *"With one voice let us support Mr. Cawley or any other gentleman who will exert himself to get the Gap bridged over. We should do away with that abominable nuisance the ferry which is a disgrace to the town and to all who have any connection with it and which makes Runcorn the wonder of the civilized world. We should establish a business and friendly union with the town fast rising on the Lancashire side of the river and so remove that tone of opposition which at present exists and which will increase if we go on in the same old way".* The writer went on to declare that a bridge would link Runcorn not only to Widnes but also to Liverpool, London and the Potteries. This would result in new factories and job opportunities on both sides of the river.

In the thirty years following the census of 1831 the population of Runcorn doubled to more than ten thousand inhabitants. Although housing development was westwards towards the Parish Church and the Top Locks, the nucleus of the township still centered upon the Old Quay area and the district around the junction of Mersey Street, High Street and Bridge Street. In the opinion of the Improvement Commissioners it was from Old Quay that a railway ought to be built in order to improve communications to Warrington and beyond. Communications to the east had suffered as a result of the closure of the Bridgewater swift packet passenger service in February 1856 and in an attempt to improve matters, the Improvement Commissioners submitted two railway schemes to the directors of the London and North Western Railway Company. In 1858 they proposed a line from Aston to cross the Mersey at Runcorn Gap proceeding to Huyton where it would join the Liverpool and Manchester Railway. The other project was a scheme for a railway from Old Quay to Walton near to Warrington on the former Grand Junction line. No doubt the Commissioners were influenced by the Bridgewater Trust representatives who saw the possibility of a branch line to their docks at Old Quay. The notion of a railway in the area of Old Quay was not new. In 1830 and again in 1838 the Grand Junction Railway sought to cross the Runcorn to Latchford Canal and the Mersey with a bridge at Marshgate about a mile to the east of Old Quay. The bridge was not built because the scheme was successfully opposed by the Mersey and Irwell Navigation Company and by merchants with shipping interests and so the Bill was dropped. The Runcorn to Warrington line proposed by the Commissioners in 1858 did not receive the sympathetic attention of the railway directors and nothing more was heard of the idea. However, about this time a major undertaking to improve communications on the waterways was commenced when the Bridgewater Trustees started work on the Runcorn and Weston Canal which linked Francis Dock to the Weaver Navigation. The canal was complete in 1860 and it enabled the Weaver flats to deliver cargoes of salt direct to the Bridgewater Docks.

While the narrows of the Runcorn Gap remained unbridged there was some truth in a popular local assertion of the time, "Runcorn is like the Dead Sea. There's a road into it but none out". Throughout the 1850s local deputations met the directors of the London and North Western Railway Company but it was not until 1861 that the Act for the railway and Runcorn Railway Bridge was passed with the work commencing in 1863. Before the railway came to the town a horse omnibus conveyed passengers twice daily between Runcorn and the railway station at Moore. An omnibus also conveyed passengers to Northwich. By way of the ferry, communications by railway to St. Helens were five times a day from the station in Widnes.

With the growth of Newtown the Improvement Commissioners had to give their attention to Savage's Bridge which was too narrow and steep to cope with the increase in the number of waggons and carts wanting to cross the canal. The old bridge had to be taken down and rebuilt and later Waterloo Bridge and its approaches were widened. Up to this time the town lay almost entirely between the Bridgewater Canal and the river. With the exception of English Row, Crescent Row and Welsh Row there was no housing in Duke's Fields and in the centre of the township at Old Quay, the fields on each side of Irwell Lane were used for farming. As previously noted, the way to Higher Runcorn was a path through the fields. The path was not suitable for vehicles, and on Sundays Miss Ann Orred, the principal landowner in Weston, walked in procession down to the Parish Church with her maidservants leading and her menservants following a few yards behind her.

With the arrival of the railway age the turnpike road system was becoming bankrupt. The scientifically-made roads of the late eighteenth and early nineteenth century were overwhelmed by the success of the railways and they were no longer profitable to their trustees. In May 1861 the Trustees of the Chester to Warrington Turnpike Road at their meeting in the Ring o' Bells in Daresbury, invited offers for the leases of the toll gates at Preston Brook, Appleton, Stockton Heath and the toll gate and side gate at Sutton. There is no record that there was any interest shown in the Trustees' invitation and within a short time the trust was wound up and the road reverted to the parish to become an open highway.

Education, Housing and Public Health

From the middle of the last century many more children began to attend school. Until 1870 education was almost entirely in the hands of voluntary bodies with the churches playing the leading role. The large population increase in the expanding towns resulted in a severe shortage of school places and when education was at last recognised as a public service at the passing of the Education Act of 1870, the main aim of the Bill was to "fill the gaps" in those localities where school places were insufficient. This was done by awarding building grants to the existing schools and if afterwards, there was still a shortage of places, by establishing locally elected School Boards which were empowered to provide new schools with support from the rates.

There was some hostility in Runcorn at the idea

of a Board school with the opposition coming from churchmen who feared that a school which received aid from the rates would pose a threat to the church schools and the undenominational, "simple Bible Instruction" which was part of the curriculum of the Board school was regarded by many people to be a diluting of Christian teaching. Runcorn resisted the establishment of a School Board until May 1874 when a final notice was served on the town.

The first meeting of the Runcorn School Board was held in January 1875 with seven elected members comprising three Anglicans, two Wesleyans, one Presbyterian and one Congregationalist member. Churchmen were to form the majority on the Board until 1901 and opposition to them was not lacking. For years there was bitterness and ill-feeling between the supporters of the Board schools and those supporting the church schools. At a Runcorn Union meeting in 1877 the Reverend Mr. Spencer, vicar of Daresbury, said that the School Board was totally unnecessary, *"The schools which were in existence at the time were educating seventy-five per cent of the children and the Board has been obtained from motives of spite. Shut it up. The burden falls on the ratepayers and I don't care tuppence for anything else. They will lay the last ounce on us which will break our backs"*. It would be decades before the resentment over the schools controversy finally disappeared.

Runcorn's first Board school was opened in the old Ragged School building on Mill Brow in 1880 with another in Bethesda chapel a couple of years later. Greenway Road Board School was opened in 1886. Later is was renamed to become Victoria Road School.

By 1850 there were a number of grand houses in the town. The present "South Bank Hotel" was the residence of Dennis Brundrit J.P., Philip Whiteway J.P. lived at Grove House whilst Waterloo House was the home of Charles Hazlehurst. Set amongst gardens and orchards, these houses were riverside villas with today's Waterloo Road being an unmade country lane leading to the ferry. In Halton Road, near to Delph Bridge, were a couple of large houses, Belvue House and Belmont House and further along Halton Road (the Runcorn to Northwich turnpike road) was a sizeable house which a few years later became Holy Trinity parsonage. But desirable residences were few and at the other end of the scale there was the "Rookery" — the wretched slum area bordered by Mersey Street, Water

Court Dwellings. Lowe's Court off Cooper Street.

Pool Lane, Nos.24 to 34

Old houses in Pool Lane at the centre of Runcorn township.
Pool Lane was sometimes called Buttermilk Lane or Sour Milk Lane.

Street and Brunswick Street.

The Rookery was a run-down district of small dwellings with many shabby lodging houses which catered mainly for Irish immigrants. In November 1857 the Improvement Commissioners invited their Chief Constable to become the inspector of common lodging houses. The Commissioners proposed to pay Mr. Blake five pounds a year to carry out the onerous duties attached to the office but on a motion proposed by Mr. Ormerod, the allowance for the assignment was reduced to £3 per annum. However, Mr. Blake had experience of the task and he declined to accept the offer stating that the job *"was of a most offensive and laborious nature ... There are forty lodging houses and as many more as ought to be ... and to do what the Act requires I have to turn down the bedclothes and thoroughly examine the whole place day and night. I have passed through fever, filth, stench and vermin. The £3 offered would not pay for sweeping the bugs off me. Ten pounds was more reasonable"*. The Commissioners appointed a Mr. Steers who reported in March the following year. Inspector Steers said that many of the town's registered lodging houses were in a filthy condition particularly those in the Rookery. He also drew attention to the undesirable practice of lines of washing being stretched across the streets. During the summer months the narrow thoroughfares were vile. In 1864 Doctor Henry Wilson was appointed medical officer to the Board of Commissioners. Within six months he was dead "to the regret of the whole town and

district, cut off by typhus fever while in the execution of and devotion to his duties". During the summer months disease was rampant and the prime cause was obvious — the lack of an efficient sewerage and drainage system. Before the commencement of building in Newtown the Improvement Commissioners determined to use their powers to ensure that the new roads and sewers would be constructed so as to avoid problems in the future. There were difficulties in plenty in the old town and the Commissioners wanted no more. They demanded to see all the plans before building began and they promptly rejected those which were submitted by Major Orred's land agent. The Commissioners required that he should present new plans with "satisfactory street levels showing the direction of sewers to be approved by the Commissioners according to the Act of Parliament". At last haphazard speculative building was subject to constraint.

But industrial Runcorn was not a particularly unhealthy place. The death rate in 1884-5 was 13 per thousand rising to 22 per thousand in 1889-90 before failing back to 14.3 per thousand in 1899-1900. This was lower than the death rate in Widnes over the same years and Runcorn's average figure at 17.9 for the ten years up to 1905 was near the national average. However, child mortality was unacceptably high. After an outbreak of diphtheria in the summer of 1898 the medical officer to the Runcorn Urban District Council was scathing in his report on the conditions in the town. *"The infant rate of mortality is painfully high ...due to defective drains ...legacies that have been handed down to the authority".* The medical officer went as far as to describe those responsible for the original sewerage work as being guilty of "criminal responsibility".

A glance at the parish magazine of any town church in the last century tells a sad story — the tragedy of child death, usually as a result of insanitary conditions. Even during the first two decades of the twentieth century child mortality was often intolerable. At All Saints church in September 1900 for instance, there were forty funerals. Twenty-two were infants and three were young people under eighteen years of age.

Small-pox was prevalent in the town in 1892 and Vicar Maitland Wood wrote a few lines in the parish magazine in order to allay the fears of his parishioners. He said that he had attempted to see the victims of the disease in hospital but that he had been forbidden entry. The authorities were adamant in their determination to isolate the sick and so contain the outbreak. The Chairman of the Improvement Commission wrote to Mr. Wood explaining the situation, *"For obvious reasons visiting is not allowed at the Runcorn Isolation Hospital and I could not feel justified in assuming the responsibility for making an exception of yourself or ministers of religion generally".* The vicar printed the Chairman's letter in the magazine but wisely decided not to make an issue of the matter.

By 1900 all newly-built houses had to have water sanitation and the conversion of older property was proceeding as quickly as possible. However, large scale slum clearance did not get under way in Runcorn until well into the twentieth century and the tiny airless court dwellings remained an unpleasant feature of the town. Long after their deaths, slum landlords were remembered by the courts which were named after them : Massey's Court, Salkeld's Court, Hedley's Court, Lowe's Court, Rigby's Court, Hitchmough's Court and Grindrod's Square. Other streets were unimaginatively named after the Duke of Bridgewater and members of his family, with Duke Street, Bridgewater Street, Egerton Street and Algernon Street. The Duke's nephew became Earl of Ellesmere and the heir to the Earl was Viscount Brackley. Sutherland Street was named after another nephew of the Duke of Bridgewater who became Duke of Sutherland and Blantyre Street is called after a Scottish estate of the Duke's. Cawdor Street gets its name from one of the titles of the Sutherland family. Some street names are those of important officials of the Bridgewater Trust such as Loch Street, Howarth Street, and Sothern Street. There is a

Gilbert Street and a Brindley Street and one named after W.H. Collier who was the manager of the Bridgewater Navigation Company. Vicar Street and Alcock Street commemorate Vicar Alcock and his brother. Treacle Row was a row of cottages in Stone Street, off Bridge Street, but why it was so called remains a mystery.

From the middle years of the 1860s there was no doubting the success of the canal port of Runcorn. Although it was still a town of small businesses, one or two imposing shops had been built in Church Street, High Street and Devonshire Square and the beginnings of the Runcorn and Widnes Co-operative Society date from shops which were opened in Regent Street and Devonshire Square in 1862. The town had a number of new chapels and churches and, always an indication of increasing commercial prosperity, there was a steady rise in the number of public houses as well as an expansion in the banking facilities. After the end of the American Civil War, local industry boomed with the soap and alkali works, the quarries and the shipyards all experiencing capacity production. New docks had been built in order to cope with the growth in shipping and from 1863 the railway bridge was under construction so that within a couple of years the town would be linked to Liverpool, the Midlands and London. Runcorn had become a thriving place which had expanded across the barrier of the Bridgewater Canal into the fields to the south. Fifteen years after the establishment of the gas works the supply had reached Weston village, Weston Point docks and also the dock on the St. Helens Canal at Woodend in Widnes.

Although atmospheric pollution was a nuisance and industrial tipping had become an unsightly feature, the Improvement Commissioners were providing effective local government which was beginning to make the town a healthier and cleaner place in which to live. When the Improvement Commission took over the management of the town in 1852 Runcorn had a total of sixty-five streets. By the end of Queen Victoria's reign there were a hundred and fifty streets and the rateable value had risen from £23,000 to £57,000.

The fields to the west of the railway viaduct were being built over by 1875 and parts of Brackley Street, Bentinck Street, Leinster Street, Portland Street, Cawdor Street and Blantyre Street were in being. There were a few houses in Ashridge Street with others on the northern side of Rutland Street where the Welsh chapel had been built in 1856. Soon the gardens and orchards of Dennis Brundrit's "Southbank" and those of Philip Whiteway's "Grove House" would be given over to building. On the eastern side of Waterloo Road there was still only one house between

Runcorn waterfront about 1870.
The white building in the centre is the old swimming baths sited next to the Belvedere shipyard.

Egerton Street and the river — that of Charles Hazelhurst.

The construction of Greenway Road in the 1860s had resulted in the creation of Newtown but later housing development in the area came slowly. There were a couple of terraces immediately above the railway bridge in Greenway Road and a number of large houses had been built in Moughland Lane whilst in Weston Road there was "Beaconfield", the home of Thomas Hazlehurst.

Weston village expanded rapidly after the building of the chemical works on the Weston Canal. The industrialisation was largely responsible for an eighty per cent increase in the population of Weston and Weston Point in the thirty years from 1851 to 1881.

For centuries there had been confusion as to the exact line of demarcation between the townships of Halton and Runcorn. The boundary was almost indefinable. Charles Nickson observed, *"Even in 1881 when the boundaries of the township were changed, one side of Bridge street was in Runcorn whilst the houses opposite were claimed by Halton. In one or two instances a single dwelling assessed to the township of Halton was surrounded by property paying rates to the authorities in Runcorn"*. By the Divided Parishes Act of 1882 and a local government order of 1885 the situation was resolved when part of Halton township was transferred to Runcorn and a part of Runcorn was added to Halton.

When the Urban District Council of Runcorn was formed in 1894 eighteen councillors were appointed to administer local government over a district of 1,275 acres with a population of 19,000 and a rateable value of £58,131. The town was divided into six wards; Mersey ward, Central, Bridgewater, Newtown, Heath and Halton wards. Runcorn was now a deep water port and the new Council adopted an emblem depicting a full-rigged ship as its official crest.

The essential atmosphere of Victorian Runcorn differed little from that of other small towns. In every street there was a grocer and a beer house with tiny shops and workshops everywhere. Independent shopkeepers and tradesmen of every kind proliferated. Clog makers, makers of hand-made boots and shoes, tailors, milliners and dress makers, saddle and harness makers, wheelwrights, chimney sweeps, lamp and oil dealers and clock makers. The directories of the time list a number of straw bonnet makers, "chymist and druggists", braziers and tinmen, nail makers and rope and twine manufacturers. Mrs. Susannah Roberts of Loch Street earned her living as a "bleeder with leeches", Thomas Taylor was a hay and fodder dealer whilst George Tomkinson of Loch Street was a cow-keeper. Joseph Heginbotham made umbrellas, Thomas Harvey made chairs and Samuel Ravenscroft was a sailcloth manufacturer. Mr. Joseph Peck, the car proprietor, offered his two and four-wheeled drags, landaus, and waggonettes for hire by the day, the hour or by the distance. Mr. Littler, the piano teacher, advertised that he was a "professor of music". For a few hours every Thursday Mr. Samuel Frazer, surgeon-dentist of Mount Pleasant, Liverpool, was available at the druggist's shop in High Street. At his stables at Top Locks, Edwin Tuckey advertised that he was "a team owner with horses for sale always on hand which may be tried before purchasing". Among the many pawnbrokers, one informed the public of a "special lot of forefeited pledges every Wednesday". Most of the town's carpenters and jobbing builders made coffins and many of the drapers supplied servants' outfits. For festive occasions such as balls and pleasure parties, the quadrille band of Mr. Thomas Woods was always in demand.

Many women and girls were employed in domestic service. In addition to those classed as "daily helps" there were resident domestics employed in the homes of the professional and business people. At Norton Priory, the one great household of the district, only two members of the family, Sir Richard Brooke and his brother, Colonel Thomas Brooke, were in residence on the day of the census of 1851. However, two dozen servants including footmen, grooms, housemaids, laundry maids, kitchen maids and gardeners are recorded as living in the Priory mansion.

To protect their gamebirds and wildlife the Brookes employed gamekeepers. There was little poaching among the villagers of Halton and Norton but it is reported that organised gangs of poachers from the towns occasionally became involved in serious fights with Sir Richard's keepers. Elderly residents of present-day Halton recall seeing rusty man-traps hanging in the stables of Norton Priory.

The local newspaper advertisements of the 1880s present a fascinating illustration of the times. Messrs. Handley and Beck, the ironmongers promoted their brass and iron bedsteads, wringing and mangling machines and also wood and wicker bassinettes. Marsh and Smith, the drapers, offered men's suits from £1 with men's shirts from one shilling (5 pence) and boys' shirts from three pence each. One notice proclaimed that Annie Tonks was "A sign and ship painter, church decorator and glazier", whilst Mr. T.H. Spender, the coal merchant supplied only the best "Arley seven feet and Pemberton coals". There were a number of mineral water manufacturers. Duttons of Greenway Road were the sole makers of the celebrated "XL Botanic Ale". The bespoke department of Whinyates, the boot and shoemaker of Church Street, specialised in "needlework slippers made up in splendid style" and Mr. Hampson of Waterloo Road made all kinds of stove pipes to order. Without doubt the chemist's advertisements are the most interesting. Some remedies are unpronounceable with "Neurash-thenipponskelesterizo", "Zylobalsamum" and "Rypophagan". There were cures for "impoverished blood", "depression of spirits and melancholy" as well as powders for "old horses badly out of condition". The most eye-catching advertisement at Smith's chemists of 7 High Street is the following from a trades directory of 1887, *"Dr Lalor's Phosphodyne. Only safe remedy ever discovered for the permanent cure of brain wreckage, paralysis, sleeplessness, harassing dreams, premature decay of vital power. Beware vile imitations".*

Crescent Row

Bibliography

This chapter relies heavily upon William Handley's study of local government in Runcorn, "After Many Years", which was published in the *"Runcorn Weekly News"* in 1902. See also Charles Nickson's *"History of Runcorn"* (1887), *"The Transactions of the Runcorn Improvement Commissioners"* (1852-1894) are to be found at the Shopping City Library, Runcorn.

County and trade directories are useful aids in the study of the Victorian era and the following were used in this chapter; *"Kelly's Post Office Directory "* to 1894; J Slater, *"Directory of Cheshire"* 1855 and 1890; White & Company *"Runcorn Directory"* 1887 and Morris & Company *"Commercial Directory and Gazetteer of Cheshire with Stalybridge"*, 1874.

Other sources included *"Brief History of Runcorn"* (1975) Halton Borough Council; *"A History of Victoria Road School "*1886-1985 by Susan Gilbert; Canon Barclay's Annual Letters to the Parishioners of Runcorn from 1860 and the parish magazine of All Saints church 1896 to 1901. The *"Warrington Guardian"* provided information on Runcorn Market Hall 13.10.1855; 19.7.1856; 9.8.1856 and 4.10.1856; the propositions for a waterworks can be found in the *"Warrington Guardian"* for 6.8.1853; 13.8.1853 and 20.8.1853; lodging houses 7.11.1857 and 6.3.1858; typhus 27.7.1864, fire engine 26.9.1857, cemetery 7.6.1858, the railway and the Improvement Commission 26.6.1858, and the development of Newtown 15.6.1861.

The details of the waterworks on Runcorn Hill are taken from *"The Reports and Estimates of the Proposed Waterworks at Runcorn"* which were presented to the Runcorn Improvement Commissioners in 1864.

The establishment of the Runcorn School Board is discussed in *"Cheshire Archaeology"* Vol.57 (1971) and also in *"Cheshire in the Twentieth Century"* (1985) by Rosalind Tigwell.

The annual Whit Monday procession in High Street in 1924.

The tableau advertising biscuits and bakery produce wins first prize in 1926.

Chapter 17
Social Activity

Before the railway came to Runcorn summer excursions on the Mersey were popular. Indeed river trips only ceased to be an attraction with the building of the Manchester Ship Canal at the end of the Victorian period. In the 1830s the general public could enjoy a sail around the "Comet" lightship off Hilbre Island or to the North Wales coast, and the local newspapers sometimes carried brief accounts of church outings or trips which had been arranged by the Friendly Societies. Typical of the newspaper reports is a paragraph referring to the Runcorn Loyal Order of Shepherds whose committee engaged the steam packet "Earl of Ellesmere" to take their members to Birkenhead in July 1858. Over four hundred members of the society, dressed in their regalia paraded through the town behind the brass band on their way to the steamer. A river trip was a favourite treat for the school children. The "Warrington Guardian" in June 1861 briefly describes the outing arranged for the scholars of the town's National Schools. Five hundred children accompanied by their teachers and Vicar Barclay crammed abroad the paddle steamer "Blanche" for a river cruise. After visiting Liverpool the boat proceeded to New Brighton where the children were thrilled to see the local artillery volunteers firing at a floating target. On their return to Runcorn the party was met by the Parish Church drum and pipe band. The temperance societies also arranged river cruises for their members. In August 1878 the Star of Widnes Lodge of the Good Templars hired the steamer "America" to take 170 members and the brass band for a sail from West Bank Dock in Widnes up the River Weaver to Northwich and back. Adults paid one shilling and sixpence and children, nine pence.

Local firms hired steamers to provide an annual cruise on the river for their employees and families. For many years the shipbuilders, Brundrit and Whiteway arranged treats for their workforce when they chartered the Upper Mersey Navigation Commissioners' buoying vessel "Preston" and every year from 1876 the Bridgewater Navigation Company carried about 450 of their work people and their families to Liverpool in the company's tug-boats. Towards the end of the last century Eastham gained some renown as a pleasure resort and the village was sometimes referred to as the "Richmond of the Mersey" for there were pleasant walks through the woods and gardens with pierrot shows and dancing. To accommodate day trippers arriving by boat, an iron pier was erected in 1874 and the cruise to Eastham became a popular day out for many Runcornians during the summer. When St. John's, Weston held their annual Sunday School and Congregational outing in July 1901 no less than 400 sailed down river to enjoy the swings, donkey rides and merry-go-rounds at Eastham.

With the coming of the railway, the holiday resorts of North Wales and the Lancashire coast became accessible for a day at the sea side and Frodsham Hill became the favourite place to spend an afternoon. The arrival of the railway made it possible for theatrical companies to visit the town and in 1869 the "Theatre Royal" was built in Duke Street. The wooden theatre could hold about 1,200 people. The theatre programme must have suited most tastes for, in addition to the usual melodramas, a number of Shakespearian productions were staged. University lecturers also came by train to address audiences at the Literary Institution and Mechanics Institute in such subjects as botany, philosophy, literature, chemistry and physics.

People made their own entertainment. There were drum and fife bands. Halton St. Mary's church had a drum and pipe band in the 1860s as did the Parish Church in Runcorn. At Weston there were two brass bands, St. John's and the Weston Wesleyan Brass Band. In an item in St. John's church magazine for 1899 the Band Committee reported that "the instruments are not in good order and they have been in use for many years and some were second-hand when first acquired". The Committee determined to raise the money to maintain a playing membership of twenty-eight bandsmen and they declared "We may expect some music during summer evenings as well as parades through the village when required. The band is a church society". There was an excellent response to the committee's appeal and £30 was raised to be spent on new instruments. On all important occasions such as the Sunday Schools' traditional Whit Monday Walk through the town the Runcorn Harmonic Band was certain to be on parade.

Queen Victoria's birthday was always celebrated in style. At Halton in May 1859 about 230 school children and fifteen elderly people from the alms houses and from Sir Richard Brooke's estate were "treated to an excellent plum pudding and roast beef dinner by the amiable Lady Louisa Brooke". The dinner was held on the bowling green of the "Castle Hotel". There were races and the Halton Friendly Female Society helped to organise the events. The occasion was enlivened by the firing of cannon. *"Cannons to the number of five were firing all day long under the command of an old man-o'-war's man who, on more than one occasion when his match went out, quietly placed the short pipe he was smoking over the touch hole to ignite the powder".*

There was plenty of entertainment when George Egerton, the son of Lord Francis Egerton of the Bridgewater undertaking celebrated his twenty-first birthday on 15th June 1844. The employees of the Bridgewater Trust and the Mersey and Irwell Company were given a holiday with pay so as to be able to enjoy the celebrations which were on an elaborate scale. The official programme of events states that proceedings were to begin early in the morning, *"At six o'clock a.m. a salute of twenty guns, which will be repeated every alternate hour during the day until six o'clock p.m. On the arrival of the steamer "Alice" from Liverpool a salute of twenty guns and three cheers will be given from the shore and returned from "Alice". At eleven o'clock the amusements will be commenced in Cooper's Meadow with a barrow race by ten men blindfolded, — distance 150 yards. The man who first wheels his barrow through a certain gap in the hedge to be the winner and to receive a garden spade as his prize. At half past eleven a donkey race for a riding whip, the last donkey to win".* There were more donkey races for prizes of a bridle and a donkey saddle and a pole climbing race with *"a cap and other prizes at the top. No shoes with nails in to be allowed in climbing".* The days of cruel sports were not completely over in 1844 for one item was *"A pig race in which any person catching the pig by the tail and holding it for five minutes by the tail will be entitled to it".* Perhaps the most spectacular event was the Grand Aquatic Tournament at the slate wharf at Bottom Locks between six Bridgewater Trust flatmen and six flatmen of the Old Quay Company. Only six months before, the Bridgewater Trust had purchased the Mersey and Irwell Company (or Old Quay Company as it was known locally) and the intense commercial rivalry of the previous seventy years no doubt produced keen competition in the jousting tournament. Two boats each of four oars and each with a platform on the bow were prepared. *"On the firing of a signal gun the boats to start from opposite ends of the dock and when they approach within five yards of each other the rowers are to draw in their oars and each antagonist to place the point of his javelin against his competitor and the one who by fair pushing throws his opponent off the boat into the water to be the victor. The prize to the winning side to be a suit of clothes. The men are to be dressed in white trousers and gandzey or other jackets which will not impede their swimming powers. The Bridgewater Trust men are to have blue caps and javelins and the Old Quay men red caps and javelins".*

At four o'clock in the afternoon refreshments were served. *"The men are to form in procession and go to dinner in the pavilion in Old Quay yard, and after dinner the men to return to Cooper's Meadow and the wife or other female friend of each man to go to the pavilion for tea".* At dusk there was a firework display on Runcorn Island followed by the burning of an old ship in the centre of the river. The festivities ended with the royal salute of twenty-one guns and "three times three cheers with the bands playing "God Save the Queen". Within a short time of this happy occasion Cooper's Meadow would be built over and with the coming of the Manchester Ship Canal, the sandy beach of Runcorn Island would become inaccessible to children and bathers.

Even when Runcorn was a village with only three thousand inhabitants there was appreciation of classical music. William Handley recalls seeing a programme of the fourth public concert presented by the Runcorn Philharmonic Society in Johnson's Hotel on 22 September 1820. Mr. Handley copied down the details of the programme. Among the items were two by Mozart with others by Pleyel and Jommelli as well as a number of popular choral works. The old programme gave no information about the performers on "instruments of musick" but a footnote suggests that the organisers of the concert expected a full house. "N.B. Gentlemen. Non-subscribers residing in or within a mile from Runcorn will not be admitted". Musical entertainment was always a regular attraction and the Runcorn Literary Institute arranged frequent concerts. Groups from outside the town came to sing. The Frodsham Vocal Amateurs were invited by the Literary Institute to perform in the Parish School before many of the town's influential personages. A performance by the Frodsham group in December 1857 received a tremendous ovation. Runcorn's own Amateur Vocal Society gave their performances in the 1850s in the Forester's Hall in Devonshire Place. This hall which was opened in 1836 occupied the upper floor of a building above shops and it had a capacity for five hundred and fifty persons. The hall was used for public meetings, dancing and entertainment and it was well used, so much so that its success prompted a limited company to build the Public Hall off Church Street in 1860. There was a need for both assembly rooms and they were well patronised over many years.

Orchestral music was popular with the Runcorn Orchestral Society much in demand for public and church functions. The church choirs of the town aimed for the highest standard of excellence. The Methodist congregations in particular had a fine tradition for choral work and in 1897 St. Paul's choir was the "Prize Choir" at the Widnes Eisteddfod in competition with many choirs from the region. Magic lantern lectures were very popular. Mr. David Speakman's celebrated illustrated talk on the Holy Land was reported as having been received with tremendous applause at Bethesda in 1859. One form of entertainment was ancient in its origin. As late as 1886 a medieval mummers' play, which was always presented on All Souls Day and known as "the Souler's Play", was performed at Halton.

The Young Men's Christian Association was active in providing classes and pursuits. Founded in High Street in 1875 the members soon had a rambling club, a naturalists' field club and a historical society which met every week "to discuss historical essays". The Association provided a reading room with five hundred books and "literary improvement classes" were organised. By 1882 the committee was trying to find a suitable piece of land on which to build a gymnasium. Over the years many of the town's well-to-do merchants and businessmen were pleased to serve as vice-presidents of the Y.M.C.A.

Patriotism and nationalism were virtues to be cherished and when France under Napoleon III appeared to be becoming a threat to the security of the country, volunteer rifle corps were organised in every town in the kingdom. Sir Richard Brooke proposed that Runcorn should have its own volunteer force and in 1859 the local corps recruited some eighty officers and men. Within two years the Second Battalion of the Cheshire Rifle Volunteers under the command of Lieutenant-Colonel Brooke was well established and their activities were frequently mentioned in the press. The Runcorn Corps had its own band and the volunteers entered shooting competitions against other corps at Shotwick Sands near Chester. No doubt the volunteers were enthusiastic but it seems their activities could be a danger to the public. The following is from a trades directory published in 1890. *"We should like to point out the dangerous position of the rifle butts. The bullets often fly beyond their mark and over a public road and in the quarry beyond, the rock is peppered with lead, and the workmen have been obliged to leave the quarry during firing time. The only wonder to us is that no accident has happened considering the number of people who walk in the summer on the hills of the quarries adjacent to Weston Road".*

Although a public library had been established in 1858 it was not until some years later that the town had a free Public Library. This was opened on 6th July 1882 with a thousand volumes which had belonged to the Literary Institute. There were a number of local newspapers. Besides the "Free Press", Mr. Charles Walker, the printer, produced the "Runcorn Observer" and in 1862 the "Runcorn Guardian" was launched The "Runcorn Weekly News" dates from 1876. The "Runcorn and Widnes Examiner" appeared in 1870 and it was advertised as being "for those of Liberal persuasion".

Almost everyone held an allegiance to a particular church or chapel and religion had an important place in people's lives. Religious debate and discussion interested most and lengthy articles on religious issues were popular items in the local press. For example in 1853 the "Warrington Guardian" reported much activity "by the Mormon sect". In August of that year there was an open meeting in Ellesmere Street at which the Methodist ministers accepted a challenge to dispute with the Mormon elders. The three Methodist ministers had their say but for some reason which was not reported in the newspaper, *"The elders who were on the platform did not have the courage to come forward even though they had addressed the challenge".* In the next issue of the paper there appeared a brief paragraph which mentioned a Methodist tea party held in the Foresters Hall *"to commemorate the victory of Mr. Shaw Brown over the President of the Mormon priesthood in the discussion on the principle of Mormonism".* On special occasions the churches could not cope with the number of worshippers wishing to attend the service. For instance at the Harvest Thanksgiving Service in the Parish Church on October 4th 1889 many parishioners were turned away because the church was full. There was seating for 1060 people but the parish magazine reported *"The Parish Church could not unfortunately hold any more people than were packed into it. It is a matter of regret that so many failed to get in but the sidesmen and churchwardens used their best endeavours to accommodate all who could get into the building".*

Undoubtedly the most popular spectacle of the year was the Whitsuntide Walk by the town's Sunday schools. This ritual originated early in the nineteenth century as a procession of witness and it grew until by the end of the century thousands were taking part. Dressed in their best attire with church brass bands in attendance and accompanied by their teachers, clergy and civic notables, the scholars paraded through the town with their banners. All the churches took part and every third year it was the turn of either the Anglican, the Methodist or Roman Catholic denomination to have the honour of leading the procession. On Runcorn Heath the various groups assembled for short services and afterwards the children were treated to cakes and buns. The walk remained a major attraction until quite recently when inevitably it faded away with the decline of the Sunday Schools. Today only a token walk is held.

Organised sporting activity developed rapidly during the 1860s. In the previous decade there had been well-attended "foot races between individuals from Widnes and from Runcorn on Runcorn Heath". With the introduction of Bank Holidays in 1871 and also as the result of improved communications to the town, regular fixtures for football and cricket teams became established and local teams and their supporters travelled some distance to away games. Weston village had a successful cricket team which played sides from Widnes, Rainhill, St. Helens and Warrington and from about 1875 the Runcorn Y.M.C.A. fielded a cricket XI which was good enough to take on the Widnes team. The local churches sponsored sport and cricket flourished at St. John's Weston where by 1898, with Major T.C. Orred as its patron, the club fielded two teams. The Parish Church also had a successful side and even the choirboys had a cricket team. There was a "Sons of Temperance" eleven which competed with the local church sides.

Football was as popular in the 1890s as it is today and there were many teams in Runcorn, Weston and Halton. The clubs were often associated with church congregations with the Mariners' Mission, St. Mary's Widnes, Frodsham Parish, St. John's Weston and All Saints, Runcorn competing in the Warrington and District Amateur League before the turn of the century. Rugby football rivalled soccer in popularity and there was fierce competition on both sides of the river. Runcorn Parish Church boasted a "Saturday Club" which was a rugby union fifteen. The Runcorn town rugby union club had two sides by 1885 and the club was recognised as formidable opposition. Many of the players were awarded a county jersey for having the honour of playing for Cheshire.

Pleasure boating on the Bridgewater and Old Quay Canals was prohibited in 1882 but it appears that before that date scullers enjoyed the waterways in the neighbourhood of Runcorn. John Corbett writing in 1907 recalls memories of his youth in his book "The River Irwell. Pleasant Reminiscences of the Nineteenth Century and Suggestions for Improvements in the Twentieth Century". Corbett says that in the 1850s scullers would travel the Mersey and Irwell to Old Quay where they would *"lift their boats out of the water at Old Quay docks and carry them up the steep streets onto the Bridgewater Canal higher up the hillside. They would stay Saturday night in the cosy rooms of the Wilsons Hotel, have a quiet game of bowls on the green and enjoy an excellent dinner followed by a smoke and song and liquid refreshment ... The row back along the Bridgewater Canal to Manchester meant keeping an eye open for fly boats and swift packets."*

Ship launches fascinated young and old. When the full-rigged ship "Dennis Brundrit" was launched from Brundrit and Whiteway's Mersey Street yard in 1856 the town was decked in bunting, cannons were fired and a carnival atmosphere prevailed. Between 1853 and 1857 a number of great iron ships were built at the Bank Quay Foundry in Warrington. When they were towed down river to be fitted out at Liverpool the whole of Runcorn's inhabitants came to cheer and Runcorn Hill, Halton Hill and the waterfront were crowded with thousands of well wishers.

From about 1885 the bicycle became fashionable and young people began to set out to explore the countryside. At William Booth's cycle depot in Runcorn a dozen different makes of bicycle were available and the proprietor advertised that "All purchasers of machines will be taught to ride free. Machines for hire by the week, day, month or hour". The "Wilsons Hotel" in Bridge Street was the headquarters of the Cyclists' Touring Club. Athletic meetings and cross country runs were popular. There were bowling greens at the "Royal Hotel", the "Vine Hotel" in Lowlands Road, the "Egerton Arms", the "Wilsons Hotel", and at the "Norton Arms" and "Castle Hotel" in Halton. Reputedly, the best green was the one at the "Bridge Hotel" in Ashridge Street which was the headquarters of the Runcorn Bowling Club. In the 1870s it was alleged that the bowling green at the "Royal Hotel" was destroyed by atmospheric fall-out from the chemical works.

There was an abundance of public houses in Victorian Runcorn. Forty-five hotels and beer houses were licensed in 1869 and this number had increased to eighty-seven, with another seven in Weston and seven more in Halton by 1891. Many of their names are now forgotten. The "Seven Stars" was in Mersey Street, the "Shamrock Inn" in Regent Street; the "Theatre Vaults" in Queen Street; "Uncle Tom's Cabin" in Mason Street; the "Welsh Harp" in Cooper Street. There was the "Sloop Inn" in Loch Street the "Three Crowns" in King Street; the "Lancer's Inn" in Wellington Street; the "Swan Inn" in Shaw Street and the "Village Inn" in Halton. Although excessive drinking was no greater problem in Victorian Runcorn than it was in other small towns, nevertheless intemperate spending on drink constituted a serious social problem. A local magistrate, Mr. Philip Whiteway, was renowned for his severity when dealing with drunkards. In its obituary to Mr. Whiteway, the "Warrington Guardian" on 23rd February 1873 declared that his strict sentences were necessary because "drunkenness was the vulgar vice which is the base and blot of this place and parish".

There was a reaction against drinking with the formation of many temperance groups. All the religious bodies, especially the Nonconformists, promoted a temperance movement. These made determined efforts to enroll children before they could acquire a taste for drink. The local Rechabites, the Good Templars, the Mersey

Mission to Seamen and the Blue Ribbon Army organised lantern lectures, sales of work, tea parties, summer outings and other diversions in order to counteract the attractions of the public houses. The newspapers carried an advertisement for "Lea's Temperance and Commercial Hotel" in High Street. In 1883 the "Old Hall" in High Street was demolished to make way for the Salvation Army's Citadel and judging by the press reports of the petty sessions, the Army's officers must have been kept very busy in and around the public houses of Victorian and Edwardian Runcorn.

There were ample opportunities for those Runcornians who wish to become involved in social activity. In 1900 the serious-minded could join the Pickwick Club, a literary society which met in the Guild Hall, or they could attend University Extension courses held under the auspices of the Library Committee. The Education Committee of the Co-operative Society offered lectures in a variety of subjects. There was the Runcorn Horticultural Society and the Naturalist Field Club. Every church supported a large choir and their public concerts were advertised on bill boards around the town and in the local press. Church debating societies were popular and notices of charity sermons were posted on advertisement hoardings. In the years leading up to the First World War there was roller skating at Hope hall. The Sons of Temperance Cycling Club had a large membership as did the Tally-Ho Athletic Club. Rugby Union football was played at Canal Street until 1895 when Runcorn became one of the twenty-two northern clubs to leave the Rugby Football Union to form a professional Rugby League.

Within a year of the destruction of the "Theatre Royal" in a fire in 1906, the town acquired a new theatre when the Public Hall was converted for stage productions. The first films were screened before the outbreak of war and within a few years cinema-going was the public's favourite leisure activity. By 1920 the town had three cinemas, the "Empress", the "Palace" ("later the Scala") and the "King's" theatre. Local cinema-goers were fortunate in having wide choice of programme as the five Widnes cinemas were within easy reach.

As the twentieth century progressed there grew an increasing interest in party politics. After 1918 with the right to vote being extended to all males over the age of twenty-one years, many more men took an active part in political affairs but women did not enjoy the full franchise until 1928. Open-air political meetings in Devonshire Square and on the market place became customary and the speakers' views were copiously reported in the local newspapers. Two local men became prominent in county and national matters in the first three decades of the century. Sir Frederick Norman, chemist and physicist of the United Alkali Company, was knighted in 1914. Sir Frederick played an important role in social and educational development in Cheshire and he served as Deputy Lieutenant for the county. Sir William Dudley O.B.E. received his knighthood in 1926. He became the president of the Co-operative Wholesale Society in 1933.

The staff of the "Palace" (later "Scala") in the 1920s.

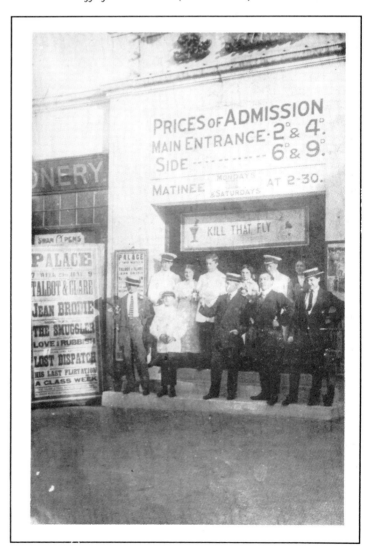

Bibliography

The description of leisure and social activity in Victorian Runcorn has been written using items culled from local newspapers. Amongst the more informative articles are those concerned with the formation of the Runcorn Rifle Corps, *"Warrington Guardian"* 11.6.1859; 18.6.1859 and 20.7.1861; Runcorn Mechanics' Institute activities 22.10.1853 and 12.2.1857. Queen Victoria's birthday celebrations at Halton are described in *"Warrington Guardian"* of 28.5.1859.

The Parish Magazine of All Saints (with Weston) 1896-1901 and the Parish Magazine of St Mary's Halton for 1886 were consulted for parochial social activity.

The celebrations of the Bridgewater Trustees is taken from "The Passing of the Bridgewater Trust. Runcorn Reminiscences of June 15th 1844" by William Handley from the *"Runcorn Guardian"* of 12th December 1903.

Chapter 18
The Twentieth Century

In spite of the despondency prevailing at the time of widespread unemployment, Queen Victoria's Diamond Jubilee was celebrated with enthusiasm. Jubilee day, the 22nd June 1897, saw the town festooned with flags and bunting. In the morning there was the grand procession of town dignitaries. The magistrates, clergy, councillors and the Guardians of the Poor led the Friendly Societies, members of the School Board and the trades unions through the crowded streets. It was the turn of the school children to parade in the afternoon and thousands of them walked in procession wearing their commemorative Jubilee medals. A free meal was provided for the elderly and there was a fête followed by a bonfire on the Common. In Weston village, Canon Wood unveiled the village cross which had been restored by Major Orred and in the evening there was a spectacular torchlight procession through the lanes and fields. Sir Richard and Lady Brooke gave a garden party at Norton Priory for their tenants and the schoolchildren of Halton and their parents. About five hundred people attended and they were entertained by the band of the 7th Cheshire Volunteers. After dusk the huge bonfire on Halton Hill was visible for miles.

At a Jubilee banquet held at the Adelphi Hotel in Liverpool, Sir John Brunner presented the Chairman of the Runcorn Urban District Council and those of Northwich and Winsford with his gift of their gold chains and badges of office. In further celebration of the Jubilee, a fund was opened for the liquidation of the debt on Runcorn's Technical Institute and this was accomplished with Sir John's generous help.

The Boer War saw a great upsurge in patriotism. A number of local volunteers left for South Africa and the Queen's War Fund was well supported. There was great jubilation at the eventual British successes. The relief of Ladysmith and Mafeking were occasions for rejoicing but there was sadness too for Colour Sergeant John Whitehead, an old scholar of the Parish school, was killed in action the day before the relief of Ladysmith.

Queen Victoria died in January 1901 and the town shared the genuine feeling of sorrow which was expressed throughout the country. On the night of the Queen's death and every night until the funeral, the church bells of Runcorn solemnly tolled sixty-three times to denote the length of her reign. At the various memorial services held throughout the district there were capacity congregations with councillors, town officials, the organised clubs, representatives of local industry and thousands of Runcorn people attending. With the coming of spring the newspapers began to anticipate the coronation of King Edward VII and Queen Alexandra. It was determined that the occasion would be celebrated with the same joyous spirit which had prevailed in Runcorn township at the young Queen Victoria's coronation in the summer of 1838.

The Warrington to Runcorn Tramway

Communications to Runcorn remained wretched into the twentieth century and in 1900 determined efforts were made to improve matters. In that year two projects were under consideration; one was for a street tramway system from Runcorn to Warrington and the other was for the construction of a transporter bridge across the river.

In May 1900 a draft provisional order under the Light Railways Act of 1896 was issued authorising the construction of the Warrington and Runcorn Light Railway which was to commence at the intersection of Old London Road and Fairfield Road in Stockton Heath and which was to pass through Walton, Acton Grange, Moore, Keckwick, Norton and Halton to terminate at Runcorn railway station at the junction of Station Road and Lowlands Road. The line was to be the standard gauge of four feet eight and a half inches and its total length was exactly eight miles. For most of its length the railway would be single track but just over a mile of it would be double track in the form of short stretches of passing-loops. The promotors of the Warrington and Runcorn Light Railway were James Mitchell Hewitt, John Philip Bedson and the International Electric Traction and Power Syndicate Ltd. The costs of construction were estimated at £61,029 and the capital to be raised was £120,000 in £1 shares. As the proposed route of the railway followed level ground no expensive cuttings or embankments were required although alteration of the road gradient to Delph Bridge would be necessary. The means of propulsion was to be by electric locomotives or cars but steam locomotives were not to be used without the consent of the local authorities. The company also had the powers to build "steam engine works and buildings, dynamos, car sheds and electrical apparatus" where they were needed in Runcorn.

Nowhere in the documents relating to the project is the word "tramway" used but the proposed Warrington and Runcorn Light Railway was in fact a street tramway having grooved lines and electric tramcars. The line was to be laid down the centre of Station Road, High Street, Bridge Street and Halton Road. Between the railway station in Runcorn and Halton Brook there were to be nine short passing loops of double track.

Special workmen's fares were to be charged with *"Cheap fares for the labouring classes. The Company shall run two carriages each way every morning in the week and every evening in the week at such hours not being later than seven in the morning or earlier than 5.30 in the evening for the convenience of artisans, mechanics and daily labourers at fares not exceeding one halfpenny per mile"*. The use of the word "railway" permitted the carriage of goods and livestock as well as passengers and the schedule of maximum rates for goods and animals includes; *"For every horse, mule or other beast of draught or burden four pence per head per mile. For every ox, cow, bull three pence per head per mile. Calves, pigs and sheep one penny-halfpenny per head per mile"*. Provision was made for the carriage of heavy bulk material : *"For all coals, coke, limestone, chalk, sand, dung, compost and all sorts of manure ... two pence per ton per mile. Iron ore, pig iron bricks and slag ... two pence halfpenny per ton per mile. Sugar, hides, grain, dyewoods, timber staves and anvils ... three*

pence per ton per mile. Fish, cotton, wool at four pence per ton per mile". Single articles of great weight such as iron boilers and cylinders up to eight tons would be charged at the rate of two shillings per ton per mile.

The Warrington and Runcorn Light Railway never became a reality. Tramways were the cheapest method of urban transport and if the line had been made there is little doubt but that both Runcorn and Warrington would have extended their suburbs along it s route and there was a plan to extend the line to Weston. Initially the Runcorn Urban District Council supported the tramway idea but a more important project — that of a transporter bridge across the Gap occupied the public mind and the Light Railway plans were shelved and then forgotten.

The Transporter Bridge

The Mersey estuary had always been a formidable obstacle to trade between north Cheshire and south Lancashire. For wheeled traffic there was a distance of twenty miles between Warrington Bridge and the Liverpool ferries. The cost of building a high level bridge across Runcorn Gap with a span high enough to clear ocean-going vessels on the Manchester Ship Canal and traffic on the river was prohibitive but by 1898 the authorities in Runcorn and Widnes had begun to explore the possibility of bridging the river by means of a transporter bridge. The principal of the travelling platform applied to a large scale bridge was novel but it was seen as the most practicable and economic means of providing a crossing for road traffic. Because no approach viaducts would be needed the cost of a transporter bridge would be far less than a high level bridge.

By the last years of the nineteenth century the transporter bridge concept had been tried and satisfactorily proved. The prospectus issued for the Runcorn and Widnes project pointed to the success of the transporter bridge across the River Nervion at Portugalette near Bilbao. This had been in successful operation for eight years under conditions which were

The last ferryman 1905.

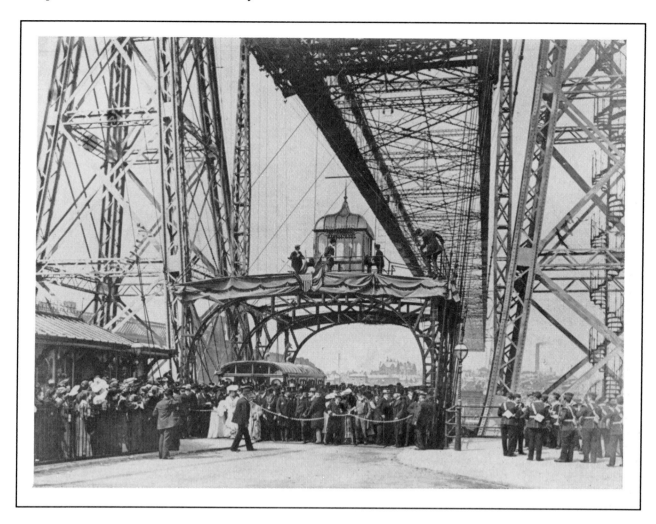

The Transporter Bridge. The first crossing, May 29th 1905.

declared to be "much less favourable than those which exist at Widnes". The promotors also drew attention to the success of another bridge which was operating over the River Seine at Rouen and they noted that Parliament had authorised the construction of a transporter bridge over the River Usk at Newport in Monmouth.

In 1899 the Runcorn and Widnes Transporter Bridge Company was formed with Sir John Brunner M.P. as Chairman and Sir Henry Seaton-Karr M.P. as Deputy-Chairman. Other directors included Joseph Beecham J.P. of St. Helens, Henry Wade Deacon J.P., Holbrook Gaskell J.P., H. Sutton Timmis J.P. and Major J.W. Wareing of Widnes. An application was made to Parliament in the session for 1900 for powers to construct the bridge. The share capital was £100,000 divided into 10,000 shares of £10 each to which the Corporation of Widnes agreed to subscribe £25,000 and the Urban District Council of Runcorn £10,000. There was considerable opposition to the Bill with eleven petitions against it being presented by authorities and individuals from both sides of the river. The

Bill received the Royal Assent on 10th July 1900. There was an unusual clause in the Act for it was stated that the Company was "to provide for the construction of a wharf at the end of the bridge on the Runcorn side alongside the Manchester Ship Canal which will enable ocean traffic to and from Widnes to be dealt with".

The work of construction began in December 1901 when the solid rock on each side of the river was cut away to a depth of ten metres and the anchorages for the cables were placed in position. The anchor pits were then filled with a ballast of concrete and railway metals. Nineteen cables each of 127 wires formed each of the two main cables the steel ropes being bound together at a distance of about fifty feet from the anchorage to become one cable to pass over the top of the towers. The weight of the steel cables was 250 tons and each was capable of withstanding a tensile stress of about 5,000 tons. The bridge towers reached a height of 58 metres above the high water level. The towers were 24 metres apart and they were braced together with horizontal and diagonal frames. On the top of the towers there were fixed saddles resting on steel rollers for carrying the cables, the rollers being adapted for variations in the length of cable due to the differing loads and temperatures. Under each of the four towers there were four steel cylinders filled with concrete, braced together and bolted into the solid rock. The transporter car was 18 metres long and 8 metres wide and it was designed to carry four 2-horse farm waggons as well as 300 passengers making the crossing in about two and a half minutes. The bottom of the car cleared the Manchester Ship Canal wall by 1½ metres and it was four metres above the river at the highest tide. The passengers were protected from the weather by means of a cabin which had sliding doors at each end. The car was suspended from a trolley which was 25 metres in length and which was carried by sixteen wheels on each rail on the span. At first the car was driven by two electric motors of 35 horse power each which were fixed within the trolley. As there was no electricity supply on either side of the river a generator was installed at the bottom of the Widnes east tower. The driver's control cabin was a conning tower on top of the car from which he had a clear all-round view. The motorman had complete control over the motors above his head and he could stop, reverse and start again at a moment's notice and in case of emergency, he could bring the car to a stop within its own length.

Before the official opening of the transporter bridge, a series of test runs was carried out when a load of 36 tons comprising seven horses and five waggons loaded with barrels of silicate was carried backwards and forwards without any sign of weakness in the structure. The work was completed in 1905 at a cost of £130,000. King Edward VII was to have performed the opening ceremony but he was unable to do so and Sir John Brunner officiated in his place. On 29th of May Sir John made a short speech to the gathering of officials and councillors of Widnes and Runcorn and then he declared the bridge open. The local school children were given a holiday to celebrate the occasion.

Few, if any of the spectators who assembled to witness the first crossing could have envisaged the tremendous volume of traffic which would eventually make demands on the bridge. In fact the official souvenir went so far as to state, *"An ordinary high level bridge would have cost at least three times the cost of the transporter and the traffic would probably not justify such a large outlay. There is little doubt that the convenience and comparatively small cost of the transporter will ensure complete success to the enterprise financially"*. This was an optimistic forecast for in its first years the bridge was not a financial success. It had been estimated that the transporter would bring in £12,000 a year in tolls and that its running costs would be less than £2,000 a year but the Company could not make it pay and in 1911 the Widnes Corporation bought the bridge from the Company for £38,000.

The Transporter Bridge. The first crossing, May 29th 1905.

The transporter bridge was to last for fifty-six years and every year the demands on it increased. In its later years the bridge carried over two million passengers annually as well as an incredible 280,000 motor cars and 145,000 commercial vehicles. Various alterations and improvements were made to the transporter. The cumbersome electric motors were removed when a main supply of electricity was available and swinging gates were installed on the car.

The bridge made a considerable contribution to the development of both towns. Similar products were manufactured in the Widnes and Runcorn factories and for the first time materials could easily be carried between the works on opposite sides of the river. Waggonettes, furniture vans, horse-drawn omnibuses and handcarts as well as motor cars, steam lorries and cyclists found the new bridge a boon and foot passengers were spared the long climb and walk across the railway bridge.

With the completion of the transporter bridge the ancient ferry was closed after being in existence for nearly eight hundred years. By a coincidence the bridge was built on the same site as the one proposed by Telford and it had exactly the same span being a 303 metres from the centre of the towers on the Runcorn side to the centre of those on the other side of the river.

Economic Recession, War and Industrial Revival

The first official census of the present century took place in the last year of Queen Victoria's long reign. Sixty-four years before when the Queen acceded to the throne, Runcorn township had a population of less than six thousand inhabitants. In the year of her death this had increased to 16,491. Halton's population in 1901 stood at 1,238 whilst that of Weston which included Weston Point had risen to 2,115.

Runcorn no longer dominated the Gap for Widnes was now more prominent. During Victoria's reign the population of Widnes had increased by nearly ten times to reach almost thirty thousand and its rate of growth continued to be greater than that of its older neighbour across the river.

At the beginning of the twentieth century the outlook for much of Runcorn's industry was not bright. The old inland waterways which were connected to the town's docks were in decline and this recession would accelerate rapidly because of the competition from the railways and even more from the growth of mechanised road transport. The shipbuilding industry had shrunk

to become a repair and barge building trade, the quarries were being worked out and the old Leblanc chemical works were struggling to survive. The days of soap manufacture were also coming to an end. For some years before the turn of the century Hazelhurst's had been producing soap for Lever Brothers. The Runcorn factory's soap making plant (as distinct from its chemical side) became an associated company of Levers, and by 1910 the official address of Thomas Hazlehurst & Sons had become Bebington, Wirral — not Runcorn.

But the future of industrial Runcorn in 1900 was not altogether gloomy. Castner-Kellner's programme of expansion included the installation of a power station in order to supply electricity for the large scale electrolytic decomposition of brine and a few years later when Salt Union at Weston Point was enlarged the Mersey Power Company was set up to supply the factory with electricity. In 1912 Mersey Power commenced the public supply of electric current to the municipalities of Runcorn and Widnes. With the installation of plant for the vacuum evaporation of brine at Salt Union in 1911, the loading facilities on the Manchester Canal were improved in order to allow ocean-going ships to receive salt cargoes. The vessels thus avoided the trouble and added costs of taking salt at Liverpool. Since the completion of the Marbury pipeline, salt production at Weston Point had vastly increased. In 1910 the pipe was enlarged and powerful pumping engines were installed so that the quantity of brine supplied to Salt Union nearly doubled to 122 million gallons in 1911. When it was predicted that the success of the Weston Point works would bring about the complete ruin of the Cheshire salt district within a decade, the salt towns began panic legal action in an attempt to stop the pipe. Their efforts were defeated by the combined opposition of the Runcorn Council, the Salt Union and the chemical manufacturers. The local authorities of Winsford, Northwich and Middlewich applied for a Parliamentary Bill to regulate the volume of brine to be supplied to Weston Point but they were unsuccessful in their plans and the Bill was thrown out in June 1912.

Around the turn of the century new industry was attracted to Runcorn with Evans Sons, Lescher & Webb Ltd. establishing a medical research laboratory in co-operation with Liverpool University at Crofton Lodge in Westfield Road. The Biological Institute produced anti-toxins, sera and vaccines for hospitals and during the First World War the company opened their Ellesmere works in Gas Street to produce synthetic pharmaceutical drugs, a field of research in which German industry had always held the monopoly. Evans, Lescher & Webb also produced photographic chemicals, insecticides and rat poisons as well as antiseptics. Another firm established in Runcorn late in the last century was the Australian Alum Company with its works adjoining Highfield Tannery. This company manufactured alum and sulphate of alum which were used in the preparation of medicines and cosmetics and also in paper making, paint manufacture and in water purifying processes.

The tanning industry did not suffer the fluctuations in demand which so bedevilled the chemical industry and which led to the laying off of men in the chemical works during periods of recession. By 1910 Runcorn was the country's leading centre for the production of leather. Highfield's capacity had grown from fifty hides a week in 1888 to five thousand a week and Astmoor Tannery was producing an average of 2,500 a week. John Ockleston & Sons of Halton Road specialised in the manufacture of belting for machines and in the making of harness leather. When Hazlehurst's Camden soapworks closed in 1914 the site was immediately adapted to meet the war-time demand for leather and with Mr. R.H. Posnett in charge, Camden Tanning Company created a large output of leather within a very short space of time.

At the start of the war the old Pierpoint Tannery in Halton Road was acquired by Henry Boston & Sons, a firm which owned tanneries in Leicester, Northampton, Leeds, in Sydney, Australia and in Boston in the United States. Boston's new Puritan Tannery was planned to be the most up-to-date in the country. It was equipped with modern machinery and was designed so as to give working conditions that were considerably better than those in the older Runcorn tanneries. Puritan's output soon became considerable and by the 1930s almost very railway station in Britain displayed the firm's well known advertisement showing a seventeenth century puritan extolling the quality of Runcorn leather. The tanneries required a constant supply of tanning material and in 1918 the old rope walk in Percival Lane was leased by the Organic Products Company of Glasgow to become a factory for the production of tanning extracts and colouring agents for the leather and textile trades.

Lea & Sons, of High Street, manufacturers of oxygen, hydrogen and nitrogen was an old established firm founded in 1849. The company also had an engineering department and in 1925 whilst boring within the works for a supply of water with which to cool the compressors, a spring which was claimed to have radio-active properties was discovered. The Official Runcorn Handbook made extravagant claims about the curative nature of the water. *"The radium spring possesses curative properties which are found to be particularly effective in case of gout, rheumatism, asthma, anaemia and even weak eyesight. The radium activities of the water amounts to 5.84 mache units per litre. Bottles packed in wooden boxes containing one sixth of a gallon are now sent to all parts of the kingdom. Already thousands of bottles have been despatched. A new service main from the pump to the retail shop has now been installed so that the freshly drawn water can be obtained from 8.30 a.m. to 7 p.m."*.

The early years of the new century saw far reaching developments in education. By an Act of Parliament of 1902 government provision was made to establish a national system of secondary education. At the same time the School Boards were abolished and the responsibility for education, both elementary and secondary was handed over to the elected County Councils. The old School Boards had managed elementary education in the limited environment of a single town or village so that their thinking had been narrow in outlook and their parochial character had often exacerbated the discord which existed between the members of the Church of England and the dissenters on the question of education. The Education Act of 1902 stirred up the last great agitation of religious sectarianism in British politics and the government's attempt to put the former Board schools and the voluntary schools on the same footing caused vehement argument and friction along sectarian lines throughout the whole country. The matter was debated with some passion in Runcorn where both sides engaged in virulent verbal attacks on their opponents. Local feeling had been running high since the late 1890s with the transfer to the School Board of the two Wesleyan Methodist Schools, Granville Street and Brunswick. The expense of taking over these voluntary schools was considerable and the School Board Rate had risen by four pence between 1896 and 1898.

The election for the Runcorn School Board of 1901 was fought with some acrimony. The adversaries flooded the town with their handbills which attacked the opposition with undisguised malevolence. The voluntary school candidates, Messrs Cunningham, Imison, Littler and Canon Wood appealed to the ratepayers. They pointed out that the church schools saved the town at least £1,000 a year and they declared that a victory for the "Progressives" would bring an immediate increase in the rate. The managers of the voluntary schools believed that they were fighting for the very existence of the church schools because the Board schools, with rate support, were spending fifteen shillings a year per child more than the voluntary schools and this was reflected in better standards and equipment. The church school managers issued a pamphlet which attempted to exploit to their advantage the patriotic spirit which was prevailing at the time. A popular song during the Boer War was "Soldiers of the Queen" and the scholars of the church schools were given a handbill with a doggerel verse to be sung to the tune. The chorus was,

> "It's the voluntary School my lads, which save the town,
>   and keep well down,
> Ugly rates for School Board purpose, lads, when our
>   pockets do not fill as pr'aps they should,
> And when we canvass for our vote, we'll all reply 'Now
>   Make a note,
> We know the names quite off by rote, For they're
>   C,I,L, and Wood".

A leaflet produced on behalf of the "Progressive" candidates, Messrs. Handley, Norman, Posnett, Pritchard and Taylor and addressed to Canon Wood attacked the vicar for his "lurid financial prophesies". The canon was accused of being a dictator in his position as chairman of the School Board. He was also charged with exaggeration and of spreading fallacies. The electors were asked to vote for the progressives who were "sound business men with large interests who have no sectarian schools to serve". The election result saw the churchmen lose their majority on the School Board after dominating the proceedings for twenty-seven years.

A Technical Institute had been built by public subscription in Waterloo Road in 1894. Sir John Brunner gave £1,000 towards the cost of the building and for equipping the laboratories. The Institute satisfied the local demand for evening classes for students who were destined for careers in industry and commerce. The Institute's premises served a dual role after 1902 when they accommodated the pupils of the new Runcorn County Secondary School.

The opening of the Victoria Memorial Hospital (known locally as the Cottage Hospital) in 1903, provided the town with a much needed amenity and during the next twenty years the hospital was enlarged to provide 32 beds for some 220 in-patients and facilities for the treatment of over 500 out-patients a year. As the demands on its services increased, the Cottage Hospital came to rely on the generous financial support of the Runcorn public. After the First World War, in order to raise funds for the hospital, the Runcorn Council sponsored the Runcorn Festival, a well organised pageant and procession which involved the schools, local industry and the leading personalities of the town. The various tableaux paraded through the streets accompanied by the Runcorn Pioneer Prize Band, the Preston Brook and District Prize Band, the Weston Wesleyan Brass Band, the Sea Cadet Corps Drum and Fife Band and various local jazz bands. Each year the Runcorn Fire Brigade, the Castner-Kellner Fire Brigade and the organised youth movements took part. The vast procession made its way to the Canal Street football ground where there were refreshments and side shows. The occasion was the spectacle of the year, a splendid display of municipal pride and voluntary effort which attracted many spectators from Widnes and from neighbouring districts.

In 1906 the public library in Egerton Street was enlarged through the generosity of Andrew Carnegie. About this time the old market hall in Bridge Street was converted into the public swimming baths. The new baths were a boon to the town for drowning tragedies were remarkably frequent occurrences. The river and the canals constituted a considerable hazard to young people and in 1905 a local newspaper reported on the work of the Runcorn and District Life Saving and Grappling Corps. In the first four years of its existence this voluntary organisation recovered fifty-two bodies from the docks and canals. The Highfield Tanning Company made a generous donation to the District Council towards the costs of building the swimming baths.

The philanthropy extended by the local industrialists had changed direction during the last decade of the Victorian era. In the early years of the Queen's reign the Brundrit, Hazlehurst, Johnson and Brooke families and others had given liberally to church and chapel building and to the various charities. Now the businessmen of the town preferred to aid social and administrative progress by funding education, medicine and civic amenities. Sir John Brunner led the way. He bought the old chapel in St. John's Street and presented it to the town to be used primarily as a Guild Hall by the trades unions and the Friendly Societies. Sir John subscribed £25,000 towards the construction costs of the transporter bridge with an additional loan of £12,000 together with his personal guarantee on a bank loan of £31,000. When, by 1911 it seemed that the bridge would always operate at a loss, he assigned his interest to the Widnes Corporation. The "Times" newspaper declared that this generous action amounted to a "virtual gift of £68,000".

Through the benevolence of Mr. Samuel Taylor a new ward was added to the Cottage Hospital whilst Mr. R.H. Posnett gave the X-ray equipment. The latter also provided three gifts of land to be used for children's playgrounds. After the First World War Mr. Posnett bought the worked-out quarry in Union Street and presented it to the town. The quarry was used for the tipping of domestic refuse after which it was covered with soil to become Rock Park with its bowling greens and tennis courts. The creation of Rock Park was undertaken in the 1920s to provide work during a period of acute unemployment. Mr Posnett also gave the land for the Memorial Gardens.

Evidence that the town was becoming a healthier place can be seen in the statistics in the annual report of the Medical Officer of Health. The expenditure on improved sanitation proved to have been money well spent. The removal of night soil had always been a major item of expense in the Council's budget and while the old open privies still existed typhoid and diptheria were endemic in parts of the town. However, at the monthly meeting of the Council in November 1909, Dr. McDougall, the Medical Officer, was able to report that there had been only eight deaths with thirty-eight births registered during the previous month. Dr. McDougall stated that he had never known such a low death rate in his forty years' service. He had no hesitation in attributing the satisfactory state of public health to improved sanitation.

The war memorial in Moughland Lane was unveiled in November 1920. Of the two thousand men of Runcorn who served in the armed forces in the First World War, one in five died. The names of four hundred dead are recorded on the memorial and the names of forty-one men from Halton who did not return are inscribed on the lych gate of Halton cemetery. Among the forty-three local men who received awards for gallantry was Private Thomas Jones who won the Victoria Cross for outstanding valour at Morval in France. During the war 3,460 wounded servicemen were treated at the Cottage Hospital and at the Parish Church Vicarage Voluntary Hospital which Canon Howard Perrin made available for casualties from the front. Over a hundred local women volunteered to nurse the wounded during the war.

Industry made a significant contribution to the war effort. One tannery alone produced enough leather to sole ten million pairs of army boots. On both sides of the river the chemical works were in production day and night and an enlarged workforce travelled from Runcorn to shift work in the Widnes works and to the cable factory at Helsby. Castners made large quantities of material to be used in the manufacture of high explosives, hydrogen for balloons and airships as well as mustard gas. Women were employed in this dangerous work and a number of employees were warded the Order of the British Empire for devotion to duty and for bravery on the occasion of a serious accident during the manufacture of mustard gas. In 1916 the Castner-Kellner company became associated with Brunner-Mond at Northwich.

Local shipping played its part during the war. When much of the Belgian and French coalfields were overrun by the German advance, Runcorn schooners were used to carry coal to French ports. At least two schooners are known to have been lost as the result of enemy action.

The region suffered the same acute war-time privations as the rest of Britain but Runcorn was fortunate in that its factories did not receive attention from enemy air attack although on 12th April 1918 the Zeppelin L61, in attempting to bomb Liverpool, lost its way and turned north over Halton to bomb the glowing furnaces of the Wigan Coal and Iron Company.

The war was to keep the United Alkali Company's uneconomic Leblanc process of chemical manufacture in being for a few more years but the technical progress which had advanced during the conflict soon brought an end to the old methods at the termination of hostilities. The extraordinary war-time demands for chemicals for explosives meant full employment but after 1918 the numbers of those in work quickly dropped to pre-war levels. By the autumn of 1921 the unemployment situation was as desperate as it had been in the great recession of 1896-1898.

The war severely disrupted Runcorn's traditional trade patterns and the town's docks never recovered from the dislocation of their coastal traffic. The salt trade to Newfoundland could not be restarted after the war and following a brief recovery in 1919, shipping at Runcorn and Weston Point went into sharp decline. Although some 1100 canal craft were registered at Runcorn in 1920 more than half of them were out of commission for traffic on the Bridgewater was much reduced.

At the end of the war Runcorn, in common with many other towns, experienced a severe shortage of houses. In an attempt to relieve the pressure the old waterworks pumping station on the Heath was converted into a number of flats and the Council began work on the building of 112 houses on the Stenhills. To provide work for two hundred unemployed men, the Heath and Runcorn Hill were laid out with paths and gardens to create a 55-acre park. In the early 1920s the Manchester Ship Canal Company presented to the Council a strip of land which bordered the canal and the construction of the new Mersey Road in 1924 provided employment for the town's out of work.

Not all the post-war plans came to complete fruition. During the war many work people had travelled to Castners and it was anticipated that eventually a railway passenger service would be inaugurated between Runcorn railway station and Weston Point. Indeed, the official Runcorn Handbook for 1920 optimistically declared, *"The Castner-Kellner Company has recently applied for permission to build a light railway to run from near Runcorn Station to their works and, at a public enquiry, stated their intention of permitting the line to be used for passenger as well as goods traffic, an innovation which will be a blessing to the residents of Weston and Weston Point"*.

Castners was responsible for the rapid development of Weston Point in the years immediately following the war. The firm built company houses for their employees and a large estate was built near to the works. A start was made on a hundred houses in 1921 and another three hundred were started in 1928. The scheme which comprised Castner Avenue, Baker Road, Roscoe Crescent, Mather Avenue and Sandy Lane was completed in 1932.

At the formation of ICI in 1926, Castners and the United Alkali Company merged with Brunner-Mond. Of the old Leblanc firms that had been part of United Alkali only Johnson's Weston works and Wiggs still survived. The old Weston works was closed in 1931.

Between the wars the boundaries of the Runcorn Urban District were enlarged when a County of Chester Review Order increased the size of the town by the addition of the parish of Weston and part of the parishes of Halton and Clifton. By this order of 1936 Runcorn's population rose to a total of 22,587 inhabitants and its area to 2,904 acres.

The town acquired a new town hall in 1932. In that year the Council completed negotiations to purchase Halton Grange, the former home of Thomas Johnson and later of the Hazlehursts. The Grange had been bought by Mr. Francis Boston in 1909 and when he died in 1930 his executors sold the house and twelve acres of land to the Council for £2,250. The transaction caused an outcry and the local press denounced the Council for its "squandermania" during a period of severe economic depression.

Between the wars there was industrial development to the east of the town with the erection of the Astmoor factory of the Chemical and Metallurgical Corporation on land between the Mersey and the Manchester Ship Canal. This company was acquired by I.C.I. in 1933 and four years later Salt Union at Weston Point merged with I.C.I.. When war threatened in 1938, Rocksavage chemical works was built on the site of the old Johnson factory. This new works was built by the Ministry of Supply for the production of chlorine and caustic soda and it was operated by I.C.I.

In the inter-war years Runcorn and Weston Point docks experienced a disastrous slump as their traditional cargoes were won by other ports and the coastal trade was captured by road and rail transport. By the late 1930s the Duke of Bridgewater's Canal had much reduced traffic, although the canalside tanneries still obtained their coal supplies by narrow-boat. In the year before the Second World War the old line of locks became disused and the schooners disappeared. The oldest of the town's industries was also nearing its end when the remaining quarry at Weston was used for the tipping of factory waste. After 1942 no stone was quarried in the district.

The Second World War

Just as in the First World War, the factories of Runcorn and Widnes were engaged in the vital work of producing chemicals used in the manufacture of munitions. Because of this and the fact that the bridges over the river were legitimate targets, it was expected that the district would be subjected to aerial attack. It is certain that the enemy knew of the importance of the area for the infamous "Soderfahndungsliste" – the Gestapo Arrest List for Great Britain – includes names of companies in which the Central Security Agency of the Reich had a special interest. The I.C.I. works are listed as "International Chemical Industries, Inhaber, Runcorn". Although deliberate air attacks were never directed against the Runcorn factories, the Weston Point works were the subject of some discussion at Luftwaffe briefings in 1940.

In anticipation of the outbreak of war, preparations were made to evacuate the children from the area and a couple of days before hostilities began thousands of mothers and their children left the town for the safer environment of Blackpool.

Runcorn prepared for action. The tunnel of the old quarry dram road at Weston had been made into an air raid shelter and many other shelters were built in the streets of the town. Schoolrooms were taken over to be used as emergency first aid posts and the Salvation Army's Citadel in High Street became an air raid wardens' post and the headquarters of the Women's Voluntary Service. Barrage balloons were sited in many of the town's open spaces and as part of the defences of Liverpool, batteries of anti-aircraft guns were positioned at Aston Lane in Sutton Weaver, at Moss Lane, Moore and at Red Brow in Daresbury. The guns were continuously in action at night from the autumn of 1940 until the following May.

Despite the proximity of Liverpool and the many air raids on the city, few bombs fell on Runcorn. Property was damaged in Latham Avenue, Halton Brow, Langdale Road and in Weston but fortunately there were few casualties. Two service personnel were killed by a landmine which wrecked Aston church on the night of 28th November 1940 and an airman died near Hallwood when a bomb struck a barrage balloon site. In 1944 when the possibility of air raids on the town became unlikely, the people of Runcorn accommodated evacuee families who had left London during the flying bomb attacks on the capital.

The routine of life in war-time Runcorn was little different from that in other industrial towns. At first there was some limitation on public entertainment but on Sunday evenings celebrity concerts in aid of charity were held in the "Empress" cinema and in St. Paul's church with famous personalities of stage and radio performing to large audiences. People made their own entertainment and church amateur dramatic societies and choral groups flourished. There were dances in aid of the Red Cross at the Citadel and at the swimming baths. As everywhere in war-time Britain, the cinema provided an escape from the drabness of life.

There was shift working in all the local factories and the labour force was swelled by thousands of women. Mustard gas was produced at "Randles" works and because of the secrecy surrounding the activities of the factory it became known as the "Hush Hush" works. The tanyards worked to full capacity with over four thousand employees producing leather to be despatched all over the world. To cater for Runcornians who were working difficult hours Brunswick Sunday school became the British Restaurant.

By 1943 United States servicemen were a familiar sight in Runcorn streets and every day scores of American aircraft from the base at Burtonwood passed over the town on training exercises. American influence remained long after the troops had gone, for it was due to United States generosity that the wards of Dutton hospital were re-equipped and modernised.

During the war earnings in industry were good and, as a result, few towns did better than Runcorn in response to the National War Savings Campaign Appeal. This patriotic response is perhaps the source of the often repeated post-war allegation that Runcorn folk are thrifty to the point of being mercenary. However, an official publication of 1951 which lists the attributes of Runcornians makes no reference to this assertion of parsimony. The following is taken from the official Runcorn Festival of Britain programme of local events and it is somewhat chauvinistic and laudatory in its appraisal of Runcorn folk, *"They are friendly, easy going, careful and yet generous. They are critical without bearing grudges. They accept difficulties because they are predominantly faithful and conscientious church-goers. Their virtues are many and their vices are few and insignificant. They now look to the future with renewed hopes, with a feeling that they are providing for it with a good will and with a purposefulness and desire earned by decent men and women"*. An extravagant statement without doubt — and yet there was an essential local exclusiveness, a difference in character which made Runcorn Gap appear to be infinitely wider than it is. Perhaps this individuality was the result of a century and a half of isolation? Whatever the nature of old Runcorn, within twenty years of the end of the war immense changes would begin to make its previous identity difficult to discern.

Post War Change and Challenge

For a few years following the end of the Second World War, urban Runcorn remained more or less confined within a triangle, the base of which can be represented by the river, one side by Heath Road and the other side by the line of Holloway and Moughland Lane. Additional housing extended along Halton Road to Halton Brook and there were separate communities at Weston, Weston Point and at Halton. The countryside reached the town hall grounds and there were still cultivated fields within half a mile of the old town centre at Old Quay. For a short distance along one side of Clifton Road there was some ribbon development but beyond that it was open countryside to Frodsham. The slopes of Runcorn Hill and much of Weston Point remained green whilst Halton village was surrounded by farmland. Viewed from Lancashire, the distant scene of the rising ground to the east and west of Runcorn was most inviting. These areas had remained untouched by development because they were almost inaccessible to commuters from the opposite side of the river due to the absence of a permanent road bridge.

Although the inter-war years had seen the spread of private housing, the Runcorn Council had not embarked on a programme of building large council estates. As a consequence of this there were still large open areas within the town's boundaries at the end of the war. The acute shortage of houses in 1945 demanded urgent action and within two years of the end of hostilities, plans were ready for the start of the Grange housing estate with its hundreds of houses and shops. Later, another large estate of council houses spread across the fields to Weston Point.

During the 1950s, inadequate housing in old Runcorn was cleared to make way for a new market and bus station. The nucleus of the ancient township which had centred around Holy Trinity church, Cooper Street and Brunswick Street was also demolished.

For more than a decade after the war's end there was severe pressure on the schools. The shortage of places following the years of high birthrate resulted in church halls and Sunday School rooms being taken over to become temporary classrooms. Helsby Grammar School which was designed to accommodate children from Runcorn and Halton as well as those from Frodsham and its neighbourhood, was nearing completion in 1939.

On the the outbreak of war the building was immediately requisitioned to be used for billeting purposes and it was to be another ten years before the school finally opened for its intended purpose. Gradually new schools were built on the housing estates and the old "All-Age" schools disappeared in the reorganisation which followed the opening of the Grange County Secondary School.

The period in the aftermath of war was a time of austerity but it was also an era of full employment. The official "Town Guide" for 1950 noted *"At present unemployment is practically non-existent. A great proportion of the female labour is being absorbed in the cable making industry at Helsby and during the seasonable period, in jam making in Frodsham."*

At this time the tanneries were at the very zenith of their prosperity. Between the wars they had saved Runcorn from the worst effects of the recession and as late as 1950 they were still trying to recruit additional labour in order to meet the demand for leather. However, this happy state of affairs was not to last and by 1955, because of the widespread use of man-made substitutes, the production of sole leather had to be reduced. The tanneries were doomed and the end came rapidly. Camden was the first to go in 1958 and four years later the Puritan and the Astmoor sites were offered for sale. Highfield tannery ceased production in 1968 and thus there passed into

history a local industry which probably had its roots in the middle of the eighteenth century.

The first decade of peace saw the Manchester Ship Canal experience a remarkable surge in business. The cargo tonnage handled at the port of Manchester soared from 5.5 million tons a year in 1946 to 18.5 million tons in 1959. This rise in traffic meant round the clock working for the crews of the Runcorn-based tug-boats as well as increased employment opportunities for local men in the ship canal workshops. But the Runcorn and Weston Point docks did not share in the general prosperity of the waterway. The coasting trade had all but disappeared leaving the local docks almost deserted and by 1960 their closure seemed possible. Access to the Runcorn docks from the Bridgewater Canal was severed in 1962 when the approach roads to the new Mersey road bridge were completed. Runcorn was no longer an inland canal port. There were no commercial craft on the Duke's canal and the famous lines of locks were filled in. About the same time the Sprinch and Castle Rock boatyards were closed and the two hundred year old tradition for building and repairing wooden river and canal craft died out.

Other industries were also in difficulties and when Timmins' Foundry and the Liverpool Borax Company's "Anchor Works" in Halton Road closed, Runcorn became wholly dependant on the I.C.I. as the one major employer of labour.

There were further post-war changes. By an act of Parliament of 1948 the constituency of Runcorn was created. Prior to this the town had been part of the Northwich division and for some years at the beginning of the century local interests had been represented by Sir John Brunner M.P. In 1950 Mr. Dennis Vosper became Runcorn's first Member of Parliament. The town was still growing and in 1955 some 212 acres of the townships of Halton and Sutton were added to the Runcorn Urban District. In 1961 the town had 26,035 inhabitants.

The greatest impact on the social and economic life of the region came as a result of the building of the present road bridge.

The transporter was forty years old when the war ended. It was by then hopelessly inadequate. The volume of traffic had increased beyond its capacity, the bridge could not be operated in high winds and a service was not provided after midnight. Furthermore the transporter had become mechanically unreliable and essential repairs necessitated its closure for some months in the early 1950s. Increasing demands for the provision of a conventional high level bridge at the Gap came from industry, the municipalities and from the general public. In 1946 the

Ministry of Transport agreed that a bridge should be built as soon as the necessary funds were available. The design chosen was for a suspension bridge but in 1956 when plans were well advanced, wind tunnel tests found that this type of structure would tend to oscillate in high winds due to the proximity of the railway bridge. The revised plan was an entirely different concept. The bridge was to be a steel arch bridge and work on the concrete piers on both sides of the river began in May 1956.

The new toll-free bridge took five years to build and it was opened by Princess Alexander of Kent on July 21st. 1961. It had cost nearly £3 million and the approach roads had added another £1.5 million. Within ten years the bridge was carrying forty times the traffic which had been carried by the old transporter bridge.

Runcorn was no longer a cul-de-sac. Centuries of isolation were at an end and the fields of Cheshire had come within the reach of north Merseyside.

A New Runcorn

In 1964 occurred the most momentous event in Runcorn's long history. Under the New Towns Act, a designation order was made to create a new town which would provide housing and employment for people from north Merseyside and which would have an ultimate population of 90,000 to 100,000 by the end of the century. Thirty-seven farms on 7,500 acres of land were to be taken.

In the preamble to the master plan the developers readily acknowledged the value of the rich heritage of Runcorn and Halton. *"It is important to recognise the contribution of the past. The town and nearby villages already have roots in history which will be valuable in bringing a sense of continuity in time and a feeling of stability. These are advantages which some other new towns do not have to the same extent. The genius loci of many old places within the designated area is something to be cherished".*

Nevertheless, it must be recorded that in spite of the fact that the proposed new factories, shops and offices promised exceptional employment opportunities in an area of rapidly contracting industry, the vastness of the project did cause anxiety and some dismay in old Runcorn. However, the famous art historian Nikolaus Pevsner, had no doubts about the desirability of change. In 1971 he opined, "Runcorn is miserable to look at, so the best of luck to the new Runcorn".

The new town came quickly. The Runcorn Development Corporation was entrusted with the responsibility of creating the new environment and gradually the master plan with its proposals for factories, schools, busway and new residential estates was implemented. The farmland was developed to provide the splendid town park and everywhere informal wooded areas were established. The magnificent landscaping is a notable feature whilst considerable care was taken to provide recreation and leisure facilities and local community centres.

Runcorn now boasts a fine modern hospital, a large shopping complex, a first-class library and a second railway station. The construction of the unique fast transit busway and the building of new factories entailed the demolition of property in old Runcorn. The designated area included the existing town which was to be integrated with the new and extensive residential redevelopment of the Bridge Street and Ellesmere Street area has brought new vitality to the heart of the ancient township.

More than a century of industrial grime has been removed from the sandstone churches of old Runcorn, the river front has been attractively landscaped and there are schemes for the enhancement of Dukesfield. The site of Norton Priory is now an impressive museum of monastic life whilst the Bridgewater Canal is given over to pleasure cruising and angling. Recently, there has been a proposal to include the environs of Runcorn in a plan for the forestation of north Cheshire.

In 1974 the Runcorn Urban District Council was merged with the Borough of Widnes to form the Borough of Halton and seven years later the Runcorn Development Corporation was dissolved, its duties being transferred to a new body, the Warrington and Runcorn Development Corporation. Recent progress has been rapid and at the time of writing the new town of Runcorn is nearing completion. It has attracted a great deal of attention at home and abroad. The town has become a place of vigorous industrial and commercial enterprise and the future points to continuing success. The new Runcorn owes little to the Runcorn of the past but it does promise an improved quality of life and security for the Runcornians of the future.

Coat of Arms

of the

Runcorn Urban District

(Granted 1956)

Or on a base barry wavy of four Azure and Argent a lymphad proper flying flags and pennon of St. George the sail also Azure charged with a garb Gold on a chief Gules two flaying-knives in saltire proper handles Or between as many fountains.

Out of a mural crown Gules a demi-lion Sable crowned with an ancient crown and supporting an abbot's crozier Or pendant therefrom by the guige an escutcheon also Gules charged with four fusils conjoined in pak each fessewise Gold.

"To fill the ship with goods"

Bibliography

A useful guide or framework to events is *"A Chronology of Runcorn and Its Environs"* produced by Runcorn library. Also helpful in discerning twentieth century developments are the Official Handbooks of Runcorn authorised by the Urban District Council from 1920 as well as Kelly's Post Office Directories.

For the account of the proposed Warrington and Runcorn Light Railway the author is indebted to Mr. John Thompson of Halton who made available the plans and documents concerning the project. The School Board versus Voluntary School controversy of 1902 has, in the main, been culled from the handbills which were issued by the protagonists of the time.

Other publications consulted included *"The Queen's Diamond Jubilee in Cheshire"* (1897) by J.H. Cooke; *"Salt in Cheshire"* (1915) by A.F. Calvert and *"A History of Cablemaking at Helsby"* by L.C. Banbury, B.I.C.C. General Cables (1980). Also used were *"A Brief History of the Chemical Industry in Runcorn"*, I.C.I. (undated); *The Evans Biological Institute 1937,* Evans Sons, Lescher and Webb Ltd.; *Widnes and Runcorn Transporter Bridge,* Official Souvenir of the Opening Ceremony, May 29th 1905 and the Souvenir Programme of the Unveiling of Runcorn War Memorial November 14th 1920 with a report of the event in the *Runcorn Weekly News* for 19th November 1920.

Twentieth century developments in local industry were obtained from Gordon Rintoul's report for the Museum of the Chemical Industry *"Chemical Manufacture in Runcorn and Weston 1800 – 1930"* which was produced in 1984. Much information on the local tanneries is available from material deposited at the Museum of the Chemical Industry. The decline of the port of Runcorn in the twentieth century is discussed in H.F. Starkey's *Schooner Port* (1981). War-time activity at Randles works is taken from "The Sheathed Sword. Gas Production in World War II" by Gordon Howarth in *Chemistry in Britain* (1984).

For reports of local events see Victoria Memorial Hospital (Cottage Hospital) *Widnes Weekly News* 23rd November 1909; Medical Officer of Health's Report for Runcorn, *Widnes Weekly News* 1909; the history of Halton Grange *(Runcorn Town Hall)* is taken from an information sheet issued by the Borough of Halton. The occasion of the Runcorn Festival is taken from the Official Programme of the event for 1931 and an account of the end of quarrying at Weston and Runcorn has been taken from the publicity material of the Mersey Valley Partnership.

Runcorn at war is mentioned in *"The Zeppelin in Combat"* (1962) by D.H. Robinson and *"The Last Ditch"* (1968) by David Lampe. For references to enemy awareness of the importance of Runcorn's industries see Luftwaffe Briefings 1940. DDX 328/4-6 Cheshire County Record Office.

A

Abbey Cottage 14
Acton Grange 2
Agriculture 147
Air raids 220
Alcock, Dr. Nathan 52,54,55,70,90,134
Alcock, Reverend Thomas .. 52-55, 70, 122, 134, 154
Alfred Dock 180
Alms houses 82
Alkali Acts 157
All Saints 95-100, 141, 143, 149, 200, 208
  (see also Runcorn Parish Church)
Anglo-Saxon Chronicle 4
Anti-aircraft defences 220
Appleton, Widnes 8, 20, 31, 102
Archery 24
Astmoor 37
Astmoor Tanning Company 154, 221
Aston 4, 7, 19, 36, 100
Aston chapel (St. Peter's) 13, 51, 60, 99, 220
Augustinian Canons 9, 35-39
Augustinian Friars 14
Australian Alum Company 216
Atmospheric pollution 157, 200

B

Baptists 103
Barclay, Reverend John 95-98, 144, 182
Barrage balloons 220
Barry, James, Earl of Barrymore 77, 82
Beacons 44
Belvedere Terrace 133, 135
Belvedere Shipyard 151
Bertelin, Saint 10-12
Bethesda Chapel 102, 120
Big Pool 3, 134
Black Prince 10, 24
Blundell, Nicholas 81
Boat House Inn (Runcorn) 125, 126, 176
Boarding Schools 135-136
Boleyn, Queen Anne 29
Boniface IX, Pope 12
Booth, Sir George 59
Bone Mills 179, 187
Bowling Greens 208
"Bowling Green Inn" 112

Bradshaw, Captain James ... 85, 86, 90, 113, 115, 117
Bradshaw, Robert Haldane 117
Brass Bands 143, 205, 217
Brazenose College, Oxford 70
Bridewell 106, 107, 114, 115
Bridlington 9
Bridgewater Canal
  .... 125-135, 165, 180, 188, 218, 219, 221
Bridgewater Trustees 116, 165, 170, 174, 176, 179
Bridgewater, Francis, Duke of 126-129, 151, 173
Bridgewater foundry 159
Bridgewater Navigation Company
  .... 99, 159, 160, 180, 184, 186
Bridgewater House 128, 129, 173
Brindley, James 125, 127, 129, 167
Britannia Telegraph Works 162
British Restaurant 220
Bronze Age 2
Brooke Family
  ..... 30, 39, 43, 44, 53, 57-59, 65, 67, 85, 90, 95, 97
  .... 113, 122, 126, 141, 144, 189, 211
Brunner, Sir John . 102, 189, 211, 213, 214, 217, 221
Brunner-Mond Company 159-160, 218, 219
Burrows, Reverend Hugh 44-45, 47
Brundrit, Dennis 97, 107, 151, 198, 200
Brundrit and Whiteway 205, 208
Brunswick Chapel 100-102, 220
Burton-upon-Stather 36

C

Caine, Sir Thomas Hall 145
Camden, William 2, 3
Camden Tanning Company 216
Camden Methodist Chapel 101
Canal packet boats 126, 127, 128, 130, 135
Capital punishment 25-26, 28
Castle Hotel 172, 176
Castle Donington 35
Castle Rock 5, 129, 130, 139
Castle Rock Shipyard 151, 152, 221
Castner-Kellner works 162, 215, 218, 219
Cawley Reverend J 86
Celts 2
Cemetery 134, 196
Census 111, 114, 121
Cinemas 209, 220
Charles II 59

Charities 139-142

Chesshyre, Sir John 77-81, 83

Chesshyre Library 51, 77, 79, 80

Chesshyre, Reverend Robert 48, 51

Cheshire Rifle Volunteers 207, 211

Chester 35, 73

Chester Cathedral 72, 149

Chester-Warrington Turnpike Road 130, 197

Chesterfield Lord 77

Cholera 116-117, 159

Cholmondeley family 70, 77, 122, 166, 168

Christ Church College, Oxford 39

Christ Church, Weston Point 98-99

Clifton 50, 73-77, 219

"*Cock and Hen Lane*" 121

Colchester Lord 75, 77

Common land 17, 25, 49, 75, 113

Cooper, John 134

Co-operative movement 145

Crecy, battle of 73

Cricket 208

Cromwell, Oliver 75

Cromwell, Thomas 38, 39

Cuerdley 5, 31, 35, 64

Cycling 209

D

Daresbury Chapel (All Saints)

.... 4, 12, 43, 46, 47, 51, 55, 96, 99

Delamere Dock 186

De Lacy, Edmund 31

De Lacy, John 31

De Lacy, Henry 17, 18, 31

De Lacy, Roger 30, 31

Delph Bridge 121, 127, 129, 211

Ditton, Widnes 4, 81

Ditton Brook Ironworks 179

Diphtheria 199

Dobbs, Reverend Robert 43, 45

Domesday Survey 7, 8, 36

Dorcas Society 141, 144

Domestic servants 202

Dutton 2, 4, 12

Dutton workhouse 117, 141

Dutton Hall 68-69

Dutton Hospital 220

Dutton family 35, 36, 38, 43, 66

Dutton Lodge 48

Dudley, Sir William 209

Duke's Dock, Liverpool 173

Duke's Gut 129, 136

E

Eanley in Norton 8, 23, 36

Eastham Pleasure Gardens 205

Earp, William 162

Eddisbury 2, 5

Edward the Elder 4

Edward the Confessor 7

Edward I 31

Edward II 22

Edward III 13

Edward IV 22

Egbert 4

Education 53, 69, 135-136

.... 144-145, 198, 216, 217

Elcock, Reverend Ephraim 45

Ethelfleda 4, 5, 10

Evans, Lescher and Webb Ltd. 215

F

Fairs 112

Famine 72-75

Farnworth, Widnes 25

Farnworth Church, Widnes 20

Farnworth Methodist Chapel, Widnes 96

Festival of Britain 220

Finmore, Reverend William 46-48, 59

Fishgarths 7, 18, 21-22

Fire engine 120

Flint implements 1, 2

Flodden, battle of 73

Floating Church Mission 99, 144

Football 208

Foresters' Hall 206

Fox, George 43

Francis Dock 179, 197

Frankpledge 25

Free, Reverend Dr. John 51-52

Freemasonry 144

Friendly Societies 139, 142-143, 205

Frodsham 1, 7, 12, 35, 74, 75, 205, 221

Frodsham Bridge 57-58, 109, 147, 151

G

Gas Company 117-118
Gaunt, John of 32
Gilbert, John 127, 173
Glacial boulders 1
Grappenhall 5, 36
Grand Junction Railway 165, 168
Grange Housing Estate 221
Grange County High School 221
Great Budworth 5, 12, 35, 36, 59
Guild Hall 217

H

Haddock and Parnell and Co. 156
Hale Ford 4, 8, 58, 59, 135
Hallwood 20, 77-78, 83
Halton
    Castle 8, 19, 22, 24, 25-29, 32, 56, 58, 61, 70
    Chapel 60
    Court 25, 70
    Common 110
    Deer Park 19-20, 29, 60, 147
    Fair 19, 62
    Grange 154, 158, 219
    Hill 3, 4, 8
    "Ladies' Day" 142-143
    Market 19, 25
Halton Road Methodist Chapel 103
"Harrying of the North" 7
Hatton 12
Handley, William 139, 217
Hardy and Wylde (Millers) 159
Hartley, Jesse 164
Hawthorne, Nathaniel 159
Hayes, Ollier and Co. 154
Hazlehurst, Charles 198, 201
Hazlehurst, Thomas 96, 101, 103, 114, 156, 201
Hazlehurst, Thomas and Sons
    .... 156, 158, 162, 215, 216
Hearth Tax 66, 68
Heath, Richard of Weston 59
Head, Sir George 176
Hearse house 88
Hedley, Robert 159
"Hempstones" 125-126
Helsby Grammar School 221

Henry III 17, 29
Henry VIII 20, 39
Hill forts 2, 5
Highfield Tanning Company 153-154, 216, 217
Higher Runcorn 125
Holy Trinity Church 98, 120, 149
Hope Hall 103
Hospital (Victoria Memorial or
    "Cottage Hospital") 217
Horticultural Society 209
Huntingtonians 102
Hutchinson, John 156, 167
Hugh Lupus 8

I

Ice Age 1
Illegitimacy 106
Imperial Chemical Industries 219, 221
Iron Age 2
Isolation Hospital 200

J

Jacobites 81-82
James I 20, 65, 74, 75
John, King 22
Johnson, John (Senr.), soap manufacturer 154
Johnson, John 122, 145, 147, 154-158, 193, 196
Johnson, Thomas .. 122, 145, 147, 154-158, 193, 196
Johnson, J & T, soap manufacturers
    .... 122, 144-145, 154-158

K

Keckwick 12, 19
Keyt, Reverend William 52, 53, 54, 91
Kilmorey, Robert, Viscount 13
Kneller, Sir Godfrey 77

L

Lea and Sons, Engineers 216
Legal quays 179
Leland, John 173
Leprosy 35
Lever Brothers 215
Libraries 207, 217
Lighthouses and light-vessels 176

Literary Institute 145, 207

Liverpool Borax Company 221

"Liverpool Blues" 81

Liverpool-Manchester Railway 179

Liverpool Town Dues 179-180

Liverpool-Runcorn steam passenger packet
.... 170, 174, 175

London, North-Western Railway Co. 165, 168

Lower Whitley 59

Lupus, Hugh 29

Lyons and Sons, alkali manufacturers 162

M

Macclesfield 73, 74, 77

Manchester Ship Canal Company
.... 2, 152, 184-190, 212, 219, 221

Marl pits 21

Marbury brine pipeline 215

Markets 112

Market Hall 196

Mariners' Mission 98, 149, 150

Mechanics' Institution 145

Master, Reverend Frederick 85-92, 115, 133

Mersey Dock and Harbour Board 179, 180

Mersey Mission to Seamen 99, 141

Mersey and Irwell Navigation Company
("*Old Quay Company*") 112, 126, 130, 131, 135
.. 147, 159, 174, 176, 177-179, 184, 185, 196, 206

Mersey Power Company 215

Mersey Salt and Brine Company 160

Mersey Street Shipyard 151, 205, 208

Methodism 100-103, 206

Middleton Grange 13

Militia 24, 43, 81, 82, 106, 133

Monmonth, James, Duke of 75-77

Moore 10, 19, 22, 23, 122

"Moore Milk Boat" 147

N

Narrow-boat people 121, 138, 145, 183, 184

National School (Runcorn Parish School) 91, 93

National War Savings Campaign 220

Newfoundland Salt Trade 180, 218

"Newtown" 196-197

Nicholas IV, Pope 13

Norman, Sir Frederick 209

Norton 1, 17, 48

Norton Priory and Abbey 9-12, 35-42, 57, 65, 66

Norton Priory mansion 39, 41, 57

Norton Priory museum 222

Norton water tower 162-163

O

Ockleston, John 152, 153

Ockleston and Son, tannery 152, 153, 216

Old Coach Road 179

"Old Gut" (Pool of Runcorn)
.... 112, 114, 121, 125, 134

"Old Hall", Runcorn 67, 125

Old Hall, Halton 68

Old Hall, Weston 68

Old Quay Alkali Works 162

Old Quay docks and canal (see Mersey and Irwell Co.)

Old Quay Pottery 159, 162

Open field system 17

Orme and Muntz quarry 151

Orred family
.... 53, 122, 134, 135, 141, 144, 197, 199, 211

P

Packet houses 176-177

Parish Church of Runcorn 87-92
(see also All Saints)

Paupers 105, 106, 108-109, 114, 141, 142

Pawnbrokers 117, 202

Peat Moss 22-23

Peover 36, 39

Perch Rock Battery, New Brighton 149

Pevsner, Nikolaus 101, 222

Pickford, Thomas 173

"Pilgrimage of Grace" 39

Pickwick Club 209

Pin factory 117

Pinfold 115

Plague 23, 26, 32, 70, 73, 83

Poachers 202

Poor Law 106, 117, 141

Poosey chapel 13

Posnett, R.H. 216, 217, 218

Public health 198

Public Hall 141, 206

Public houses 176

Puritan Tannery (Henry Boston and
Sons Ltd.) 216, 221

Q

Quakers (Society of Friends) 47-48, 55
Quarries 147-151

R

Ragged School 144, 156, 198
Railways 165-170, 197
Recusancy 44-45, 55, 75
Rickman, Thomas.................................... 11
Rivers, Thomas, Earl of Rocksavage 76
Rock Park 218
Rocksavage 57, 73-77, 83
Roman occupation 2-4
Roman Catholics 43, 44, 48, 55, 59, 102-103, 189
Roofing slates 173, 178
Rooke and Hunter, alkali manufacturers ... 156, 162
"Rookery" 118, 141, 199
"Royal Hotel" ("White Hart")
.... 21, 102, 112, 125, 128, 139, 166, 176
Rowing club 208
Rugby football 208, 209
Rupert, Prince 57-58
Runcorn :
    Castle 5
    Common (Runcorn Heath) 113, 121, 134
    Ferry 9, 10, 16, 19, 35, 81, 114, 134, 166
    .... 167, 168-170, 190, 191, 215
    Gas Company 139
    Improvement Commission
    .... 158, 170, 184, 193-202
    Laybye 187
    Life-saving and Grappling Corps.................. 217
    Market 112
    New Town 222
    Parish Church 10-12, 53, 88, 89-91, 92, 95-98
        (see also All Saints)
    Penny Bank 144
    Philharmonic Society 206
    Railway Bridge 4, 5, 168-170, 190
    School Board 216-217
    Town Bridge 113, 121, 134, 138, 197
    Vicarage house 45, 91
    Vicarage Voluntary Hospital 218
Runcorn-Northwich Turnpike Road ... 114, 131, 135
Runcorn Urban District Council
    .... 200, 201, 211, 219, 221, 222, 223

"Runcorn Road" Railway Station 165
Runcorn and Weston Soap and Alkali
    Company 158, 160, 162
Runcorn and Weston Canal 186, 197

S

St. Edward's R.C. Church 102-103
St. John the Evangelist Church,
    Weston 100-101, 141, 205
St. John's Presbyterian Church 102, 149, 150
St. Luke's Congregational Chapel 102
St. Paul's Wesleyan Methodist Church 100-101
St. Mary's Church, Halton 60
St. Mary's Church, Nantwich 149
St. Peter's Mission, Dukesfield 98-99
St. Michael and All Angels 98, 100, 143-144, 149
St. Helens-Runcorn Gap Railway.................. 165, 167
Salt Trade 151, 174
"Saltport" 186-187
Salt Union 162, 190, 215
Salt water baths 135
Salvation Army 160, 209, 220
Sanctuary 13
Sankey Canal 167, 172, 173
Savage family 23, 43, 48, 63, 73-77, 81
Schooners 182-183, 218
Scott, George Gilbert 60
Sea fishing 184
Shaw, William 99
Shipbuilding 151, 176, 189, 208, 215
"Ship money"..................................... 45, 55
Shipowners 184
Silting 180-182
Skinner, Reverend John 135
Smallpox 200
Smiles, Samuel 167
"Sour Milk Lane" 121
South African War 211
Sothern, Benjamin 173
Sprinch brook 21, 112, 120, 125, 139, 193-194
Sprinch boatyard 221
Stanlow Abbey 31, 35
Statute of Labourers.............................. 26
Steam towage 182
Stenhills 134, 219
Stockham 4, 12, 23, 39, 65, 66
Stocks 107

Stoke-on-Trent 174, 180
Street lighting 117-118
Street tramway 211
Summer excursions 177, 205
Sundial 97
Sutton 4, 14, 68, 105, 165, 170, 221
Sutton Hall.. 14, 36
Swift packets.. 176, 197

T

"Tally-Ho" coach 176
Tanneries 152, 153, 221
Taylor Samuel 217, 218
Technical Institute 217
Telford, Thomas 166-167, 215
Telegraph line 180
Temperance movement 209
"Theatre Royal".. 205, 209
Thelwall.......................... 5, 21, 35, 46, 47, 51, 55, 99
Timmins and Sons Ltd. 159, 221
Tithes.. 47-51, 90, 91, 94
Toleration Act 47
Tollemache Dock, Weston Point 184
Tomkinson, John 102, 122, 149
Top Locks.. 124, 127, 176
Town Bridge (Savages Bridge or Doctors Bridge)
.... 113, 121, 134, 138, 197
Town Crier 97-98, 112, 115, 120
Town Hall.............. 115, 116, 122, 139, 150, 219, 220
"Towngate" 125
Transporter Bridge 212-215, 221
Treacle Row 200
Trent and Mersey Canal 129, 165, 173
Trinity Wesleyan Methodist Church, Halton 103
Typhus.. 199

U

Upper Mersey Navigation Commission 180, 184
United Alkali Company 162, 218, 219

V

Vale Royal 13
"Valor Ecclesiasticus" 38
Vagrants.. 72, 107
Veratinum 2
Victoria, Queen 14, 139, 187, 205, 211

Vikings... 5

W

Walsh, Reverend John 117
Warburton family 24, 35
Warrington 35, 170, 208
Warrington and Runcorn Development
      Corporation 222
War memorial 218
"Waterfall Lane" 121
Waterworks 193-196
Waterloo Bridge 114, 197
Weaver Navigation Company 98, 160, 173, 180
Wedgewood, Josiah...................................... 127, 130
Weeton, Ellen 174
Wesley, John 100
Welsh Chapel 102
Wesk Bank Dock, Widnes 159
Weston 4, 8, 13, 14, 66, 110, 111, 114, 121
.... 122, 125, 144, 201, 211, 215
Weston Point................. 1, 2, 111, 173, 201, 219, 220
Whalley Abbey 31
Whit Monday Walk 205, 207
Whiteway, Philip 122, 139, 151, 170, 200, 208
Widnes 8, 10, 19, 20, 23, 24, 25, 35, 108, 159
.... 165, 167, 169, 170, 184, 212-215
Wigg, Charles... 156
Wigg Brothers and Steele 157, 160
Wigg Works 190, 219
Wilderspool... 2
Wilsons Hotel 125
William I... 7
William IV 91
Wind and water corn mills......... 18, 19, 21, 119, 159
Witchcraft 70
Women's Voluntary Service 220
Wood, Reverend Alfred Maitland .. 54, 211, 216, 217
Wright, William 151

Y

Y.M.C.A.. 141, 207, 208
Yorfrid 8

Z

Zion Methodist Chapel 101
Zeppelin raid 218